FOURTH EDITION

Transition Education and Services for Students with Disabilities

Patricia L. Sitlington
The University of Northern Iowa

Gary M. Clark
University of Kansas

Boston   New York   San Francisco
Mexico City   Montreal   Toronto   London   Madrid   Munich   Paris
Hong Kong   Singapore   Tokyo   Cape Town   Sydney

Executive Editor: *Virginia Lanigan*	**Editorial Production Service:** *Lynda Griffiths*	
Series Editorial Assistant: *Scott Blaszak*	**Composition Buyer:** *Andrew Turso*	
Executive Marketing Manager:	**Manufacturing Buyer:** *Andrew Turso*	
Amy Cronin Jordan	**Electronic Composition:** *Peggy Cabot*	
Editorial Production Administrator:	**Cover Administrator:** *Kristina Mose-Libon*	
Annette Joseph		
Editorial Production Coordinator:		
Holly Crawford		

For related titles and support materials, visit our online catalog at www.ablongman.com.

The previous edition, by Patricia L. Sitlington, Gary M. Clark, and Oliver P. Kolstoe, was published under the title *Transition Education and Services for Adolescents with Disabilities,* copyright © 2000 by Allyn & Bacon. Earlier editions by Gary M. Clark and Oliver P. Kolstoe were published under the title *Career Development and Transition Education for Adolescents with Disabilities,* copyright © 1995, 1990 by Allyn & Bacon.

Between the time website information is gathered and then published, it is not unusual for some sites to have closed. Also, the transcription of URLs can result in typographical errors. The publisher would appreciate notification where these errors occur so that they may be corrected in subsequent editions.

Library of Congress Cataloging-in-Publication Data

Sitlington, Patricia L.
    Transition education and services for students with disabilities / Patricia L. Sitlington, Gary M. Clark.—4th ed.
        p. cm.
    Rev. ed. of: Transition education and services for adolescents with disabilities / Patricia L. Sitlington, Gary M. Clark, Oliver P. Kolstoe. 3rd ed. c2000.
    Includes bibliographical references and index.
    ISBN 0-205-41642-X
    1. Students with disabilities—Education (Secondary)—United States. 2. Teenagers with disabilities—Education (Secondary)—United States. 3. Students with disabilities—Vocational education—United States. 4. Teenagers with disabilities—Vocational education—United States. 5. People with disabilities—Vocational guidance—United States. I. Clark, Gary M. II. Sitlington, Patricia L. Transition education and services for adolescents with disabilities. III. Title.
LC4031.S58 2005
371.9'0473—dc22

Printed in the United States of America

10 9 8 7 6 5 4 3 2 1   HAM   10 09 08 07 06 05

CONTENTS

PREFACE

The 1990s will be known as the years in which the concept of transition services made its debut into educational practice. The preceding decades, especially the 1960s, 1970s, and 1980s, laid the groundwork for what happened in the 1990s with regard to the initial transition services mandate in the Individuals with Disabilities Education Act of 1990 and its subsequent amendments and reauthorization in 1997. We now have the Individuals with Disabilities Education Improvement Act of 2004 with changes that affect transition services directly. In addition, educational reform and other major legislation, such as the No Child Left Behind Act, have had major indirect impacts on transition services delivery and transition planning. The first three editions of this text have tried to describe, elaborate on, and reflect on these years and events and what educational practices are appropriate for youths with disabilities during their secondary school experience.

A recent cartoon in *The New Yorker* magazine (September 6, 2004) showed a gentleman telling a man and woman, "The feds have authorized me to leave your child behind." This is clearly a humorous play on words for readers who have no stake in educational policy or practice, but for many of us, it is a political observation that speaks to the growing reality for many youths in school these days. In this fourth edition, we address both the ideal and the real in a variety of ways. The first chapter begins with an ideal framework for approaching the challenges of *transition education* (what we do instructionally to prepare students for the transitions in their lives) and *transition services* (what we do in linking our students to supports they need for the transitions in their lives). The second chapter focuses on the reality of what legislation requires of us in schools today. It also reflects on how the provisions of various laws provide both opportunities and challenges for students, families, and schools in the transition planning process. Chapter 3 discusses the reality of who the major stakeholders in transition education and services are—students and families. Its goal is to get the focus for schools back on the consumers of transition education and transition services. Chapter 4 goes back to the ideal, since it addresses the need for transition planning and transition education at the K–8 levels of schools and the logic for beginning early in transition preparation. The remaining chapters relate to practical ideas for the real world in implementing transition education services and some ideal strategies we recommend for practice.

Overview of Changes

The title of the fourth edition of this book, *Transition Education and Services for Students with Disabilities*, reveals the first change to mention. The three earlier editions all had a focus on adolescents with disabilities. We believe strongly that any serious effort to address the issues of identifying and addressing transition service needs must include some discussion of the elementary and middle school levels. These years are too critical to ignore. We acknowledge the importance of good foundations laid as early as possible during the preschool through middle school years and are pleased to include a chapter for the first time on this issue.

This edition of the text also extends its coverage to all levels of severity. The focus of previous editions was on adolescents with mild to moderate disabilities. This decision was made early on because youths with high incidence disabilities seemed to be left out of the transition literature of the mid-1980s and early 1990s. In addition, personnel preparation programs during that period were more divided than they are today in addressing the needs of youths with mild to moderate versus severe disabilities. We believe it highly appropriate for this edition to include research, discussions, and recommendations for a more complete range of students going through the transition process. These beliefs are reflected throughout the chapters.

A third change in the organization of this new edition is the addition of more resources and websites for readers who are seeking more in-depth information on certain topics. Rather than include these as part of the chapters, these resources are available on the Allyn and Bacon companion website for our book at **www.ablongman.com/sitlington4e.** The appendices referred to throughout the text are also available on this website. We encourage you to access these resources for the rich content they provide and the in-depth coverage of topics that this text could not include because of page limitations.

For the first time, an instructor's manual accompanies the text to provide instructors with targeted student learning objectives, sample instructional content, and sample essay questions keyed to the learner objectives for assessing student learning outcomes.

Acknowledgments

We acknowledge those individuals and groups who contributed to our thinking and efforts for this fourth edition. First, we thank our support systems at the University of Northern Iowa and the University of Kansas, including our department administrators and staff. Both, in their own ways, pushed us and encouraged us to stay abreast of the field and be responsible for the task of keeping the transition education and services process vital.

We particularly thank those graduate students who worked directly with us through the various stages of the revision. Their tireless, enthusiastic assistance kept us going. These individuals include Krista Morrison and Shyla Deutmeyer, who updated the resource agency list, coordinated the website and reference lists, and assisted with revisions; Jenny Johnson, who assisted with the subject and author indexes; and Amy Gaumer, who took the lead in developing the instructor's manual.

We also acknowledge undergraduate and graduate students in the vocational and transition programming classes at the University of Northern Iowa and the University of Kansas who provided reviews of the previous edition and suggestions for improvement. These individuals make up a list too numerous to name, but we took their ideas seriously and they should feel that they made contributions toward this work. In addition, we also thank the following reviewers of this edition for their extremely helpful suggestions and comments: Kimberley Fatata-Hall, Nova Southeastern University; Janice Ferguson, Western Kentucky University; Margaret Hutchins, Illinois State University; Dawn R. Speidel, West Liberty State College; and Lynn M. Walz, Eastern Illinois University.

Additionally we thank the publishers who gave permission to use the copyrighted materials that we have included. We also thank Virginia Lanigan at Allyn and Bacon and Lynda Griffiths for their editorial assistance in getting this fourth edition in its final form.

Our appreciation also goes to all of the individuals with disabilities, family members, teachers, administrators, support staff, and adult providers with whom we have worked and continue to work. They provided us with the questions that needed to be addressed and many of the proposed answers to these questions. Finally, we thank our families and friends. They have supported us not only as we wrote this edition but also in all of our experiences that provided us with the information included here.

We are excited about the content of the pages that follow. We hope that this book will help you as you assist individuals with disabilities and their families in their transitions to all aspects of adult life.

P. L. S.
G. M. C.

Transition Education and Services in Perspective

From the standpoint of the child, the great waste in the school comes from his inability to utilize the experiences he gets outside the school in any complete and free way within the school itself; while, on the other hand, he is unable to apply in daily life what he is learning at school. That is the isolation of the school—its isolation from life. Nothing is more absurd than to suppose that there is no middle term between leaving a child to his own unguided fancies and likes or controlling his activities by a formal succession of dictated directions.

— John Dewey

To regard youths with disabilities as a potentially valuable resource requires a belief in human potential and a recognition that potential must be discovered, developed, and nurtured. To be certain that each youth with a disability has a chance to discover his or her potential, belief must be backed up by educational programs that are realistically designed to allow all students to pursue options to reach their goals. This requires, of course, a willingness to invest time, effort, patience, and support.

For the students, their families, the teachers, and others in the training program, the investments of time and energy are substantial. Yet, the returns are more than worth it. To assist youths with disabilities to discover new feelings of self-worth, to convert dependents on tax dollars into taxpayers, to offer better preparation for postsecondary education to students, to provide anxious parents with emotional strength and some measure of hope, to provide employers with able workers, and to send to communities more competent citizens all create a labor of considerable value.

Under the educational system in the United States, state education agencies and local school districts are responsible for charting the educational plans for its own population of students. They do this, however, under existing federal and state laws and continuing (and changing) calls for reform. At the heart of these laws and reform proposals is an attempt for quality education for all students. The problem is the lack of agreement on what quality education is. Currently, the prevailing reform model is the improvement of academic knowledge and skills of all students. Reform success outcomes are acceptable academic achievement scores.

This book presents a case for reform that values reform success in terms of adult outcomes, not just in terms of academic achievement scores. We present this case, recognizing that public policy does not currently respond adequately to its multiple commitments to educating children of diverse backgrounds. It is pursuing a "one program fits all" philosophy, even though the principles of special education services under federal law not only permit but mandate individualized educational programming. The basis for an adult outcomes reform approach comes out of what we know from our history and documented efforts that show success.

This chapter sets the stage for the remainder of the book. First, it discusses some major historical attempts to train youths and young adults with various disabilities. Next, it examines the guiding principles of secondary education programs. The chapter then highlights the development of special education programs as these efforts have been focused to provide training (within the limits of the U.S. high school) to prepare people with disabilities for the adult world of working, living, and further education. Finally, we present a comprehensive model for transition education and services to give a framework for everything that follows in the book.

Historical Overview

Importance of a Historical Perspective

People who have some characteristic in common can be studied in any society and in any historical period relative to their place in society and the esteem accorded them. This is true for individuals with disabilities, even though they vary considerably in the types of disabilities that are represented and the range of severity within and across disability groups.

A historical record of persons with disabilities participating as adults in a society is a concrete example of interpreting society's view of them at any point in time. Chronologically, historical records reveal changes in values that societies have held toward people who have disabilities. From those changes, one should be able to see patterns on which future directions for action can be built. The best of the past becomes the basis for blueprints for the future, whereas the failures are the warning signs of pitfalls to be avoided.

Development of Programs in the United States

As the United States matured, prevailing social climates had their effects on the treatment of persons with disabilities. From the first development of asylums in New England for people with severe disabilities who were blind or who were classified as mentally deficient until the mid-1800s, there was little change in early U.S. values or practice in care and treatment. Essentially, the prevailing practice was providing food and shelter. The period of the Civil War brought great concern for human rights. The mechanism for assuring these rights came from federal laws and private efforts, both probably unevenly administered. Concern for the welfare of slaves was extended to others who were afforded limited human rights, among them people with disabilities. The attitudes toward Civil War veterans with physical disabilities due to war injuries reflected this in more positive treatment toward all persons with disabilities.

The Victorian era brought marked change to the social climate in a negative direction. Attitudes toward crime and degeneracy became more sharply focused, and new concerns about morality arose. Coincidentally, the emergence of information on the heritability of traits led to the identification of a disability as not only the punishment for presumed behavior transgressions but also as a heritable trait (Goddard, 1912; Dugdale, 1910). Whether by sterilization or segregation, the prevention of procreation among people with mental disabilities and, by extension, any other person with disabilities whose morals were suspect, quickly put the brakes on any societal movement toward liberal social policies.

In the early 1900s, public education for children with disabilities began to develop according to two principles that seemed to have universal applicability: (1) the principle of opportunity and (2) the principle of proof. The *principle of opportunity* simply meant that any child should be allowed to enroll in any class open to other children, with no prior restrictions placed on participation. The *principle of proof,* however, provided that continuance in a class, school experience, or school activities would be contingent on meeting the standards used to determine satisfactory performance. Unlike the principle of opportunity, the principle of proof imposed a qualitative expectation on the behavior of the student. Thus, each child had to prove his or her ability and willingness to meet the standards set for each class.

The application of these two principles in governing programs for people with disabilities has a curious history. Earliest records of secondary programs for people with disabilities, as described by Descoeudres (1928) and Duncan (1943) in Europe and Ingram (1960) and Hungerford (1943) in the United States, implied that all persons had to demonstrate progress to stay in their programs. Although no qualitative standards were mentioned, the progression of activities from simple to complex and from concrete to abstract made it easy to implement a hierarchy of performance objectives. The principle of proof seemed to be operating. However, this practice should not be construed to imply that special education programs were really much different from regular programs. Both have a long history of using tests and other methods of evaluation to assign grades (A, B, C, D, and F) as an index of a person's level of achievement. Those students who get Fs are presumed to be demonstrating that they have no right to continue in the program. Clearly, the principle of proof has been used for some time with children who have no disabilities for determining who can continue and who cannot, although inter- and intra-school standards vary considerably in their subjective views as to what constitutes failure. It seems possible that the principle of proof played a role in programs for students with disabilities also but probably was tempered considerably in application.

Another manifestation of the principle of proof is the accumulation of units of credit. In 1899, a Subcommittee on History as a College Entrance Requirement made a report to the National Education Association. In that report, the subcommittee used the term *unit* and defined it arithmetically and precisely (Savage, 1953). However, it was not until 1906 that the Carnegie Foundation for the Advancement of Teaching (1909) described how a unit of credit could be established. The foundation described a unit (which became known as the *Carnegie unit*) as the satisfactory completion of a class dealing with some subject that met five days per week for a minimum of 40 minutes each day or a minimum of 120 hours per year. It is clear from several historical accounts (Carnegie Foundation for the Advancement of Teaching, 1909; *Encyclopedia of Education*, 1971; Savage, 1953) that the Carnegie unit was designed solely to provide a quantitative device for appraising school instruction for college admission. Schools began to recognize 14 Carnegie units of credit as the requirement for graduation as of 1906. The number has increased over the years to the 20 to 24 units required today. It seems reasonable to assume that these units made it easier for college officials to determine eligibility for admission. By embracing the unit concept, colleges and advocates of reform in higher education contributed to the movement to recognize the Carnegie unit as the standard of credit for high school coursework and significantly affected the nature of high school requirements.

Although the agreed-upon measurement of accomplishment in secondary education is a Carnegie unit or some variation of it, the mere accumulation of units is not enough to ensure graduation. The units must have some core focus and reflect an acceptable body of knowledge. Nearly all states have their respective core academic requirements. Even though the requirements are minimal, they include classes in English, science, mathematics, and history— the basic blocks of knowledge required to make an industrial society function. In addition to this redefining the meaning of a high school education, there is yet another measure of accomplishment that schools are using with increasing frequency. High school exit exams are emerging as a parallel measure of accomplishment. The combination of core curriculum credits and exit exams are redefining a high school education. Accountability for higher achievement scores in core academic courses is associated with schools decreasing the number of electives in order for students to spend more time on basic academic literacy.

Such is not the case for the principle of opportunity. Education has practiced exclusivity from its beginning. Although this point is not within the scope of this book, you can find documentation in Jordan (1973). Suffice it to say that equal educational opportunity has never been universally practiced in the United States, and the possession of a disability imposes limitations on educational opportunities, even in today's inclusive education philosophy.

Until the 1950s, few, if any, special educational provisions were made in public schools for persons with disabilities, but educational opportunities were, theoretically, fairly unrestricted except for those with the most severe levels of disability. Furthermore, they continued to be unrestricted so long as the standards of expected achievement continued to be met. Obviously, the principles that controlled participation in programs included both the principle of opportunity and the principle of proof.

With the outbreak of World War I, another swing in the attitude toward people with disabilities occurred. First, the development and widespread use of IQ tests (the Army Alpha and Beta tests) revealed that the number of persons with scores below what was thought to be "normal" was much larger than originally expected (Anastasi, 1976). For the first time, a national picture of subnormality appeared, and it was found to be a large problem. Second, the sudden appearance of many war veterans whose combat wounds left them with permanent disabilities prompted people to recognize the problem as universal. The sudden visibility of people with disabilities acquired in combat may also have had the effect of attacking the myth of the heritability of a disability. Certainly, the time was one of compassion, and the result was a scramble to provide services of all kinds.

The Special Class Movement. Often billed as "opportunity" classes or programs, the educational model prevailing after World War II was an exclusive one. Self-contained classes and even schools composed of children sharing the same or similar disabilities proliferated for those children and youth whose disabilities or family situations did not warrant placement in special schools or institutions. *Equal opportunity* was interpreted to mean "modified to compensate for the disability." Thus, equal educational opportunity required instruction to be modified to deal with the difficulties imposed by a disability. At the same time, standards of achievement uniquely appropriate to the goals of the instruction were used. This service-delivery model was dominant until well into the 1970s.

Opportunity for participation in segregated programs increased almost exponentially beginning in the 1950s (U.S. Department of Education, 1983). Over the next two decades, most youngsters with a mild disability living anywhere in the United States had a class or a program available. By the early 1960s, it scarcely made sense to advocate for more services, because they were nearly universally available to those with mild and moderate disabilities.

From the earliest efforts, it was recognized that educational curricula used with students without disabilities did not provide the kind of content that would help some persons with disabilities learn to become independent adults. Unfortunately, the same was true regarding many of the segregated programs, with their lack of rigor and emphasis on "happiness" and arts and crafts. This led to placement in special classes where the emphasis was on self-development and work skills. Special education teachers in these programs essentially rejected the "watered-down" academic approach and concentrated their efforts on preparing students for work. Looking at some of the data on vocational performance during this period, one can get a picture of rather remarkable success.

In Altoona, Pennsylvania, Dinger (1961) found that

1. Eighty-five percent were employed four years after leaving school.
2. Forty-two percent earned more than a beginning teacher's salary.

Findley (1967) followed up performance of adolescents and young adults in Texas and Colorado and found that

1. IQ was an influencing factor in employment when comparing persons with IQs above 60 with persons with IQs below 60.
2. The above-60 group needed less help and got better jobs, but an equal per-centage from both groups got jobs. Most importantly, both groups returned the cost of training in income tax alone in less than 10 years.

Chaffin, Spellman, Regan, and Davison (1971) found that

1. Sixty-eight percent of a non-work-study group were employed versus 94 percent of work-study groups.
2. Two years later, 75 percent versus 83 percent of persons in these respective groups had jobs. This was not a significant difference in employment rate, although the work-study group had significantly higher wage rates than the non-work-study group.

In Kent County, Michigan, Warren (1976) found that

1. More than 95 percent of the students from the program were employed.
2. Average starting wage was $2.65 (when minimum wage was $1.65), and the highest wage was $4.85.

These and other landmark studies of work experience and work-training programs during the 1960s and 1970s were basically optimistic, and the lack of sophistication in the research methodology was largely overlooked. One important exception to this neglect was a critique by Butler and Browning (1974) of the studies most often quoted. However, the studies did nothing to raise questions about the work-study model. This was not the case with special education model program research, particularly research that focused on the effectiveness of special classes.

Evolving Program Philosophies

The major outcome of the proliferation of special education program research was confusion over what the programs were actually accomplishing for people with disabilities. Although many studies tried to assess the effectiveness of special education programs (thus named *efficacy studies*), most of the findings were equivocal. One obvious reason for this is that if there is no agreement on what is supposed to be accomplished, effectiveness cannot be demonstrated. Confining the criterion of success to academic achievement provided the chance for a host of people to criticize the programs (Johnson, 1962; Dunn, 1968; Kolstoe, 1972; MacMillan, 1977). Unfortunately, no amount of in-depth analysis can help programs that really have no agreed-upon goals or directions in the first place, particularly if the analyses examine only the means and ignore the ends, or vice versa.

The 1960s and the Normalization Concept.   One goal did emerge as a by-product of the civil rights movement that began in the 1960s. The 1960s were years of idealism in which the major thrust was one of assuring every segment of society the right to participate in the American way of life. Out of this movement came the principle of normalization, the goal of which was to ensure a normal existence for people with disabilities. Although much controversy surrounded the meaning of the normalization principle (Roos, 1970; Throne, 1975), there is little doubt as to its effect. The normalization principle established the goal for all people with disabilities to have the right to as normal an existence as possible using the most normal means possible. Essentially, the principle of normalization reestablished the principle of opportunity and the principle of proof as rights for people with disabilities to achieve as normal an existence as possible using means that are as normative as possible. For many people, however, the traditional academic program is viewed as the most "normalizing" environment available, and academic achievement has again become the school criterion for success for everyone in that environment.

Historical Development of Work-Training Programs

It fell to John Duncan in England to develop a systematic program of training that would help people with disabilities become prepared for jobs in society. Duncan's school at Lankhills, Hampshire, England, was a residential school for youngsters sent by the social services agencies of Hampshire. Although many may have had disabilities, many others were children of the streets who had few assets to help them merge into society. In today's terms, they would probably be categorized as *students at risk*. Duncan (1943) discovered that, although the verbal IQs of his young charges averaged about 66, their performance IQ scores were about 30 points higher, averaging 96. He interpreted that discrepancy to mean that the youngsters had greater concrete than abstract intelligence, and he designed a program to capitalize on that fact. Duncan analyzed the jobs in the community that demanded concrete intelligence. Jobs such as beekeeping, carpentry, baking, cooking, as well as other domestic jobs were analyzed and developed as training areas.

The analysis of community jobs into their component skills and then the incorporation of those skills into the curriculum as practiced by Duncan was also the hallmark of the program developed by Richard Hungerford in New York City in the early 1940s. As the director of the Bureau for Children with Retarded Mental Development, Hungerford (1941, 1943) published a series of tradelike journals called *Occupational Education* between 1941 and 1944. They provided teachers with step-by-step instructions for teaching skills in the needle trades, service occupations, light industry, and various unskilled and semiskilled jobs in which Hungerford had observed youngsters with mental retardation working.

In 1958, Kolstoe and Frey initiated a series of studies that yielded data on successfully and unsuccessfully employed young men with mental retardation. The extensive records kept on the young men made it possible to compare them on personal, academic, social, and occupational skills. The analyses enabled the investigators to go considerably beyond job skills to include the behaviors, knowledge, and attitudes that were displayed by the successfully employed young men. These attributes (Kolstoe, 1961) were incorporated into their work-preparation curriculum and subsequently into similar programs across the nation. Thus, in addition to the job performance skills, those academic, personal, and social skills so important to satisfying life-styles were also recognized. These were presented in the book *A High School Work Study Program for Mentally Subnormal Students* (Kolstoe & Frey, 1965). Even though the needs of students with mental retardation were specifically addressed, the curriculum and techniques were presented as being applicable to a much broader range of persons with disabilities. Because many of the young men studied had associated physical and sensory disabilities, those with visual, auditory, motor, perceptual, sensory, and linguistic problems were also included. Thus, the basic work skill development approach became much more widely applicable and acceptable, with the inclusion of the academic, personal, and social skill training that had been found to differentiate between the successful and unsuccessful young men.

Most of the emphasis during the decades before 1970 was on persons with mild mental retardation. Today, many of those persons would be diagnosed and classified as having learning disabilities or behavior disorders.

Until this time, the group classified as having moderate to severe mental retardation was rarely singled out for attention in occupational or job training. It
was this group that Gold targeted in the late 1960s to demonstrate that even
the lowest-functioning individuals in sheltered workshops could perform
complex assembly tasks with training (Gold, 1972, 1973). His "Try Another
Way" theme caught the imagination of many professionals in secondary special education and rehabilitation and began a trend toward an ideology and
technology that culminated in the major movement now associated with the
term *supported employment*. Gold's early work was extended and refined into
community-based competitive work settings by the seminal work of such
investigators as Bellamy, Peterson, and Close (1975), Rusch (1986), and
Wehman (1981).

Beginnings of Vocational Education

Another movement to identify curricula appropriate for youths with disabilities had its roots in the 1960s, but it did not become widely accepted until the
1970s. Criticisms of special education services were generally directed at
elementary-level programs, partly because there were not many secondary
programs of which to be critical. Nonetheless, some criticisms of secondary
work-training and vocational rehabilitation programs did surface. Nearly all
the criticisms alleged that the training efforts were restricted to only a few jobs
in each area of exceptionality and that the levels of training were so low that
they precluded people with disabilities from all but the most low-skill entry-
level jobs. People who were blind were often restricted to learning how to tune
pianos, cane chairs, or become street musicians. Individuals who were deaf
were trained to be linotype operators, dry cleaners, or bakers. Persons with
mental retardation were trained for food service or janitorial tasks, and those
with physical disabilities were relegated to watch repair or office work (Brolin
& Kolstoe, 1978).

   The charges that training programs limited students with disabilities to
few career options and jobs that underutilized their skills were forcefully presented to lawmakers at state and national levels. This caused them to turn their
attention to the need for legislation that would free people with disabilities
from these restrictive practices.

   One other source of major concern in special education was that self-
contained special education teachers taught not only the academics but also
the vocational skills and the skills of independent living. They also did the job
placement and follow-up supervision. Although it could be readily acknowl-
edged that the teachers were reasonably well trained to teach academic skills,
it was more difficult to justify their teaching of work skills and skills of independent living while doing work placement and follow-up. Few, if any, college
training programs provided opportunities in those years for would-be teachers
to learn those skills, and those programs that did address those skills did so

minimally (Clark & Oliverson, 1973). Vocational educators, on the other hand, were trained to teach work skills, but they often were reluctant to work with students with disabilities. Some feared that if people with disabilities were admitted and successful in vocational education programs, those programs might be thought to have low requirements or standards compared with other, more academic programs. Student safety and their assumed inability to read were other common sources of concern.

Despite these concerns, Congress passed the Vocational Education Act of 1963 (see Chapter 2 for more detail on laws mentioned in this section), which specified that persons with disabilities could be included in ongoing vocational education along with their peers without disabilities. The intent of the law was to ensure that students who have disabilities should have opportunities to learn their work skills from people who were experts at teaching work skills (vocational educators) and their academics and daily living skills from experts in those skills (general and special educators).

Unfortunately, no funds were appropriated in the 1963 act that would make it financially attractive for vocational educators to serve students with disabilities. As a result, these students were not served in any great number. That began to change, however, when Congress passed the Vocational Education Act Amendments in 1968. Among the many provisions, two were significant. First, 10 percent of the funds for vocational education were set aside to serve youths with disabilities. Second, each state was required to file a plan with the Bureau of Adult and Vocational Education that described how the funds that were set aside were to be used to serve students with disabilities.

Many states made no more than a token response to the financial incentives of the set-aside funds and did not use all available funds. It was not until the passage of PL 94-142, the Education for All Handicapped Children Act (1975), that some leverage could be applied to this situation. PL 94-142 stipulated a free and appropriate education for all youths with disabilities. The penalty for noncompliance was more stringent—loss of *all* federal funds to any state that failed to comply. The combination of money to provide services and the threat of the loss of all federal funds for not serving students with disabilities in regular vocational education programs had its desired effect: From 1973 to 1978, enrollment figures increased by 66 percent (U.S. Department of Education, 1983). Chapter 2 gives an update on vocational education (now called *career and technical education*) and its evolving role with students with disabilities since the mid-1970s.

The Career Education Movement

Career education was considered an alternative to the narrow job-preparation approach of vocational education at that time and was also a response to the problems associated with the basic general education course of study in the nation's high schools. (Basic general education was essentially the course of study leading to minimal graduation requirements and included anything that was not college preparatory or vocational education.) The career education concept, first presented by Sidney Marland in a speech to school administrators in Houston, Texas, in 1971, was conceived by members of the National Advisory Council on Vocational Education. When Marland introduced the concept of *career education,* he defined it broadly—that is, not only as preparation to earn a living but also as a way to learn about living itself. Very early in the movement there was general agreement that career education was not a high school program model, but rather a K–12 program model.

Hoyt (1975) defined *career education* as "the totality of experiences through which one learns about and prepares to engage in work as part of her or his way of living" (p. 4). He defined *work* (paid or unpaid) as a "conscious effort (other than that involved in activities whose primary purpose are either coping or relaxing) aimed at producing benefits for oneself and/or for oneself and others" (p. 3). In this context, career education was conceptualized as considerably less than all of life or one's reason for living, as Marland had visualized it, but clearly more than paid employment.

In a later elaboration, Hoyt (1977) defined *career education* as "an effort at refocusing American education and the actions of the broader community in ways that will help individuals acquire and utilize the knowledge, skills, and attitudes necessary for each to make *work* a meaningful, productive, and satisfying part of his or her way of living" (p. 5). He clarified his use of the term *work* by indicating that it "is individualistically decided by the person, not the nature of the task. What is *work* to one person may well be play to another and drudgery to another. The human need to work will, hopefully, be met by others in productive use of leisure-time, in volunteerism, or in duties performed as a full-time homemaker who is not employed for wages" (p. 7). Thus, Hoyt clarified his position on what constitutes productive work—something many conceptualizers have failed to do.

Many conceptualizers of career education for students with disabilities defined *career education* as education that focuses on the roles a person is likely to play in his or her lifetime. These include student, paid worker, recreator, family member, and citizen. Career education is what people do to learn how to engage in these roles. This view is exemplified by the definition approved in December 1977 by the Board of Governors of the Council for Exceptional Children (Brolin & D'Alonzo, 1979).

Development of Career Education Models

So many program variations have been developed that it is impossible to describe all of them. Even when the names of the programs are the same, details differ from school to school and even within the same school from year to year. Rather than this being a cause for concern, it may well be a tribute to the sincerity of the professionals who continuously evaluate their efforts, changing, adding, and discarding elements, materials, and practices as they seek better ways to help young people who have disabilities become better prepared to work and live in a complex and changing society. Three models characteristic of most program development during the 1970s and 1980s are mentioned in the following sections.

Life-Centered Career Education Model. Brolin and Kokaska presented a model (Brolin & Kokaska, 1979; Kokaska & Brolin, 1985) that captured many features of special education work-study programs with their variations and modifications, but broadened them to encompass the concept of career education for all ages. They defined *career education* as a purposeful and sequential planning approach to help students in their career development. A three-dimensional model of competencies was proposed by the authors: (1) stages of career development; (2) school, family, and community experiences; and (3) a set of 22 basic life-centered competencies that collectively contribute to the maturity of youngsters with disabilities.

The 22 major competencies students need to master to become successful as adults were identified from research in the field (Brolin & Thomas, 1971). These were grouped into three major areas: daily living skills, personal-social skills, and occupational guidance and preparation. The groups are broken down as follows:

Daily Living Skills
1. Managing family finances
2. Selecting, managing, and maintaining a home
3. Caring for personal needs
4. Raising children and living as a family
5. Buying and preparing food
6. Buying and caring for clothes
7. Engaging in civic activities
8. Using recreation and leisure
9. Getting around the community (mobility)

Personal-Social Skills
10. Achieving self-awareness
11. Acquiring self-confidence
12. Achieving socially responsible behavior
13. Maintaining good interpersonal skills
14. Achieving independence
15. Achieving problem-solving skills
16. Communicating adequately with others

Occupational Guidance and Preparation
17. Knowing and exploring occupational possibilities

18. Selecting and planning occupational choices
19. Exhibiting appropriate work habits and behaviors
20. Exhibiting sufficient physical-manual skills
21. Gaining a specific occupational skill
22. Seeking, securing, and maintaining employment

Rather than being presented initially as a specific curriculum, the Life-Centered Career Education (LCCE) curriculum was designed as an outline or model for the concepts embodied in the 22 competencies to be *infused* into the general education curriculum, beginning with the kindergarten level and extending well into adulthood. Experience with the infusion approach for the past decade led Brolin (1988) to a modified view, however, when he proposed that for some students an alternative curriculum, such as the Life-Centered Career Education curriculum, must be provided instead of primarily academic programs, the goals of which are unattainable for them. The LCCE curriculum (Brolin, 1997; Brolin & Loyd, 2004) and the adaptation for students with moderate mental disabilities (Loyd & Brolin, 1997) was developed to be used through infusion or through separate instruction. The LCCE Revised Edition (Brolin, 2004) is the latest revision and provides some new features for implementing the LCCE model.

Career Education for Exceptional Children and Youth. Gillet (1981) presented a developmental model specifically for exceptional youngsters that centered on a core program modified to fit the type and degree of disability. It suggested a continuum of services beginning at the elementary level. Learning the meaning of the world of work and developing social competencies form the bases upon which students learn about the requirements of many jobs from which occupational choices are made. Personal adequacy, work habits, skill development, decision-making ability, and the opportunity to participate in a job with constructive supervision were systematically developed. The program required the cooperation of pupils, teachers, service staff, parents, administrators, and community leaders to successfully relate special education to career development. The scope and sequence of the program certainly made it a very attractive proposal, but it clearly focused on work and occupational roles, ignoring personal and social skills and independence in daily living tasks outside of employment.

School-Based Career Development and Transition Education Model. The School-Based Career Development and Transition Education Model was originally a career education model developed for students with disabilities, adapting the Marland Career Education Model described by Goldhammer and Taylor (1972). The initial versions of the model appeared in Clark (1979, 1980). In the late 1980s, the model was revised to incorporate the concept of *transition* and appeared in earlier editions of this book (Clark & Kolstoe, 1990, 1995) and other sources (cf. Gajar, Goodman, & McAfee, 1993; Brolin, 1995; Wehman, 1992, 1996). The latest version of this model will be presented later in this chapter as the conceptual basis for our current thinking about career development, transition education, and transition service delivery.

Functional and Community-Based Models for Students with Severe Disabilities

A spin-off from the career education models during the late 1980s and early 1990s were some models designed for students with moderate and severe disabilities. Dever (1988) published the *Community Living Skills Taxonomy,* Smith and Schloss (1988) developed the *Community-Referenced Curriculum,* and McDonnel and associates developed the *School and Community Integration Project* (1992). McDonnel, Wilcox, and Hardman (1991) affirmed the need for community-based programming for those students who had not been included in many of the life skills and community work-based programs prior to that time. Since the early 1990s, Valletutti, Bender, and Sims-Tucker (1996) and Wehman and Kregel (2004) have provided new curriculum models across all age levels.

Development of Career Education Programs

National acceptance of the concept of *career education* was facilitated by the appointment of Kenneth Hoyt in 1972 to coordinate program efforts in the U.S. Office of Education. The effect was to significantly increase opportunities in secondary programs for students with disabilities because for the first time there was a larger movement within general education with which special educators could identify and make connections. However, career education programs never were fully implemented nationally. At the crest of the career education movement, Reichard (1979) analyzed programs in a five-state area; each state reported having a career education curriculum for students with disabilities. He found that nearly 70 percent of the programs stated they did not schedule field trips to business and industrial settings, even though 60 percent reported they had cooperative work programs through local businesses. Also, 55 percent said they did not provide any job placement help for their students. Most disappointing was that only 25 percent of the students with disabilities at the junior high school level participated in a career education program; at the high school level, only 42 percent of the students with disabilities were involved.

Reichard's (1979) findings were essentially the following:

1. Career education is too frequently viewed synonymously with vocational education or rehabilitation.
2. Of those existing efforts, there appear to be no agreed-upon competencies, philosophies, guidelines, or functional intraagency communications.

3. Knowledge of—or the provision and/or development of—career education materials is nearly nonexistent.
4. Definitions of career education appear to vary significantly among vocational programs.
5. Philosophical differences between administrators and teachers of regular and special classes are evident.
6. Noneducational personnel apparently are not being included in the process.
7. For those programs in existence, accountability—that is, competencies and programmatic evaluations and publications of results—is taking a low profile.
8. Agreement with the career education concept appears to be widely accepted, but implementation is varied.

There is no reason to believe that the problems discovered by Reichard were locally unique or that they were characteristic of a specific period of the late 1970s. It was not the discouraging results of Reichard's study, however, that led to the demise of career education. When the federal office of Career Education Programs closed, it had finished its legal mission of providing incentives, initiatives, and technical assistance to states and local programs. The federal role was over and, unfortunately, when the money disappeared for states and local districts, so did career education programming to a significant extent.

Independent Living for Persons with Disabilities

Special educators once thought that the state vocational rehabilitation agency was the natural and appropriate bridge to employment and "happily-ever-after" community living for their graduates. This expectation developed during the 1960s, when schools saw state vocational rehabilitation agencies taking a new look at special education populations, particularly those classified with mild mental retardation. The number of cases closed successfully by vocational rehabilitation increased dramatically from 1960 to 1975. This served only to heighten special educators' expectations that there was someone to assume responsibility for students after they left or completed school. School personnel welcomed the commitment that divisions of vocational rehabilitation were making to the rehabilitation closures (defined as "closed in employment status") of special education graduates and assumed that it was a permanent policy commitment.

At the heart of this optimism was the rather spectacular success of many state departments of education and state vocational rehabilitation agencies in working together through local school districts in programming and funding school work-study programs. Interestingly, even the term *transition* was used in the late 1960s to describe an orderly passage from school or institutional programming to adult services and full community participation (Chaffin, 1968; Younie, 1966). Unfortunately, the momentum waned in the late 1970s as state education agencies and schools became immersed in implementing PL 94-142. It became increasingly difficult to claim teachers' salaries for third-party reimbursement from state vocational rehabilitation funds when less time was spent in the work experience phase of the work-study programs. During that time, state vocational rehabilitation agencies began quietly withdrawing from school cooperative programs and turning their attention to the demands for services for persons with more severe disabilities.

Two separate yet parallel movements set the stage for the field to move to the current concept of *transition.* These movements rekindled hopes for an organized, effective process for students and their families. Both occurred in the context of ending school programming and beginning adult living. The first of these was the career education movement, as described in the previous section. The second was the independent living movement. While the career education movement was reaching its zenith in the U.S. public education system, the independent living movement was unfolding in the field of rehabilitation with adults. Both have contributed to a return to the goal of interagency cooperation but through a new and improved delivery system—transition programs and services.

Like the word *transition,* the term *independent living* has both a generic meaning and a symbolic meaning. The generic connotation of independent living may be thought of as the choice, opportunity, and ability to participate actively in the community through home and family life, work, and civic and recreational involvement (Nosek, 1992). Symbolically, however, independent living implies much more than this. One of the early and definitive statements of the meaning of independent living was provided by the Independent Living Research Utilization Project–Texas Institute for Rehabilitation Research (1978). *Independent living* was defined as

> control over one's life based on the choice of acceptable options that minimize reliance on others in making decisions and in performing everyday activities. This includes managing one's own affairs; participating in day-to-day life in the community; fulfilling a range of social roles; and making decisions that lead to self-determination and the minimization of psychological or physical dependence upon others. Independence is a relative concept, which may be defined personally by each individual. (p. 1)

Independent living rehabilitation (ILR) started as a disability-rights movement in the early 1970s by persons with severe physical disabilities in reaction to years of federal and state legislation and rehabilitation policies that stopped too short of meaningful *vocational* rehabilitation and way short of community accessibility and independent living. From the beginning, vocational rehabilitation services were restricted by federal policy to the provision of services only to those for whom there was a "reasonable expectation" that the services would result in remunerative employment. It was the view of many vocational rehabilitation professionals that independent living services were developed for those for whom a vocational goal was thought to be impossible or unfeasible (DeJong, 1980), rather than a means of making vocational goals feasible. It was the view of many persons with disabilities, on the other hand, that accessible housing, transportation, and communication were the key elements to realizing preferences and opportunities in employment

During the period from 1959 to 1972, Congress made several attempts to pass legislation for special comprehensive rehabilitation services to improve the independent living of persons with disabilities without regard to their ultimate employability. Consumers of rehabilitation services, especially those with the most severe physical disabilities, challenged this concept with the notion that gainful employment is one of *several* ways an individual can become truly independent. They argued that both comprehensive independent living rehabilitation services *and* vocational rehabilitation services not only were needed but were a basic right.

The Rehabilitation Act of 1973 was the first legislation to pass that clearly made a commitment to the provision of vocational rehabilitation services to persons with disabilities who needed more than assistance in gaining employment. Although the Act not mandate independent living rehabilitation or even vocational rehabilitation services, it did provide a legal base for prohibiting denial of services and discrimination through Sections 501, 502, 503, and 504. It also directed the secretary of the Department of Health, Education, and Welfare to conduct a comprehensive needs study, including research and demonstration projects of various methods of providing rehabilitation and related services to individuals who were the most severely handicapped (Arkansas Rehabilitation Research and Training Center, 1978). "Most severely handicapped" was interpreted by most rehabilitation personnel as persons with severe physical or sensory disabilities.

Because it was a logical extension of the civil rights movement of the 1960s, the independent living movement was influenced by other social movements of the 1970s. Among these were consumerism, or self-advocacy, demedicalization and self-care, deinstitutionalization and normalization, and mainstreaming (DeJong, 1983). In spite of being affected by these various movements, there is still a split between the advocates of persons with severe physical and/or sensory disabilities and those with severe cognitive or mental disabilities. To some degree the separateness between them is a result of two issues: (1) the strong self-advocacy concept within the independent living movement and (2) the issue of "independent" living. Those with severe cognitive or mental disabilities are not as able to be active, articulate, self-advocates in the political arena and, in most cases, expect "interdependent" living situations. As a result of these factors, the independent living movement typically focuses on those with physical and sensory disabilities. The severe cognitive disabilities group is championed by The Association for Persons with Severe Handicaps (TASH), and those with severe mental health disabilities have mental health organizations as their advocates. At the heart of all of these independent living efforts, however, has been the theme of discrimination or rejection by the prevailing social system. Their impact on both educators and rehabilitation personnel alike set the stage for a readiness for the concept of *transition.*

Transition Programs and Services

Just as the career education movement of the 1970s was an expansion of the work-study movement of the 1960s, in 1984, Madeline Will, director of the Office of Special Education and Rehabilitative Services, championed the transition movement that extended the career education issue into the realm of transition programs and services in schools and linkages with adult community services.

Like its predecessors, work-study and career education, the early stages of the transition movement owed much of its acceptance to the fact that it was introduced as a federal initiative. As such, the initiative carried the weight of legislative legitimacy and substantial funding to support innovative and imaginative programs. It emphasized the preparation of people with disabilities for work, and made possible such innovations as supported employment and job coaching. However, it paid little attention to preparation for independent living and the notions of self-determination.

Fortunately, there has been a broadening of the view of the transition concept beyond merely a transition from school to work, just as there was eventually a broadening of the concept of career education beyond an occupational focus (cf. Brolin & Kokaska, 1979; Clark, 1974). The current perspective of transition held by the Division on Career Development and Transition and framed by Halpern (1994) presents the idea that the transition concept should include concerns for employment, postsecondary education, independent living, community participation, and social and interpersonal relationships. This shift of thinking about transition from the narrow concern about employment to all quality-of-life areas was influenced by the state and national follow-up and follow-along studies of the period from 1985 through 1995. Seminal studies from among the 20 or more that appeared during this 10-year period began with the landmark studies of Mithaug, Horiuchi, and Fanning (1985), Hasazi, Gordon, and Roe (1985), Wehman, Kregel, and Seyfarth (1985), and Kranstover, Thurlow, and Bruininks (1989). Studies in the early to mid-1990s were characterized by their impressive sample sizes and systematic inquiry techniques (Affleck, Edgar, Levine, & Kortering, 1990; Frank & Sitlington, 1993; Frank, Sitlington, & Carson, 1991; Sitlington & Frank, 1990, 1993, 1994; Sitlington, Frank, & Carson, 1992) and the SRI National Longitudinal Transition Study and its numerous analysis reports (cf. Valdes, Williamson, & Wagner, 1990; Marder & D'Amico, 1992; Wagner, Blackorby, Cameto, Hebbeler, & Newman, 1993). Most of these studies focused on high-incidence populations (learning disabilities, mild mental retardation, or behavior disorders) who were in high school special education programs or received special education services while in school. These findings had direct bearing on current targeted issues of transition from school to adult living. The federal funding of the National Longitudinal Transition Study–2 in 2001 will provide a more current look at outcomes after 10 years of effort).

The early unidimensional view of transition from school to working life is often attributed to Madeline Will as a result of her initiatives and influence of federal priorities as head of the Office of Special Education and Rehabilitative Services of the Department of Education (Will, 1984). Actually, this single-focus view goes back to the influence of Gold (1980) and others, who staked early claims in vocational training of persons with severe disabilities and the supported employment concept (Bellamy, Peterson, & Close, 1975; Rusch, 1986; Wehman, 1981). In any case, it is clear that Will's priority for federal support in transition efforts was targeted on employment and influenced the general perceptions many people had about transition programs. Politically, there are any number of reasons for linking transition as a concept to employment outcomes, but it caused some professional debate early on over the interpretation of the concept of transition (Clark & Knowlton, 1988; Rusch & Menchetti, 1988).

We affirm again in this edition the position of Halpern (1994) and numerous others (cf. Brolin & Loyd, 2004; Browning, 1997; Flexer, Simmons, Luft, & Baer, 2005; Wehman, 2001) that transition from school to adult living is a life-career focus that families, school personnel, and adult service agencies should have in developing transition programs. Ending all debate, in the Individuals with Disabilities Education Act of 1990 (IDEA; PL 101-476), Congress institutionalized the life-centered outcome focus of transition services. Congress most recently (Individuals with Disabilities Education Improvement Act, 2004) defined *transition services* as a service-delivery system in the following way:

> Transition services means a coordinated set of activities for a child with a disability that:
>
> (A) is designed to be within a results-oriented process, that is focused on improving the academic and functional achievement of the child with a disability to facilitate the child's movement from school to post-school activities, including post-secondary education, vocational education, integrated employment (including supported employment), continuing and adult education, adult services, independent living, or community participation;
>
> (B) is based on the individual child's needs, taking into account the child's strengths, preferences, and interests; and

> (C) includes instruction, related services, community experiences, the development of employment and other post-school adult living objectives, and, when appropriate, acquisition of daily living skills and functional vocational evaluation. (Sec. 602)

The definition of *transition* by the Division on Career Development and Transition of the Council for Exceptional Children (DCDT-CEC), framed by Halpern (1994), is the definition we prefer because it does not limit the concept of transition to a service-delivery notion. It emphasizes transition from school to adult life as a *process*. Halpern's definition states:

> Transition refers to a change in status from behaving primarily as a student to assuming emergent adult roles in the community. These roles include employment, participating in post-secondary education, maintaining a home, becoming appropriately involved in the community, and experiencing satisfactory personal and social relationships. The process of enhancing transition involves the participation and coordination of school programs, adult agency services, and natural supports within the community. The foundations for transition should be laid during the elementary and middle school years, guided by the broad concept of career development. Transition planning should begin no later than age 14, and students should be encouraged, to the full extent of their capabilities, to assume a maximum amount of responsibility for such planning. (p. 117)

Transition from School to Adult Living and the Individuals with Disabilities Education Act and Its Amendments

Chapter 2 presents the provisions of the IDEA and its amendments in detail, but it is important in this section on historical context to note the primary changes. In the IDEA of 1990, Congress established age 16 as the beginning point for requiring transition services, but allowed for the possibility of transition planning to begin at an earlier age (i.e., ages 14 to 15, or earlier when appropriate). Subsequent to 1992, some states, on their own initiatives, took positions in their transition guidelines or state regulations to include students who were age 14 or 15. The DCDT definition (Halpern, 1994) took the strong position that age 14 was a minimum age for beginning transition planning and services. In response to these actions, concerns about dropout rates for students with disabilities (U.S. Department of Education, 1995), and lobbying efforts by advocacy groups, Congress amended the IDEA of 1990 in the 1997 reauthorization amendments to include students ages 14 and 15 in a transition planning process. It also made explicit what had previously been implicit—that is, related services are included among the transition services that should be considered in developing a statement of needed transition services.

IDEA 2004 retreated from the progressive stance of the 1997 Amendments to move the mandated age for initiating planning back to age 16. IDEA legislation (including all amendments) made it clear that programs and services needed by a student should be highly individualized, based on individual strengths, needs, preferences, and interests. Programs and instructional arrangements are not to be based on currently available programs and services. The individualized education program (IEP) requirements under PL 94-142 and later amendments was expanded under the IDEA and its amendments to ensure better individual planning for transition outcomes. The provisions specify that all goals, objectives, instruction, and related services must be planned and delivered within a results-oriented process.

Transition and Education Services Models

We believe that a transition services model for programming for the needs of all secondary special education students must be one with multiple options. As a consequence of that belief, we found it necessary in the third edition to propose two models rather than one. The models reflect the two views that we value about the transition process. First, we believe that instruction or an educational component is absolutely critical in facilitating not only the development of knowledge and skills related to making the transition from school to the adult community but also self-determination skills that are needed after leaving school. Second, we believe that transition services, particularly related services and linkages to support services, are critical for students and their families to have some knowledge about and access to support services at school and in the community. The models are linked by their common reference to transition outcome domains.

Assumptions for a Comprehensive Transition Education and Services Approach

The transition education and services models presented in the next section are based on certain assumptions that we derived from looking at our history and the relevant research on adult adjustment for people with disabilities. These assumptions include the following:

1. Lifelong career development and transition education are needed for *all* persons—young and old, with and without disabilities, male and female, poor and affluent, and of all races and ethnic groups.
2. One's lifelong career is one's progress, or transition, through life as a family member, citizen, and worker. It is a developmental process and is subject to planning, educational opportunities, choices, and changes.

3. Transition education for lifelong career development and life transitions is concerned with age-appropriate independent and interdependent living. As such, it promotes protecting each developing person's freedom to make choices and decisions, while assisting him or her to learn what alternatives there are and how to make decisions about them.

4. Significant neglect or adversity in any aspect of human growth can affect one's lifelong career development. Significant neglect or adversity during any of life's basic transition periods or during a person's unique transition periods can affect his or her adult living outcomes.

5. Society still imposes limits on the lifelong career development and transitions of persons with disabilities. These factors restrict their independent and interdependent living and will require long-term attention to social change.

6. Any person choosing to participate as a producer or consumer in today's complex and changing world must possess a variety of life skills in adaptability.

7. Lifelong career development and transition education for persons with physical or mental disabilities differ significantly enough in nature or degree from those of persons without disabilities that some special attention to training and services is required.

8. Just as there is a need for different programming between people who have disabilities and those who do not, there is also a need for some differentiated programming among the individuals identified for special education services.

9. Lifelong career development and transition planning and education for any person should begin during infancy and continue throughout adulthood. Early training is especially critical for individuals with disabilities.

10. A democratic philosophy of education and a realistic philosophy of normalization dictate that all students have the same educational opportunities. These philosophies do not dictate, however, that all students have the same specific educational experiences, be in the same instructional programs, or achieve the same educational outcomes.

Proposed Comprehensive Transition Education and Services Models

The Career Development and Transition Education Model used in the first two editions of this book targeted some basic program content elements and possible school and community delivery alternatives at a time when the field needed that kind of focus. Our understanding of life transitions and the process of planning and delivering transition education programs and services since 1995 led us to move to another level of thinking in the third edition. The proposed models presented in Figures 1.1 and 1.2 are a reflection of our continuing perspective of critical student outcomes across age/developmental levels, transition exit points for students as they move from one educational level to the next, and the educational and service systems needed to deliver transition education and transition services.

The present models reflect an outcome-oriented set of performance areas or domains that must be *addressed* as transition planning areas for students rather than as specifically designated curriculum and instruction areas that schools must provide. We believe there is a major difference in what happens when a model is used to organize and implement programs and services if the model focuses on knowledge and skill outcomes rather than knowledge and skill curriculum content. Figure 1.1, Comprehensive Transition Education Model, features this idea in the list of Knowledge and Skill Domains. Nine domains are proposed as the framework for responding to the individualized education program (IEP) requirement under the IDEA for determining what a student needs in order to meet his or her transition services needs in the areas of *instruction, related services, community experiences, employment,* and *other postschool adult living objectives.*

Another major shift in this model from the career development and transition education model of earlier editions of the book is the recognition that there is not just one transition in life, but many. A comprehensive model of transition education and services must take into account the idea that success in one transition increases the likelihood of success in later transitions. We believe strongly in that part of the Division on Career Development and Transition (DCDT) definition (Halpern, 1994), expanded in other DCDT position statements (Clark, Carlson, Fisher, Cook, & D'Alonzo, 1991; Clark, Field, Patton, Brolin, & Sitlington, 1994), that states that education for life transitions and support in making life transitions needs to begin as early as possible. Figure 1.1 reflects this view in the Exit Points and Outcomes component. Developmental or life phases include all phases of life and a life span continuum, beginning with infants and toddlers. Each phase has its own set of benchmark outcomes and/or exit points so that families and teachers can see their targeted outcomes for short-term planning. Too often, transition advocates emphasize the long-term adult outcomes of transition when communicating about the concept of transition and the nature of transition services. Long-term outcomes are too far removed for many families and teachers of young children, and so there is a tendency to assume that those outcomes will be addressed adequately at a later age.

The third and final major shift in the present models from the previous model used is the notion that educational systems are not the only desirable or responsible educational or service-delivery systems in transition considerations. Stakeholders in transition decision making and problem solving have become increasingly aware that collaborative, interdependent efforts are much more effective than independent, isolated efforts. Public schools are required by law to be responsible for transition planning for children with disabilities moving from infant/toddler programs to early childhood programs at age 3 and for students 16 years of age and older preparing to leave school between the ages of 17 and 22. There is no mandate for transition planning or services for elementary-aged and middle-school aged children, but these are critical years that should be included in a comprehensive model. Regardless of the age level, however, schools cannot assume responsibility for planning or supporting the transition process alone. The students, their families, and appropriate community service agencies must be involved, as well. To that end, the model reflects a comprehensive range of educational and support service systems as part of the process. Figure 1.2, Comprehensive Transition Services Model, reflects the connection between knowledge and skill domains and the multiple service delivery alternatives that can be considered in any individual's transition planning.

The language used in describing the various components of the models should be clear to those who are familiar with current transition literature. Some of the terms, though, may need clarification for our particular use of them in the context of transition education and services. For that reason, we will discuss briefly each of the three components of the models and the language used within them.

Knowledge and Skill Domains

Knowledge and skill domains refer to those skills or performance areas that are important for successfully coping with life demands across developmental levels. We think of knowledge and skills as a response to the question, What do we want our students to know (knowledge) and be able to do (skills) when they leave school? That is, at every stage of life, from birth to death, there are demands or expectations of people that require certain kinds and amounts of knowing or doing to adjust successfully to that stage of life. For example, young children normally develop a functional use of their family's language system by the age of 5. Before that, they know a lot of words through their receptive vocabulary, but cannot express ideas or concepts at the same level. One is comprehension and the other is expressive skill. For older students, they may know and be able to list the steps for calling 911, but when asked to perform the skill, it becomes another task. Most skills involve some knowledge, but knowledge does not require skills until it has to be demonstrated or applied.

Each of the nine knowledge and skill areas presented in both Figures 1.1 and 1.2 are briefly defined and explained here. Hopefully, it will be clear how there is a direct relationship between knowledge and skills in each domain and content areas for curriculum and instruction in a range of educational settings.

Communication and Academic Performance Skills. *Communication skills* refer to expressive skills (e.g., speaking, signing, and augmentative communi-

Exit Points and Outcomes

Knowledge and Skills Domains

Communication and Academic Performance

Self-Determination

Interpersonal Relationships

Integrated Community Participation

Health and Fitness

Independent/Interdependent Daily Living

Leisure and Recreation

Employment

Further Education and Training

Developmental /Life Phases	Exit Points
Infant/toddler and home training	Exit to preschool programs and integrated community participation
Preschool and home training	Exit to elementary school programs and integrated community participation
Elementary school	Exit to middle school/junior high school programs, age-appropriate self-determination, and integrated community participation
Middle school/junior high school	Exit to high school programs, entry-level employment, age-appropriate self-determination, and integrated community par ticipation
High school	Exit to postsecondary education or entry-level employment, adult and continuing education, full-time homemaker, self-determined quality of life, and integrated community participation
Postsecondary education	Exit to specialized, technical, professional, or managerial employment, graduate or professional school programs, adult and continuing education, full-time home maker, self-determined quality of life, and integrated community participation

FIGURE 1.1   Comprehensive Transition Education Model

Education and Service Delivery Systems

Home and neighborhood

Family and friends

Public and private infant/toddler programs

General education with related and support services

Special education with related and support services

Generic community organization and agencies (employment, health, legal, housing, financial)

Specific community organization and agencies (crisis services, time-limited services, ongoing services)

Apprenticeship programs

School and community work-based learning programs

Postsecondary vocational or applied technology programs

Community colleges

Four-year colleges and universities

Graduate or professional schools

Adult and continuing education/training

Knowledge and Skills Domains

Communication and Academic Performance

Self-Determination

Interpersonal Relationships

Integrated Community Participation

Health and Fitness

Independent/Interdependent Daily Living

Leisure and Recreation

Employment

Further Education and Training

FIGURE 1.2   Comprehensive Transition Services Model

cation skills) and listening skills (e.g., oral comprehension, sign reading, and speech reading). *Academic skills* range from basic reading skills for acquiring information or pleasure to advanced reading speed and comprehension of difficult materials, as well as written language (grammar, syntax, and spelling), math comprehension, and math computation skills. Communication and academic skill outcome goals should be age or grade-level appropriate for current and next anticipated performance settings.

Self-Determination Skills. Field and Hoffman (1994) stated in their model that self-determination begins with an awareness of one's self and valuing one's self. From that stage, an individual has the basic information to make decisions and set personal goals, plan actions to meet those goals, and anticipate some specific results. Self-determined action follows planning and sets the stage for experiencing outcomes and learning from the entire process. *Self-determination skills* obviously vary in relation to the complexity of the outcome goals and the environments within which they occur. Still, as a developmental skill that one hopes will gain in power over time in life, it is important to view it as a teachable skill. Educational and support-service systems must be attentive to the self-determination skill-development process over time and not wait until the last stages of the school experience to address it. Field, Hoffman, and Spezia (1998) expanded and clarified the concept of self-determination and strategies for developing self-determination knowledge and skills in adolescents. Field, Martin, Miller, Ward, and Wehmeyer (1998a) presented some major models of self-determination and existing curricula and materials. Their publication is a superb practical source for teachers in curriculum and instructional planning for knowledge and skills in self-determination.

Interpersonal Relationship Skills. *Interpersonal relationship skills,* or *socialization skills,* vary across age levels but comprise the basic interpersonal skills used in family, school, and community relationships. Skills include positive social behaviors, such as sharing, cooperating and collaborating, respecting others' privacy and property, being sensitive to others' feelings and preferences as well as cultural differences and values, and exhibiting specific environment social behavior expectations. Knowledge includes knowing socially appropriate and inappropriate behaviors and understanding how cultural, moral, ethical, legal, and religious influences guide one's individual social behavior as well as one's community and government public policies.

When skills and knowledge of interpersonal relationships are described in this way, it is difficult to omit the role that values, attitudes, and habits play in social interactions. People's values and attitudes are the basis for what they find worthy in themselves and in others. Values and attitudes undergird codes of conduct, preferences, beliefs, ideas, habits, and even decision making. On the other hand, the mention of values worries some people who believe that this is an area that schools cannot afford to address because of the controversial issues inherent in values education. We are persuaded by the eloquence of

Noddings (1992) in *The Challenge to Care in Schools: An Alternative Approach to Education* and Brendtro, Brokenleg, and Van Bockern (1990) in *Reclaiming Youth at Risk: Our Hope for the Future* that the school can and should model and teach caring and personal responsibility.

Integrated Community Participation Skills. *Integrated community participation* skills range from knowledge about how to access community interest settings to actual knowledge or skills in participating in those settings. Examples of community participation activities are unique to specific communities and neighborhoods, but common interest and preference areas include accessing and participating in shopping alternatives, community special events (e.g., festivals, parades, fairs, etc.), parks and recreation centers, religious organizations or community activities, volunteering, voting, advocacy for disability rights, public libraries (e.g., free loan of books, compact discs, videos, and audiocassettes), and the like. The school's responsibility to assess a student's preferences and interests should go beyond occupational or postsecondary education preferences and interests. The nature of a student's preferences and interests in relation to participating in his or her neighborhood or community should guide the school on that student's instructional needs.

Health and Fitness Skills. The area of *physical health and fitness* covers the expected areas of general health concerns (e.g., health status, nutrition, weight, chronic illnesses or symptoms, and medications) as well as physical fitness (e.g., physical condition related to wellness and prevention of health problems and physical condition related to strength, stamina, endurance, range of motion, and mobility). Knowledge of one's health status and fitness is important for preventing health problems or self-injury as well as the need for medications, consistency in following treatment procedures, periodic examinations or medical procedures, and the possible need for physical therapy, prosthetics, orthotics, or assistive technology. Skills in self-care and fitness are important for wellness.

Students and families who are not informed or educated about the relationship between nutrition and general health, exercise and fitness, diet and weight control, and mental or emotional stress and physical symptoms may not show a high level of interest in health and fitness as a transition education planning issue. Schools that have good health education programs and use health services personnel to observe and evaluate student needs can take the initiative in assessing health and fitness concerns and reporting these to students and their families. Schools that do not necessarily have good health education or health services can still address health and fitness concerns in careful and creative curriculum decisions and/or linkages to appropriate health services.

Independent/Interdependent Daily Living Skills. *Independent living skills* are highly valued in U.S. society. With appropriate training or support, most persons with disabilities achieve satisfactory levels of independence. Indicators of independent living vary across age levels. For young children and older youths with severe cognitive or multiple disabilities, independent behaviors are essentially what is referred to as *adaptive behaviors*—dressing, eating, bathing, taking care of personal belongings, performing simple chores, and the like. In adolescence, adaptive behaviors begin to take on the form of daily living skills and independent living skills—advanced dressing skills and decision making on clothing, personal hygiene skills, basic food preparation, care and maintenance of clothing, driving or use of public transportation, managing one's own money, taking responsibility for one's own medications or support requests, and complying with the rules of authority at home, school, and in the community. Adult adaptive behavior skills are much the same as independent living skills, including all areas of daily living at home, community participation, employment, personal decision making, and taking responsibility for one's own financial, legal, and personal-social life.

The concept of *interdependence* is also important because few individuals are totally independent in life. Most people, with or without disabilities, do not live truly independently, but rather conduct their individual affairs through mutual reliance with other people. Interdependent living skills across all ages may refer to (1) being able to know one's self and understand when one needs support or assistance, (2) knowing that different people in families and living groups play different types of interdependent roles, and (3) understanding the roles of personal attendants or professional support people in interdependent relationships.

Leisure and Recreation Skills.   The importance of satisfying use of *leisure time* for rest, recreation, and renewal is often neglected in transition programs that focus exclusively (or predominantly) on transition from school to work or school to careers. Brannan (1999) made the case that leisure, recreation, and play are inherent aspects of the human experience and are essential to health and well-being. Certainly, persons with disabilities that limit their participation in home, school, and community activities have the same needs for and right to leisure, recreation, and play. Access to leisure, recreation, or play events or facilities is critical for this, but from the individual's perspective, access is not enough. Students with disabilities must develop and expand their awareness and knowledge of leisure alternatives, and understand the value of asserting their needs and rights for leisure opportunities as well as skills relating to activities, social expectations, and self-determination.

Employment Skills.   Within the model presented here, *employability skills* for students with disabilities making the transition from school to adult living refers to general employability skills, occupational skills, and vocational skills. *General employability skills* are general work skills such as following directions, exhibiting on-task behavior, showing concern for quality work as well as work rate, recognizing and correcting errors or problems, understanding attendance and punctuality, and having the ability to take instruction and criticism. Learning these employability skills begins in early childhood. *Occupational skills* include skills in seeking and obtaining a job; exhibiting marketable entry-level skills in reading, math, communication, and interpersonal relationships; demonstrating speed, accuracy, and precision in job tasks assigned; adapting to work environment changes; adjusting to repetition and monotony of job performance; and demonstrating skills in job maintenance. *Vocational skills* are specific skills learned through training or experience in job performance, such as industrial skills (welding, machine operation, etc.), business and office occupations (bookkeeping, secretarial, computer operation, etc.), construction trade skills (carpentry, plumbing, electrical, masonry, etc.), health occupations, and the like.

Further Education and Training Skills.   *Further education and training* as a knowledge and skill or instructional content area refers to readiness for any formal education or training experiences after leaving the public education system. The most common of these options include preparation in school for postsecondary vocational and technical schools, community colleges, four-year colleges and universities, graduate and professional education, education and training provided in the military or business and industry, adult education, and personal or vocational continuing education. Preparation of students for taking advantage of postsecondary education and training options includes awareness of application procedures and admission requirements as well as successfully completing all the academic courses or programs possible that will help ensure successful postsecondary education or training.

Increasingly, the need for assuming the role of a lifelong learner is being accepted in society. Too many changes occur in work and societal demands to depend solely on any one level of educational attainment. Individuals with disabilities have enough difficulties in accessing and maintaining satisfying roles in the workplace and in the community without getting farther behind others because they discontinue their education and training. This model also emphasizes the importance of continuing education and training, regardless of the basic choice after high school of going to college or some type of vocational training school versus going directly to work or being a full-time homemaker. Continuing education highlights the importance of knowing how to learn about and access information related to family and community living and all aspects of integrated community participation via the media, the Internet, public libraries, and other information sources.

Exit Points and Outcomes

The exit points and outcomes shown in Figure 1.1 reflect the lifelong process of vertical transitions of life, using developmental or life phases as a continuum. On the other hand, developmental or life phases connected with educational benchmarks or life outcomes also involve lifelong horizontal transitions. *Tran-*

sition education, a term used in the title of this book, implies that although vertical and horizontal transitions in life are natural and inevitable, people can be more prepared for those transitions if they learn what they need to know about life demands and expectations during each transition period of life. Since the late 1980s, the term *transition* has been used so frequently and in so many contexts that it seems important to anchor an understanding of life transitions here not only by domains of concern (knowledge and skills) but also by transition exit points.

A comprehensive model of transition education and services that embraces a lifelong transitions approach must take into account all the major exit points in transition education and services from infancy through adulthood. Professionals and families need to be reminded that at each major educational level, there is a transition process with age-appropriate and environment-specific expectations. For example, elementary school children receiving special education and/or related services will, at a certain grade level or socially determined decision point, move on to middle school or junior high school in a public or private school program. The decision to exit is not always based on mastery of all elementary school standards; rather, it usually is based on age appropriateness and readiness for a more advanced level of education. Good transition education and services, however, would extend its academic preparation of a student not only to be ready for middle or junior high school but to ensure that the student is also ready for more advanced levels of integration in community participation.

The emphasis in this book is on transition education and services for all children and youths with disabilities from elementary grades through graduation or exit from school. The comprehensive models presented here reflect exit points that range from exit and transition expectations for children leaving elementary school into middle school to exit from high school and transition into postsecondary education or entry-level employment, adult and continuing education, full-time homemaker roles, and a self-determined quality of life and integrated community participation. This may sound lofty and ideal, but the two models are meant to focus on the ideal so as not to settle for something much less. We believe it is better to have models with high standards laying out some specific exit-point accomplishments rather than have no model or vision at all and viewing the school's responsibility as merely getting students through a series of grades.

Education and Service Delivery Systems

The education and comprehensive delivery systems presented in Figure 1.2 are meant to emphasize the collaborative nature of transition education. Too many secondary special education teachers feel alone in the effort to provide transition education and services in multiple knowledge and skill domains. One reason teachers feel this way is a result of an administrative delegation of responsibility for transition services without adequate support or training.

Another reason teachers might feel alone is that they have an awareness of the responsibility of the need and the federal requirement to provide transition services, but feel neglected and abandoned by administrators. Congress requires local education agencies (not just teachers or designated transition specialists) to provide transition services through instruction (general or special education) and related services.

No one who understands the challenges of providing transition education and services believes that teachers, or even schools, can successfully accomplish the goals of results-oriented transitions alone. Even from the outset, the 1990 federal mandate for transition services under the IDEA (PL 101-476) called for linkages with appropriate nonschool agencies and service-delivery systems. In the 1997 IDEA Amendments, Congress added related services, which are school-based service-delivery systems, as additional linkage alternatives. To address the issue of doing the job of transition education and services, our models present an array of formal and informal systems that should be involved in developing knowledge and skills for one or more of the many transitions that individuals with disabilities will face in their lifetimes.

Home, family, neighborhood, and friends vary in availability and effectiveness as educational and support systems for students in special education programs. We know that many home situations are excellent environments for learning about and reinforcing skills in the outcome areas of our comprehensive models. Other times, parents or family members are actual barriers to learning and development. The same is true for neighborhoods and friends and all the other programs, agencies, and systems cited in the transition services model. Some sources will be available, accessible, and highly supportive, and others will be difficult to access and limited in what they will offer. All of the systems cited need to be included, though, because each has potential. If one of the system options is not functioning well as a source for learning, encouraging learning, or support for learning at any one point in time, there are ways to make systems change. When change does not occur, or does not occur quickly enough for an individual student's benefit, other educational and support delivery system alternatives must be selected.

Conclusion

The model or approach used by a high school special education program to provide the best transition services possible will depend on the vision and task commitment of its staff and administrators. This book is intended to provide new visions or to provide support for existing visions. It is also intended to supply, through the comprehensive models and most of the chapters that follow, some specific strategies for how to implement one or both of the models or a school's own variation of it. The content of instruction for students is the key to effective knowledge and skills outcomes. Targeted goals and objectives that are tied directly to a student's age-appropriate preferences, interests, and needs and that are supported by multiple education and support system delivery options lead to satisfying outcomes for each student's next exit point.

It is our intent in proposing these comprehensive transition education and service models to (1) emphasize the major knowledge and skill domains that are evolving in transition services, (2) highlight the lifelong aspects of transitions and the different expectations for various transition exit points, and (3) stress the shared responsibility and potential of a variety of transition education and service-delivery systems. We realize that a dual model such as this (Figures 1.1 and 1.2) does not cut to the heart of a plan of action, since the model used by most schools is not a transition education model. Rather, most schools are structured around a predetermined academic core curriculum, specified electives, and some established criteria for satisfactory achievement.

A wide range of flexibility exists both within and across states on how local schools provide a "free and appropriate education" for students with disabilities. Students with disabilities who are able to meet the expectations of a traditional academic general education curriculum, with or without support, are encouraged to do that, but often with the assumption that if they can do that, they do not need any transition education or special considerations for transition planning.

Can the comprehensive transition education and services models presented here work in today's schools? We believe they can work in those states and local school districts that allow flexibility in curricular options. That is especially true in modified curriculum options and alternative curriculum options (functional skills or community-based instruction programs). More challenging is the task of making the models work for students in general education diploma tracks under strict compliance with prescribed curriculum content and standards-based assessments. Kochhar-Bryant and Bassett (2002) advocated for a combined standards and opportunities-based education system that addresses (1) increased standards for all students included in the general education curriculum; (2) curriculum options that blend academic, career-technical, and community-based learning; (3) multiple outcome measures in multiple domains for all students; and (4) appropriate aids and supports that help students participate in general education. Until such time as these features are in place in all schools, it may be more feasible in high-stakes programs to try to apply our models creatively to the individual needs of students through electives, extracurricular activities, innovative summer programs, before- and after-school programs, and home and community learning opportunities.

The ultimate accountability criterion for a school system is that its educational programs prove useful to its students in all aspects of their lives. As a thematic goal around which curriculum content and instructional approaches are woven, a functional, life-centered, lifelong learning competencies approach speaks to the ultimate issue of *usefulness*. The theme presented in this chapter is such that it may alienate educators or critics of education who are concerned only about academic excellence, academic accountability, and achievement standards. For those individuals, we would defer to Marland (1974, p. 13), who quoted Alfred North Whitehead as saying, "Pedants sneer at an education that is useful, but if it is not useful, what is it?" Without apology, that view is supported in presenting our ideas on transition education and services in this book.

2

Legislation and Guidelines for Secondary Special Education and Transition Services

DEBRA A. NEUBERT

What the best and wisest parent wants for his own child, that must the community want for all its children. Any other ideal for our schools is narrow and unlovely; acted upon, it destroys our democracy.

—John Dewey

Career, vocational, academic, and school-to-adult life transition programs for students with disabilities have evolved over the years in response to legislation, research, and educational reform movements. Federal laws in the fields of special education, rehabilitation, vocational-technical education, and workforce training have provided legal mandates for the provision of various academic, vocational, and transition services to individuals with disabilities. If you work with students with disabilities, you must be familiar with these mandates to ensure that your students have access to a range of educational and vocational secondary options, receive appropriate transition planning services, and are provided with interagency links as they exit the school system. Researchers have also sought to identify recommended practices in secondary special education and transition services. These findings have served as benchmarks for practitioners and policy makers to develop and revise guidelines for secondary programs and transition services.

This chapter reviews legislation in the fields of special education, rehabilitation, vocational-technical education, and workforce training that have affected the development of programs, services, and policies found in secondary settings. This is followed by a discussion of educational reform movements and their effect on curricula and diploma options for secondary students over the past two decades. Finally, a review of recommended practices for secondary special education and transition services is provided.

Legislation

Educational, vocational, and transitional services for individuals with disabilities are mandated in legislation that spans the fields of special education, vocational-technical education, rehabilitation, and workforce development. Current laws in these fields call for interdisciplinary efforts to serve individuals with disabilities in educational, vocational, and employment settings. The following sections provide a historical review of legislation to provide you with a framework for understanding patterns of federal initiatives and how the nation has progressed to this point. The current laws will help you understand the differences in the funding and the structure of various programs available to students with disabilities (see Figure 2.1). A good understanding of the law will ultimately enhance transition planning for students with disabilities during the middle and high school years.

Special Education

The Education for All Handicapped Children Act of 1975, PL 94-142. Signed into law in 1975, PL 94-142 was the landmark legislation that provided all children with disabilities the right to a free and appropriate public education in the least restrictive environment. The Education for All Handicapped Children Act (EHA) mandated that each child have a written individualized education program (IEP) that addressed the present levels of functioning, long- and short-term goals, services to be provided, and plans for initiating and evaluating services. The evaluation process for each student was to be nondiscriminatory and made by a multidisciplinary team. Parents had to be notified when their children were to be evaluated for and placed in special education services.

Much of the literature and research concerning EHA was initially focused on younger students with disabilities. During the late 1970s, there was a growing awareness that secondary special education students needed increased vocational training and independent living skills. Almost two decades ago, Phelps and Frasier (1988) pointed out that the least restrictive environment provision clearly suggested that for secondary students, the least restrictive and most responsive environment included placements where students could work on vocationally related goals and objectives. In fact, the Final Rules for PL 94-142 specifically stated that both state and local education agencies had to take steps to ensure that students with disabilities were able to access the same

FIGURE 2.1   **Selected Legislation-Secondary Special Education and Transition Services**

Special Education Legislation

- The Education for All Handicapped Children Act of 1975, PL 94-142
- The Education of the Handicapped Act Amendments of 1983, PL 98-199
- The Education of the Handicapped Act Amendments of 1986, PL 99-457
- The Individuals with Disabilities Education Act of 1990, PL 101-476
- The Individuals with Disabilities Education Act Amendments of 1997, PL 105-17
- The Individuals with Disabilities Education Improvement Act of 2004, PL 108-446

Rehabilitation and Civil Rights Legislation

- Vocational Rehabilitation Act of 1973, PL 93-112
- Rehabilitation Act Amendments of 1983, PL 98-221
- Rehabilitation Act Amendments of 1986, PL 99-506
- Rehabilitation Act Amendments of 1992, PL 102-569
- Rehabilitation Act Amendments of 1998, PL 105-220 (Title IV:Workforce Investment Act of 1998)
- Americans with Disabilities Act of 1990, PL 101-336

Vocational-Technical Education Legislation

- The Smith-Hughes Act of 1917, PL 347
- The Vocational Education Act of 1963, PL 88-210
- The Vocational Education Act Amendments of 1968, PL 90-210
- Education Amendments of 1976, Title II, PL 94-482
- The Carl D. Perkins Vocational Education Act of 1984, PL 98-524
- The Carl D. Perkins Vocational and Applied Technology Education Act Amendments of 1990, PL 101-392
- The Carl D. Perkins Vocational and Applied Technology Educational Act Amendments of 1998, PL 105-332

Workforce Training Legislation

- Comprehensive Employment and Training Act of 1973, PL 93-203
- Comprehensive Employment and Training Act Amendments of 1978, PL 95-524
- Job Training Partnership Act of 1982, PL 97-300
- Job Training Partnership Act Amendments of 1986, PL 99-496
- Job Training Reform Amendments of 1992, PL 102-367
- Workforce Investment Act of 1998, PL 105-220

Other Significant Legislation

- Goals 2000: Educate America Act of 1994, PL 103-227
- The School-to-Work Opportunities Act of 1994, 103-239
- Improving America's Schools Act of 1994, PL 103-382
- Higher Education Amendments of 1998, PL 105-244
- The No Child Left Behind Act of 2001, PL 107-110

types of programs and services available to students without disabilities. At the time, these programs generally included industrial arts, home economics, and vocational education. Researchers also began to document the poor post-secondary outcomes of students with disabilities in terms of employment and independent living. This, in turn, provided an increased focus on the needs of secondary students with disabilities and provided some of the basis for the school-to-work transition movement that became prominent in the 1980s.

The Education of the Handicapped Act Amendments of 1983 and 1986.   Section 626 of the Education of the Handicapped Act Amendments of 1983, PL 98-199, was the first act that authorized $6.6 million in funding to develop and support school-to-work transition services for youths with disabilities in the form of model demonstration programs, research projects, and personnel preparation projects (Rusch & Phelps, 1987). These projects served as starting points for others to develop transition programs and to shape future policy regarding school-to-work programming. The federal Office of Special Education and Rehabilitative Services also spotlighted school-to-work transition as a national priority and provided a model for secondary special educators to bridge the gap between school and work (Will, 1984). However, there were no specific mandates for transition planning in this Act and state and local education agencies were allowed to develop and fund transition services at their own discretion. During this time, it was also suggested that the school-to-work concept be broadened to include school-to-adult life components, such as personal-social adjustment and community participation (Halpern, 1985). This followed the same pattern of the federal initiatives of the 1970s for career education, emphasizing occupational aspects of life-career development and subsequent calls for emphasis on personal-social adjustment and daily living skills (Brolin, 1978; Clark, 1974).

The Education of the Handicapped Act Amendments of 1986, PL 99-457, reauthorized the funding for discretionary programs (model demonstration, research, and personnel preparation projects) under Section 626 and authorized funding for research projects to investigate postsecondary outcomes for students with disabilities who had dropped out of school. Most importantly, PL 99-457, Part H, mandated the provision of services to infants and toddlers with disabilities. This increased the spectrum of services offered to individuals with disabilities from birth to age 21 (or 22) and focused on the need for inter-disciplinary efforts during the early years of life. Parallels between the transition process at the early childhood and secondary levels have been discussed (Repetto & Correa, 1996), along with the need to provide seamless and inter-disciplinary services for all students with disabilities. Public Laws 98-199 and 99-457 did not actually mandate transition services for students with disabilities, but the foundation was intact for the sweeping changes that took place with the Individuals with Disabilities Education Act of 1990.

The Individuals with Disabilities Education Act of 1990, PL 101-476. The Individuals with Disabilities Education Act of 1990 (IDEA) was the first federal legislation mandating that a statement of needed transition services be included in students' IEPs by age 16 (or at a younger age when appropriate). This Act clearly designated that special educators were responsible for initiating the transition planning process. The IEP was also to include (when appropriate) a statement of each public agency's responsibilities or linkages before the student exited the school system. This mandate clearly stated that transition planning was to include individuals and organizations who provided postsecondary services to individuals with disabilities.

Transition Services. The definition of *transition services* included in IDEA clearly broadened the concept to include multiple postsecondary outcomes. Transition services included the following:

> A coordinated set of activities for a student, designed within an outcome-oriented process, that promotes movement from school to post-school activities, including postsecondary education, vocational training, integrated employment (including supported employment), continuing and adult education, adult services, independent living, or community participation. (Department of Education, 1992, p. 44804)

The *transition services* definition also stated that students were to be involved in the transition planning process and that assessment data were to be used in formulating transition goals:

> The coordinated set of activities must be based on the individual student's needs, taking into account the student's preferences and interests; and include instruction, community experiences, the development of employment and other post-school adult living objectives; and acquisition of daily living skills and functional vocational evaluation (if appropriate). (Department of Education, 1992, p. 44804)

Student Involvement. The IDEA of 1990 highlighted and mandated the need for students to be involved in planning their transition services and goals at IEP meetings. This mandate provided a policy basis for the self-determination movement that called for students to become actively involved in expressing their needs and goals, and in planning for the future (Ward, 1992). PL 101-476 stated:

> If a purpose of the meeting is the consideration of transition services for a student, the public agency shall invite the student; and a representative of any other agency that is likely to be responsible for providing or paying for transition services. If the student does not attend, the public agency shall take other

steps to ensure that the student's preferences and interests are considered; and if an agency invited to send a representative to a meeting does not do so, the public agency shall take other steps to obtain the participation of the other agency in the planning of any transition services. (Department of Education, 1992, p. 44814)

Interagency Planning.   The IDEA stated that transition services and planning be considered by a team of individuals, which could include personnel from community and adult service agencies (e.g., rehabilitation counselors). Interagency planning was to be initiated by special educators, and personnel from outside agencies were to be invited to students' IEP meetings when appropriate. The IDEA also addressed the need for secondary special educators to reconsider a student's needs and goals if an outside agency could not provide the agreed-upon services:

> If a participating agency fails to provide agreed-upon transition services contained in the IEP of a student with a disability, the public agency responsible for the student's education shall, as soon as possible, initiate a meeting for the purpose of identifying alternative strategies to meet the transition objectives, and if necessary, revising the student's IEP. Nothing in this part relieves any participating agency, including a State vocational rehabilitation agency, of the responsibility to provide or pay for any transition service that the agency would otherwise provide to students with disabilities who meet the eligibility criteria of that agency. (Department of Education, 1992, p. 44815)

The Individuals with Disabilities Education Act Amendments of 1997, PL 105-17.   Whereas the IDEA of 1990 provided the first federal mandate for transition planning in special education, the Individuals with Disabilities Education Act Amendments of 1997 (IDEA Amendments of 1997) and the Final Regulations for this Act (Department of Education, 1999) broadened the scope of transition planning. In addition, the IDEA Amendments of 1997 have had far-reaching implications for students with disabilities in terms of participation in state and district assessments and access to general education courses.

Transition Services.   The definition for *transition services* remained the same as in the IDEA of 1990 (Section 602), with the exception that the coordinated set of activities could include related services such as transportation and support services such as speech and language pathology and audiology services, psychological services, physical and occupational therapy, recreation, social work services, counseling services (including rehabilitation counseling), orientation and mobility services, and medical services (for diagnostic and evaluation purposes). Providing related services may be especially significant to students with low-incidence disabilities who participate in community-based transition programs until the age of 21 (or 22).

A significant change in the IDEA Amendments of 1997 related to when transition planning must begin for students. PL 105-17 (Section 614) stated,

> Beginning at age 14, and updated annually, a statement of the transition service needs of the child under the applicable components of the child's IEP that focuses on the child's courses of study (such as participation in advanced-placement courses or a vocational education program). (IDEA 1997, p. 84)

This mandate required special educators, students, and families to be aware of curricula and diploma options, prerequisites for vocational-technical programs, and college entrance requirements as early as the middle school years (Neubert, 2003). For example, if a student desires to attend college, the IEP team should determine what courses are needed throughout middle school and high school that will enable the student to enter a postsecondary institution. The IDEA Amendments of 1997 also continued to mandate that a statement of needed transition services for the child, including, when appropriate, a statement of the interagency responsibilities or any needed linkages, be included in the IEP by age 16.

A final point relevant to transition planning was the option that states had concerning the transfer of rights at the age of majority. "In a state that transfers rights at the age [of] majority, beginning at least one year before a student reaches the age of majority under state law, the student's IEP must include a statement that the student has been informed of his or her rights" (Department of Education, 1999, p. 12442). If students are determined not to have the ability to provide informed consent with respect to their educational and transition programs, the state had to establish procedures to appoint the parent of the student or another appropriate individual as a legal guardian (IDEA, 1997).

There is great variability in how schools have complied with the transition mandates. In a study of IDEA-related federal monitoring and enforcement activities between 1975 to 1997, the National Council on Disability (2000) reported that one of the largest areas of noncompliance was transition, where 44 states failed to ensure compliance. For example, 35 states (70 percent) did not indicate transition services as a purpose included in the IEP meeting notice and 34 states (68 percent) did not include a statement of needed transition services. McAfee and Greenwalt (2001) described transition due process hearing and court trials that also point to problems with implementing transition services in the schools. Clearly, secondary educators, guidance counselors, school psychologists, and other related personnel need to understand and comply with the legal requirements for transition services. As more secondary students with disabilities access general education courses, it is especially important to ensure transition services are integrated within educational efforts and are not seen as an "add-on" service for students with disabilities.

State and District Assessments.   State education agencies and local school systems have instituted various high-stakes assessments for the past two decades (Johnson & Thurlow, 2003; Thurlow, 2000). However, until the IDEA Amendments of 1997, students with disabilities were often excluded in these reform efforts (National Center on Educational Outcomes [NCEO], 2003a). This Act mandated that students with disabilities participate in state and district assessments and required a statement of individual modifications in the IEP regarding the administration of assessments (IDEA, 1997). Many states developed recommendations for specific accommodations on state and district assessments (Thurlow, 2002). For students with disabilities to receive appropriate accommodations on assessments, it must be documented on students' IEPs, 504 plans, or on plans for English Language Learners (ELL).

If the IEP team determined that an assessment is not appropriate, a statement regarding why the assessment is not appropriate and how the student will be assessed had to be included in the IEP. In response, states developed or revised alternate assessments, which often focused on functional skills (National Center on Education Outcomes, 2003a). Documentation of skills and standards achieved through alternative assessments was generally accomplished through portfolios, performance assessments, checklists, or a collection of student work linked to achievement of IEP goals.

Access to General Education.   The U.S. Department of Education (2002) reported that 95.9 percent of students with disabilities were served in regular school buildings during the 1999–2000 school year; of these students, 47.3 percent were served outside of the regular classroom for less than 21 percent of the school day. Students with high-incidence disabilities (e.g., learning disabilities, speech and language disabilities, etc.) are more likely to receive services in the regular classroom, whereas students with low-incidence disabilities (or severe disabilities) are more likely to receive services and instruction outside of regular eduction classes. The IDEA Amendments of 1997 and the Final Regulations required a number of provisions for students with disabilities to participate in and progress in the general education curriculum.

Although the mandate since 1975 has been to serve students with disabilities in the least restrictive setting, the IDEA strengthened and mandated participation in general education. For example, the IEP must include documentation of the student's present levels of performance describing involvement and progress in the general curriculum, and the student's need for special education, related services, and supplemental aids and services to access and participate in general education and extracurricular activities (U.S. Department of Education, 1999).

The makeup of the IEP team meeting included the parents, a *general education teacher* (if the student is or may be participating in general education); a representative of the local education agency (LEA) knowledgeable about general curriculum and availability of resources in the LEA; the student, if he or she chooses to participate; an individual who can interpret the instructional implications of evaluation results; and other individuals at the discretion of parents or the agency. The mandate to include general education teachers in IEP meetings reinforced the need for students with disabilities to be included in classes available to the entire student population in secondary settings. If the student was not participating in general education, the IEP needed to include a statement of why this decision was made. In addition, the IEP needed to contain a statement of how the student's progress toward annual goals was measured and parents were to be informed of this progress as often as parents of students without disabilities. For example, if students received four progress reports and four report cards throughout the year in a middle school, students with disabilities were also to receive progress reports at these points.

Assistive Technology. The IDEA Amendments required that assistive technology be considered by the IEP team (Fisher & Gardner, 1999). Assistive technology *devices* are items, equipment, or product systems that can be acquired commercially, modified, or customized to increase or improve students' "functional capacities" (IDEA, 1997). Assistive technology *services* allow the student and the IEP team to select, acquire, or use an assistive technology device. This can include assessing the student in the environment in which he or she will use the technology, purchasing or leasing technology, or providing training to teachers and parents to assist students use the assistive technology. Secondary special educators should identify the contact person or team in their school system that provides assistive technology evaluations for students and actual assistive technology devices. The Internet also has a wealth of resources for assistive technology devices and specific suggestions for accommodating students with disabilities in various tasks. To get ideas about assistive technology to enhance academic and job performance, visit the Job Accommodation Network, a free service offered through the Office of Disability Employment Policy, U.S. Department of Labor at www.jan.wvu.edu/.

In summary, the IDEA Amendments of 1997 were framed to encourage students with disabilities to participate in general education and to meet the standards and expectations that were increasingly being set by school systems for all students (Council for Exceptional Children, 2003). In addition, earlier transition planning and interagency planning were required during the IEP process.

Individuals with Disabilities Education Improvement Act of 2004. President Bush signed into law the Individuals with Disabilities Education Improvement Act of 2004 (IDEA 2004), PL 108-446, in December 2004. This reauthorization of IDEA continues to reinforce the need for students with disabilities to be provided with transition services, to have access to general education, and to participate in state assessments. In addition, IDEA 2004

addresses issues associated with the No Child Left Behind Act of 2001 by defining "highly qualified" special education teachers and by revising the definition
of transition services. At the time of this writing, the final regulations for this
Act had not been published. Readers are encouraged to update the information
on IDEA 2004 in this section by using the companion website.

Transition Services.   The definition for *transition services* has changed slightly
from IDEA 1990 and 1997. Transition services means a coordinated set of activities for a child with a disability that:

> (A) is designed to be within a results-oriented process, that is focused on
> improving the academic and functional achievement of the child with a dis-
> ability to facilitate the child's movement from school to post-school activities,
> including post-secondary education, vocational education, integrated employ-
> ment (including supported employment), continuing and adult education,
> adult services, independent living, or community participation;
>
> (B) is based on the individual child's needs, taking into account the child's
> strengths, preferences, and interests; and
>
> (C) includes instruction, related services, community experiences, the develop-
> ment of employment and other post-school adult living objectives, and, when
> appropriate, acquisition of daily living skills and functional vocational evalua-
> tion. (IDEA, Sec. 602, H.R. 1350)

The requirements for addressing transition in the IEP process have also
changed. The requirement to address a statement of transition service needs
for students at age 14 has been deleted and is replaced with the following:

> beginning not later than the first IEP to be in effect when the child is 16, and
> updated annually thereafter—
>
> (a) appropriate measurable postsecondary goals based upon age appropriate
> transition assessments related to training, education, employment, and,
> where appropriate, independent living skills;
>
> (b) the transition services (including courses of study) needed to assist the
> child in reaching those goals; and
>
> (c) beginning not later than one year before the child reaches the age of
> majority under State law, a statement that the child has been informed of the
> child's rights under this title, if any, that will transfer to the child on reach-
> ing the age of majority under section 615(m). (IDEA, Part B, Sec. 614, H.R.
> 1350)

It should be noted that this language still addresses the need to specify a
student's course of study to reach his or her goals but does not include language to identify interagency linkages if needed by age 16 (as did the IDEA

Amendments of 1997). The additions to IDEA 2004 include *measurable* postsecondary goals for students with disabilities and *age-appropriate transition assessments* upon which to base postsecondary goals.

Access to General Education and Participation in State Assessments.   IDEA 2004 retains the language to address how a student with a disability will be involved and progress in the general education curriculum and how he or she will participate in state and district assessments during the IEP process. Some changes to the IEP process include:

- A statement of measurable annual goals in the IEP remains in this Act; however, benchmarks and short-term objectives are now required only for a student who takes an alternate assessment aligned to alternate achievement standards.
- A description of how the student's progress toward meeting annual goals must be described, *measured,* and reported on periodic reports.
- A statement of special education, related services, and supplemental aids/services in the IEP is to be based on *peer-reviewed research* to the extent practicable.
- A statement of individual appropriate *accommodations to measure the academic achievement and functional performance* on state and district assessments must be given.

The IDEA 2004 provides an opportunity for secondary special educators and transition specialists to continue the provision of transition services. The challenge is to ensure that students with disabilities are provided with appropriate career education and transition assessment activities in elementary and middle school so they can identify individual interests, strengths, and needs. This is necessary for students to identify postsecondary goals and to participate in secondary general education and career and technical education courses that will assist them in meeting these postsecondary goals.

Rehabilitation

The legislative history of vocational rehabilitation services for people with disabilities dates back to 1918 when the federal government sponsored rehabilitative services for veterans of World War I. Rehabilitation services initially served persons with physical disabilities, with a goal of returning adults with disabilities to employment. Over the years, the scope of rehabilitation services has expanded to serve a diverse group of individuals with disabilities. Many students with disabilities will need time-limited services (e.g., counseling, vocational training, work adjustment services) through vocational rehabilitation after they exit the school system. Therefore, secondary educators need to understand the eligibility requirements for rehabilitation services and the types of available services (see Chapter 11). Secondary educators must also be familiar with the legal mandates in rehabilitation that provide the basis for reasonable accommodations in educational settings through Section 504 plans (explained below).

The Vocational Rehabilitation Act of 1973, PL 93-112.   The Vocational Rehabilitation Act of 1973 was landmark legislation, for it included mandates calling for equal opportunity and nondiscrimination in workplace and education settings for individuals with disabilities. This Act required an individualized written rehabilitation plan (IWRP) to be developed for each person, which documented the long-range rehabilitation goals, the types of services to be provided, the dates for services, and the evaluation procedures (Shafer, 1988). It is interesting to note that this element of the mandate closely resembles its counterpart found in the EHA of 1975, the individualized education program.

Section 503.   Section 503 of the Vocational Rehabilitation Act established not only federal policy but also federal leadership in the practices of hiring, training, advancing, and retaining qualified workers with disabilities. The provisions of Section 503 covered all governmental employment as well as any employer under contract to the federal government for more than $2,500. Every business or agency covered under this Act needed an affirmative action plan for all employment openings. Also, any government contractor holding a contract for $50,000 or greater, or who had at least 50 employees, needed an affirmative action plan.

Section 504.   Section 504 of the Vocational Rehabilitation Act had an impact on education and training opportunities for persons with disabilities. It included a statement that "no otherwise qualified handicapped individual in the United States, as defined by Section 7(6) shall, solely by the reason of his handicap, be excluded from the participation in, be denied the benefits of, or be subjected to discrimination under any program or activity receiving Federal financial assistance." This excerpt shows the intent of the law was to provide nondiscriminatory access to programs, services, and employment. As a result, secondary and postsecondary schools receiving federal funds initiated and continue to offer an array of services that provide reasonable accommodations to students with disabilities. For example, Section 504 provides the legal basis for individuals with disabilities to receive reasonable accommodations in postsecondary institutions (Brinckerhoff, McGuire, & Shaw, 2001). Although individuals with disabilities are not entitled to receive special education services in postsecondary settings, they are able to receive reasonable accommodations such as extended time on tests, use of assistive technology, and interpreters.

In secondary settings, students with disabilities who are not eligible for special education but who have a disability pursuant to Section 504 of the Vocational Rehabilitation Act of 1973 also may receive services or reasonable accommodations. Each local school system should have someone designated to oversee Section 504 policies who can provide teachers with guidelines. Students with disabilities will still have to go through an assessment process to determine if they are eligible to receive accommodations and services under Section 504. In most cases, a team will then develop a Section 504 plan for the student that specifies which accommodations and services he or she must receive in school (deBettencourt, 2002; Smith & Patton, 1999). The students most likely to receive services under Section 504 are those with attention deficit disorder, visual or hearing impairments, or physical disabilities (President's Commission on Excellence in Education in Special Education, 2002). Examples of reasonable accommodations include untimed tests, enlarged print in books and assignments, note-takers, use of a notebook computer, and interpreters. Finally, Section 504 also provides the foundation for reasonable accommodations (e.g., providing directions in various formats, redesigning workspace) in the workplace for students and adults with disabilities.

The Rehabilitation Act Amendments of 1983 and 1986. The Rehabilitation Act was amended in 1983 (PL 98-221) and in 1986 (PL 99-506). The Rehabilitation Act Amendments of 1986 were important in terms of providing funds for supported employment services to individuals with low-incidence or severe disabilities. Supported employment was an opportunity for adults with disabilities to work in integrated settings, earn wages, and receive ongoing support in the employment community. This Act provided funds for personnel training, model demonstration programs, and systems change grants for states to convert sheltered workshops and day activity programs to supported employment programs. The implementation of supported employment programs in rehabilitation programs, along with a growing awareness that individuals with low-incidence disabilities could work in the community, provided the foundation for many of the community-based secondary programs that serve students with more significant disabilities (ages 14 to 22) in high schools today.

The Rehabilitation Act Amendments of 1992, PL 102-569. The Rehabilitation Act Amendments of 1992 have been hailed as a consumer empowerment bill. The purpose of this Act was "to empower individuals with disabilities to achieve economic self-sufficiency, independence, and inclusion and integration into society" (NISH, 1996, p. 5). In addition, the Rehabilitation Act mirrored the self-determination and inclusion movements in special education to involve individuals with disabilities in actively planning and implementing their educational, vocational, and transitional services in integrated environments. This Act also (1) created Consumer-Majority Rehabilitation Advisory Councils, (2) mandated that IWRPs be jointly developed and signed by the rehabilitation counselor and the consumer, (3) strengthened the priority to serve individuals with severe disabilities, and (4) substituted the term *community rehabilitation program (CRP)* for *community-based rehabilitation facility* to reflect the movement to provide services to individuals with disabilities in the community.

The Rehabilitation Act Amendments of 1992 were significant for secondary students with disabilities for a number of other reasons. First, the definition of *transition services* duplicated the definition included in the IDEA of 1990 and mandated that "the State plan must assure that the IWRP for a student with a disability who is receiving special education services is coordinated with the individualized education programs (IEP) for that individual in terms of the goals, objectives, and services identified in the IEP" (Department of Education, 1997, pp. 6354–6355). This encouraged greater collaboration between secondary special educators, rehabilitation personnel, and students with disabilities.

Second, there was a significant change in determining eligibility for rehabilitation services. Up to this point, most individuals were determined eligible for services when rehabilitation counselors examined selected psychological reports, vocational evaluation reports, and/or medical reports from highly qualified and approved professionals. The Rehabilitation Act stated that existing assessment data—provided by the individual with a disability, the family, an advocate, or an educational agency—could be used for determining a person's eligibility for rehabilitation services. This meant that assessment data collected on a secondary student in work and community settings should be passed on to rehabilitation personnel if that student is referred to vocational rehabilitation. Therefore, it is important that secondary educators collect and compile assessment data that can be used to support a student's needs and goals for employment outcomes (Neubert & Moon, 2000). Many states have developed cooperative agreements between the departments of special education, rehabilitation, and vocational-technical education to facilitate a smooth transition of eligible students from school to rehabilitation programs. In fact, there has been evidence of collaborative partnerships between special education and rehabilitation programs since the 1960s (Kolstoe & Frey, 1965; Neubert, 1997). However, it is important for educators to understand that rehabilitation services are based on eligibility criteria. These criteria include a documented disability; the fact that the disability requires rehabilitation service to prepare for, enter into, or retain employment; and the presumption that the individual can benefit in terms of an employment or independent living outcome from rehabilitation services. It is also important for educators to understand that rehabilitation services are based on the availability of federal and state funds and must follow established "order of selection" policies. All educators need to be aware of their states' policies and procedures for order of selection. It is estimated that rehabilitation services are provided to only 7 percent of the 13.4 million potentially eligible people (NISH, 1996).

The Rehabilitation Act Amendments of 1998, Title IV of PL 105-220 (Workforce Investment Act of 1998).   The Rehabilitation Act Amendments of 1998 were included under legislation that links the state vocational rehabilitation system to the state work force investment system. The Rehabilitation Act

Amendments, Title IV of the Workforce Investment Act of 1998, were signed into law on August 7, 1998. Employment and training programs for all individuals are to be coordinated and administered through a state workforce investment system. This is important for individuals with disabilities who do not meet state order of selection criteria for rehabilitation services, since they will also be able to access other services and programs through their workforce investment system (e.g., Job Corps, employment training programs). States have developed one-stop centers that house personnel from various vocational, labor, and rehabilitation programs that serve local communities. (Check www.servicelocator.org/ to determine where these centers are located in your state and community.)

Although the intended outcome of vocational rehabilitation services in the Rehabilitation Amendments of 1998 remains employment, the definition of *employment* is broad, including (1) full- or part-time employment in the integrated labor market, (2) satisfying the vocational outcome of supported employment, and (3) satisfying any other vocational outcomes such as self-employment, telecommuting, or business ownership. Teachers who work with individuals with significant disabilities should also be aware of the term *presumption of benefit.* This term implies that all individuals can benefit from vocational rehabilitation services unless the state unit can demonstrate by clear and convincing evidence that an individual is incapable of benefiting in terms of an employment or independent living outcome due to the severity of the disability of the individual (Section 102).

The Rehabilitation Act Amendments of 1998 have a number of themes that are carried over from the Rehabilitation Act Amendments of 1992. First, the concept of *empowering* individuals with disabilities is strengthened and emphasizes the need for informed choice. This is similar to the concept of self-determination that is used in secondary special education. Individuals with disabilities are to be involved in choosing assessment strategies, determining training options, designing individualized employment plans, and determining independent living options. The term *individualized written rehabilitation plan (IWRP)* was changed to *individualized plan for employment (IPE)* under this Act. Second, the definition of *transition services* remains the same as the definition found in the Individuals with Disabilities Education Act of 1997. Finally, the need to use existing assessment data for determining eligibility and in planning the individualized plan for employment is emphasized and expanded from the 1992 Rehabilitation Amendments. The term *assessment for determining eligibility and vocational rehabilitation needs* includes a review of existing data to determine whether an individual is eligible for vocational rehabilitation services and to assign priority for an order of selection. This definition also highlights the need to collect information from the individual, family, and other programs. If additional assessment data are needed to determine eligibility, this law is specific in describing the types of assessment activities that can take place, including:

- An assessment of personality, interests, interpersonal skills, intelligence and related functional capacities, educational achievements, work experience, vocational aptitudes, personal and social adjustments, and employment opportunities of the individual.
- An assessment of the medical, psychiatric, psychological, and other vocational, educational, cultural, social, recreational, and environmental factors that affect the employment and rehabilitation needs of the individual.
- An appraisal of the patterns of work behavior of the individual and services needed to acquire occupational skills and to develop work attitudes, work habits, work tolerance, and social and behavior patterns for successful job performance. This can include work in real job situations.
- Referral for rehabilitation technology services to assess and develop the capacities of the individual to perform in a work environment.
- An exploration of the individual's abilities, capabilities, and capacity to perform in work situations, which are assessed periodically during trial work experiences (which can include training and support).

A final point for secondary special educators and transition specialists to be aware of is that individuals with disabilities who receive Supplemental Security Insurance (SSI) may be eligible for vocational rehabilitation services under the definition of a *significant disability.* Supplemental Security Insurance is an income support program and provides monthly payments to an individual with a disability who has limited income. If eligible, SSI can provide students and young adults with disabilities with an income while they are involved in a job-training program or while working part time (National Center on Secondary Education and Transition, 2003). Teachers should encourage students with disabilities and their families to explore SSI and related work incentive programs through their local social security office or through the Social Security Administration's website (www.ssa.gov/work).

The Americans with Disabilities Act of 1990

The Americans with Disabilities Act (ADA), PL 101-336, provides broad civil rights protection to individuals with disabilities across education, employment, public services, public accommodations, transportation, and telecommunications. The ADA extends Section 504 of the Rehabilitation Act of 1973 to the private sector in terms of access to and reasonable accommodations in employment, schools, and community facilities. Educators should be able to acquaint students and their parents with the ADA so they can access employment opportunities and community services. This responsibility can be met by altering curriculum content (e.g., teaching about the ADA and Section 504 in the social studies curriculum) and by providing parents with pertinent information at transition planning meetings. For example, Title I of ADA, Employment, extends the provisions of Section 504 by requiring both private (over 15 employees) and public employers to provide *reasonable accommodations* to qualified individuals with disabilities. Title I mandates that employers must only make reasonable accommodations if they are informed of a person's disability. For some students, this means that they must decide when to disclose a disability and how to describe their needs in terms of reasonable accommodations. For other students, teachers, parents, or advocates will have to assume the responsibility of informing employers about the need for reasonable accommodations. In addition, secondary teachers must work with students to identify their strengths, abilities, and needs in order to determine if they can perform the *essential functions of the job.* Essential functions of the job relate to the actual tasks that are required in specific jobs.

Title II of the ADA, Public Services, "provides for extension of Section 504 prohibitions against discrimination to all programs, activities, and services of state and local governments regardless of whether they receive federal financing" (Linthicum, Cole, & D'Alonzo, 1991, p. 2). Title II also includes provisions for making public transportation systems accessible. Title III, Public Accommodations, expands the scope of Section 504 to include businesses and community services that are used every day by most people (e.g., department stores, grocery stores, laundromats, parks, movie theaters, schools, public community agencies, theaters, hotels, and recreational facilities). Title IV includes telecommunications (voice and nonvoice systems), and Title V, Miscellaneous, contains provisions that individuals with disabilities do not have to accept offered accommodations, services, or benefits that they choose not to accept (Linthicum, Cole, & D'Alonzo, 1991). The ADA has far-reaching implications for employment and community living opportunities for people with disabilities. However, students with disabilities and their families need to be educated about how to advocate for their rights under ADA; otherwise, those rights will remain unfulfilled or denied.

Vocational-Technical Education

Federal support for vocational education has long recognized the need to prepare students to participate in the workforce. The Smith-Hughes Act of 1917, PL 347, provided funding for public schools to develop secondary vocational education programs. Vocational education during this period focused on skill training in the areas of agriculture, trade and industry, and home economics. Since that time, legislation has targeted the expansion of vocational-technical programs, the need to serve diverse and special populations, and the impetus for reform efforts to integrate challenging academic content in programs that lead to postsecondary education and skilled employment opportunities. Including this option in the IEP transition planning process can ensure that students with disabilities who have an interest in vocational training are prepared to enter the workforce. Equally important, it meets the requirement for students with disabilities to participate in regular education under the IDEA. It should be noted that state and local school systems may use the term *career and technical education (CTE)* when referring to current vocational programs.

The Vocational Education Act of 1963 and the 1968 Amendments. Congress passed the Vocational Education Act, PL 88-210, in 1963, broadening the definition of *vocational education* to provide funding for business education and cooperative work-study programs. In addition, this Act provided support for students with special needs (which included students with disabilities and disadvantages) to participate in vocational education programs and related services (Cobb & Neubert, 1998).

The Vocational Education Amendments of 1968, PL 90-576, continued to broaden the range of vocational programs offered to students in secondary and postsecondary settings and to emphasize the need for improved access for all students to vocational opportunities. Public Law 90-576 was important because it introduced the practice of providing set-aside funding for special populations in vocational education. This funding included 10 percent of all the state grant vocational education funds designated for supporting programs for youths with disabilities and 15 percent to support programs for youths with disadvantages. The 1968 Amendments required each state to have an advisory committee made up of parents, business personnel, special educators, teachers, higher education leaders, and vocational educators to monitor state plans and practices for compliance with the provisions of the Act. This practice contributed to the development of vocational programs and services to serve individuals with disabilities. Although it took some states as many as five years to develop programs within their states, others used the full set-aside allotments immediately for vocational evaluation services and, in some cases, separate vocational programs for individuals with disabilities.

The Vocational Education Amendments of 1976, PL 94-482. Students with disabilities were generally underrepresented in vocational education programs during the 1970s. For example, in 1971, only 2.1 percent of students enrolled in vocational education had disabilities and 70 percent of these students were placed in separate classes (Hagerty, Halloran, & Taymans, 1981). The Education Amendments of 1976, PL 94-482 (which included amendments to the Vocational Education Act), increased the funding for these students in vocational programs. These amendments required the 10 percent set-aside funds for students with disabilities to be matched with state and local funds. In addition, the set-aside funding for students with disadvantages was increased to 20 percent.

The purpose of this Act was to improve and expand vocational education programs, to overcome sex discrimination and sex stereotyping, and to improve the accountability of vocational education with the development of the Vocational Education Data System. Public Law 94-482 mandated that vocational education programs be coordinated with other federal vocational and education programs. These amendments, together with the EHA of 1975 and the Rehabilitation Act of 1973, served as cornerstone legislation for providing interdisciplinary services such as assessment, training, and employment activities to students with disabilities in vocational education programs (Neubert, 1997).

The Carl D. Perkins Vocational Education Act of 1984, PL 98-524. Conway (1984) reported that the number of students with disabilities in vocational education programs increased 95 percent between 1976 and 1982. The Perkins Act of 1984 continued to focus on the need to serve students who had traditionally been underrepresented in vocational programs. Dominant themes in this Act related to equal access of all programs and to services that would assist individuals with special needs in entering and/or succeeding in vocational programs. The following provisions applied to students with special needs under Title II of this Act:

1. Of the funds allocated to states for vocational education, 57 percent had to be spent on supplemental programs and services for special groups. These groups included individuals with disabilities (10 percent), individuals with disadvantages (22 percent), adults in need of training or retraining (12 percent), single parents and displaced homemakers (8.5 percent), individuals in training for nontraditional occupations based on their sex (3.5 percent), and persons in correctional institutions (1 percent).

2. Annual federal appropriations to states for students with special needs had to be matched equally by state and local funding. These appropriations were designated to support the costs of special supplemental services or modified programs for such students (e.g., vocational support services to assist students in succeeding in vocational programs). Other changes in the funding formula of the 1984 Perkins Act helped eliminate many of the separate vocational education programs and facilities for students with disabilities, resulting in increased mainstreaming.

3. Section 204 of Title II contained assurances that individuals with disabilities be offered equal access to a full range of vocational education programs, including recruitment, enrollment, and placement activities. Local schools had to provide supplemental services to students with special needs, which included (a) an assessment of interests, abilities, and special needs with respect to successfully completing the program; (b) special instructional services such as adaptations of curricula, instruction, equipment, and facilities; (c) guidance, counseling, and career development activities; and (d) counseling services to facilitate the transition from school to postschool employment and career opportunities. In addition, parents and guardians were to be informed of available options in vocational education programs prior to students entering the ninth grade. Finally, programs and services had to be coordinated for students

with IEPs in the spirit of the least restrictive environment provisions in PL 94-142.

The Perkins Act of 1984 also began the process of redirecting states to improve and expand their programs to train workers in occupations needed by the existing and future workforce (Cobb & Neubert, 1998). This Act also required that the outcomes of vocational education for all students be reported to Congress through the National Assessment of Vocational Education (NAVE). The NAVE report provides data about all students' participation and access to vocational education programs (to access the most recent NAVE report, see www.ed.gov/rschstat/eval/sectech/nave/index.html).

The Carl D. Perkins Vocational and Applied Technology Education Act Amendments of 1990, PL 101-392.   While the Carl D. Perkins Vocational and Applied Technology Education Act Amendments of 1990, PL 101-392, continued the themes of improving the quality of vocational education and providing supplemental services to special populations (Boesel & McFarland, 1994), significant changes occurred in the funding patterns. The use of set-aside funding for special populations was eliminated, but strong language remained in the Act, declaring that all students were to have access to vocational education programs. Title II, Section 118, contained provisions similar to the 1984 Perkins Act, calling for assessment activities, supplemental instructional services, career-development activities, and counseling to facilitate the transition from school to postschool employment and career opportunities. Section 118 also mandated that states and locals "assist students who are members of special populations to enter vocational education programs, and with respect to students with disabilities, assist in fulfilling the transition requirement of Section 626 of the IDEA."

Although many feared that the removal of set-aside funding would negatively affect students with disabilities, the NAVE report (Boesel, Hudson, Deich, & Masten, 1994) documented that students with disabilities took more vocational credits than other students. However, they were predominantly enrolled in agriculture, home economics, and trades occupations. Therefore, the mandate for equal access to all programs and services remained a challenge to students with disabilities in secondary vocational education.

Finally, this Act emphasized the need for greater integration of academic and vocational content through efforts such as Tech-Prep programs (articulated programs between a vocational content area in high school and the community college). The 1990 Amendments, in concert with the School-to-Work Opportunities Act of 1994, also provided the impetus for other models currently found in high schools, such as career academies, technical magnet high schools, and youth apprenticeship programs. Finally, greater local accountability was mandated in that schools were to evaluate the effectiveness of vocational-technical education programs each year according to statewide measures and standards of performance.

The Carl D. Perkins Vocational and Applied Technology Education Act Amendments of 1998, PL 105-332. The purpose of the Carl D. Perkins Vocational and Applied Technology Education Act Amendments of 1998 (Perkins Act of 1998) was to develop the academic, vocational, and technical skills of secondary and postsecondary students who elect to enroll in vocational technical education by doing the following:

- Building on the efforts of states and localities to develop challenging academic standards;
- Promoting the development of services and activities that integrate academic, vocational and technical instruction and link secondary and postsecondary education;
- Increasing State and local flexibility to provide services and activities designed to develop, implement, and improve vocational and technical education, including tech-prep education; and
- Disseminating national research and providing professional development and technical assistance that will improve vocational and technical education programs, services, and activities. (American Vocational Association, 1998)

The term *special populations* remains in the definition section of the Perkins Amendments of 1998, and includes individuals with disabilities, individuals from economically disadvantaged families, individuals preparing for nontraditional training and employment, single parents, displaced homemakers, and individuals with other barriers to educational achievement, including people with limited English proficiency. Individuals with academic disadvantages and individuals in correctional facilities are no longer included in this definition (Brustein, 1998). Mention of *special populations* is also found in the provisions for state and local plans (and uses of funds). To receive federal funding, each state must develop, submit, and implement services outlined in the state plan. In terms of special populations, the contents of the state plan (Section 122) are to include a description of the eligible agency's program strategies for special populations and a description of how individuals who are members of special populations will (1) be provided equal access to activities (2) not be discriminated against on the basis of their status as members of special populations, and (3) be provided with programs designed to meet or exceed the state's levels of performance, prepare for further learning, and prepare for high-skill, high-wage careers. Local recipients of federal funds also submit a plan that includes a description of (1) how individuals with special needs will not be discriminated against on the basis of their status as members of special populations and (2) how parents, students, teachers, representatives of business and industry, labor organizations, representatives of special populations, and other interested individuals are involved in the development, implementation, and evaluation of vocational and technical education programs and how these individuals are informed about and assisted in understanding these requirements. As with other recently enacted legislation, PL 105-332 requires educators and administrators to be held accountable for student outcomes and establishes a state performance accountability system that is similar to the system in the Workforce Investment Act (Brustein, 1998).

The most recent NAVE report (U.S. Department of Education, 2004a) found that in 1998 students with disabilities earned substantially more credits in vocational education than did students without disabilities (24.9 percent and 3.9 percent, respectively). Students with disabilities still tend to be over-represented in traditional vocational programs such as agriculture, construction, mechanics, and materials production.

The Carl D. Perkins Secondary and Technical Education Excellence Act of 2004 was proposed by the Bush administration in May 2004 to reauthorize the Perkins Act (U.S. Department of Education, 2004b). A key objective in reauthorization efforts is to ensure that career and technical education complements the academic mission of the No Child Left Behind Act of 2001 and the workforce mission of the Workforce Investment Act of 1998. In addition, career and technical education (CTE) pathways are to provide a challenging academic education and smooth transition into postsecondary training, education, or employment. Secondary special educators should keep abreast of reauthorization efforts because students with disabilities can access CTE in preparation for work and college (e.g., U.S. Department of Education, Office of Vocational and Adult Education, www.ed.gov/about/offices/list/ovae/index.html).

Workforce Training

Workforce training programs have a long history in providing training and employment opportunities to individuals with economic disadvantages. Individuals with disabilities are often eligible for these programs. The following legislation is discussed in terms of the services and programs provided under workforce training and how secondary students with disabilities might benefit from these programs.

The Comprehensive Employment and Training Act of 1973 and the 1978 Amendments.   In December 1973, PL 93-203, the Comprehensive Employment and Training Act (CETA), was passed to aid people with economic disadvantages to gain access to job training and employment opportunities. This Act was amended with PL 95-524, the 1978 CETA Amendments, and included individuals with disabilities.

Comprehensive Employment and Training Act programs were required to establish cooperative links with other agencies providing training and employment opportunities. As a result, many special educators referred students to CETA programs for further training after students exited the schools or to gain work experience through the summer youth employment programs during the high school years. The programs received intense criticism for their faulty administrative procedures and for training programs that were unresponsive to local employment needs. This, in concert with comprehensive career education practices in the late 1970s, led to improvements in employment training, which were recognized by Congress when the CETA program was replaced in the 1980s.

The Job Training Partnership Act, PL 97-300.   The Job Training Partnership Act (JTPA), PL 97-300, was passed in 1982 to replace CETA and to improve the role of business and industry in training youths and adults with disadvantages. The purpose of the JTPA (Section 2) was to establish programs to prepare youths and unskilled adults for entry into the workforce by providing job training to individuals with economic disadvantages and other individuals facing barriers to employment. Each state was required to identify designated service delivery areas (SDAs) where JTPA programs would be established and administered by local private industry councils (PICs). Representatives on the PICs included employers and education personnel. Training for employment reflected the local job market and funds were used to provide a variety of services, including Adult Programs as well as Summer Youth Employment and Training Programs. Typical services in these programs included job search, remedial and basic education, work experiences, vocational exploration, and literacy training. Part B of this Act also reauthorized the Job Corps, which still operates today. Job Corps programs include residential and nonresidential centers in which individuals participate in programs of education, vocational training, work experience, and counseling. The purpose of Job Corps is to assist young individuals by providing intensive programs in group settings and to contribute to the needs of local and national workforces.

Although JTPA programs were designed to serve individuals with economic disadvantages, individuals with disabilities could qualify for JTPA if their income met either of the following two criteria: (1) received or was a member of a family that received cash welfare payments or (2) was a member of a family that had received a total family income for the six-month period prior to application for the program that was at the poverty level.

The Job Training Partnership Act Amendments of 1986 and Reform Amendments of 1992.   The JTPA was amended with the Job Training Partnership Act Amendments of 1986 (PL 99-496) and the Job Training Reform Amendments of 1992 (PL 102-367). The most recent amendments, PL 102-367, modified the previous JTPA acts with a purpose of

> establishing programs to prepare youth and adults facing serious barriers to employment for participating in the labor force by providing job training and other services that will result in increased employment and earnings, increased educational and occupational skills, and decreased welfare dependency, thereby improving the quality of the workforce and enhancing the productivity and competitiveness of the Nation. (Section 2, p. 1023)

The 1992 Amendments continued to fund Adult Programs and Summer Youth Employment Programs while expanding services for students in secondary settings with the addition of Title II-C Year-Round Youth Training Programs. These programs served in-school youths, 16 to 21 years old (students as young as age 14 or 15 may participate if it is stated on their job training plan), who had economic disadvantages, participated in compensatory education programs under Chapter 1, or were eligible for free meals under the School Lunch Act. This program also targeted youths with economic disadvantages who are out of school and in need of remedial education and job training. The final rules for PL 99-496 expanded opportunities for youths and adults with disabilities to participate in JTPA programs by modifying other eligibility requirements. For example, people who received Supplemental Security Income (SSI) could no longer have SSI counted as income when eligibility was determined, and individuals with disabilities could be considered as a "family of one" (the entire family's income is not taken into account) for the purposes of determining eligibility (National Transition Network, 1993).

Under PL 102-367, service delivery areas were to establish links with educational agencies, including formal agreements to identify procedures for referring and serving in-school youths. Many secondary special education students continued to benefit from JTPA through Summer Youth Employment and Training Programs (for students ages 14 to 21), which could include remedial education, work experience, occupational training, and employment counseling. School systems also used JTPA funds to run Year-Round Youth Training Programs for students who were at risk of dropping out and needed remedial education and work experience. People who participated in JTPA programs had an individualized plan, which may have included an assessment of basic skills, a list of supportive service needs (e.g., child care), and a review of work experiences, interests, and aptitudes. This provided another opportunity for special educators to share assessment data that they had collected in school and the community with personnel from an outside agency. Finally, JTPA was an appropriate postsecondary option for some students with disadvantages and/or disabilities who needed further job training through the Adult Programs or Job Corps.

The Workforce Investment Act (WIA) of 1998, PL 105-220.   The purpose of PL 105-220 is to consolidate, coordinate, and improve employment, training, literacy, and vocational rehabilitation programs in the United States. The Act creates a comprehensive job-training system that consolidates many federally funded employment and training programs. The intent of this consolidation is to improve employment and training programs for all individuals, including those with disabilities, and to assist the consumer in identifying a range of workforce options through a one-stop delivery system. The WIA contains five titles:

- Title I: Workforce Investment Systems
- Title II: Adult Education and Literacy
- Title III: Workforce Investment-Related Activities
- Title IV: Rehabilitation Act Amendments of 1998
- Title V: General Provisions

Title I contains provisions for implementing state and local workforce investment boards, youth councils, one-stop delivery systems, youth activities, Job Corps, and youth opportunity grants (National Center on Secondary Education and Transition, 2002). Secondary educators should become familiar with the one-stop delivery centers in their state (check www.servicelocator.org).

One-stop centers should be designed to streamline job-training programs in one location, so consumers (including students) can find out about local job-training opportunities, employment opportunities, vocational rehabilitation, and other adult services for individuals with disabilities. Becoming familiar with WIA and one-stop centers can enhance transition planning for students with disabilities by providing interagency linkages and encouraging students and their families to explore job-training opportunities in the local area.

The Workforce Investment Act is designed to serve all individuals but emphasizes underserved populations such as low-income individuals, out-of-school youths, individuals with disabilities, and older or dislocated workers (National Center on Secondary Education and Transition, 2002). The Act also funds youth services for individuals in and out of school, between the ages of 14 to 21 (National Collaborative on Workforce and Disability, 2003). These services and activities are coordinated through state and local workforce investment boards and can include tutoring, occupational skill training, mentoring, work experience, and other supportive services. Youth activities can be found in local schools during the academic year and in summer programs. Low-income youths (ages 18–21) may be eligible for both youth and adult programs through WIA. Adults who receive services may have individual training accounts (ITAs), which allow them purchase services from eligible providers in their one-stop systems. As with recent special education and rehabilitation legislation, WIA emphasizes consumer choice and involvement in planning services. In addition, greater accountability for service providers is mandated in terms of documenting outcomes for individuals who participate in their program.

In terms of transition planning, students with disabilities and their families should find it easier to access information on a range of employment and training opportunities through a one-stop delivery system. Understanding the WIA and one-stop centers is especially important for linking students with high-incidence disabilities who are interested in obtaining skilled employment training after school and for students who are at risk of dropping out of school. In addition, low-income young adults and students who have dropped out of school may want to investigate job training and general equivalency diploma (GED) opportunities through Job Corps.

Other Significant Legislation

The legislation reviewed in the fields of special education, vocational rehabilitation, vocational-technical education, and workforce development form the basis for providing and funding specific services and educational opportunities. In addition, school systems have had to comply with legislation that targets educational reform efforts. In short, educational reform efforts have raised academic standards, instituted state and district assessments, and held schools accountable for students' progress measured through these assessments. Finally, the Higher Education Amendments of 1998 merit mention as reauthorization efforts are underway to increase access to postsecondary education, provide appropriate financial assistance, and ensure that students with disabilities are successful in pursuing this postsecondary goal.

Reform Efforts: Assessments, Standards, Accountability

Educational reform efforts in the 1980s resulted in students taking an increased number of academic courses and minimum competency tests. In 1983, the National Commission on Excellence in Education issued the landmark report, *A Nation at Risk,* which recommended an increase in the number of Carnegie units needed for graduation. Educational reform efforts in the 1990s focused on the need to raise academic standards for all students, to hold schools accountable when students did not improve performance, and to institute state and district assessments. These reform efforts were also extended to vocational-technical education and work-training programs in an effort to raise standards in these programs and ensure better postsecondary outcomes for students. In the case of statewide assessment systems, both traditional assessments (paper-and-pencil tests with a focus on students' achievement) and alternative assessments (performance assessments and portfolios) were included. Often, the provision of transition services for students with disabilities mandated in IDEA 1990 and IDEA Amendments of 1997 had to compete with the mandates to raise academic standards.

The standards-based education and accountability movement continues with the No Child Left Behind Act (NCLB) of 2001. State education agencies have had to develop high standards for all students and hold schools accountable if students cannot meet these standards. This reform effort has the potential to include more students with disabilities in general education and in state and district assessments. However, these students will need increased supports and accommodations to access and succeed in such ventures. In addition, transition services must be integrated within the standards-based movement to ensure students with disabilities are provided needed transition services in a climate of academic achievement (Johnson, Stodden, Emanuel, & Luecking, 2002; Kochhar-Bryant & Bassett, 2002b).

Several legislative acts are reviewed here, highlighting issues for secondary educators, including Goals 2000, the School-to-Work Opportunities Act of 1994, Improving America's School Act, and the No Child Left Behind Act of 2001.

Goals 2000, PL 103-227. Goals 2000: Educate America Act of 1994, PL 103-227, set eight national goals to improve schools: (1) school readiness; (2) school completion; (3) student achievement and citizenship; (4) teacher education and professional development; (5) mathematics and science; (6) adult literacy and lifelong learning; (7) safe, disciplined, alcohol- and drug-free schools; and (8) parental participation. Goal 2 called for the high school graduation rate to increase to 90 percent by the year 2000, meaning a significant reduction would be needed in the number of students who drop out of school. Dropout rates for students with disabilities have been estimated to be about 32 percent (Wagner, 1991). Although this goal was not realized, the U.S. Department of Education (2002) reported that dropout rates for students with disabilities declined from 34.1 percent to 29.4 percent between 1995–1996 and 1999–2000. Dropout rates must be interpreted with caution due to variations schools use in defining *dropouts* and variations among disability categories (e.g., 51.4 percent of students with emotional disturbances drop out of school).

Under Title II of the Educate America Act, the National Education Goals Panel was created to report on schools' progress toward achieving national education goals. Title III of this Act established a five-year grant program for the improvement of state and local education systems. Section 306 mandated that state improvement plans include strategies for improving teaching and learning (including standards for content, student performance, and opportunity to learn) and strategies for coordinating school-to-work programs along with the integration of academic and vocational instruction. Finally, Title V of PL 103-227, the National Skill Standards Act of 1994, established a National Skill Standards Board to identify clusters of major occupations and then develop skill standards, assessment and certification systems, and information dissemination systems. Although this Act had the potential to provide standards for how secondary students are prepared for the workforce, it is not evident in many of the state standards that have been set to comply with the No Child Left Behind Act of 2001.

The School-to-Work Opportunities Act of 1994, PL 103-239. The School-to-Work Opportunities Act of 1994 (STWOA) was passed by the Clinton administration to establish a national framework for states to create school-to-work systems. The overall purpose of the STWOA was to prepare students for work (to enter first jobs in high-skill, high-wage careers) and postsecondary education (Benz & Lindstrom, 1997). While the STWOA addressed the need for *all* students to have access to school-to-work programs, including students with disabilities was highlighted in this reform effort. The STWOA was administered by the U.S. Departments of Education and Labor and provided grant monies to states to plan and implement school-to-work systems. These school-to-work systems were to build on existing promising practices, such as Tech-Prep education, career academies, school-to-apprenticeship programs, and other work-based learning opportunities (Cobb & Neubert, 1998). Although the STWOA legislation expired in 2002, the intent was for states and local schools to reorganize and upgrade their vocational-technical programs. For example, some schools reorganized their vocational offerings around career themes or pathways (e.g., health occupations, communications, technology), with an emphasis on integrating vocational and academic instruction.

Improving America's Schools Act of 1994, PL 103-382. Title I of the Improving America's Schools Act amended the Elementary and Secondary Education Act of 1965, which focused on educational opportunities for students with disadvantages. This Act emphasized the development of standards and provided funds for school improvement activities. For example, Title I of the Act authorized programs for helping students with disadvantages to meet high standards and for prevention and intervention programs for youths who are neglected, delinquent, or at risk of dropping out of school. States who received funding under this Act had to describe in their state plan how these efforts were coordinated with Goals 2000 activities. Sarkees-Wircenski and Scott (1995) detailed how other activities, such as vocational-technical education, school-to-work, cooperative education, and apprenticeship programs, were coordinated with efforts under Improving America's Schools Act of 1994. These reform efforts clearly mandated greater collaborative efforts and laid the foundation for improved standards in academic and vocational courses.

No Child Left Behind Act of 2001, PL 107-110. Accountability has been the hallmark of education reform efforts over the past decade, but the No Child Left Behind Act takes it to a new level. The NCLB governs elementary and secondary education in the United States and provides significant changes to the Elementary and Secondary Education Act of 1965. The NCLB has four education reform principles: (1) accountability for results, (2) increased flexibility and local control, (3) expanded options for parents, and (4) use of teaching methods that have been proven to be effective (National Center on Educational Outcomes, 2003b).

States must develop *content standards* for content areas (e.g., English, science). Assessments must be tied to academic content standards, which identify *what* students will learn, and academic achievement standards, which specify *how well* students must learn. All students must be tested in reading and math in grades 3 through 8 by 2004–2005 and once in high school; by 2007, all students must also be tested in science.

Assessment results must be shared with the public each year. Teachers should look for brochures or reports that describe state and district assessment results or check the State Department of Education website. Schools are *accountable* for Adequate Yearly Progress (AYP), a term used for measuring students' improvement in achieving standards each year. This information must be reported for all students, but AYP must also be reported *separately* for students with disabilities with IEPs, students with disabilities with 504 plans, and English language learners, and by race, ethnic group, and socioeconomic status (No Child Left Behind, 2002). This will allow schools and parents to determine if students with disabilities or disadvantages are being held to the same standards as other students and if they are making progress toward meeting these standards. Sanctions and rewards are to be offered to schools depending on their AYP.

The No Child Left Behind Act also reinforces the need for alternate assessments; however, they must be aligned with state content standards and are to be used for students with significant cognitive disabilities (about 1 percent). The U.S. Department of Education (2003) issued a rule that allows these students to be assessed against standards appropriate for their intellectual level and allows schools to count the "proficient" scores of students with significant cognitive disabilities. This provides more flexibility in meeting AYP and allows more than 1 percent of students to participate in alternative assessment given that schools demonstrate they have a large population of students with significant cognitive disabilities.

The NCLB requires states to document that "highly qualified" teachers deliver instruction in content areas such as English, math, and science so students are able to master content standards. *Highly qualified* means that a teacher meets state certification requirements, holds at least a bachelor's degree, and has demonstrated subject-matter competency in each academic content he or she teaches (U.S. Department of Education, 2004). Middle and high school teachers will have to complete an academic major, graduate degree, advanced credentialing, or pass a state-approved test in the academic subject for each content area taught. Under NCLB, parents in Title I schools have the right to request a teacher's credentials to determine if he or she is highly qualified in a content course. In addition, parents can request that their child be transferred out of a low-performing school at the expense of the school system. The role of the secondary special educator in terms of "highly qualified" is a topic of debate. Secondary special education teachers should check with their State Department of Education website to determine how to meet the requirements for "highly qualified" under NCLB.

The Higher Education Amendments of 1998, PL 105-244.   By raising academic standards in schools, there is an expectation on the part of policy makers that greater numbers of students will consider postsecondary education and skilled training opportunities. Although the number of students with disabilities entering postsecondary education institutions has increased over the past 20 years, the type, range, and availability of supports services varies widely between insititutions (Stodden, Whelley, Harding, & Chang, 2001). In addition, problems with coordinating finanical assistance from multiple sources, such as vocational rehabilitation, federal loans, and work-study, are often problematic for students with disabilities. Therefore, there are a number of efforts underway to lobby that these issues be addressed as the Higher Education Amendments of 1998 are reauthorized in the near future. (See National Council on Disability, 2003, and Wolanin & Steele, 2004, for a discussion of these issues and related references.)

For students with disabilities who are considering postsecondary education as a postschool outcome, it is especially important that they are familiar with legislation that governs the provisions of reasonable accommodations at higher education institutions. This would include an understanding of Section 504 and the Americans with Disabilities Act in terms of eligibility for reasonable accommodations and the definition of a disability. In addition, students and their families should be familiar with the Higher Education Amendments of 1998, which are amendments to the Higher Education Act of 1965. Under this law, the term *disability* has the same meaning as the American with Disabilities Act of 1990; *disability* means a physical or mental impairment that substantially limits one or more of the major life activities of an individual; there is a record of the impairments or the person is regarded as having such an impairment. In addition, Title VII-Graduate and Postsecondary Improvement Programs, Part D of this Act provides funding for Demonstration Projects to Ensure Students with Disabilities Receive a Quality Higher Education. These projects provide technical assistance or professional development for faculty and administrators in higher education in order to provide students with disabilities a quality postsecondary education experience. Materials developed through these projects may assist students with disabilities and faculty in postsecondary education. Additional information on the reauthorization of the Higher Education Amendments of 1998 and projects targeted to improve postsecondary programs for students with disabilities can be found through the Office of Postsecondary Education, U.S. Department of Education, at www.ed.gov/about/offices/list/ope/index.html.

Understanding High School Requirements

Educational reform efforts have resulted in many changes in high school graduation requirements, including the number of academic courses required, the length of school days, minimum grade-point averages, high school exit exams, and diploma options. Middle and high school teachers must be familiar with the requirements for a diploma in their states so they can advise students with disabilities and their families on the various diploma options during transition planning, beginning no later than age 14. It is best to check your State Department of Education's website for specific and updated information on graduation requirements, exit exams, assessments, and instructional strategies to support educational reforms on a regular basis.

Differientated Diploma.   Over the years, state and district assessments and graduation requirements have led to differentiated diploma options. The U.S. Department of Education (2002) reported that the standard diploma graduation rate for students with disabilities was 56.2 percent during the 1999–2000 school year. Diploma options generally include a standard diploma or honors diploma with criteria that all students must meet; a standard diploma with multiple criteria (e.g., students complete their IEP goals; a certificate of attendance or achievement); and a special education diploma or certificate available only to students with IEPs. However, even with standard diplomas, the criteria vary greatly from state to state.

States have often used assessments to make decisions about student promotion or high school graduation (deFur, 2002). The National Center on Educational Outcomes (NCEO) (www.education.umn.edu/NCEO/) has been tracking and analyzing state policies on participation in assessment and accommodations for over a decade (e.g., Thurlow, Lazarus, Thompson, & Robey, 2002). A recent trend in assessments is to require students to pass content exit exams in order to earn a diploma. In a survey of 46 states and the District of Columbia, 27 state education agencies were reported to have or will have exit exams that require students to take a high-stakes assessment to receive a diploma (Johnson & Thurlow, 2003). The NCLB does not mandate graduation requirements or diploma options, but it does require school systems to report graduation rates as one measure of AYP. Therefore, it is likely that the use of differentiated diplomas will continue to grow.

Secondary students generally have to complete specific courses or credits to earn a diploma. For example, Thurlow, Ysseldyke, and Anderson (1995) found that 44 states used Carnegie course unit requirements, ranging from 10.25 credits to 24 credits for graduation requirements. The average number of credits required for graduation is 3 to 4 credits of English, 2 to 3 credits of math, 2 to 3 credits of social science, and 2 credits of science. In addition, most states require 1 to 2 credits in physical education, art, or health education. Students generally are able to select electives (ranging from 2 to 9 credits) during the high school years. Some states require foreign language or vocational-technical education credits during the secondary years and some require students to perform community service as part of their secondary experience.

At this point, little is known about the consequences of different diploma options in terms of access to employment and postsecondary education or students' motivation during the secondary years (Johnson & Thurlow, 2003). At this time, it would appear prudent to develop a course of study that leads to a standard diploma as part of the transition planning process for most students with disabilities.

Curricula Options. In addition to increased credits required for graduation and differentiated diplomas, students with disabilities and their families are also faced with choosing curricula options during the secondary years. In the past, secondary students generally had three options: college preparatory, general education, or vocational-technical education. In recent years, many state and local school systems have reorganized their curricula options around a college preparatory option and a career and technical education option due to educational reform initiatives. Some have opted to delete the general education track in hopes of preparing non-college-bound youths for better jobs and postsecondary training opportunities through restructured vocational programs. Some states may offer a vocational or occupational diploma. Students with low-incidence disabilities or those in separate special education classrooms may participate in community-based training programs with an emphasis on functional skills and work experience during the secondary years. Although there is some degree of overlap among the college preparatory and vocational-technical curricula due to common graduation requirements, some differences in the purpose, course requirements, and anticipated outcomes merit discussion.

College Preparatory Option. The college preparatory track provides a broad foundation of courses in English, math, science, social studies, and foreign language. The outcome for students in this track is obviously to continue in postsecondary education after graduating from high school. Students may take electives in vocational-technical education, although this is not the focus of their studies. College preparatory programs impose rigorous standards in both content difficulty and level of performance expectations. Some schools also provide advanced placement courses in academic areas, allowing students to earn college credit in some courses. The rigorous academic content classes in concert with state requirements for content assessments requires careful planning at the IEP meetings; accommodations, supports, and assistive technology should be carefully considered for each student with a disability at IEP meetings. In addition, a student's strengths, interests, preferences, and needs should be considered in terms of the type of postsecondary institution the student expects to enter after high school (e.g., community college, university) and the type of major the student is interested in pursuing. Not only are these considerations desirable for good planning but they are also necessary to comply with the transition requirements in the IDEA 2004. One of the challenges associated with the college preparatory option for some students with disabilities is the lack time to engage in vocational or work experiences and functional skill instruction.

Career and Technical Education Option. Students who select the career and technical education (CTE) curricula option must still meet state and local graduation requirements. In the past, programs were often organized around specific occupational areas, including agricultural education, business and office education, health occupations education, home economics or consumer sciences education, marketing and distributive education, trades and industrial education, and technical/communication (Sarkees-Wircenski & Scott, 1995). In addition, out-of-school work experience programs were generally delivered under Cooperative Work Education (CWE). Students in CWE programs are supervised by a work experience teacher in an employment setting for half a day and spend the other time in school earning their academic credits. An obvious strength of this curriculum is the combination of studying about a job and the opportunity to experience an actual job situation under the guidance of school personnel and an employer.

In some states, CTE programs may be organized around career clusters or career pathways (e.g., business management and finance, health and biosciences, transportation technologies). Work-based options may also include Tech-Prep programs, career academies, youth apprenticeships, and school-based enterprises. For a discussion of work-based learning options, see Chapter 6. It is important for secondary special educators to assist students with disabilities in exploring the requirements of these programs, participate in assessment activities that will identify areas of interest, and suggest appropriate, reasonable accommodations as students enter these programs. Since CTE programs vary from state to state, it is important to explore which programs are offered in specific states and local school systems. For students with disabilities interested in pursuing this option, their postsecondary goals should be tied to preparation for employment and/or further postsecondary education during transition planning meetings.

Recommended Practices in Secondary Special Education and Transition Services

Legislative mandates have clearly laid the foundation for students with disabilities to access diverse career, academic, vocational, and transition programs. Researchers have tried to identify what constitutes effective and validated practices in these programs in secondary settings by identifying quality indicators, best practices, and a conceptual organization for transition-focused education and services. This research has contributed to the development of program guidelines for students with disabilities in many secondary settings. Although few exemplary programs exist that use all of the quality indicators or recommended practices that we affirm as effective, there is no reason for any secondary special education teacher or transition specialist to be working without direction or focus. It is important that practices or guidelines are reviewed and updated periodically to reflect practices that have been validated through research.

Quality Indicators

In the 1980s, the literature in secondary special education and transition programs focused on four basic domains of instruction: academic, vocational, independent living, and social/interpersonal knowledge and skills. These student outcome indicators and related program characteristics indicators were validated in a study in Oregon (Halpern & Benz, 1987) and in an independent external study by Darrow (1990). Halpern (1988, 1990) and others refined the set of indicators to address six major categories of standards: curriculum and instruction, coordination and mainstreaming, transition, program documentation, administrative support, and adult services. These indicators were generated from the literature in the field and a systematic statewide evaluation of secondary special education programs in Oregon. A number of states (Oregon, Washington, Nevada, Arizona, and Kansas) endorsed Halpern's indicators and standards for the development of a system for follow-along transition programs in their states' secondary special education and transition programs. The indicators and standards were accompanied by a system of assessment and data collection, making the approach highly useful for program planning, program implementation, program evaluation, and, ultimately, program accreditation.

Another example of indicators can be found in *The NYEC Ednet Criteria: Indicators of Effective Practice,* which was developed through a literature review, expert opinion, and field-testing of the criteria in actual program. The National Youth Employment Coalition (NYEC) (2004) identified a set of indicators of effective practice that includes a self-assessment tool to assist schools in improving academic and transition practices. The indicators are organized around three broad categories:

- Teaching and Learning (e.g., academic program, transition, faculty/staff, learning climate)
- Essential Supports, Opportunities, and Services (e.g., youth voice, youth/adult relationships, building responsibility, supportive services)
- Purpose, Organization, and Management (e.g., mission, activities, continuous improvement, community connections, data collection, evidence of success)

These indicators reflect mandates in the NCLB Act of 2001 and may be particularly useful to those educators who work with youths in community-based and alternate education programs. The self-assessment approach allows schools or teams to target specific needs in their settings and work through changes systematically.

Recommended Practices in Transition.   A number of recommended practices or quality indicators for transition services have been identified through survey research or literature reviews. Several are briefly reviewed to provide an overview.

In the 1990s, researchers (e.g., Banks & Renzaglia, 1993; Kohler, 1993; Kohler, DeStefano, Wermuth, Grayson, & McGinty, 1994; Phelps & Hanley-Maxwell, 1997; Sale, Everson, & Moon, 1991) identified recommended practices, which included:

- Vocational training
- Parent involvement
- Interagency collaboration
- Social skills training
- Paid work experience
- Follow-up employment services
- Integrated settings
- Community-based instruction
- Vocational assessment
- Community-referenced curricula
- Career education curricula and experience
- Employability skills training
- Academic skills training

Hughes and colleagues (1997) validated transition practices teachers used in Tennessee. They surveyed teachers to determine if they accepted empirically derived strategies that support the transition from school to adult life and identified eight secondary transition support strategies as follows:

- Identify and provide social support.
- Identify environmental support and provide environmental changes.
- Promote acceptance.
- Observe the student's opportunities for choice.
- Provide choice-making opportunities.
- Identify the student's strengths and areas needing support.
- Teach self-management.
- Provide opportunities to learn and practice social skills.

A conceptual organization of practices for transition-focused education and services that has been updated over the years has been presented by Kohler and associates (Kohler, 1993; 1998; Kohler et al., 1994; Kohler & Chapman, 1999). The Taxonomy for Transition Practices was developed based on reviews of research literature, evaluation studies, and model transition project outcomes (Kohler & Field, 2003). Effective practices are organized by the following categories: (1) student-focused planning, (2) student development, (3) interagency and interdisciplinary collaboration, (4) family involvement, and (5) program structure and attributes.

Although secondary and transition practices have been associated with better outcomes for students after they exit school, there has been sharp criticism for the gap between what the literature identifies as "best" or recommended practices and what researchers have actually documented as effective practices (e.g., Greene & Albright, 1995; Kohler, 1993). Another problem with recommended practices is that there are few standards associated with a specific practice, making it difficult for practitioners or researchers to evaluate if a practice is used effectively in a specific setting (Redd, 2004). It will be important for secondary educators to stay abreast of research that continues to document which practices are effective under what conditions.

Transition Outcomes Project

The Transition Outcomes Project, developed by O'Leary, assists school districts and states in meeting the IDEA transition service requirements, evaluate the effectiveness of providing transition services through the IEP process, and use results to identify strategies to improve graduation rates and postschool outcomes of students with disabilities (Mountain Plains Regional Resource Center, 2003). Although this approach does not target specific practices to be used in the transition process, it does provide a framework for secondary educators and administrators to examine if they are meeting the IDEA transition service requirements and to target areas for improvement. The Transition Outcome Projects is reported to be used in over 23 states/regions and 1,000 school districts across the country. For information on this project, materials, online resources, and preliminary results, see www.usu.edu/mprrc/curproj/sectrans/sectrans.cfm.

Conclusion

Legislation, educational reform efforts, and research on practices will continue to affect secondary education for all students. It is important to understand legislative mandates so that students with disabilities (1) receive instruction and accommodations in general education classrooms to master content included on state and district assessments; (2) receive appropriate supports and accommodations in general education; (3) engage in early transition planning; (4) understand their rights in education, community, employment, and postsecondary settings; and (5) understand the services and eligibility procedures for interagency linkages. Educational reform efforts will also continue the debate on how secondary special education and transition services are provided in middle and high schools. This debate is not new in secondary special education, but it is controversial (e.g., Bodner, Clark, & Mellard, 1987; Clark,

1994; Edgar, 1988, 1992). At this point, it is critical that transition services be recognized in current educational reform efforts and that state standards reflect instruction and practices that promote optimal transition planning. Finally, understanding practices that contribute to better postsecondary outcomes for students with disabilities will enhance the transition planning process and assist secondary educators in complying with the transition service mandates in IDEA 2004.

3 Students and Families

Key Participants in Transition Education

There is no one who cannot find a place for himself in our kind of world. Each of us has some unique capacity waiting for realization. Every person is valuable in his own existence—for himself alone.

—George H. Bender

Although the participants in school programs for students with disabilities include a number of people, including student population, school personnel, and families, this chapter focuses on students, the subgroups that comprise them, and their families. No two school programs are alike, even in the same district, because of the diversity of these subgroups. This chapter describes, defines, and explains some of the diversity that makes planning for educational programs for students who have disabilities so satisfying, challenging, interesting, and, at times, difficult. This will be done by first presenting findings from the National Longitudinal Transition Study (NLTS2) (Wagner, Cameto, & Newman, 2003), highlighting the changing demographics and characteristics of youths with disabilities from 1987–2001; then presenting a perspective on school-aged students and the various student subgroups with disabilities; followed by the roles of parents as participants, as well as the family influences on students through their cultural, language, ethnic, and socio-economic characteristics.

Students as Participants

There is no doubt that among the stakeholders in the transition process, the students we serve are the most important; their lives should be our focus. Students will range from high to low motivation, from enthusiasm for the future to despair, and from sheer pleasure to be around to outright aversion. They come to us in large numbers, they come to us with different needs and strengths, and they come to us year by year, whether we are ready for them or not. It is the school's challenge to have teachers who are ready. This chapter is designed to inform, if not inspire, so that you will be more ready—professionally and psychologically—for the task. The next two sections review students in various developmental perspectives as a grounding for knowing your students better.

Elementary and Middle School Years

The elementary and middle school years represent the broadly defined period ranging from childhood through emerging or even early adolescence. Technically, school-aged students can include early childhood preschool programs for children with disabilities, but the emphasis here will be on grades kindergarten through eight. Legally, there is no mandate for schools under the IDEA provisions for transition planning per se, but an *appropriate education* is required and we believe that an appropriate education includes early planning and instruction in transition knowledge and skills as well as self-determination.

Childhood is seen by most families and the school as the period of early development in basic academic skills and socialization. It is characterized by dependence on parents and other adults for decisions, for the most part, but with natural efforts by the children to take on more and more decision making for themselves. Although many of those decisions are selectively related to children's self-interests (e.g., bedtime, foods and snacks, clothing, play activities, choice of friends, and independent activity outside the home), adults still assume full responsibility for final decisions in these areas as well as decisions regarding personal behavior, educational choices, religious influences, health, mobility in the community, and levels of self-determination.

It is well accepted that entering school is a major developmental transition for young children. The experience results in a significant shift in children's view of the world, starting with their own families. Intellectual and social development are the areas where children show the most gains. They are expected to learn the basics of reading, writing, arithmetic, communication skills, and an expanded view of their physical and social worlds.

As children develop intellectually and socially and gain more independence, they move from a natural drive to learn and master tasks to an orientation that is more complex. While they are developing some motivation to achieve (i.e., learn, make, do, perform, etc.), they are also experiencing an interest in competition and a sense of competence. Erikson (1963), some four decades ago, referred to this period as the time when a child's sense of industry (competence) can be enhanced or his or her sense of inferiority (incompetence) reinforced. Success at school and in social relationships generally enhance a sense of competence, and lack of success results in a sense of failure or incompetence. Families have a major role in how this plays out, but the school does also. If home experiences are strong, they can do much to undo what the child experiences at school and vice versa. Either way, the elementary years are crucial in establishing a solid foundation for later successful transitions in life.

It is during the elementary school years that most children with mild to moderate disabilities are identified for services. Those with more severe disabilities or multiple disabilities are usually recognized much earlier and are placed into infant/toddler programs or early childhood programs. This means that for a large percentage of children who are identified for services through special education, no thought is given to either the nature of possible problems or any intervention options until the child is 8 or 9 years of age. Most certainly, little serious thought is given to transitions in the future, especially school-to-adult living issues.

Once identified, however, schools should provide families appropriate information about the educational implications of the disabilities they identified and how this can play out in children's adolescence and adulthood. Getting these families together with parents and families of older students with disabilities may be the best way to orient new families to the issues of transition from elementary to middle/junior high schools, from middle/junior high schools to high schools, and from high schools to postschool programs or postsecondary education and employment opportunities. Chapter 4 presents a more detailed discusssion of this age group in relation to what teachers can and should be doing as early as possible in the K–8 transition education process.

Adolescence

Adolescence may be broadly defined as the transition period from dependent childhood to self-sufficient adulthood. It is a time of conflict, redefinition, and pushing for independence. Adolescence may be difficult even for the most intelligent, advantaged, and popular students, given the right conditions. For those with disabilities, adolescence may become a major task for which these young people are neither prepared nor capable of dealing. Thus, educators working with adolescents with special needs must be reminded of the characteristics and struggles associated with adolescence in general and the possible effects of this transition period on an adolescent's behavior and personality.

The beginning of adolescence is marked by the genetically and biologically produced onset of puberty. *Puberty* is the time span of physiological development during which the reproductive functions mature. The physiological changes take place over a period of approximately two years. The rate of physical change during this period is frequently greater than at any other time during a person's maturation, with the exception of the first year or two of life. The adolescent must deal with a new body and new roles in a very short period of time. New relationships with people of the opposite sex and of the same sex emerge out of both necessity and desire. Masculinity and femininity as well as a new body and self-image are explored. Thus, the adolescent is, in essence, involved in the struggle to develop a new sexual identity. This is apparent in the "nondating game" versus the "dating game," conformity versus nonconformity in dress and hairstyles of peers, new relationships with peers and adults, uncommon modesty versus blatant immodesty, and experiments in flirtation and sexual relations.

The biological change is not the only cause of adolescent conflict, however. The adolescent also is being programmed to fit the expectations of his or her culture. Cultural anthropologists have found that in primitive cultures, the period of adolescence is very short (Aries, 1962). Upon reaching puberty, the individual is considered an adult and may be initiated into the adult society through rites and rituals. In Western society, adolescence is an extended period of time during which young people are expected to pattern themselves, over time, after adult standards.

One adult standard of Western culture is for adolescents to begin to demonstrate a work ethic—and the sooner, the better. Because of the change in the family structure, with one or both parents working outside the home, and the formalization of the workplace, the burden is placed on the school to keep students in school and prepare them for adult roles. Keeping students in school and life preparation status extends the adolescent period through secondary and, often, postsecondary years. This extension may lead to conflicts concerning independence and self-sufficiency between parents and their adolescent child. Although the adolescent desires to become self-sufficient, he or she may not have the means to accomplish this goal. Parents, still providing financial support, may impose too many restrictions on the adolescent striving for independence.

Havighurst (1953) identified some developmental tasks that adolescents must complete in order to become successful (i.e., "normal") adults. Using some of Havighurst's tasks and adapting others to more current cultural values, the following tasks are presented:

1. Achieving new and more mature relations with age-mates of both sexes
2. Achieving a sexual identity
3. Accepting one's physique and using the body effectively
4. Achieving emotional independence from parents and other adults
5. Achieving economic independence
6. Selecting and preparing for an occupation

7. Preparing for marriage, family life, and intimate relationships
8. Developing intellectual skills and concepts necessary for civic competence
9. Desiring and achieving socially responsible behavior
10. Acquiring a set of values and an ethical system as a guide to behavior

Given a set of challenging developmental tasks such as those listed, adolescence is more than a matter of hormones and physical maturation. It is also a period of psychological and social change. This change involves a great deal of stress for adolescents with disabilities because the pressures of childhood to conform to or achieve intellectual and academic standards expand to include physical, social, and emotional expectations and standards as well. What makes these demands especially stressful for some adolescents with disabilities is that there is an increasing discrepancy between the physical development that is so obvious, and the social and emotional development levels that are not so obvious. Parents, teachers, neighbors, employers, and other significant adults frequently tend to respond primarily to the physical maturation and assume or expect an equal amount of maturational development in the social and emotional areas.

This book addresses all age groups in public schools, but there is no doubt that the emphasis throughout favors secondary-aged students. Part of the reason for this is that this is the age group specified for transition services in the law. It is also a fact that there is so much more in the literature on this age group. Research studies, including the federally funded National Longitudinal Transition Studies, provide more detailed information on adolsescents and young adults. The most current data are from the NLTS2 report (Wagner et al., 2003) on the changes since 1987 in characteristics of students targeted for the study (15- through 17-year-old youths with disabilities). Some of their findings are presented here as background information for this book.

Demographic Characteristics.   The composition of the group or demographics in 2001 in comparison to the 1987 NLTS study has changed markedly in a number of ways:

- Significantly fewer students classified with mental retardation as their primary disability appear in the 2001 group. In contrast, there was a significant increase in the proportion classified as having "other health impairments." Some of the growth in "other health impairment" resulted from large increases in the number of youths diagnosed with autism or attention deficit/hyperactivity disorder.
- Boys in both the 1987 and 2001 groups comprised about two-thirds of all youths with disabilities.
- The racial/ethnic composition of youths with disabilities is now more like that of the general population of youths 15 to 17 years of age. Youths

of color accounted for similar proportions of those with disabilities and those in the general population in 2001. They had been overrepresented by about 4 percentage points in the 1987 group.

- There was a significant increase in the diversity of languages used by youths with disabilities, with a considerable increase in the percentage of youths who did not speak primarily English at home. More than half of Hispanic American youths with disabilities did not speak primarily English at home.
- The proportion of youths who were at the typical age for their grade level increased from one-third of the youths to more than one-half between 1987 and 2001.
- Despite earlier identification and service, small yet significant declines since 1987 were reported by parents in the area of daily living skills of the youths.
- Support services increased from 1987 to 2001 in all disability categories, with the largest increase occurring for students with emotional disturbances. Boys and girls both experienced significant increases in receiving services from their schools, as did all income groups. Youths from lower-income households had increases in a wider range of services than those from higher-income households. White and African American youths had a similar pattern of increase in services, with significant increases in speech/language therapy, vocational and mental health services, and transportation.
- In 2001, youths with disabilities were more likely to be living in households with at least one biological parent present than in 1987 and the heads of households were much less likely to be high school dropouts or unemployed.
- Youths with disabilities in 2001 were less likely to be living in poverty than in 1987. Exceptions to this were those youths with mental retardation or emotional disturbances who were more likely to live in poverty with unemployed heads of households and in households that participated in benefit programs.

Student Outcomes. There was a mix of "good news" and "bad news" in student outcome data:

- The one-year dropout rate (students dropped out and remained out for at least a year) made a dramatic change. The overall dropout rate for youths with disabilities was cut in half between 1987 and 2001 and was significantly lower than the rate for the general population, ages 15 to 17. Only the mental retardation category rate showed a statistically significant decline in dropouts over time. Youths with emotional disturbances had the highest dropout rate in 1987 (over 50 percent) and had no decrease over time.

- Overall participation rates of youths with disabilities in extracurricular activities was below that of the general population and showed no increase over time, but did show increases for youths with disabilities in volunteer or community service activities, which more than doubled over time.
- Youths with disabilities experienced a significant increase in one-year paid employment rate in 2001 compared to the 1987 group. This increase brought the overall one-year employment rate for youths with disabilities to 60 percent and in line with that of the general population of youths (63 percent). However, a decline in the rate of current employment suggests that youths with disabilities had more sporadic work experiences as opposed to continuous employment.
- More youths with disabilities had work-study jobs, fewer hours per week worked, and significant increases in pay. Two-thirds of the youths with disabilities in 2001 were earning more than the minimum wage, a 50 percent increase over time since 1987.
- By 2001, 20 percent of youths with disabilities had experienced one or more of the following: suspension or expulsion from school, fired from a job, or arrested. This percentage is up 6 points from the 14 percent negative social adjustment outcomes in 1987.
- Girls with disabilities showed significantly larger increases in extracurricular participation than boys. They also had larger increases in employment than boys, closing the gap in employment rates that favored boys in 1987. Girls in 2001 had increased more than boys in the likelihood of having money of their own to spend. Still, in spite of their significant increases in the area of earning more than minimum wage, boys were still more likely than girls to meet or exceed the minimum wage rate.

Children and Youths with Disabilities

Some of you will be generally familiar with the nature and characteristics of each of the major disability groups under the IDEA. Others may be familiar with only one disability group or even think in noncategorical terms. There even may be some who are new to the field and need an introduction to the general definitions, characteristics, behaviors, and special needs of the variety of students who might be found in school special education programs or services. Regardless of which group you might fit into, the information on students in high school special education programming reviewed here is important, for it brings into focus the young people who need special services at a critical transition time in their lives.

A number of states are moving away from the process of assigning specific disability labels to students, yet still identifying students who require special education services. Some of these states have adopted the label of *non-*

categorical. Other states are using broad terms such as *students in need of special education services, students requiring an adaptive curriculum,* or *students requiring a functional curriculum.* Although we recognize this trend in labels, we believe it is important for you to be aware of the specific disabilities identified in the Individuals with Disabilities Education Act (IDEA) and the effects these disabilities may have on your work with these students. When one considers the specific student outcome data in the preceding list from the NLTS2 report (Wagner et al., 2003) relative to certain categorical groups, the logic of continuing to focus on some of the unique needs and strengths of certain groups is more clear.

The definitions provided in your state plan under the IDEA for each disability condition provide a starting point for any person who may be unfamiliar with certain disability groups. The major conditions that are the review focus of this text include the following:

1. Visual impairments
2. Deafness and hearing impairments
3. Orthopedic or chronic health impairments
4. Other health impairments
5. Speech or language impairments
6. Specific learning disabilities
7. Emotional disturbance
8. Mental retardation (mild and moderate)
9. Traumatic brain injury
10. Autism
11. Severe and/or multiple disabilities

In the early days of special education, segregated programs for each of these groups were the rule rather than the exception. Today, there is less segregation and more heterogeneous, inclusive groupings in most school programs. The consequence of this is that teachers may have a much wider range of ability level and diversity of students than ever before.

Visual Impairments

Visual impairments under the IDEA refer to both blindness and low vision. Students with visual problems may be placed in local public schools without regard for the severity of the visual impairment. That is, a student who is totally blind or who has a visual acuity of 20/400 with only light perception could be as likely to be in a neighborhood public school program as a student who is partially sighted with a visual acuity of only 20/70 with correction. The major considerations are family goals, independence, mobility skills, available resources, and academic potential rather than degree of loss or severity of impairment.

Individual student characteristics vary greatly, but teachers should be aware that adolescents with visual impairments *may* have one or more of the following characteristics or special needs:

1. Subaverage reading speed and level
2. Limited mobility and orientation skills
3. Restricted range of life experiences
4. Limitations in interactions with the environment
5. Underdeveloped abstract reasoning
6. Peer acceptance and social adjustment problems

The population of students who have visual impairments in public schools is difficult to estimate because of the low incidence of visual impairment generally (7 in 1,000 school-aged children), but the dispersal of students across residential and local community programs and all grade levels makes the probability of working with students who are even partially sighted at the high school level rather low. Even so, the possibility for any schools to have students with visual disabilities exists, and educators should be prepared to accommodate these students' needs and assist them to move through school programs successfully.

The unique instructional needs of students with visual impairments and the extra time that it takes for instruction and student learning may be a key barrier to the transition planning and transition education for this group. Teachers serving these youths in public schools have a wide age range of students and are frequently itinerant consultants to general education teachers. Teachers serving youths in residential or day schools for the blind are finding that the school populations tend to have multiple disabilities. For whatever reasons that affect outcomes, the NLTS2 data (Wagner et al., 2003) indicated that youths with visual impairments were the only group to experience a significant decline in their overall rate of participation in extracurricular activities and were among the few groups to show no increase in the work-study or one-year or current paid employment rates. Those students who were working, however, had large gains in earnings in comparison to their 1987 group. Independence, particularly mobility, and employment continue to be challenging areas for this population. *Transition Issues Related to Students with Visual Disabilities* (Erin & Wolffe, 1999) is a helpful resource for learning more about the unique issues of students with visual impairments. *Skills for Success: A Career Education Handbook for Children and Adolescents with Visual Impairments* (Wolffe, 1999) gives numerous strategies for transition education for elementary and middle school students.

Deafness and Hearing Impairments

Students with auditory impairments range from those who have no hearing ability to those who have difficulty hearing speech, from those who have no speech to those who have near-normal speech, and from those who use manual communication to those who read lips and use speech. There are those who are born deaf and those who lose hearing in childhood or adolescence. There are those who choose to identify primarily, or solely, with the deaf community and there are those who want to be accepted as a part of the hearing community. With such diversity, it is difficult to define or characterize students in this population.

The degree to which a hearing loss results in personal, social, intellectual, and occupational adjustment problems is related partially to the severity of the hearing loss and the age at onset. The key factors in life adjustment for students who have hearing loss, however, are communication skills and social acceptance. Both of these are influenced by the following characteristics, which occur with greater frequency in groups of people with hearing loss, but which are not present in all persons with a hearing loss:

1. Language development may be affected markedly in terms of oral and written expression. Vocabulary, verbal comprehension, grammar, syntax, and spelling may be significantly different from those individuals without a hearing loss.
2. Reading level is lower than expected for age and grade level.
3. Intelligence scores on verbal tests are lower. This does not, however, suggest a direct cause-and-effect relationship between hearing loss and intellectual ability, but rather the significant effect verbal reasoning, comprehension, and vocabulary skills have on performance with verbal tests of intelligence.
4. Emotional and behavioral problems interfere with school, peer, and family relationships.

Successful transitions for students who are deaf are often in the eye of the beholder. This is a group whose preferences and interests may very well be more in line with the values of the deaf community than what hearing educators or the public might want for them. Those who want to be fully immersed in the deaf community where they live or where they can find a deaf community may not be nearly as concerned as some hearing teachers are about oral communication and community participation skills. Others might find their places in public schools and develop preferences and interests similar to their hearing peers in terms of planning for college, occupational training, or a wide range of interpersonal relationships. Regardless of cultural values, however, unemployment and underemployment have been persistent problems, especially among women (Schirmer, 2001). The key to transition planning for this group, like other groups, is to help these students identify their strengths, preferences, and interests, and then work with them to be good self-advocates to achieve their goals. *Self Advocacy for Students Who Are Deaf or Hard of Hearing* (English, 1997) and *Facilitating the Transition of Students Who Are Deaf or Hard of Hearing* (Luckner, 2002) are excellent resources with strategies for transition planning and programming.

Orthopedic or Chronic Health Impairments

The population of students with orthopedic or chronic health impairments represents such a range of physical disabilities that no single quantitative, legal, or medical definition can describe it. In general, this classification encompasses all those who have neuromuscular disorders, musculoskeletal disorders, congenital malformations, chronic health problems, or disabilities resulting from disease, accidents, or child abuse. The nature of the disabling condition or health impairment is not as significant to educators as are its effects on cognitive, emotional, and social development. In fact, unless the impairment does affect learning and achievement in school, a student will not likely be identified for special education services and would be considered for accommodations under Section 504 of the Rehabilitation Act. On the other hand, educators must remember that students and families will frequently be most concerned about the presence of pain, discomfort, medication side effects, and the secondary emotional debilitation resulting from the medical problems and not as concerned about schooling. The school's sensitivity to family priorities is critical.

The effects of orthopedic or chronic health impairments are related to age at onset, the severity of the condition in terms of restricting activity and interaction with others, the extent of visible signs of a disability, and the extent of services and support. The actual limitations are more important than the specific name of a condition. For example, the *Disability Statistics Abstract* (1991) provided statistical data on people with *activity limitation,* rather than a general classification or naming of orthopedic or health impairments.

It is the limitations in activities of life that truly define this area as a disability that requires or does not require special education services. Only those students who have been referred and determined to need an individualized education program because of their physical disabilities or health problems or who request accommodations under Section 504 will come to the direct attention of school personnel. Unless a physical disability or health condition interferes with functioning in a regular classroom, there is no reason to identify or attempt to serve this group. Many students and their families choose not to request educational services under an IEP and instead use Section 504 accommodations as needed. Section 504 provisions do not require transition planning from school to employment or postsecondary opportunities, however, and students and families need to know they are rejecting planning, services, and linkage assistance.

We have no substantial indication that persons with impaired physique or health differ as a group from any other disabled or nondisabled group in their general or overall adjustment. Any blanket generalizations about characteristics would be inappropriate. There is also no clear evidence of an association between types of physical disability and particular personality traits. There is evidence, however, that indicates that physical disability has profound effects on a person's life. These effects come through the process of reaction and adjustment to the disability itself and through the various sources of stress (parental reactions, hospitalization, limitations in activity, dependence on others, sexual development, and limitations in social relationships) on students who have physical disabilities. The case study of Kathy Koons illustrates the individual characteristics that can emerge from type of disability, individual characteristics, and family characteristics.

Kathy Koons

Kathy is a 19-year-old young woman with spina bifida. She has an electric wheelchair that she can control in a very limited way. An instructional assistant works with Kathy to ensure that she is able to get around the school and to assist her with classroom activities. She requires assistance in writing and getting her supplies ready for class, getting her lunch and feeding herself, and controlling her wheelchair.

Kathy is a middle child; she has an older, married sister and a brother who is age 14. Her father is an electrician and her mother does not work outside of the home. The family lives in a very nice house, which has had some modifications made for the wheelchair.

Her school attendance has been very poor. Mrs. Koons has kept Kathy at home for extended periods of time throughout the years, stating that Kathy was not well enough to attend school. The family was told that Kathy would not live to be 5 years old and they have taken care of her every need. The mother does many things that Kathy could do on her own, but it would take her a long time to get it done. When Kathy is at home, she spends the majority of the time in her wheelchair in front of the TV or stretched out on a blanket on the floor. There is nothing that Kathy does at home for herself or the family.

Kathy is in four resource classes (math, language arts, social studies, and vocational exploration), is in two regular education classes (computers and home economics),

and spends one hour a day with the instructional assistant working on daily living and functional living skills. Kathy is working on grooming skills, kitchen skills, making change, telling time, and mobility. She has good verbal skills, but has very limited written language skills because of her limited mobility. She is learning to use a computer so that she can increase her written expressive skills. Kathy has indicated an interest in doing a job that would utilize telephone skills, which is something she feels she could learn to do. She has several friends at school. She says that she would like to have a boyfriend and talks about relationships quite often. She is very concerned about not having someone to marry, being able to leave home, and living on her own.

Kathy's Verbal Scale IQ is 84, Performance Scale IQ is 64, and Full Scale IQ is 75. Curriculum-based assessment results indicate skills functioning at the 7.5 grade level in reading and at the 6.8 grade level in math. She is aware of her academic limitations, but wants to do something with her life. Kathy indicates that she wants to learn to live more independently and to develop job skills. She is older than most of the students in the high school and plans are being made for her to go to a residential independent living center for young adults with physical disabilities, where she can have the opportunity to learn many of the things that will allow her to live in a group home and have a job. Kathy is very excited about these plans, but her parents are somewhat hesitant.

Teachers and counselors can contribute meaningfully to the transition of students with physical disabilities if they can make a clear distinction between a *disability* and a *handicap* in their own interactions with the students. A teacher must remember that, although the disability persists, a handicap can be eliminated or diminished by intervening with the tasks to be performed, the person, the person's environment, or any combination of the three. Helping students recognize that disabilities do not always produce handicaps may allow them to develop confidence that they have some control over their lives. This may have a critical effect on their personal feelings of worth and sense of destiny. Although there are many sources of information teachers can turn to for suggestions to help them work effectively with students who have orthopedic or health impairments, *Teaching Individuals with Physical or Multiple Disabilities* (Best, Heller, & Bigge, 2005) is an excellent resource for instructional strategies and Haslam and Valletutti (2004) is a useful guide to medical problems in the classroom for teachers.

Other Health Impairments

Recent focus on attention deficit disorders (ADD) and attention deficit/hyperactivity disorders (ADHD) by physicians, psychiatrists, mental health professionals, and educators has posed diagnostic and classification problems for schools and even more difficult problems in intervention approaches. Considerable debate continues about the causes of ADD and ADHD, which leads to a variety of placements in special education programs. Some individuals are placed in programs for students with learning disabilities, some in programs for emotional disturbance, and others in programs/services for "other health impairments." At this time, there are not enough specific research data available to have a great deal of useful information on how to provide these students with appropriate career development and transition programming. Most information relates to social and attentional behavior.

Parents and educators have frequently turned to medications for control of inappropriate and exasperating behavior, but there is increasing agreement that this is no cure and that some side effects are more serious than the attention deficits or hyperactivity. In most cases, there will need to be close coordination between career education specialists and medical personnel until such time as research data point to more effective methods of treatment and training. In the meantime, simply recognizing that the behavior or attention disorders are neither willful nor controllable by the youngsters can go a long way toward moving teachers and other professionals into meaningful relationships with the youngsters and their families. A student with ADD or ADHD may or may not be determined eligible for special education and related services. Local schools must follow state and federal regulations in determining eligibility or accommodations under Section 504 and the Americans with Disabilities Act.

Authorities now recognize that up to 70 percent of individuals diagnosed with ADD/ADHD in childhood will continue to have significant symptoms in adulthood (Rief, 1998). Although persons with ADD/ADHD are at risk for less positive outcomes after school exit, especially in employment and in marriage and family life (Hallowell & Ratey, 1996; Weiss, Hechtman, & Weiss, 2000), many adults with this condition achieve highly successful careers and jobs and have happy, successful marriages.

Speech or Language Impairments

Speech and language problems for school children are common. In excess of 25 percent of all students receiving special education or related services have communication disorders as their primary disability, making it the second highest of the disability populations (Hegde, 2001). Speech disorders involve articulation problems, fluency disorders, and voice disorders. Language disorders result from language delay or specific language impairments due to neurological, cognitive, or hearing impairments.

Teachers need to be alert to the existence of communication disorders and must be ready to ensure that the students who have them have the best diagnoses and intervention possible. This begins with an understanding of what constitutes a speech or language problem. Some practical questions to ask in determining whether a person has a speech problem severe enough to warrant referral include:

1. Can I understand this person?
2. Does this person sound strange?
3. Does this person have any peculiar physical characteristics when speaking?
4. Is the communication in a style inappropriate to the situation?
5. Is this speaker damaging his or her vocal chords?
6. Does the speaker experience pain or discomfort when attempting to communicate?

Language disorders are much more complex than speech defects, since they involve not only speech but also receptive, integrative, and expressive activities. A student who has difficulty in comprehending questions or directions has a receptive language problem. A student who clearly has greater ability to receive messages than to express them has an expressive language problem. A student who can demonstrate some receptive ability and some expressive ability but has difficulty in coordinating the two is assumed to have some type of integrative deficit in perception, recall, or retrieval of sensory or perceptual input. Language disorders usually affect both oral and written communication, but proper use of facial expressions, gestures, and body language can make oral communication deficits less noticeable.

Speech and language interventions for students of transition planning age should make sure that functional communication—using appropriate conversation skills, dealing with the public in stores and service offices, using public transportation, and engaging in employment-related conversation on a job—is the focus of transition goals (Klein & Moses, 1999; Rogers-Adkinson & Griffith, 1999).

Specific Learning Disabilities

Students with specific learning disabilities make up the largest and most heterogeneous of all high school students with disabilities. Abilities range from slow learner to gifted levels, and behavioral characteristics are so diverse as to leave little doubt why this group has practically defied definition. Teachers usually focus on the academic and behavioral problems of students with learning disabilities. The academic failures of these students in reading, writing, math, language, or spelling are major obstacles in school adjustment, and the personal-social problems that accompany them (or emerge as a consequence of them) are the primary targets of school concerns. These academic and social difficulties make it nearly impossible to differentiate students who have learning disabilities from students who are low achieving. Researchers do seem to agree on the following:

1. There is a discrepancy between what a student should be able to do and what he or she is actually doing.
2. Learning disabilities are lifelong problems.
3. Students do respond and improve in performance with appropriate instruction.
4. There are some specific tasks that others can do that students with learning disabilities cannot do.
5. Students' difficulties are centered on one or more basic psychological processes involved in using and understanding language.
6. Students are not learning adequately in spite of the basic integrity of their senses, cognitive ability, emotional state, or lack of opportunity to learn.

The case study of Craig Turner is an example of one student with specific learning disabilities. Keep in mind that Craig's characteristics and history are not meant to represent a typical student with specific learning disabilities. There is no such typical student.

Craig Turner

Craig is 17 years of age and in his third year of high school. His father is an insurance executive and his mother is socially active in Junior League and a local sorority. Craig is an only child and is very verbal and socially adept. He was in classes for dyslexic children at a private school for five years prior to returning to the public high school. During his junior high school years at the private school, he was successful in athletics, earning letter awards in football and track.

Reading has always been difficult for Craig; his current reading achievement level is 1.8. His math performance is 3.6. These grade-level scores are verified through performance on both curriculum-based assessment and commercial achievement measures. He does poorly in spelling and writing and is beginning to refuse to do any assignments that require composition and handwriting. In social studies and science, Craig contributes orally and demonstrates a wealth of information that indicates he acquires information aurally and has good memory skills. He is managing to pass all his subjects and is on schedule to graduate next year.

During the past two years, Craig has frequently been in trouble at school. He has not been eligible to participate in athletics because of poor grades and periodic suspensions due to infractions of school rules. He has been truant on numerous occasions and has been caught at school with liquor and various drugs in his locker. He seeks out friends in regular classes from his affluent neighborhood but is not very successful in his attempts. Those who do choose to be with him are those who are having similar problems with grades and school adjustment.

Craig presents two role identities at school. One is the assertive, outgoing, cooperative but "cool" student who has everything under control, including the teachers, as they respond to this role positively and cater to his mood and wishes. The other role is the restless, impatient, negative student who communicates nonverbally to everyone, "Stay out of my way—don't hassle me." His classmates do not trust him, and some are afraid of him. Teachers have tried to establish a relationship with Craig that is positive, and have succeeded in preventing any classroom conflicts. Most of his misbehavior occurs outside the classroom in other parts of the school.

Craig's parents are well known to school officials because of their response to the school's disciplinary policies. They do not deny the infractions but believe that the school environment is to blame. They have refused to permit Craig to enter into any vocational or exploratory community-based training experiences during his first two years of high school. They believe he has the ability to work in some occupation that has much higher status than what they associate with the school vocational programs. They insist that the school should remediate his reading problem and provide an academic program that will qualify him for high school graduation and possible admission to a community college. Both parents are college graduates and find it difficult to accept any low-status school or employment alternatives.

Craig does not verbalize any occupational interests and has not wanted to be in any high school vocational or prevocational options. His interests appear to focus on cars, movies, professional football, and his stereo equipment. The only part-time job he has ever had was a summer job as a recreation assistant for a children's soccer league. This was obtained for him by his father. Craig's work was satisfactory, but he did not ask to do it again. His parents provide him with a generous allowance each week of $50, so he has spending money all year long.

Hallahan, Lloyd, Kauffman, Weiss, and Martinez (2005) stated that researchers have developed and refined increasingly effective instructional procedures for students with learning disabilities. Among the major approaches are the following:

- Cognitive training (includes such procedures as self-monitoring or self-instruction)
- Mnemonics (includes using key words and other means of assisting memory)
- Direct instruction (includes careful sequencing of instruction, rapid and frequent responding, and immediate feedback and correction of errors)
- Metacomprehension training (provides students with strategies for thinking about remembering content they read)
- Scaffolded instruction (includes gradual reduction of assistance and reciprocal teaching)

Hallahan and associates (2005) recommended an instructional approach that makes sure that students initially receive the most effective instruction available and that those who are *not* making reasonable progress under such instruction should be provided prereferral services or special education services. They affirmed Zigmond's (1997) view that special education must be not only carefully planned, but "intensive, urgent, relentless, and goal directed" (p. 384).

Bender (2001) indicated that there are seven general curricular approaches to meeting the needs of students with learning disabilities: functional skills, work-study, basic skills instruction and remediation, tutorial in subject-matter areas, learning strategies, inclusion or co-teaching, and consultation. The first two of these are appropriate for those students wanting to go to work after completing school; the others are appropriate for students wanting to go on to some type of postsecondary education or training. Transition planning needs to determine early on the student's strengths, preferences, and interests regarding future plans so that appropriate courses of study can be arranged.

Emotional Disturbance

Definitions of *emotional disturbances* typically revolve around two major issues: (1) the inability to establish appropriate, satisfying relationships with others and (2) demonstration of behavior that either fails to meet or exceeds the expectations of those with whom the person comes in contact (Kauffman, 1997). Since these characteristic behaviors are found to a certain degree in many "normal" children and adolescents, emotional disturbances must be viewed differently from those in adults. According to societal standards, the fine line between normal behavior and disordered behavior is drawn among the degree or magnitude of severity, the rate or frequency of occurrence, the duration of the behavior, and the unique form of the behavior.

The definition of *emotional disturbance* used in the IDEA excludes a student with a social maladjustment, unless it is determined that the student has a serious emotional disturbance. Some authors have challenged this exclusion (Walker, Ramsey, & Gresham, 2004) on logical grounds. That is, they argue that the behaviors associated with social maladjustment (truancy, hostile and aggressive behavior, cruelty to others, destruction of property, etc.) provide the basic descriptors for conduct disorder, which is a psychiatric diagnosis used to describe a condition involving agression, property destruction, and deceitful behavior over time (American Psychiatric Association, 2000).

It is clear that the IDEA definition is a political and economic one. Eddy, Reid, and Curry (2002) stated that conduct disorders, when combined with oppositional-defiant disorder (both American Psychiatric Association diagnoses), characterize between 2 percent and 16 percent of the U.S. youth population. Although school-aged students can and do access mental health services both within and outside of schools, schools typically refer and ultimately serve slightly less than 1 percent of the school population with emotional and behavioral problems through IDEA (Walker et al., 2004). Although the large percentage of the students served at school in special education services for students with emotional and behavioral disorders have agressive, antisocial behaviors, this means that there are many other nonagressive students needing services who might not be receiving them because of students' or parents' fear of being in classes with these students.

Emotional disturbance ranges from mild to severe, although some would say that, by definition, even mild emotional or behavior disorders are so markedly inappropriate, socially unacceptable, or personally unsatisfying that they are obvious to most observers. In other words, the behaviors must be severe, excessive, and persistent before a student is classified as having an emotional disturbance or behavior disorder. The relative terms *mild, moderate,* and *severe* are appropriate only when used as a continuum of severity within the population already diagnosed as having an emotional disturbance. Following are some general descriptions distinguishing levels of severity of emotional disturbances:

1. *Mild* emotional disturbance is characteristic of students who are involved in some type of crisis causing dysfunctional behavior, but still able to function within the regular school system with a minimum of support help from a crisis teacher, counselor, itinerant resource teacher, and/or medication. Disorders that fall within the mild category tend to be transient and may disappear with time-limited interventions or sometimes even without specific intervention.

2. *Moderate* emotional disturbance requires some type of intensive intervention (e.g., individual or group therapy, medication, special or resource room placement). These types of disturbances tend to be longer lasting and more debilitating, and they interfere more with functioning at home or school.

3. *Severe* emotional disturbance is based on a student's inability to function in a high school environment. The adolescent who has severe emotional disturbance may have difficulty maintaining contact with reality. The behaviors exhibited are more exaggerated and bizarre. The adolescent with a severe disturbance frequently needs a self-contained classroom or possibly temporary placement in a homebound, hospital, or residential treatment situation.

The case study of Amy Sanders gives an example of a student with unique manifestations of an emotional disturbance.

Amy Sanders

Amy is 12 years old and in the seventh grade in a suburban community. She is the youngest of four children and the only girl. Only one brother lives at home, but he is in and out, depending on his employment. Amy's mother works in a factory and is married to her third husband. Amy's current stepfather works in the same factory but in a supervisory position. He is actively involved in Amy's school and medical problems.

Amy is a low achiever in school, but it has been her emotional and behavioral problems that have dominated school responses. Early on, she was assessed as not needing a special class, but she was still seen as different from the other children in her classroom. She demonstrated withdrawal, extreme shyness, immaturity, and excessive dependency throughout elementary school. Amy made no academic progress during the elementary years, but she made significant progress in her personal and social development during sixth grade. Her current reading and math skills are at a fourth-grade level.

After one semester in the seventh grade, Amy started to withdraw, showed symptoms of depression, and was unable to function or perform as she previously had at home and at school. She was hospitalized twice for depression, hallucinations, and

hearing voices. She is currently taking three medications for her emotional state, but these have been changed frequently in attempts to regulate the dosage. Her behavior at school and home is erratic and she is described by her teachers as "deteriorating" and regressing in all areas and skills where she had earlier shown much positive growth.

It is known that Amy was a victim of sexual abuse by her natural father, second stepfather, and the brother who is still at home occasionally. Amy's mother reports that she is at the end of her rope. Recently, when Amy wandered from home and asked a stranger for a ride, the family found it necessary to seek respite care for Amy after school.

Amy is now demonstrating manipulative and passive-aggressive behaviors at school. She refuses to respond verbally at times, frequently cries over trivial incidents, and wants to call her "mommy" to come get her when school staff attempt to deal with her inappropriate behaviors. She is lacking in positive community experience outside the school. She has demonstrated some positive occupational development at school by asking to assist in the school office or library.

Transition from school to work and adult life in the community is especially difficult for adolescents with emotional or behavioral disorders (Bullis & Fredericks, 2002). They frequently do not have the basic academic skills to seek employment beyond the entry level and families, neighbors, and the public have a difficult time dealing with their inappropriate behavior. This is particularly true for those who grow up with conduct disorders or antisocial behaviors. Successful transition to adult life is often complicated by neglectful, abusive, or inadequate family relationships and by the lack of appropriate educational programs. Bullis and Frederickson presented the challenge clearly when they stated that costs to society of *not* providing this population with effective programs and services is obvious in communities and that the problems go beyond the moral responsibility inherent in the school system.

Mental Retardation

In only three characteristics are all children and youths classified as having mental retardation or developmental disabilities alike: (1) they have intelligence quotients of two or more standard deviations below the mean of 100, (2) there is evidence of two or more types of adaptive behavior deficit, and (3) these characteristics manifest themselves before age 18 (Luckasson et al., 1992). Otherwise, these children and youths vary considerably in most characteristics. This introductory statement is important for you to put into perspective; it comes from the American Association on Mental Retardation (AAMR) and is the most accepted definition used for identifying this population. This latest revision of the definition for mental retardation places more emphasis than previous definitions on adaptive behavior. The definition by Luckasson and colleagues specifies that there must be "related limitations in two or more of the following applicable adaptive skill areas: communication, self-care, home living, social skills, community use, self-direction, health and safety, functional academics, leisure, and work" (p. 1).

Any generalization about those diagnosed as manifesting mental retardation is an artifact of the definition and is very subjective. For example, assume that two persons have significant deficits in intellectual functioning and adaptive behavior. Knowing that one has an IQ of 65 reveals no single clear notion of what the person's capacity to learn, solve problems, acquire knowledge, or think abstractly is, compared to someone with an IQ of 55. Neither does it mean that the person with the higher IQ has a higher level of adapted behavior. Both persons are identified as having "mental retardation," but they may be evaluated quite differently—not only on the two factors required for the diagnosis but also in their interests, aptitudes, personalities, physical attributes, and health. The case study of Darrell Cook gives an example of this.

Darrell Cook

Darrell is 17 years of age and is in his first year of high school. His mother does commercial cleaning with a janitorial service in a city high-rise office building. His father is serving a long-term sentence in prison. Prior to incarceration, he had been absent from the home more frequently than he had been in it and had not held a steady job in 10 years. Both of Darrell's parents are uneducated and unskilled, and have not been able to work steadily at the same time to generate two incomes for the family.

Darrell is the oldest of five children. He has had difficulty in school from the very beginning. His junior high school years were especially difficult. Curriculum-based assessment results for Darrell reveal that he is functioning at about the third-grade level in reading and math (3.1 and 3.2, respectively) but the diagnostician noted that these scores may not reflect his ability, as he did not appear to be showing any sincere effort while taking the tests. His intellectual functioning was assessed as Verbal Scale IQ of 64, Performance Scale IQ of 72, and Full Scale IQ of 68. His vocabulary is limited and language immature, and he has poor oral communication skills.

Darrell demonstrated some work potential when he began selling newspapers at age 9, and did this for nearly two years. He has worked part time for a neighborhood grocery. He also worked part time for a roller skating rink when he was 15 years old. During that time, he won several cash prizes ($25–$50) in skating contests. He is interested in getting back into the skating contests and winning a lot more money.

The Cook family lives in a slum area in extremely substandard housing. Food at home is basically nutritious, but there is not much variety or quantity. Darrell rarely eats more than one meal a day at home. The family lives in a two-bedroom house with his grandmother and an aunt. Privacy is impossible, and tensions from crowding and other factors associated with poverty make family interactions difficult and sometimes volatile. This has encouraged much of the life in the street that Darrell participates in and that his younger brothers and sisters are beginning to experience.

It is fair to generalize, as with the other disability groups discussed, that the severity of mental retardation leads to differences in performance characteristics. The more severe the mental retardation, the more one can expect to find accompanying physical limitations, problems in language and communication skills, comprehension and reasoning problems, and a wide range of inappropriate social behaviors.

As with emotional disturbances, labels such as *mild, moderate, severe,* and *profound* are used frequently by professionals and others to communicate general expectations of those with mental retardation without specifying behavior deficits. Such labeling led to inappropriate generalizations, therefore is no longer part of the AAMR classification system. The new classification system is much more "transition-friendly" in that the focus in the classification gives direction for transition planning in relation to needs for support. The new classification based on levels of support needs (Luckasson et al., 1992) are as follows:

- *Intermittent support:* Support on an "as needed" basis
- *Limited support:* Support characterized by consistency over time and time limited, but not intermittent
- *Extensive support:* Support characterized by regular (e.g., daily) involvement of support persons in at least some environments and not time limited
- *Pervasive support:* Support characterized by constancy, high intensity, provided across environments, and possibly life-sustaining

It is important to remember that a person can need intermittent support in one area and limited, extensive, or possibly pervasive support in another area. This is an example of the importance of not overgeneralizing from a psychological report that places an individual in only one general support level as part of the diagnosis and classification process.

Traumatic Brain Injury

A separate category of eligible disabilities under PL 101-476 (IDEA, Section 300.7 [B] [12]) was established for students with traumatic brain injury (TBI). *Traumatic brain injury* refers to an *acquired brain injury* caused by some external physical force (open- or closed-head injuries), resulting in total or partial impairments in one or more areas, including cognition, language, memory, attention, reasoning, abstract thinking, judgment, problem solving, sensory or motor abilities, perceptual abilities, psychosocial behavior, and communication. Injuries can result in mild, moderate, or severe impairments and frequently involve complex interaction of physical, psychological, and social problems.

Although individuals with some type of acquired brain injury (ABI) have been in schools and public life for decades, it is only recently that schools have begun to address the condition. Transition from the school environment into adulthood, particularly postsecondary education or training and employment, is difficult for many students with TBI/ABI (Bergland, 1996; Wehman, 1992). Without question, soon after the injury, a student with TBI/ABI will experience impaired ability in learning new information. This affects continued progress academically in school. In addition, change in student behavior and decision making can affect general performance, self-esteem, and social relationships—usually in a negative direction. These students naturally tend to hold on to their preinjury self-identities and may have real difficulty in recognizing or accepting the need for changes in their lives at school, at home, or in the community.

In their comprehensive publication on educational dimensions of acquired brain injury, Savage and Wolcott (1994) related some unique characteristics of this population in contrast to persons born with congenital impairments (see Figure 3.1). The sudden intrusion of a loss of functioning significantly changes an individual's life. In many cases, the individual is aware of these changes and what they mean. Although there are usually surviving skills on which to rebuild one's life, the memory of "who I used to be" serves as a continual reminder of the loss that occurred. Teachers need to recognize such characteristics, be flexible to respond appropriately, and never give up. The case study of Tony Lupino is an example of unpredictable recovery effects.

FIGURE 3.1   Range of Disabilities Resulting from Acquired Brain Injury

Cognitive Problems May Involve

- Communication and language
- Memory, especially for learning new information
- Perception
- Attention and concentration
- Judgment, planning, and decision making
- Ability to adjust to change (flexibility)

Social and Behavioral Problems May Involve

- Self-esteem
- Self-control
- Awareness of self and others
- Awareness of social rules
- Interest and social involvement
- Sexuality
- Appearance and grooming
- Family relationships
- Age-appropriate behavior

Neuromotor-Physical Problems May Involve

- Vision and hearing
- Speed and coordination of movement
- Stamina and endurance
- Balance, strength, and equilibrium
- Motor function
- Speech
- Eye-hand coordination
- Spatial orientation

Source: Adapted from *Educational Dimensions of Acquired Brain Injury* (p. 10) by R. C. Savage and G. F. Wolcott, 1994, Austin, TX: Pro-Ed. Copyright 1994 by Pro-Ed. Adapted by permission.

Tony Lupino

Tony is a 15-year-old student who was struck by a car while in-line skating. He made excellent physical recovery from his head injury and presents himself as an attractive, active teenager. Since the injury, however, he has been more impulsive than he was prior to the injury and often makes poor decisions, taking unnecessary risks to show that he is "cool" and not afraid of getting hurt.

Tony returned to his general education classroom two months after his injury. His school had no specific plan for his reentry and little information on the effects of brain injury. Due to the effects of his injury on his cognitive abilities, Tony is currently unable to understand what is expected of him in class nor can he work independently on assignments. He has reacted to these changes by refusing to do his work, clowning with his peers, and skipping classes.

Recent curriculum-based assessment and formal testing revealed that Tony has low-average intellectual functioning and performs in the average range, compared with his peers, on measures of academic achievement. The school psychologist rec-

ommended special education services and the parents agreed. At the first IEP meeting, Tony's behavior was the focus of concern, and, at the school's recommendation and with the parents' approval, he was placed in a classroom for students with behavior disorders. Tony's behavior quickly deteriorated further. He viewed the placement as a punishment and was angry that he was separated from his friends.

Tony's continued and accelerated behavior problems caused great concern for the school and Tony's parents. After reviewing the situation, a neuropsychological consultant was invited in to assess the situation. The consultant determined that Tony had returned to school fully expecting to resume his normal school routine. The school expected the same thing. It appeared that no one was prepared for the cognitive or behavioral effects of the injury. Tony was frustrated with his school problems in academics, but either denied his loss of cognitive ability or was unaware of his memory loss and difficulty in learning. His acting out was interpreted by the school and his parents as normal adolescent rebellion.

Very few data are available regarding adult outcomes for students with TBI/ABI. Roessler, Schriner, and Price (1992) reported employment data on a population sample of persons with ABI, indicating employment rates ranging from 52 to 97 percent, depending on the level and length of the postinjury comas. They also reported that of those who were employed, 75 percent were working only part time.

Smith and Tyler (1997) stressed that there can be no single plan used in transition planning for students with TBI/ABI. This is true, of course, for all disability groups. Of all disability groups, TBI/ABI require especially careful joint planning with the student, family, and any medical rehabilitation personnel associated with the student. The plans need to be flexible, reviewed frequently, and adjusted when necessary to respond to the dynamic nature of this group of individuals.

Autism

Like traumatic brain injury, autism was added to the list of eligible disability groups under the IDEA in 1990. It is a condition that is seen much more frequently in schools than in years past and presents some new challenges to educators. The visibility of Asperger syndrome, in particular, has brought out the wide range of characteristics and expectations in the autism spectrum disorder classification.

Autism spectrum disorder is a general term that refers to the range of conditions that represent the area of autism. *The Diagnostic and Statistical Manual of Mental Disorders–Fourth Edition–Text Revision (DSM–IV–TR;* American Psychiatric Association, 2000) and the *International Statistical Classification of Diseases and Related Health Problems–Tenth Edition* (ISD–10; World Health Organization, 1992) both refer to all levels of autism under the diagnostic classification of *pervasive developmental disorders.* This term refers to persons who are "characterized by severe and pervasive impairment in several areas of development: reciprocal social interaction skills, communication skills, or the presence of stereotyped behavior, interests, and activities" (American Psychiatric Association, 2000, p. 69).

Most of the literature relating to autism has focused on research, case studies, and practice with young children. Until recently, the literature focused more on low-functioning individuals with autism rather than those whose abilities help them compensate for their autistic behavior, such as those with Asperger syndrome. The difficulty in long-term prognosis for even Asperger syndrome was reflected in the *DSM–IV–TR* statement: "Asperger Syndrome is a continuous and lifelong disorder" (APA, 2000, p. 82), but "the prognosis appears significantly better than in Autistic Disorder, as follow-up studies suggest that, as adults, many individuals are capable of gainful employment and personal self-sufficiency" (APA, 2000, p. 82). In spite of the growing agreement that some individuals with autism or autistic behaviors are clearly able to lead more independent lives, there is also a recognition that positive outcomes rarely come without appropriate education, treatment, and support (Myles & Simpson, 2003).

There are some dramatic success stories, such as Temple Grandin, the autistic woman who has a successful international career designing livestock equipment and is an assistant professor of animal science at Colorado State University. There are also autistic savant cases, such as Kim Peek, who was the inspiration for the movie *Rain Man,* and Jessy Park, the artist. And, finally, there are those who have satisfying, successful lives, with continued encouragement, caring, and support but whose stories are not presented in the media or research literature. The primary point is that autism is highly individual in its manifestations and that every student you have with this diagnosis deserves your best efforts to assist them in their needed transitions as they prepare for adult life. The case study of Simon Huang is not presented as a typical example, but it accurately reflects one student with high-functioning autism.

Simon Huang

Simon is 20 years old and still in his neighborhood high school. He has average intelligence, with better verbal than performance skills. He does well on rote learning tasks, but his parents and teachers continue to be puzzled by his poor comprehension of abstract ideas and his social naiveté and vulnerability to hazards in everyday life.

Simon has demonstrated some signs of autism since age 1. Very early he became socially aloof and isolated. He spent most of his preschool years gazing at his hands, which he moved in complicated patterns before his face. He passed the major development motor tasks at the appropriate age, but would spend hours running in circles with an object in his hand. Any attempts to stop him resulted in screaming. He performed many stereotyped movements as a young child, including jumping, flapping his arms, and moving his hands in circles.

At age 3, Simon recognized the letters of the alphabet and rapidly developed skill in drawing. He did not speak until age 4, and then for a long time used only single words. After age 5, his speech and social contact improved dramatically. Until age 11, he attended a special school, where teachers and the staff tolerated a range of bizarre, repetitive routines. Despite his problems, Simon was able to use his excellent rote memory and absorbed all he was taught. He could recall and reproduce facts verbatim when asked. He was transferred to a public school at age 11.

Simon uses good grammar and has a large vocabulary, but his speech is naive and immature and he is concerned mainly with his own special interests. He has learned not to make inappropriate remarks about other people's appearance, but tends to ask repetitive questions. He is socially withdrawn but prefers adults to age peers. He enjoys simple jokes, but cannot understand more subtle humor. Simon is often teased by his classmates and finds it difficult to understand the unwritten rules of teenage social interactions. He says of himself, "I am afraid I suffer from bad sportsmanship."

Simon's main interest is in maps and road signs. He has an exceptional memory for routes and can draw them rapidly and accurately. He is adept at using a citizens band radio and regularly contacts a wide network of other radio enthusiasts. He also makes large, complicated, abstract shapes out of any material he finds and he shows much ingenuity in getting them to stay together. His finger dexterity is good, but he is clumsy and poorly coordinated in large motor movements.

Progress is beginning to be seen in Simon's ability to verbalize his awareness of his problems, but he is still unable to resist some of his routines and rituals. He is quiet and easy to get along with at home and his parents and sister are very fond of him. He has no friends with whom he associates. Simon is beginning to talk about his dreams for the future, which is to be a cartographer. He has been unable to find work on a part-time basis, and the school has never tried a community-based program because of his unwillingness to participate. Simon's parents are very concerned about what will become of their son in the future.

Severe and/or Multiple Disabilities

Severe and multiple disabilites in children and youths are viewed as a low-incidence condition that cuts across many of the other single disability classifications previously discussed. For example, students with severe and profound mental retardation, severe autism, or multiple disabilities combining one or more disability conditions (e.g., deaf-blind, blind-cerebral palsy, mental retardation and multiple physical, sensory, and neurological problems) pose a variety of unique challenges for families and students. These children and youths as a group have more significant communication and/or mobility problems, are more medically fragile, more likely to have seizure disorders, and more likely to demonstrate stereotypic and/or self-injurious behaviors than any other disability group.

Unfortunately, having a population description like the one just given reinforces the myths that persons with severe and multiple disabilities have problems so severe that the best any one of these individuals can ever hope for is to live under close supervision in an institutional facility or be employed in a sheltered workshop. That is not our intent at all. In fact, we affirm the evidence that shows that with intensive and extensive instruction, many persons with severe and multiple disabilities are able to live semi-independently and/or interdependently in supported living settings in the community and be employed in integrated work settings with supported employment services. With appropriate augmentative or alternative communication systems, individuals who cannot speak may learn to carry on a normal conversation or at least communicate basic needs. As research has indicated the potential of this group, expecations of parents reflect a growing optimism for their sons or daughters to work in the community and live in apartments with friends or in their own homes (Grigal & Neubert, 2004).

Families as Participants

Even if the parents' rights and responsibilities for participation in the education planning for their sons or daughters with disabilities were not clearly established in PL 94-142, the emphasis on transition services in the 1997 and 2004 Amendments to the IDEA make it very clear that a partnership is absolutely critical. It is much easier during the elementary years for parents to yield to the school's considerable authority for educational decisions, particularly on the content of the curriculum. For some teachers and parents, school is more or less an end in itself and the content and substance of what is taught in school is of secondary importance to being there for the expected period and graduating. When a student with disabilities nears the age of entry into high school, the decisions parents and students make are much more critical in that they are no longer focused on the short-term goal of moving through the educational system reasonably successfully, academically and socially. From age 14 on, the education meter is ticking and choices that are made regarding courses of study (and even specific courses) should be made with outcomes in mind for postsecondary life. We are learning increasingly how much influence the family actually has in terms of transition planning and outcomes (deFur, Todd-Allen, & Getzel, 2001; Lindstrom, Benz, & Doren, 2004; Mercer & Mercer, 2001; Morningstar, Turnbull, & Turnbull, 1995).

The seminal work of Turnbull and Turnbull (2001) on family collaboration with schools and service agencies to empower families and their children is highly relevant to family participation in the transition process. Because Turnbull and Turnbull are both parents and professionals, they view the process in very personal terms and acknowledge that for many parents the future "looms like a frightening unknown" (p. 171). All of us want and need support when facing uncertainty, and families may want to rely on the strategy that they have used from the beginning of their parenting of a child with a disability—taking it "one day at a time." The realities of day-to-day living consume many families, especially those who are poor, unemployed or underemployed, and unaware of support services. Others forge ahead and take on life with hope, persistence, and self-determination. These are the ones that Geenen, Powers, and Lopez-Vasquez (2001) found to have positive influences on their sons and daughters in very significant ways.

The provisions of the IDEA state that educational decisions regarding a student's transition from school to adult living should be made based on the student's strengths, needs, preferences, and interests. However, families must be active participants in the determination of what those needs, preferences, and interests are. Grigal and Neubert (2004) reported some very interesting and surprising responses of parents regarding what they value in instructional domains and postschool expectations that should remind us of how important parent input is. They found significant differences in values and expectations between parents of high-incidence disability groups and low-incidence disability groups. Some of these were predictable; others were not.

Parents also need to be involved in the guidance and teaching process that the schools cannot do alone. Parent/family roles and responsibilities as participants in a transition education school program include the following:

- Encourage student self-determination and independence at home.
- Encourage and facilitate setting goals.
- Teach, and assist in teaching, daily living and personal-social skills.
- Encourage the student to work at home and at a neighborhood or community job.
- Reinforce work-related and independent living behaviors at home.
- Explore and promote community resources for transition.
- Assist in the student assessment process.
- Assist the student in developing personal and social values, self-confidence, and self-esteem.
- Work with legal and financial experts, as appropriate, to plan financial, legal, and residential alternatives.

Families cannot perform these roles and responsibilities without information and support from professionals. Turnbull and Turnbull (2001) offered the tips in Figure 3.2 for empowering parents to enhance successful transitions for their children. You should review *Family Involvement in Transition Planning and Implementation* (Wehmeyer, Morningstar, & Husted, 1999) and *The Role of Fam-*

FIGURE 3.2   Enhancing Successful Transitions for Families

Early Childhood

- Encourage parents to begin preparing for the separation of preschool children by periodically leaving the child with others.
- Assist families in gathering information and making arrangements to visit preschools in the community.
- Encourage participation in Parent-to-Parent programs.
- Familiarize parents with possible school (elementary, middle, and secondary) programs, career options, or adult programs so they have an idea of future opportunities.

Childhood

- Provide parents with an overview of curricular options.
- Ensure that IEP meetings provide an empowering context for family collaboration.
- Encourage participation in Parent-to-Parent matches, workshops, or family support groups to discuss transitions with others.

Adolescence

- Assist families and adolescents to identify community leisure-time activities.
- Incorporate into the IEP skills that will be needed in future career and vocational programs.
- Assist families in visiting or becoming familiar with a variety of career and living options.
- Develop a community mentoring program for individual students.

Adulthood

- Provide preferred information to families about guardianship, estate planning, wills, and trusts.
- Assist family members in transferring responsibilities to the young adult with disabilities, family members, or service providers as appropriate.
- Assist the young adult or family members with career or vocational choices.
- Address the issues and responsibilities of marriage and family for the young adult.

Source: Turnbull, Ann; Turnbull, H. Rutherford, *Families, Professionals, and Exceptionality: Collaborating for Empowerment,* 4th edition, © 2001. Adapted by permission of Pearson Education, Inc., Upper Saddle River, NJ.

ilies in Secondary Transition: A Practitioner's Facilitation Guide (Wandry & Pleet, 2004) as valuable resources on strategies in working with families in transition planning and programming.

Variations in Student and Family Characteristics

Students requiring special education programming and their families vary considerably—geographic variables, cultural and ethnic variables, and socio-economic variables. A full discussion of these variables is not possible, or even appropriate, here, but they are important for educators to understand in today's mobile society. It is common for teachers to move from home states and familiar cultural features of an area to new, unfamiliar working environments. The following sections are designed to provide some initial awareness of some of the unique factors that influence teaching situations in working with students with disabilities.

Geographic Variables

People living in the United States have long been aware of geographical factors related to population characteristics. Interests, values, and life-styles are historical phenomena that persist today in spite of the increased mobility of the nation's population. Yankee ingenuity, Southern hospitality, Midwest work ethic, East Coast liberalism, Southwest rugged individualism, and Northwest conservationism are examples of regional stereotypes that are based to some degree on myth, historical tradition, and observed differences. Although these regional values and life-styles may be recognizable among adults, they may or may not be reflected in students' attitudes and behavior during their school years. These influences tend to be adult culture factors that may be resisted by children and youth, then assumed later as adults. When youths with mental or physical disabilities are more attuned to values and life-styles of their parents than of their peers, then some of these regional influences may be observed during the school years, especially in the upper grades.

Urban-rural factors probably have more direct and lasting effects than do regional factors. For example, the prevalence and incidence of disability conditions is higher in urban areas than in rural areas. The reason for this may be an artifact of proportionately more diagnostic referrals as well as availability of programs for serving people with disabilities. Perhaps it is because of urban pollution, poverty, or population density leading to high stress. This does not mean that urban families have problems and rural families do not. There are also rural poverty areas, rural areas polluted by toxic agents in water and soil, issues of isolation, and scattered or distant health-care services for families.

Urban Issues.   Urban schools are usually large enough to be able to offer a range of special education programs and services. However, some issues or problem areas for urban districts include the following:

1. *Multicultural populations.* Metropolitan areas particularly have been magnets for poor and multicultural populations, especially migrants and immigrants (St. John & Miller, 1995). Two decades ago, Hodgkinson (1985) projected that by the year 2000, one of three persons in the United States would be a member of a racial or ethnic minority. Today, his projections are currently on target nationally and have been exceeded in cities such as Los Angeles, San Diego, San Antonio, and Houston. *Migrants* are of two types: those who move from one part of the country to another to live and those who move around frequently, following crops or other jobs. *Immigrants* are those who migrate from another country to this country. There appears to be a trend for some college-educated immigrants to choose permanent visas or work permits in the United States because of special education services that are not available in their home countries. The parents of some immigrant students are challenged to cope with the complexities of urban life in a new environment and to provide adequate support for their children in special education programs at the same time.

2. *Language barriers.* The survival language learned by immigrants to the United States is quite different from school language. The technical vocabulary and precision of school and vocational programs may be overwhelming. Students with learning disabilities or mental retardation, who also may have English language deficits, often find school programs in urban areas extremely demanding and beyond their abilities. The parent/school communication is also a problem because of language difficulties.

3. *Cultural and value differences.* Youths who have disabilities and who live in urban settings present a wide range of values toward school in general and vocational programs in particular. Affluent urban or suburban families, who may not see skilled or semiskilled occupations as being appropriate for their sons or daughters, sometimes insist on an academic emphasis. Families in poverty or lower middle-class working groups may want their children to rise above skilled or semiskilled levels of occupations offered in special education programming and hold higher academic or occupational aspirations. Or, some students feel no family pressures to achieve in school or work and may have learned a negative attitude about work of any kind and do not enroll in any available vocational programs even when they stay in school.

4. *Size and complexity.* Another issue of urban education that affects students and families is the size and complexity of the urban environment, especially in large metropolitan areas. Whether inner city or suburban, the diverse needs of urban students result in highly complex and sometimes almost overwhelming administrative and instructional problems. These include the following:

- Identification and appropriate placement of students who are educationally disabled versus poor achievement due to limited English proficiency
- Appropriate curriculum offerings that deal with language barriers, cultural pluralism, and retention of dropout-prone youths
- Deteriorating school facilities and inadequate supplies of texts and library books
- Transportation resources that permit mobility out of inner city or distant suburban neighborhoods and access to unique community resources
- Selection and retention of qualified teachers to work with urban students who are behind academically and losing hope
- Dropout rates that remain the highest in the nation
- Large class sizes
- Maintaining safe school environments
- Dealing with the effects on children as a result of poverty

5. *Survival behavior.* The struggle to survive in heavily populated urban areas reaches deep into families of all racial, ethnic, and cultural groups. Economic survival is basic to physical survival, and many students with disabilities are experiencing early the pressures of being an adult in the real world. Having enough money to have a place to live and food to eat is a daily challenge for too many families, and compromises are made in order to have the basics of shelter and food. Just as important, though, is the struggle to survive the social and psychological stresses of poverty, noise, pollution, lack of privacy, and fear. Gangs, child abuse, and both random and directed violence loom as such major problems and concerns that a school may be seen only as a temporary escape, and even then not always as a safe one.

Rural Issues.   The factors influencing the nature and characteristics of students and families in rural areas are numerous and varied. Economically stable rural communities may be characterized as conservative and tending to adhere to traditional family values. These attitudes may provide a positive environment in terms of basic morality, ethics, and personal values that rural youths understand and learn very early. Many of these values, attitudes, and personal and social behaviors are taught in the home, in the local churches, and in community youth organizations such as scouting, 4-H clubs, and Future Farmers. Since rural schools are so attuned to the values of the community, they can at times, however, reflect conservatism and resistance to change that affects the development of resources and programs.

Some isolated and economically depressed rural communities exhibit certain characteristics similar to those of developing countries. Rural areas, just as metropolitan areas, have poverty, alcoholism, inadequate housing, unemployment, and underemployment—but without many resources to remedy or improve the situation. These circumstances influence students and families in many of the life decisions they make concerning employment, further education and training, community participation, and health.

Many rural communities that are economically tied to agriculture have migrant workers. Some of these communities are the rural home bases of the migrant families and some are the seasonal homes. Families may leave south Texas, for example, in March or April, boarding up their doors and windows and removing their children from school. They follow the crops, moving north until the end of the fall harvests of the northwest and upper midwest states, then return to their homes in late September or October and return their children to school. Depending on their ages, the children and youths spend decreasing amounts of time in school (even temporary enrollments) and increasing amounts of time in the fields. Schooling back at the home base may last no longer than four or five months a year. Obviously, this pattern is difficult for all children, but especially for those who have special learning needs. Consequently, many rural schools find themselves facing the need to offer an increasing number of support services—social work, special education, bilingual education, and guidance. Most of them face these needs without adequate financial resources.

Cultural and Ethnic Variables

Cultural, social, and ethnic influences on values, self-concept, and personality development are well established (Akan & Grilo, 1995; Steward, Giminez, & Jackson, 1995; Thompson, 1995). These influences are at work irrespective of the geographic location or size of a community. That is, cultural, social, and ethnic forces are operating in regional locales and in both urban and rural settings across regions. Urban areas will have many cultural or ethnic groups. Rural areas may have one or two cultural or ethnic groups in relatively small numbers or perhaps a single, predominantly ethnic community. In fact, the United States is the most ethnically diverse nation in the world.

Some urban and rural factors are probably more influential in personality development than are cultural or ethnic variables, so one cannot generalize for any racial, cultural, or ethnic sample without knowing the regional location and size or nature of their community. This is seen in the differences especially between urban and rural African Americans, Native Americans, and Hispanic Americans.

Special education professionals must be responsive to different cultural and ethnic values, styles, and traditions. Unfortunately, there is very little research on the meaning of disability or its impact on various ethnic groups. The lack of information in this area puts special educators in the position of taking responsibility for finding out the cultural and ethnic perspectives of the parents of their students and how these perspectives affect parent/teacher and student/teacher communication as well as alternatives in educational interventions. Over a decade ago, Ogbu (1994) argued that neither the core curriculum movement nor the multicultural education movement adequately addresses the problem of minority students who do not do well in school. Minorities whose cultural values are oppositional to the American mainstream cultural frame of reference have greater difficulty crossing cultural boundaries to learn. Geenen, Powers, and Lopez-Vasquez (2001), Simon (2001), and Combes and Durodoye (2002) confirm this more recently, but do give some evidence that parental involvement with schools makes a positive difference in transition planning for adult outcomes.

Walker (1991) and D'Amico and Maxwell (1995) provided a helpful perspective for addressing some important cultural issues that emerge in school and rehabilitation programs preparing individuals for independence and work. The cultural assumptions that educators and adult service agencies bring to their work (e.g., assessment, planning instruction, placement in jobs, etc.) may be quite different from those of their students or clients from other cultural backgrounds. Some of those assumptions and the implications of those assumptions for work include the following:

Cultural Assumptions	*Implications for Education and Employment*
Family boundaries	Life crises and events affect attendance since family is a priority
Quality of life	Independence may be rejected in favor of family interdependence
Importance of social status	Different responses may be given to supervisors
Importance of religion	Generosity and community support may be more important than "profit" or advancement
Meaning of work	The purpose and the nature of work may be viewed differently
Decision-making style	Group decision making or authoritarian style may be preferred to avoid individual decision making
Belief in change	Individual control may not be desired; situations may be seen as fatalistic
Work routines/expectations	The main meal of the day may be eaten at mid-day with a rest period; the type of clothing that is congruent with their health and safety may be preferred

Socioeconomic Variables

The nature of suburban middle-class families has changed considerably from the "Dick and Jane" image of the 1940s and 1950s. The white-collar exodus from the cities to the suburbs led to a stereotyping of suburbia that was characterized by income and life-style. By the 1970s, a broad middle class emerged, making up more than half of the metropolitan population. The primary change of this class expansion was the upward mobility of blue-collar workers. Their incomes increased significantly—enough to enable them to match incomes and status symbols with white-collar workers (suburban homes, numerous household appliances, season tickets to sports events, recreational vehicles and campers, snowmobiles, boats, popular designer label clothes, etc.).

The life-styles of middle-class families in urban and suburban communities have produced a generation of children and youths with a range of values, aspirations, and life-style dreams. Students with disabilities today are confused by the mixed messages of home, school, and society about what is desirable and what is possible. Societal changes have placed stresses on middle-class families. The force of these changes has greatly weakened some parents' authority and diminished their enthusiasm for parenting. As these parents have yielded their authority and responsibility—sometimes literally, sometimes symbolically—students with disabilities are seen by many educators as the school's responsibility by default. The students, on the other hand, are increasingly influenced by their peers' values, attitudes, and behavior. Many are more interested in the themes played up by the mass media—glamour, sex, affluence, and entertainment (escape) as solutions to problems—than the themes of school, which include academic achievement, responsibility, and occupational goals, interspersed with athletic events, proms, and school-related extracurricular activities.

The description of low socioeconomic populations and poverty is more familiar, yet most educators are far removed from the realities of real poverty. Those teachers who did grow up in poor families and lived in lower socioeconomic neighborhoods remember well the lives they experienced as children or youths and are highly sensitive to their students' concerns for hunger, safety, health, and decent environments in which to work and play.

Poverty is difficult to define or establish in exact dollar terms, but the U.S. Census Bureau attempts to do this with its "poverty threshold" system. A family is considered poor (in poverty) when the family's total income is less than the income threshold set by the U.S. Census Bureau (Dalaker, 1999). Poverty thresholds are based on expenses judged basic and necessary for *minimal* acceptable amounts for food, clothing, housing, and other essentials and they are updated each year to account for inflation. For one person the poverty threshold for 2003 was $9,573 (U.S. Bureau of the Census, 2004), for a family of three (one child under age 18) it was $14,810, and for a single parent with three children under age 18 it was $18,725. Putting this into perspective, a graduate of a special education program earning a minimum wage (federal) of $5.15 would earn $10,712 for 52 weeks of work. This would be enough to miss the Census Bureau poverty threshold of $9,573. However, a single wage earner for a family of three or four at the federal minimum wage level would fall considerably below the poverty thresholds for that size family unit. Still, the graduate could not make it alone or be financially independent with an annual gross income of $10,712, even if he or she received some benefits from food stamps, Medicaid, or low-cost federal housing.

Park, Turnbull, and Turnbull (2002) suggested that there are five family life domains that are affected by poverty:

1. *Health:* Limited access to health care; hunger and inadequate nutrition
2. *Family productivity:* Impacts children through delayed cognitive development and underachievement at school; limited access to recreation and leisure
3. *Physical environment:* Inadequate housing, overcrowding, lead-based paint, unclean premises; concerns for safety; lack of community support and positive role models
4. *Emotional well-being:* Increased stress due to physical environment, low self-esteem, and lack of hope for any change
5. *Family interactions:* Inconsistent and/or unresponsive parenting; marital conflicts over money and parental roles; increased sibling responsibilities

Teachers recognize the symptoms of these poverty factors when students come to school hungry, unclean, and inadequately clothed for the weather; show little interest in school learning; relate alarming events or situations in the home or neighborhood; and show their frustration and anger at their lives. Teachers also see some resilient children and youths from poverty situations who bloom in school beyond all expectations. The school's responsibility is to do what it can to lessen the impacts of poverty and "keep hope alive."

Conclusion

The participants in secondary special education programming are an extremely heterogeneous population. The variations of size, location, population characteristics, and local and state laws and policies make for extremely different educational situations. These variations have implications for differences that you can expect as you are introduced to a given program as a newly employed professional or a prospective employee. If educators understand differences in students and their families and use that understanding in providing the best transition planning and programming possible for identi- fied youths with disabilities, students and families can participate more freely and effectively. It is ironic that most educators would agree in principle that the student and family are key participants in the transition process, yet as long as the teacher or case manager is the one to take full or major responsibil- ity for transition planning, the reality is that the school representatives are the key participants.

4

Grades K–8 in the Transition Process

A Critical Foundation

BETTY AMOS

There is nothing in a caterpillar that tells you it's going to be a butterfly.
—Buckminster Fuller

Since the 1980s and Part H of Public Law 99-457, early childhood professionals have been mandated to develop transition plans with parents and families to help young children transition between infancy and toddler, toddler and preschool, and preschool and kindergarten. Meetings and plans are made to involve all the necessary people and agencies to assist in making these transitions successful. Early childhood professionals have involved the family in making plans for each step forward, each transition to the new experience in the child's life. This is the way it should be.

The amendments of IDEA 2004 require schools to begin long-term transition planning at age 16, or earlier when appropriate. So what happens in that gap between kindergarten and age 16? Is transition simply an early childhood and secondary function? Or should transition be part of a seamless educational system from infancy to postsecondary? Although legislation changes are not pending to fill this K–8 gap, this chapter will discuss the importance of continuing the early childhood planning into the elementary grades and implementing interventions that can pave the way for secondary and post-secondary transitions planning. Former position papers advocating the filling of this gap will be reviewed to document how important the early years are. Even though transition planning is not mandated during these elementary years, this chapter will establish conceptually what could and should be done in transitions education and in developing appropriate services for students with disabilities during those K–8 school years. To make a case for transitions education and services in these elementary and middle school grades, we will discuss actual developmental transitions during these school years. Strategies for integrating transitions education instruction in the inclusive environment will complete the chapter.

We recognize that schools use a variety of configurations for grades K–8. For simplification in this chapter, we will consider primary grades as K–3, intermediate grades as 4–6, and middle school or junior high grades as 7–8. When the word *elementary* is used, we mean grades K–8 inclusively. We hope that you are able to apply the overlapping concepts and strategies noted in this configuration to your own school organization formats.

Pertinent History

Professionals in the transitions education field have noted the elementary school transition gap in past history in two position papers (Clark, Carlson, Fisher, Cook, & D'Alonzo, 1991; Repetto & Correa, 1996). Paralleling educational history and the transition movement at the time the papers were written, each position paper focused on the pertinent issues in transition. Although the major implementation of the Individuals with Disabilities Education Act of 1990, PL 101-476, occurred between the two noted position papers, the position papers were strikingly alike in their rationale and proposals.

1991 Position Paper

The position paper "Career Development for Students with Disabilities in Elementary Schools: A Position Statement of the Division on Career Development" (Clark et al., 1991) was published on the heels of IDEA (1990) at the time special educators were making the move from career development services and programs of career education to the new terminology of transition services determined by IDEA. At that time, IDEA (1990) mandated transition planning starting at the age of 16 (or at a younger age when appropriate). Specifically, the authors responded to the plentiful information being generated about the transition planning process and what that would mean to educators working in established career development programs and "new" transition programs. They noted the barriers educators would be facing as they implemented IDEA and called for a priority change: "the need to begin the process of career development, transition planning, and transition intervention strategies much earlier than at the secondary level" (Clark et al., 1991, p. 110). Some of the force behind the 1991 position paper was established by the former Division on Career Development (DCD) position statement by Razeghi, Kokaska, Gruenhagen, and Fair (1987) on the transition of youths with disabilities to adult life. In the 1987 position statement, issues of early ongoing programming were emphasized as they related to the life-span career development concepts of the time, noting that not only were the preschool and secondary periods in the lives of children and youth with disabilities critical but so were other periods of time between these time periods (Razeghi et al., 1987).

The emphasis for the 1991 position statement was to include kindergarten through grade 6 into any career development and transition programming, specifically in the areas of stages of career development. The authors of the position statement used the life-centered career competencies of Brolin (1978, 1983, 1989), the life stages of vocational development by Super (1953; Super, Crites, Hummel, Moser, Overstreet, & Warnath, 1957), the school survival skills of Garnett (1984), the employment adaptability skills of Mithaug, Martin, and Agran (1987), and the employability factors of Karan and Knight (1986) and Chamberlain (1988) to reiterate the need for transition programs to begin earlier than the secondary level and continuously through the lives of children with disabilities. The implicit reasoning included recognizing that learning continues throughout life, and that children and youths, especially those with disabilities, do not benefit from an interruption in this learning of coping skills. The position paper noted the following:

> These skills need to be taught directly, *while students are still in the elementary school setting.* Waiting until junior or senior high school to begin career development instruction significantly delays the development of knowledge and skills required for success in employment and adult living. . . . Elementary school is the level where the critical foundations for career development and transition skills must be considered as important as basic academic skills. (Clark et al., 1991, p. 113)

Further discussion in the position paper (Clark et al., 1991) centered on how the development needs of students, differentiated instruction, and least restrictive environment fit together, particularly at the elementary level. Additionally, the position paper included discussion of each of the basic assumptions and principles of that time period that supported career development and transition education at the elementary levels:

1. Education for career development and transition is for individuals with disabilities at all ages.
2. Career development is a process begun at birth and continues throughout life.
3. Early career development is essential for making satisfactory choices later.
4. Significant gaps or periods of neglect in any area of basic human development affect career development and the transition from one stage of life to another.
5. Career development is responsive to intervention and programming, when the programming involves direct instruction for individual needs. (pp. 115–117)

The authors of the position paper reiterated the need for elementary-level transition education and services in their conclusion:

> A commitment to life-centered career development and transition preparation for students exclusively at the secondary level is not only inadequate, it is counterproductive. Such an exclusive approach ignores the possibility that school programs have not succeeded in the past because of providing too little, too late. Such an exclusive approach also ignores the mass of data supporting early intervention with children who have disabilities and are at risk. (Clark et al., 1991, p. 118)

1996 Position Paper

Repetto and Correa (1996) advocated for a seamless model of transition from birth through age 21 in special education in the position paper "Expanding Views on Transition." As support for this continuous and seamless approach to transition services, the life-span approach of Clark and colleagues (1991) and the wrap-around service model approach of Edgar, Parker, Siegel, and Johnson (1993) were noted. Like the 1991 position paper, Repetto and Correa (1996) reiterated the need to fill the elementary gap because of the interruption of learning between early childhood and secondary programs. They further referred to the "void of service coordination" (p. 552) in this gap. To fill this void, the authors discussed common transition components from the early intervention and secondary transition programs: curriculum, location of services, futures planning, multiagency collaboration, and family and student focus. These commonalities pointed out the need for a continuous and seamless approach to formal transition planning in the preschool and elementary gap for ages 4 to 15, particularly in the area of multiagency collaboration. Repetto and Correa promoted interagency cooperative councils (ICC) as the basic managers of the multiagency coordination from birth to adulthood for children with disabilities. Additionally, this position paper emphasized (1) the "sense of abandonment" (p. 558) felt by parents during this gap when the child with disabilities is from ages 4 to 15 and (2) the need to have uninterrupted service coordination for the student and families based on future outcomes. Uninterrupted service coordination allowed students and parents to be in control of the transition education and services throughout the students' lives. This position paper cited the following barriers to a seamless transition model:

1. Curriculum based solely on nonintegrated academics does not foster the precepts of the transition model.
2. Discontinuity of the curriculum, fragmentation of services, and miscommunication among program personnel can cause failure in transition planning.
3. Educational planning teams who do not respect the use of the IEP as a working document will find it difficult to support expanding that document to include transition planning.

4. Personnel who have concentrated on the student as the single unit of intervention planning may find it more difficult to accept a broader view of intervention that includes families, communities, and schools.
5. Some families may find long-term transition planning unsettling and have difficulty actively participating in their child's program. (p. 559)

Repetto and Correa (1996) concluded with detailed guidelines to implement the comprehensive seamless transition planning and the warning, much like the 1991 position paper, that "not accepting this model will only perpetuate further fragmentation in curriculum, family under-involvement, dropout casualties, and personnel isolation" (p. 561).

A Case for Filling the Gap, K–8

As alluded to in both position papers (Clark et al., 1991; Repetto & Correa, 1996), not responding to the need for transitions education and services between early childhood and secondary leaves a gap in student learning, particularly for children and youth with disabilities. Making a case for filling the transitions education and services gap, K–8, includes starting with the definition of *transition* as outlined in IDEA, understanding the current early childhood transitions, then moving on to the development of a continuous, cohesive transition system for the students with disabilities, parents and families, and agencies, and what this means to educators and present systems. You will find detailed information about secondary transitions, transition education, and services for adolescents with disabilities throughout this text. Some of the basic information on transition generalizes across all age levels, but this chapter focuses on the unique aspects of grades K–8.

Definition of Transition

The IDEA Amendments of 2004 defined *transition services* as "a coordinated set of activities for a student, designed within a results-oriented process." Dealing with "results" and a coordinated set of activities for grades K–8 should involve an ongoing developmental model in place much like Super's life-span, life-space theory discussed by Szymanski (1994), environmental factors in this developmental process (Szymanski, Hershenson, & Power, 1988; Miller-Tiedeman & Tiedeman, 1990), and social learning theories emphasizing the importance of career development through a lifetime (Mitchell & Krumboltz, 1990).

As an example of the usefulness of some theoretical basis for providing transitions education at the elementary level, consider this. If one of the desired outcomes for a person with disabilities is a career, then Hershenson's model of work adjustment development advances the developmental need for the three domains of work skills, work personality, and work goals to interact with the work environment over time (Hershenson, 1981, 1996; Szymanski et al., 1988; Turner & Szymanski, 1990). Because the three domains develop over a lifetime, the dynamics of this model focus direct attention to each domain at every level of development, not just early childhood and secondary. The proponents of this life-span theory have determined that the development of the work personality actually occurs during the preschool years followed by the work competencies developing in the school years, and last, the work goals developing in the later school years (Szymanski, 1994). Sociocognitive, developmental contextual, and sociological approaches note the importance of contributions toward career development over a time span.

The concept of "a coordinated set of activities" indicates that these transition activities will not only span time but should also systematically integrate instruction on specific adult outcomes at the appropriate developmental time. This age-appropriate or cognitively appropriate time often falls in the present K–8 gap. Having some continuity of this set of activities accentuates the need to allow these activities to be coordinated throughout the life of the person with disabilities and based on his or her needs, interests, and preferences. A commitment to this continuity would lead to revamping both secondary programs and the "student's entire educational experience, beginning in early childhood" (Rusch & Millar, 1996, p. 329). A review of early childhood research over three decades reveals agreement that those who support transition planning should "stress that all children need continuity in their lives. Calling attention to transitions planning considerations and transitions education as a universal for *all* children, rather than a targeted program, may help attain a broader base of public support for them" (Kagan & Neuman, 1998, p. 372). This is an excellent example of the power of universal design efforts in educational curricula.

Transition, as a lifelong process beginning at birth, can be considered a societal empowerment for students, their families, and the communities if handled appropriately and given the attention it warrants through life. The life-span and life-space considerations perpetuate the belief that early experiences and childhood influences do indeed determine career choices and goals in later life (Szymanski, 1994). If this theory holds true for all other desirable adult outcomes, it is imperative that transition be addressed throughout the elementary years, not just the early childhood and secondary years.

A Look at the Early Childhood Transition Mandate

The early childhood (ages 0 to 3 years) individual education plan is known as the *individualized family service plan (IFSP)*. As initially mandated in Part H of Public Law 99-457 and reauthorized under Part C of the IDEA of 1990, individualized transition planning must occur at least 90 days before the young preschool child with disabilities is 3 years old, at which time the public school is responsible for the child's education through an individualized education program (or plan) (IEP). The family is intimately involved in developing and implementing the transition plan with the early childhood professional as a facilitator and family mentor, training the families for these changes in settings. The purpose of the transition plan is to make necessary preparations for the child with disabilities to be able to adjust to any changes in the service delivery and make needed adjustments to assist the child to function in the new setting. This includes family-centered assessments concerning their resources, priorities, and concerns. Advising and assisting the state education agencies are the state interagency coordinating councils (ICCs). Program planning follow-up of the transition planning is done routinely to ensure parents' satisfaction and to determine if the child's needs are being met. These programs must include developmentally appropriate practices that fit the individual child's needs (Wolery, Strain, & Bailey, 1992). These transitions may begin, if needed, from the hospital to home for infants and their families, with appropriate medical follow-up (Bruder & Walker, 1990).

Although transition planning at age 3 has existed for three decades, research notes that more continuity and support is needed for these transition efforts (Kagan & Neuman, 1998). Even within these early childhood transition efforts, there is fragmentation. Kagan and Neuman (1998) reported that part of this fragmentation evolves from (1) a misunderstanding of what transition means for young children, (2) barriers such as lack of consistency and high quality among early childhood programs, (3) "pedagogical discontinuity" (p. 365), and (4) dismal links between preschool programs and school settings. The National Longitudinal Transition Study (NLTS) of 1988 determined that schools varied greatly in their implementation of transition activities, schools with more low-income families needed to find new ways to ensure continuity between preschool and kindergarten, and school administrators and teachers needed more education and professional development in the area of developmentally appropriate practices (Love, Logue, Trudeau, & Thayer, 1992). Kagan and Neuman (1998) recommended "that a comprehensive approach be adopted to promote continuity in the lives of all children and families . . . a multipronged action plan to (1) explore new approaches to research, (2) galvanize public support, and (3) promote action in the field" (p. 372).

The Kagen and Neuman (1998) comprehensive approach included continuity in both horizontal and vertical transitions for young children and their families. Continuity in horizontal transitions included those transitions that occurred at a certain time and involved home, school, community, and agency representatives meeting and making decisions. Continuity in vertical transitions included those changes between settings and keeping the child, home, school, community, and agency representatives linked as those transitions between settings occurred, such as the preschool to kindergarten transition. Keeping horizontal and vertical continuity is essential to the child's success in handling change (Kagan, 1992; Patton & Dunn, 1998).

Continuity in early childhood transitions was the focus of a study (Mangione & Speth, 1998) that included structured interviews and focus groups with 36 early childhood partners, including home, school, and the community. This study determined that these partners in transition planning and the materials they used should be family centered and sensitive to family culture, home language, and community diversity. The authors determined eight elements of continuity in the transitions framework: families as partners, shared leadership, comprehensive and responsive services, culture and home language, communication, knowledge and skill development, appropriate care and education, and evaluation of partnership success.

"Family as partners" was the number one element in determining continuity of transition for early childhood (Mangione & Speth, 1998). The importance of parents and families for all levels and ages of students is noted as one of the most important factors in determining success of transition activities (deFur, Todd-Allen, & Getzel, 2001; Lindstrom, Benz, & Doren, 2004; Mercer & Mercer, 2001; Wandry & Pleet, 2004; Wehmeyer, Morningstar, & Husted, 1999).

Importance of Parents and Families

The importance of families and their involvement in the IEP process as well as transition activities has been researched extensively (Epstein, 2001; Garriott, Wandry, & Snyder, 2000; Lytle & Brodin, 2001; Muscott, 2002; Turnbull & Turnbull, 1997; Wehmeyer et al., 1999). The concept of "parent abandonment" was noted in the Repetto and Correa (1996) position paper discussed previously. Parents and families should not only be members of the IEP and transition team but they should also be actively involved in the process, directing and guiding the discussions toward the desired outcomes (Clark, 2000; Kroeger, Leibold, & Ryan, 1999; Morningstar, 1994; Salembier & Furney, 1998). Developing this trust and mutual respect between families and educators is an important process that takes time and commitment.

McNair and Rusch (1991) noted that parents often take one of three roles: facilitator, nonparticipant, or difficult parent. They also noted that it is the job of educators and transition professionals to involve the parents in the transition process. The researchers found that, although nearly all parents wanted to be more involved in the transition process of their offspring, only about 30 percent were involved. Once families are actively involved, they should receive continued support to remain actively involved. Presently, the K–8 years allow (and even encourage) parents to become passive in their involvement, responding only when requested, and participating as an outsider on the IEP team. Why, then, do educators expect them to be excited and be actively involved when students turn age 16? If they have been allowed to be passive and the trust is lost, parents must start the whole process of involvement again. Time is wasted and outcomes are lost. Partnerships with parents should be the aim and goal of transition professionals so that they can become empowered and see their dreams and goals come to fruition (Szymanski, 1994).

The involvement of agencies during the K–8 years parallels the involvement of families. If agencies providing mental health, children's social rehabilitation services, foster care, and protective or judicial services are actively involved during the early childhood phase, then dropped during the K–8 years, and contacted again during the high school years, information and resources are lost. Already agencies experience turnover of employees and changes of policy. However, if efforts are made by the school at an early age and continued throughout the elementary years, it is more likely agencies will take some ownership in the success of students and will expect to be involved throughout the students' lives. Collaboration is more likely to occur when teams have been allowed to be part of the process over time. Once system linkages are made at an early level, those linkages need to be nurtured and maintained, changing with the needs of the student. Johnson, Stodden, Emanuel, Luecking, and Mack (2002) gave these approaches to improving collaboration and system linkages:

1. Promote general education and special education collaboration.
2. Establish cross-agency evaluation and accountability systems.
3. Develop innovative interagency financing strategies.
4. Promote collaborative staff development programs. (p. 528)

Functioning as an effective and cohesive team across the school-aged years can lessen the present fragmentation of education and services provided to students with disabilities. Networking, coordination, cooperation, and collaboration are necessary for integrated services for students with disabilities. Although bureaucracy might be challenged, the impact on the students and the system would be positive (deFur, 1997).

Students in the Transition Gap

Ultimately, students are the primary ones affected by the K–8 gap in transition services. The participation of students with disabilities in the IEP process is a relatively recent idea, but it is certainly emerging as a critical concept. In fact, Zhang and Stecker (2001) asserted that the recent "focus of research on self-determination has shifted toward involving students with disabilities in their transition planning activities" (p. 1). They also found that individuals "need to be more actively engaged in the development of student-directed behaviors before, during, and after transition-planning meetings" (p. 6). In fact, Kroeger and associates (1999) found that when the student is involved in the IEP process, the other team members interacted directly with the student for more information, leading to the student becoming the "author of the process," resulting in "greater success" (p. 5). The importance of the student as the primary consumer with ownership in the process cannot be overemphasized (Kroeger et al., 1999). Additionally, Barrie and McDonald (2002), who worked on a joint initiative for student-led IEPs in Arizona, found that collaborative efforts improved with parents, general education staff, and participating agencies when the student invited the team members to the IEP meeting. These researchers also found that older students with disabilities who had learned to lead their IEPs could work with much younger students with disabilities as role models, teaching them how to participate in their own IEPs. Students in preschool through fourth grade had varied involvement in their IEP meetings, such as being asked to introduce those people attending the meeting and explaining their likes or dislikes at school. With this early involvement of students at their own IEPs, students would learn the importance of being at their own IEP meetings and making decisions about their future. As students progressed into the intermediate grades, they would participate more in their IEP meetings, including introducing themselves and talking about their strengths, needs, adaptations, and modifications (Barrie & McDonald, 2002).

Special educators need to be willing to spend the preparation time in the elementary grades to work with students, which should indeed save time in the high school years. Student led IEPs and collaborating with families and agencies take time, preparation, and planning. By starting early in the process to focus on the transition needs and continuing this process through the elementary grades and into high school, we believe fragmentation of services and education would be lessened. We also believe that more cohesive special education systems would evolve, thereby facilitating the transition process.

An overview of research on secondary education and transition services shows that many students are not involved in their IEP meetings, and this could be the result of students not feeling prepared to be involved (Johnson et al., 2002). Although teachers and parents understand the need for starting early in preparing for transition into employment, independent living, or postsecondary education, this is not being done in practice (Johnson et al., 2002). However, transition services and education could be and should be integrated into the elementary gap.

Elementary and Middle School Transitions

To make the case another way for filling in the gap with transition services and education in the elementary years, one must look carefully at the K–8 population. With the wrap-around services of an elementary school building and classroom, usually with one main teacher and minimal moves during the day, why do elementary students need access to transition services and education? We have already discussed the concepts of continuity, coordination, seamless services, cohesive services, parent involvement, and outcome-orientation. We now suggest that another reason for providing transitions education during this period is the nature of childhood at the early stage of the twenty-first century. Although elementary students in the past might have experienced some changes in their homes and educational experiences, today's students face many changes and instability.

> Since the 1970s the early adolescent experience has become more complex, and critical life issues have catapulted into the earlier stages. The media-influenced images of fashion, self-fulfillment, and sensual experiences coupled with the frightening warnings about smoking, drinking, sex, and even decibel levels and an evaporating ozone layer permeate their real and imaging view of the world. (Simpson, 1999, p. 5)

Middle school was designed to be a better transition for elementary students than a junior high school. The overall purpose of a middle level education that does not combine intermediate grade levels with ninth-grade students is to have a developmentally appropriate curriculum in a safe environment (Dickinson, 2001) and the idea of educating the "whole child" in an environment that promotes critical thinking, industrious work, contributions to the community, and caring about oneself and others (Jackson & Davis, 2000). This environment, if established and implemented well, provides a unique and timely opportunity for students with disabilities to benefit from transitions education opportunities and assistance for both dealing with current life demands as well as preparing for the changes ahead in their lives.

Some apparent changes for elementary students are moving from teacher to teacher, class to class, building to building, as well as family changes with new siblings, step-parents and extended families, or foster home situations. Additionally, students find themselves changing from one desk in one room to living out of a locker. They might have one teacher in an early elementary classroom, but have many teachers the next school year. These students move from teacher reminders throughout the day to independent planning and studying. In the past, classroom teachers largely determined what was studied and at what time, but this is fast changing to the students depending on themselves for planning and implementing study habits, moving independently among learning centers, and using their time after school wisely when parents are working and not available.

Obviously, peer issues and peer conformity grow as students move through the elementary grades into middle school. Expectations for social behaviors and the social events rapidly change. Society and media propagate the "hurried child" and "miniature adult" syndrome right along with the high rates of divorce and separation in families (Elkind, 1981). With the changes in family structures, intense family involvement in the elementary grades has gradually diminished and continues to do so as the child moves on. The changes in family structures often involve the judicial system. Many of these changes for elementary students can be devastating and contribute to what Wakefield, Sage, Coy, and Palmer (2004) called "unfocused kids." Many of these possible changes at the elementary school level are transition issues that need to be confronted through a seamless transitions planning approach.

The whole issue of independence is a transition process that needs to be addressed in the early grades and followed specifically into the middle school years. Many students without disabilities find the middle school adjustment difficult. Middle school success is often determined by individual student performance as compared to the elementary focus on the classroom of students completing tasks with teacher assistance (Midgley, Anderman, & Hicks, 1995). The achievement loss associated with the transition to middle school and high school has been researched (Alspaugh, 1998). Previous research determined this consistent student achievement loss was associated particularly when the students moved to an intermediate-level school from self-contained elementary schools in larger school districts (Alspaugh & Harting, 1995). An added problem would be the "double jeopardy situation" where students make a move from elementary to middle school and then from middle school to high school, noted by Seidman, Allen, Aber, Mitchell, and Feinman (1994). These students who experienced this "double jeopardy" also experienced achievement losses during both moves. The researchers also noted that these same students with double transitions suffered self esteem and self-perception problems as well as higher dropout rates in high school (Seidman et al., 1994). These findings were consistent with former studies showing that transitions did relate to achievement losses. Although the researchers suggested that small, cohort groups be formed with fewer transitions between schools and grade levels to alleviate this achievement loss, the research also lends support for filling the transition gap for students with disabilities, a vulnerable group in a changing system.

With the critical middle school adjustment for all students, this transition can be overwhelming for students with disabilities. McKenzie and Houk (1993) suggested that this transition from elementary to secondary settings for students with disabilities was comparable to "crossing the great divide." They concluded, "Ideally, instructional priorities related to transition should be established at least 2 years prior to the change in settings" (pp. 18–19). This once again points out that there are transition issues in the K–8 years and these transition issues need to be addressed throughout these years. Some states have attempted to fill that transition gap with transition education and services for K–8 students (Clark, 1996; Utah State Office of Education, 1998; Regents of the University of Minnesota, 1996).

Transition Education and Services, K–8

Most states continue to be noncompliant at the secondary level with the transition service requirements (National Council on Disability, 2000b; Johnson & Sharpe, 2000). These states continue to concentrate on transition education and services at the secondary level and are not addressing these issues at the elementary level. Clark (1996), under the auspices of the Utah STUDY Project, developed transition guides for four age-specific groups to include all students with disabilities from birth to age 22. In these transition guides, developmentally appropriate transition activities were proposed to ensure "a seamless transition from one age level to the next and from each environmental setting to the next" (p. ii). Additionally, these guides were developed to give direction and clarification to all school administrators, teachers, and transition coordinators in the state of Utah and assist these individuals "to empower each individual to be a caring, competent, and contributing citizen in an integrated, diverse, and changing society" (Utah Agenda for Meeting the Needs of Students with Disabilities, 1991, mission statement).

Clark (1996) proposed including direct instruction in life-centered career education competencies as well as the academic areas. The legal perspective espoused by Utah concerning transition services at the elementary school relates to the interpretation made of IDEA and carried a strong message:

> Professionals and parents who feel transition is not needed in elementary school planning are ignoring the fact that they expect schools to provide a coordinated set of learning activities and experiences. . . . If basic academic skills are taught systematically through direct instruction and socialization, and independent living skills are taught only incidentally, this leaves a gap in a "coordinated set of activities" designed to provide a seamless system of transition. This gap highlights the importance of beginning early to provide direct, integrated instruction at the elementary school level in all the adult (life-centered) outcome areas. . . . From a legal perspective of a free and appropriate education, parents and professionals have not only the right but also the responsibility to determine whether the school's set of coordinated activities should be limited to direct instruction in basic academic skills only or should include other life-centered outcomes as well. (p. 3)

Example steps for transition planning in the proposed IEP process at the elementary level included the same basic steps as for older students: (1) identifying desired future environments or planning areas and the demands in each area of employment, education/training, communication, living arrangements, social relationships, life skills, community participation, health, recreation/leisure, and self-determination; (2) listing priority needs, interests, and preferences as well as identifying potential programs, services, and support options to be considered by the IEP team; (3) preparing for the IEP team meeting by preparing the student to participate actively in the meeting and working with the student to invite appropriate participants; (4) developing the transition plan with appropriate goals, objectives, specific linkages, time-lines, responsibilities, and communication guidelines for future meetings in place; and (5) implementing, monitoring, and reviewing the IEP on a regular basis (Clark, 1996).

Additionally, the proposed guidelines for Utah (Clark, 1996) included three distinct steps in the "Role of Curriculum in Planning and Programming for Transition":

1. Review what is currently offered in the school's K–6 curriculum, giving specific attention to whether or not the subjects taught (reading, language arts, arithmetic, social studies, science, music, art, etc.) provide preparation for functional life skills for the student's life at school, at home, and in the community.
2. Identify the gaps between what is being taught in all instructional settings (general education, resource programs, special classes or schools, etc.) and what students with disabilities need.
3. Develop resources and strategies for bridging the gap in the curriculum and students' needs. (pp. 15–16)

"Examples of Transition Services' Goals, Objectives, and Activities" were included in the guidelines such as (1) a goal in the area of occupational readiness might be that a student will increase his or her occupational vocabulary, (2) a goal in the area of socialization might be that the student will demonstrate socially appropriate behaviors in a variety of settings at school and in the community, (3) a goal in the area of community participation might be that the student will demonstrate community participation skills in at least two settings outside the neighborhood, and (4) a goal in the area of daily living skills might be that the student will demonstrate home living skills required for assuming two new work responsibilities at home.

In support of the idea of providing K–8 transition planning and education, the Utah Model for Counseling and Comprehensive Guidance (1998) included career development competencies for all students at the elementary and middle/junior high school levels as well as the high school and adult levels in three areas, including (1) self-knowledge, (2) educational and occupational exploration, and (3) career planning. The Utah Code (Utah State Office of Education, 1998) included the following mandate:

> Each school district, in consultation with its teachers, school community councils or similar entities, and the State Board of Education, shall establish policies to provide for the effective implementation of a personalized student education plan (SEP) or student education/occupation plan (SEOP) for each student at the school site.
>
> The policies shall include guidelines and expectations:
>
> (A) for recognizing the student's accomplishments and strengths;
>
> (B) for planning, monitoring, and managing education and career development;
>
> (C) for an ongoing partnership involving students, parents, and school personnel in the process, to include at least two annual SEP conferences at the

elementary level, involving the student, the student's parent or guardian, and school personnel, and at least one individual conference in grade 12, involving the student, the student's parent or guardian, and school personnel, and at least one individual SEOP conference held annually in grades 7–11 . . . and

(D) for identifying and obtaining adequate resources, such as time and training, required for a successful program. (p. 53)

This level of state commitment for a universal design approach for instruction and guidance is a lighthouse example for states that want to align state standards with evidenced-based transition education needs of students with disabilities.

The School-to-Work Outreach Project (Regents of the University of Minnesota, 1996) at the University of Minnesota, funded by the U.S. Department of Education, focused on improving school-to-work opportunities for students with disabilities starting in kindergarten and continuing through twelfth grade. This nationwide, three-year project emphasized educational reform that addressed the need for children of *all* ages to experience school-to-work activities and to gain workplace skills while still in school.

These examples from two states demonstrate that having a comprehensive, universal design for the mission of education is possible if parents, the public, and state leaders will commit to a plan of action to implement a vision of what its schools are for across all grades. These states deserve recognition for their bold initiatives.

Strategies for Integrating Transition Education in Grades K–8

Having a state or district policy committed to achieving a meaningful, seamless instructional program across all grade levels is important. However, even without such policies, individual teachers or building faculty can initiate strategies on their own. We recommend the following strategies for the two elementary grade divisions, K–4 and 5–8.

Grades K–4 Transition Strategies
- Include "Who I Am" and "What I Will Be When I Grow Up" activities and discussions in reading, language arts, social studies, or science.
- Discuss what parents and family members do for a living. Talk about various careers in a nongender-specific way. Include careers that may be unique to the location, such as a marine biologist in the middle of Kansas. Find books about various careers in different fields.
- As stories are read, talk about what the vocations and jobs are of the characters in the book. Role-play and simulate situations in the books.
- Select a "Student of the Week" and have that student complete a bulletin board about himself or herself and family. Include the child's strengths

and what his or her hopes and dreams are on this bulletin board. Invite the parents to come to the class during the week to share information about their jobs or to take the class to their job site.

- Talk about interests, preferences, and talents. Share these interests, preferences, and talents with one another by staging a class "talent show."
- Plan fields trips that will integrate into any study area—for instance, discussions of careers, jobs, and volunteer opportunities noted on the trip.
- Study the community and the volunteer roles, jobs, and careers in the community and how these roles keep the community progressing.
- Utilize the counselor and resource people to study careers, jobs, and ways to participate in the community.

Grades 5–8 Transition Strategies

- Include service-oriented projects in the community as part of studies. Discuss the roles and collaboration needed to implement service-oriented projects.
- Have students involved in the community learn about roles and the interrelationships of community roles.
- Research and study various jobs, careers, and volunteer opportunities.
- Use the Internet to explore jobs and career ideas.
- Plan author, artist, and performer visits.
- Ask speakers with different jobs, careers, and volunteer roles to talk to the students.
- Discuss subject-related careers (scientists, writer, historian).
- Study famous and not-so-famous people and their careers.
- Arrange for each child to "job shadow" an adult for the day.
- Simulate in the classroom various jobs in the community.
- Visit job sites.
- Visit vocational and postsecondary schools.
- Attend job fairs.

The Administration and Resource Guide of the *Transition Planning Inventory* (Clark & Patton, 1997) includes upper-elementary instructional examples in the areas of employment, further education/training, daily living, leisure activities, community participation, health, self-determination, communication, interpersonal relationships (see companion website Appendix 4A). These examples can be implemented in schools along with the preceding proposed strategies to integrate transition education into inclusive school settings.

The National Occupational Information Coordinating Committee (1996) published a set of competencies and indicators for elementary, middle school, high school, and adults in their career development handbook. These career development guidelines for elementary, middle, and high school can also be aligned with the strategies used in schools to further integrate and include transition education and services and career planning for students with special needs (see companion website Appendix 4B).

Self-Determination Development in Grades K–8

A discussion of filling in the transitions gap for K–8 would not be complete without noting the need for self-determination development throughout these formative years. Just as transitions services and education are needed in these years, self-determination knowledge and skills should be part of transitions planning. Students with disabilities early on need to learn to accept and value themselves, advocate for themselves, participate actively in their IEP and transition meetings, set goals realistically, develop a plan of action, and adjust and modify according to the results of the implemented plan (Field & Hoffman, 1994). If these self-determination skills (making choices, solving problems, setting and attaining goals, taking risks, regulating self, promoting self-advocacy, and realizing self-awareness) are needed to connect educational outcomes with goals and objectives in transition planning (Steere & Cavaiuolo, 2002), then these self-determination skills are needed by *all* students at *all* levels. Although author David Elkind (1981) lamented the fast pace children live today, he agrees with students making judgments and decisions as long as these decisions are appropriate to the child's level and understanding. Many of these skills in self-determination and self-advocacy are easily integrated into the elementary curriculum. Educators have already integrated many of these concepts and skills into their present instructional delivery systems. Sample school and family-based interventions to support the development of self-determination in early childhood through elementary levels are included in Figure 4.1 (Sands & Wehmeyer, 1996).

Conclusion

The need to fill the transitions services and education gap in K–8 should be conceptually confirmed from the presented information and aligned research. The provisions of No Child Left Behind endorse this position. The call for assessment of all students with disabilities on the elementary and middle school levels prompts educators to take a long, hard look at what could be done to ensure success for these students who experience transitions without transition programming during the K–8 years. Although these transitions services and education are not mandated, students, parents and families, communities, agencies, and all educators should team together to make them possible for these students left in the gap. Educators owe it to themselves and their students to advocate for continuity in transitions services and education. The benefits these students, and everyone involved with these students, will gain will far outweigh the factors that might interfere with the implementation of this seamless, cohesive transitions process.

FIGURE 4.1   School- and Family-Based Interventions to Support the Development of Self-Determination

Early Childhood (Ages 2–5)

- Provide opportunities to make structured choices, such as, "Do you want to wear the blue shirt or the red shirt?" Extend choices across food, clothing, activity, and other choices.
- Provide opportunities to generate choices that are both positive and negative, such as, "We have 10 more minutes. What could we do?" and "You spilled your milk. What could you do to clean it up?"
- Provide formative and constructive feedback on the consequences of choices made in the recent past, such as, "When you pushed hard on the pencil it broke. What might you want to do the next time?" and "When you used an angry voice, I didn't do what you wanted. What could you do differently?"
- Provide opportunities for planning activities that are pending, such as, "You need to choose a dress to wear to the wedding," or "Decide what kind of sandwich you want to take for lunch tomorrow."
- Provide opportunities to self-evaluate task performance by comparing their work to a model. Point out what they've done that's like the model, such as, "Look, you used nice colors too, just like this one," and "Do you see that you both drew the man from the side?"
- As directive questions so that the child compares his or her performance to a model, such as, "Are all of your toys in the basket, too?" or "I'll know you're ready for the story when you are sitting on your mat with your legs crossed, your hands on your knees, and your eyes on me."

Early Elementary (Ages 6–8)

- Provide opportunities to choose from among several different strategies for a task, such as, "Will you remember your spelling words better if you write them out, say them to yourself, or test yourself?" or "What is the easiest way for you to figure out what this word means?"
- Ask children to reconsider choices they've made in the recent past, in light of those choices' subsequent consequences, such as, "This morning you decided to spend your lunch money on the comic. Now it's lunchtime and you're hungry. What decision do you wish you'd made?' or "I remember when you decided to leave your coat in your locker. What happened because you made that decision?"
- Encourage children to "think aloud" with you, saying the steps that they are taking to complete a task or solve a problem, such as, "Tell me what you're thinking in your head while you try to figure out what the word means," or "You've lost your house key. What are you thinking to yourself while you decide what to do?"
- Provide opportunities for students to talk about how they learn, such as, "Is it easier for you to tell me what you want by saying it or by writing it down?" or "Do you remember better if you study for a test all at once or a little bit on several different days?"
- Provide opportunities for students to systematically evaluate their work, such as, "Here's a very neat paper, and here's your paper. Is your paper as neat as this one? What are the differences between this paper and yours? How are they alike?"
- Help students set simple goals for themselves and check to see whether they are reaching them, such as, "You said you want to read two books this week. How much of a book have you read so far? Let's color in your goal sheet so you can see how much you've done."

Source: From Doll, B., Sands, D. J., Wehmeyer, M. L., & Palmer, S. (1996). Promoting the development and acquisition of self-determined behavior. In D. J. Sands & M. L. Wehmeyer (Eds.), *Self-determination across the life span: Independence and choice for people with disabilities* (p. 80). Baltimore: Paul H. Brookes Publishing Co.; reprinted by permission.

5 Assessment for Transition Education and Services

Observe what a man does; listen to what he says; how then can you not know what he is.

—Attributed to Confucius

As individuals with disabilities make the transition from school to adult life, the process of assessment is critical in all areas and stages of planning. Assessment in career development, vocational decision making, and transition planning is an essential process that is often overlooked, ignored, or misunderstood. The purpose of this chapter is to provide information on (1) the concept of transition assessment, including history, person-centered planning, and areas to be assessed; (2) transition assessment and standards-based reform; (3) methods of gathering assessment information on the individual; (4) methods of analyzing his or her future living, working, and educational environments; (5) tying assessment into transition planning; (6) issues to consider when conducting assessments; and (7) people involved in the transition assessment. The chapter then concludes with recommendations that will help you incorporate transition assessment as a key component of your current or future program. Additional resources on transition assessment are included on the companion website to this text. As recommended practices in assessment are advanced, we hope that individuals with disabilities will be actively involved in appropriate, meaningful, and effective assessment activities that will enhance their personal growth and quality of life as they make their transitions to future living, working, and educational environments.

Overview of Transition Assessment

The Division on Career Development and Transition (DCDT; Sitlington, Neubert, & Leconte, 1997) advocated transition assessment for all students moving through the education system to careers and other activities. Transition assessment is especially needed for individuals with disabilities. As individuals with disabilities, their families, and other members of the planning team move to identify postsecondary goals, they must also identify effective assessment practices and understand that assessment is an ongoing process. This does not mean that entirely new methods and approaches of assessment are needed to facilitate transition planning. Considerable information exists on effective methods of assessment that identify vocational, educational, independent living, community functioning, and personal and social preferences and strengths of individuals with disabilities. Transition assessment, however, does require appropriate methods of assessment at various transition points for individuals with disabilities in order to make appropriate programming and planning decisions.

History of Assessment

The transition assessment process builds on the earlier concepts of vocational evaluation and assessment and career assessment (Sitlington, 1996a). Having a history of all of these assessment approaches may help you better understand the concept of transition assessment and how to use this process with your students.

Vocational Evaluation and Assessment.   The vocational evaluation and assessment techniques first used in U.S. schools were borrowed from the field of vocational rehabilitation and programs operated in rehabilitation facilities. These techniques first entered the schools through separate work experience and vocational training programs for individuals with disabilities. They also emerged in vocational-technical education programs. The majority of the vocational evaluation and assessment practices in vocational rehabilitation emerged from the parent disciplines of psychology (including industrial psychology), industrial engineering and production management, and medicine (including the related fields of occupational therapy, medical case management, and physical therapy) (Leconte, 1994a, 1994b). Curriculum-based vocational assessment (CBVA; Albright & Cobb, 1988a, 1988b; Cobb & Larkin, 1985; Stodden, Ianacone, Boone, & Bisconer, 1987) was one of the most significant models that emerged out of vocational-technical education programs. This model proposed that assessment data be collected directly on the students while they were enrolled in vocational-technical education programs or in other vocational training programs.

A number of attempts have been made to take an interdisciplinary approach to the area of vocational evaluation and assessment. In 1981, the Commission on Certification of Work Adjustment and Vocational Evaluation Specialists (CCWAVES) was established as an independent commission. As stated in the CCWAVES *Standards and Procedures Manual for Certification in*

Vocational Evaluation (1996), "The primary purpose of this certification process is to provide assurance that those professionals engaged in vocational evaluation meet acceptable standards of quality" (p. 6). In 1991, the Interdisciplinary Council on Vocational Evaluation and Assessment was formed. This council was a national coalition of over 10 organizations that represented the issues and concerns of personnel involved in vocational evaluation and assessment across a variety of settings and disciplines (Schuster & Smith, 1994). The council proposed seven principles to serve as a guide to recommended practices in vocational evaluation and assessment across all settings (Smith, Lombard, Neubert, Leconte, Rothenbacher, & Sitlington, 1994).

A third effort involving collaboration and communication across disciplines in the area of vocational evaluation and assessment was the *Glossary of Terminology for Vocational Assessment, Evaluation and Work Adjustment* (Dowd, 1993). This glossary was a project of the Vocational Evaluation and Work Adjustment Association, which solicited and included input from all the major disciplines involved in the assessment and evaluation process.

Career Assessment.   As the focus shifted from vocational education to the broader concept of career education, the focus of assessment also broadened. A position paper on career and vocational assessment in the public school setting, endorsed by the then Division on Career Development (Sitlington, Brolin, Clark, & Vacanti, 1985), focused on the concept of career assessment and defined it as "a developmental process beginning at the elementary-school level and continuing through adulthood" (p. 3). Career assessment relates to lifelong career development, which affects all life roles. The specific content to be assessed in the career assessment process should be dictated by the components of the career education model being implemented.

In the school years, career assessment provides information on which to make decisions related to all areas of adult life. This process directly parallels the career education stages of awareness, exploration, and preparation as well as provides information on which to make decisions as soon as the individual enters the educational system. The career assessment process encompasses vocational assessment and the occupationally related information gathered as part of this process. Career assessment also gathers information on the individual's other life roles, such as family member, citizen, and participant in leisure, recreational, and avocational activities (Sitlington, Brolin, Clark, & Vacanti, 1985).

Transition Assessment.   Just as the concept of career assessment was proposed to address the information needs of career education, transition assessment addresses the information needs of transition planning and implementation. Transition services encompass career education, vocational education, and other life skills development. The Division on Career Development and Transition endorsed the following definition of *transition assessment:*

Transition assessment is the ongoing process of collecting data on the individual's strengths, needs, preferences, and interests as they relate to the demands of current and future working, educational, living, and personal and social environments. Assessment data serve as the common thread in the transition process and form the basis for defining goals and services to be included in the Individualized Education Program (IEP). (Sitlington, Neubert, & Leconte, 1997, p. 71)

Clark (1998) proposed the following broader working definition of *transitions assessment*, which was meant to address all of the transitions encountered by an individual, from early childhood through adulthood:

Transitions assessment is a planned, continuous process of obtaining, organizing, and using information to assist individuals with disabilities of all ages and their families in making all critical transitions in students' lives both successful and satisfying. (p. 2)

Clark went on to state that good transitions assessment addresses for each individual the goals and expectations that he or she has for a transition period or event. Good transitions assessment also suggests areas of planning, preparation, or decision making that would increase the likelihood of the individual reaching those goals and being satisfied with the outcomes.

Sitlington (1996a) attempted to present the relationship among transition assessment, career assessment, and vocational assessment as a beginning point of discussion. As can be seen in Figure 5.1, *transition assessment* is the umbrella term that encompasses both career assessment and vocational assessment.

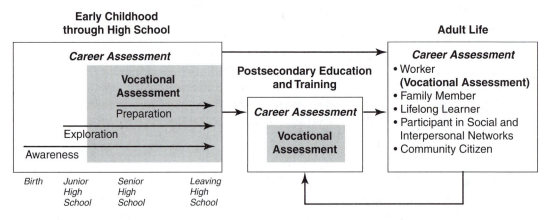

FIGURE 5.1   Transition Assessment

Source: From "Transition Assessment—Where Have We Been and Where Should We Be Going?" by P. L. Sitlington, 1996, *Career Development for Exceptional Individuals, 19,* page 163. Copyright 1996 by the Council for Exceptional Children. Reprinted by permission.

Transition assessment relates to all life roles and to the support needed before, during, and after the transition to adult life. Figure 5.1 also provides information on the relationship among transition, career, and vocational assessment.

Assessment data collected during the transition assessment process should be used to assist individuals with disabilities in making informed choices. Thus, assessment activities serve as the basis for determining an individual's strengths, needs, preferences, and interests related to career development, vocational training, postsecondary education goals, independent living, community functioning, and personal and social goals. This requires that assessment occur in a variety of environments that are natural to the individual's life. Special and general education personnel must be prepared to work cooperatively with individuals with disabilities, their families, related school personnel, and community service providers to determine what types of assessment data need to be collected and which methods will facilitate the process. In addition, local school district or building policies must be in place to support these activities. Most important, the results of the assessment process need to drive the IEP process and be integrated into the overall assessment process with the student.

Person-Centered Planning

Individual choice is a primary policy theme reflected across all of the legislation discussed in Chapter 2. To guide planning processes effectively, students must be aware of their strengths, needs, preferences, and interests and how these relate to work and careers, postsecondary education, independent living, community activities, and personal and social relationships.

The person-centered planning approach can play a major role in incorporating student choice into the transition assessment process. Flannery and colleagues (2000) defined *person-centered planning* as "an approach to designing support that is guided by the individual with disabilities (or his/her advocates) that receives support, builds from personal strengths and vision, and results in practical action plans" (p. 123). This concept began as a vehicle for including individuals with mental retardation in the process of planning for transition, and to involve family members and other unpaid support people in the process (Hagner, Helm, & Butterworth, 1996). The hope was to maximize the level of community inclusion for these individuals by changing agency-driven services.

The concept is now applied to a broader population of individuals with disabilities, but it is still viewed too often as a *program* rather than as a philosophy-based *approach* (Sax, 2002). Person-centered planning requires "equal participation, positive and clear communication, and active involvement of the focus individual" (Sax, 2002, p. 15). Person-centered planning, personal futures planning, and the McGill Action Planning System (MAPS; Vandercook, York, & Forest, 1989) were created with the expectation that they would be implemented according to the philosophy and values on which they were based—that no one has a right to plan for another person's life without that individual's participation, permission, or request (Sax, 2002). The commitment must be to a long-term process, rather than a single meeting, and facilitators and participants must be willing to listen to the focus individual and should be prepared to hear statements that may not always be what they want to hear.

As Clark (1998) stated, person-centered planning brings together the focus person with a variety of stakeholders in that person's life and future, and helps loosen the constraints of school and service agency approaches to working with students with disabilities. The process results in a plan of action that is based on preferences and strengths of the individual and is developed so specifically that IEP goals also serve as documentation for the IDEA requirement that the student be a part of the transition planning process.

Schwartz, Holburn, and Jacobson (2000) identified eight key features of person-centered planning, regardless of the approach:

1. The person's activities, services, and supports are based on his or her dreams, interests, preferences, strengths, and capacities.
2. The person and people important to him or her are included in lifestyle planning and have the opportunity to exercise control and make informed decisions.
3. The person has meaningful choices with decisions based on his or her experiences.
4. The person uses, when possible, natural and community supports.
5. Activities, supports, and services foster skills to achieve personal relationships, community inclusion, dignity, and respect.
6. The person's opportunities and experiences are maximized and flexibility is enhanced within existing regulatory and funding constraints.
7. Planning is collaborative and recurring and involves an ongoing commitment to the person.
8. The person is satisfied with his or her relationships, home, and daily routine. (p. 238)

The concept of person-centered planning is closely linked with the transition assessment process. Kim and Turnbull (2004), however, proposed a merger of person-centered planning and family-centered planning (prevalent in early intervention and early childhood circles) into an approach they called "person-family interdependent planning" for young adults with severe disabilities. This approach emphasizes thinking about transition into adulthood from the perspectives of persons with disabilities, their parents, and other family members. Although the authors stressed that planning should consider the choices and preferences of young adults with disabilities, this approach also strengthens the capacity of these young adults and their families together to build formal and informal support circles that ensure that the young adult will be active in family and community life.

Primary Assessment Areas for Transition Planning

The types of information gathered in the assessment process should relate directly to the areas the IEP team is addressing in the transition planning process. The questions asked in transition planning should translate directly into the information to be gathered. Conversely, the information gathered in the assessment process should be incorporated into the statement of the student's present levels of academic achievement and functional performance in the IEP, and drive the IEP and transition planning process.

Chapter 1 provided an overview of the development of the field of transition planning and presented a number of models upon which this planning can be based. The competencies and outcome areas contained in these models have particular implications for assessing students' present levels of performance for IEP planning. They also give direction to both assessment and intervention for all students with disabilities.

The focus areas for transition assessment that we propose are the Knowledge and Skills Domains presented in the Comprehensive Transition Education Model (Figure 1.1) discussed in Chapter 1. Figure 5.2 presents these areas and their relationship to the transition assessment process.

One resource that you may find helpful in conducting an informal assessment in some or all of these nine content areas is the Comprehensive Informal Inventory of Knowledge and Skills for Transition (Clark, Patton, & Moulton, 2000). This inventory presents 46 competencies organized under nine areas, very closely resembling the areas of the Comprehensive Transition Education Model. Under each competency are a number of knowledge and skill statements related to the specific competency.

Transition Assessment and Standards-Based Reform

The process of transition assessment must be viewed within the overarching assessment processes emanating from the legislative mandates presented in Chapter 2, especially No Child Left Behind (NCLB, 2002) and the Individuals with Disabilities Education Improvement Act of 2004 (IDEA 2004). For the past two decades, state education agencies and local districts have instituted various high-stakes assessments (Johnson & Thurlow, 2003; Thurlow, 2000). Before the IDEA Amendments, however, students with disabilities were often excluded from these reform efforts (National Center on Educational Outcomes [NCEO], 2003a).

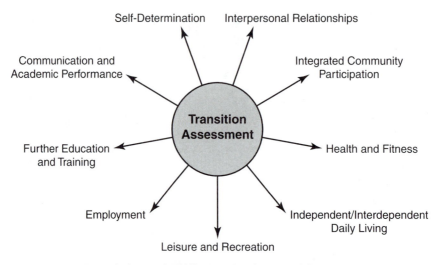

FIGURE 5.2   **Knowledge and Skill Domains for Transition Assessment**

Involving Students with Disabilities in State and District Assessments

IDEA 2004 mandates that students with disabilities participate in state and district assessments, and requires a statement in the IEP of accommodations needed in order to participate in these assessments. If the IEP team determines that the student shall take an alternate assessment, the IEP must include a statement of why the student cannot participate in the regular assessment and why the particular alternate assessment is appropriate.

Schools are accountable for *adequate yearly progress (AYP),* a term used for measuring students' improvement in achieving standards each year. This information must be reported for all students, and separately for students with disabilities with IEPs, students with disabilities with 504 Plans, and students who are English language learners, and by race, ethnic group, and socioeconomic status (NCLB, 2002). Sanctions and rewards are given to schools depending on their AYP.

In surveying the secondary schools involved in the National Longitudinal Transition Study 2 (NLTS2), the U.S. Office of Special Education Programs (2004) found that 80 percent of students with disabilities (ages 14 through 18) took the mandated standardized tests, 11 percent were given alternate assessments, and 9 percent were exempted from testing. There were no differences in participation rates at different grade levels. Almost three-fourths (71 percent) of the students with disabilities who took the mandated standardized test received some type of accommodation or modification. By far, the most common accommodation was additional time to take the test (57 percent), followed by taking the test in an alternative setting (45 percent), or having someone read instructions and/or test items aloud to the students (33 percent).

In our view there are a number of opportunities and challenges in involving students with disabilities in state and district assessments. Among the opportunities offered are:

- For the majority of students with disabilities, information will show how their performance compares to students without disabilities.
- Students with disabilities may be aided in their transition to postsecondary education if they perform satisfactorily on the assessments.
- Educators will be forced to examine the content they teach and the standards to which they hold students with disabilities.
- If the progress of students with disabilities is not measured, there will be little incentive for school districts to support the curriculum and instructional needs of these students.

There are also a number of challenges that IEP teams must consider as they develop courses of study and plan for the transition of students with disabilities to all aspects of adult life. The task as educators committed to transition is to work to include in state standards areas related to the transition to all areas of adult life.

- Strong potential exists for pressure to "teach to the test." Unless transition-related content is included in state standards (and thus the test), transition-related instruction may receive little attention in the classroom.
- The self-concept of the student with disabilities may be at risk if he or she has not been exposed to the content included in the test.
- Administrators may be less willing to have students with disabilities served within their school or district if they feel that these students will lower their school or district scores.
- Over the years, assessments and graduation requirements have led to differentiated diploma options. The effect of these diplomas on the transition to employment and postsecondary education is not known. At this time it would appear prudent to develop a course of study—as part of the transition planning process—that will lead to the earning of a standard diploma.

The American Educational Research Association (2000) issued a position statement on high-stakes testing. In this statement they outlined the following 12 conditions essential to the sound implementation of a high-stakes educational testing program for all students. We feel that implementation of these conditions would make the results of such testing more valid.

1. Protection against high-stakes decisions based on a single test.
2. Adequate resources and opportunities to learn the tested content and cognitive processes.

3. Validation for each separate intended use of a high-stakes test, whether it be for individual certification, school evaluation, or curricular improvement.

4. Full disclosure of likely negative consequences of high-stakes testing programs to policy makers.

5. Alignment between the test and the curriculum, in terms of both the content of the test and the cognitive processes engaged in taking the test.

6. Validity of passing scores and achievement levels that have been established.

7. Opportunities for meaningful remediation for examinees who fail high-stakes tests. This remediation should focus on the knowledge and skills the test is intended to address, not just the test performance itself.

8. Appropriate attention to language differences among examinees. Special accommodation for English language learners may be necessary to obtain valid scores.

9. Appropriate attention to students with disabilities. Steps should be taken to ensure that the test score inferences accurately reflect the intended construct rather than the student's disability.

10. Careful adherence to explicit rules for determining which students are to be tested. Such policies must be uniformly enforced to assure the validity of score comparisons. The reporting of test score results should accurately portray the percentage of students exempted.

11. Sufficient reliability of the type of score for each intended use.

12. Ongoing evaluation of intended and unintended effects of high-stakes testing.

High School Exit Exams and Diploma Options

In a survey of 46 states and the District of Columbia, 27 state education agencies reported to have or plan to have exit exams that require all students (including students with disabilities) to take a high-stakes assessment to receive a standard diploma (Johnson & Thurlow, 2003). Two additional states require local education agencies to select and administer exit exams for that purpose. Results also indicated that a range of diploma options continued to be made available to students with and without disabilities in most states. The authors found that in only 13 states is a standard diploma (or a standard diploma and honors diploma) the only option available to all students. One state had as many as seven diploma options available, and another 3 states had up to five options. The differentiated diploma options include honors diplomas, regular/standard diplomas, IEP/special education diplomas, certificates of attendance, certificates of achievement, occupational diplomas, and other variations (Johnson & Thurlow, 2003).

The Center on Education Policy (2003) collected information from the states with current or planned exit exams. They found that although No Child Left Behind does not mandate graduation requirements or diploma options, it is influencing the performance goals, content, and timetables of state exit exam systems. A majority of states with current or planned exit exams intended to use these exams to comply with the Act's high school testing mandates. Most states, however, will need to modify their testing systems to do so. States with exit exams that cannot be easily adapted to NCLB requirements must decide whether to scrap their exams or forge ahead with two sets of high school tests.

Also, the Center on Education Policy (2003) found that exit exams appear to encourage school districts to cover more of the content in state standards, better align curriculum with these standards, and add remedial and other special courses for students at risk of failing. They concluded, however, that a moderate amount of evidence suggests these exams may be associated with higher dropout rates.

Accommodations

As mentioned in Chapter 2, IDEA 2004 mandates that students with disabilities must participate in state and district assessments and that the IEPs of those students must include a statement of any needed accommodations. You and other IEP team members will be faced with the task of working with each student to identify the accommodations he or she will need to participate in these assessments. Nearly every state has developed a list of allowable accommodations for its statewide tests. However, there is limited consensus across states in terms of which accommodations they allow on statewide tests, in order to treat the results in the same way as a "standard" test administration. In addition, state accommodation policies are continually being adapted (Thurlow, House, Boys, Scott, & Ysseldyke, 2000).

Bolt and Thurlow (2004) indicated that there are typically two parts to each definition of *accommodation:*

- An accommodation is understood to be a change in the way a test is administered under standardized conditions. This change could be in the manner in which the test is presented, scheduled, or responded to; where the test is administered; or the type of special equipment allowed during the testing.
- An accommodation is intended to facilitate the measurement goals of the assessment. (p. 142)

Educators at this point are often unable to make evidence-based decisions about which accommodations to endorse for each student, because relatively little experimental research has examined the effects of accommodations on students' test scores (Elliott & Marquart, 2004). Tindal and Fuchs (1999) compiled one of the first syntheses of the existing research on assessment accommodations. They used the term *differential effectiveness* to discuss accommodations that enabled students with disabilities to perform better but did not benefit those without disabilities. In other words, the accommodation "leveled the playing field," while preserving the meaningfulness of the scores for students with disabilities. Among their findings are the following:

- Extended time may be an appropriate accommodation for students with disabilities.
- Change of test setting had a positive effect for students with disabilities but not for students without disabilities.
- Changes related to computer-based testing must be interpreted with caution because of rapidly changing technology and the lack of large-scale studies.
- Research findings favor the use of familiar examiners, typically the student's classroom teacher, to provide accommodations and administer the test.
- The use of large print or Braille and reading aloud of math problems have consistently been shown to be differentially effective.
- Dictation to a proctor or scribe appears to be effective in improving performance for students with and without disabilities.
- Marking responses in test booklets is an accommodation that shows no positive or negative results and does not differentially benefit students with disabilities. At best, it is effective only for some individual students.
- Findings on the use of word processors in writing tests are contradictory. Many variables need to be considered—for example, type of computer, use of features such as spell-check, and student experience with the computer.
- Using calculators during testing is not consistently helpful nor differentially effective.
- Performance is greatly enhanced by reinforcement during the testing situation
- Training in test taking may help those who lack experience in testing. Research in this area, however, has not focused on students with disabilities.

Bolt and Thurlow (2004) reviewed the existing research from the past 12 years on the five accommodations that were the most frequently allowed in state policies: dictated response, large print, Braille, extended time, and interpreter for instruction. (Individual and small-group administration were not included because they were not considered to be highly controversial.) They found that very limited research was available for Braille and interpreter accommodations. Several studies indicated that the dictated-response accommodation was effective in boosting the scores of students with disabilities, although some researchers expressed concern that it may result in implausibly high scores. They also found that research had produced mixed support or nonsupport for the remaining accommodations.

Some excellent recommendations related to accommodations were made by Bolt and Thurlow (2004):

1. Determine the skills to be measured by the test before you make a decision regarding the accommodations to be provided. (For example, if a writing test is intended to measure only a student's ability to express thoughts, a scribe may be appropriate. If the test is intended also to measure capitalization, spelling, and punctuation, a scribe would probably not be appropriate.)
2. Use an accommodation that augments standard conditions to the least extent possible. (For example, if a student is not capable of completing a paper-and-pencil test, but is capable of typing responses into a computer, a computer response may be more appropriate than a dictated response since it removes the potential for a scribe to alter student responses.)
3. Ensure the alignment of the accommodations made in instruction and those made during assessment. Students need to have an opportunity to experience accommodations prior to using them in testing situations. In addition, if a student receives certain accommodations in instruction, it is important to ensure that they are available during testing, if appropriate.
4. Provide appropriate training to those who administer the accommodations.
5. Anticipate and prepare for additional challenges associated with providing accommodations, such as appropriate page breaks in large-print tests.
6. Monitor the effects of accommodations for individual students.

Related to this last point, it is important to collect data on whether the accommodation increases your student's performance. Fuchs, Fuchs, Eaton, Hamlett, and Karns (2000) described a system called the Dynamic Assessment of Testing Accommodations (DATA) that can aid teachers in determining whether an accommodation is appropriate for an individual student, by monitoring the student's performance with and without the accommodation. Another system proposed for increasing teachers' efficiency in recommending accommodations is the Assessment Accommodations Checklist (Elliott, Kratochwill, & Schulte, 1998). Both systems rely on increasing the amount of information available to make such decisions.

Alternate Assessment

As stated earlier in this chapter, the Individuals with Disabilities Education Improvement Act of 2004 (IDEA 2004) mandates that students with disabilities be included in state- and districtwide assessment programs. If the IEP team determines that the student shall take an alternate assessment, the IEP must include a statement of why the student cannot participate in the regular assessment and why the particular alternate assessment is appropriate. States must also report the numbers and performance of students participating in the alternate assessment. This mandate will require you to become familiar with the alternate assessment procedures used in your state as well as the methods of gathering the information that is required.

As discussed in Chapter 2, the No Child Left Behind legislation (2002) reinforces the need for alternate assessments, and requires that they be aligned with state content standards and be used only with students with significant cognitive disabilities (about 1 percent). The U.S. Department of Education (2003) issued a rule that allows these students to be assessed against standards appropriate for their intellectual level, and allows schools to count the "proficient" scores of these students as part of their school's performance. More than 1 percent of students may participate in alternate assessments if schools can demonstrate that they have a larger population of students with significant cognitive disabilities.

Planning alternate assessment for students with significant disabilities is complex for two reasons: (1) all students with significant disabilities within a district do not have a common curriculum and (2) districts frequently lack a definite curriculum for these students that is comparable to the districts' standard course of study in academics (Browder, 2001). Although the use of one of the life skills curricula presented in Chapter 1 may help in planning the domains for alternate assessment, it does not fully resolve the dilemma because (1) curricula for students with significant disabilities must be personalized, (2) students with significant disabilities may be actively engaged in the general education curriculum through their inclusive education settings, and (3) life skills and functional equivalents of academic skills do not lend themselves well to standardized testing (Browder, 2001).

As Browder, Fallin, Davis, and Karvonen (2003) stated, two major influences have occurred in planning curriculum for students with severe disabilities in the last three decades. The first has been to identify curriculum that relates to real life—a functional or life-skills curriculum approach. The second influence has been the inclusion of students with severe disabilities in general education settings. This inclusion has led to the development of a parallel curriculum in which students learn either adaptations of the general curriculum or ways to participate in class activities using their life skills.

This dual focus was illustrated by the experience of Kleinert and Kearns (1999) when they were validating Kentucky's alternate assessment with 44 national experts in severe disabilities. Although the respondents gave "functionality" the second highest rating as a performance indicator (after the top-rated "integrated environments"), their written comments indicated some ambivalence about basing an alternate assessment on functional life skills. The respondents noted the need to use academic settings to achieve functional outcomes and the need not to underestimate the ability of students with significant disabilities to participate in the general education curriculum.

Thompson, Quenemoen, Thurlow, and Ysseldyke (2001) described both legal and practical reasons for not having separate standards for students with disabilities. Increasingly, states are seeing the extension of state standards to all students with disabilities and the development of alternate assessments as interrelated activities. In 1999, 32 percent of states were using only functional skills for their alternate assessments with no link to state standards; in 2001, only 8 percent were doing so (Browder et al., 2003).

Browder and colleagues (2003) stated that for students with severe disabilities, performance on alternate assessments could have the potential of increasing expectations or of competing with instructional time and producing meaningless results. Kentucky was the first state to include all students in a statewide accountability system, including the use of an alternate assessment portfolio (Kleinert, Kearns, & Kennedy, 1997; Kleinert & Kearns, 1999). A statewide survey indicated that teachers reported gains in student learning, but that alternate assessment was a time-intensive process (Kleinert, Kennedy, & Kearns, 1999).

Kleinert, Haig, Kearns, and Kennedy (2000) identified seven key conceptual and methodological issues that have arisen as states have developed alternate assessments:

- Why assess (background, context, and foundations)?
- [Whom] to assess (eligibility)?
- What and how to assess (outcomes, standards, goals)?
- When to assess (multiple versus single measures)?
- How to separate and report performance (scoring criteria and procedures)?
- How to use scores (data management)?
- How to continuously improve the process? (p. 52)

Kleinert and associates (2000) discussed each of these issues in view of statewide alternate assessment programs in Kentucky and Maryland—two states where alternate assessment is a component of a comprehensive educational and accountability system that addresses the learning of all students. They strongly recommended that all aspects of the alternate assessment be aligned as much as possible with the regular assessment so that general educators who are working with students completing alternate assessments can effectively communicate with their counterparts in special education. Many states have developed guidelines for teachers to follow in extending state standards to students with severe disabilities. The purpose of these guidelines is to create a bridge between functional life-skills curricula and traditional general education curricular topics such as reading, math, science, and social studies. States often use such terms as *extended standards* and *real-life indicators* (Browder et al., 2003).

Researchers (Kampfer, Horvath, Kleinert, & Kearns, 2001) have found that a powerful predictor of student scores on alternate assessments was the extent to which the assessment was integrated into daily instruction, as well as the extent to which students were actively involved in the construction of their own assessment portfolios. Kleinert, Green, Hurte, Clayton, and Oetinger (2002) provided the following guidelines to assist teachers in this process:

1. Relate student IEP objectives to your state's standards for all students.
2. Ensure that students are able to access standards in multiple ways. This may be (a) in the same way and at the same level as all students; (b) at the same level but with an alternative response format (such as sign language); (c) in a modified form or content level (learning definitions of 5 rather than 20 terms); or (d) participating in an activity with the individualized goal of learning a basic or access skill (learning to follow two-step directions in the context of a cooperative social studies group).
3. Plan for your state's alternate assessment requirements from the beginning of the school year, building the requirements into your ongoing data collection and IEP monitoring sheets.
4. Use student planning, monitoring, and self-evaluation forms so that students can be more involved in their learning.

Methods of Gathering Assessment Information on the Individual

Transition assessment is an ongoing process that focuses on an individual's current and future roles as a worker, lifelong learner, family member, community citizen, and participant in social and interpersonal networks. We support the position of the Interdisciplinary Council on Vocational Evaluation and Assessment (Smith, Lombard, Neubert, Leconte, Rothenbacher, & Sitlington, 1994), which advocates that the assessment process be student centered and be designed to emphasize individual capabilities rather than disabilities. In addition, working, educational, and living environments should be adapted to accommodate the individual, rather than the individual trying to adjust to fit the environments. A number of methods have been used in the past three decades to conduct career, vocational, and transition assessment. These methods can be conceptualized in two broad domains: (1) those used to assess the *individual* and (2) those used to assess or analyze *future working, educational, and living environments.*

This section will focus on methods for gathering information on an individual's strengths, needs, preferences, and interests. These methods include techniques such as (1) analysis of background information, (2) interviews/questionnaires, (3) psychometric instruments, (4) work samples, (5) curriculum-based assessment techniques, and (6) situational assessment. Although we do not endorse specific methods in the process of transition assessment, we do emphasize the need for personnel to move beyond methods that are isolated from actual life contexts (such as psychometric tests) and to move toward methods that are conducted within natural or actual employment, postsecondary, or community settings. For instance, if an individual is participating in transition assessment to identify employment options, assessment activities should take place in a variety of real work settings to determine strengths, needs, preferences, interests, and compatibility with the skill demands and social interactions of each setting. During the assessment process, it would also be necessary to determine the individual's compatibility with the transportation options (e.g., transferring to a subway or riding a bus) required to travel to and from work in the community or to address lack of transportation in rural areas.

Sitlington, Neubert, and Leconte (1997) suggested the following guidelines for selecting methods used in the transition assessment process:

1. Assessment methods must be tailored to the types of information needed and the decisions to be made regarding transition planning and various postsecondary outcomes.
2. Specific methods selected must be appropriate for the learning characteristics of the individual, including cultural and linguistic differences.
3. Assessment methods must incorporate assistive technology or accommodations that will allow an individual to demonstrate his or her abilities and potential.
4. Assessment methods must occur in environments that resemble actual vocational training, employment, independent living, or community environments.
5. Assessment methods must produce outcomes that contribute to ongoing development, planning, and implementation of "next steps" in the individual's transition process.
6. Assessment methods must be varied and include a sequence of activities that sample an individual's behavior and skills over time.
7. Assessment data must be verified by more than one method and by more than one person.
8. Assessment data must be synthesized and interpreted to individuals with disabilities, their families, and transition team members.
9. Assessment data and the results of the assessment process must be documented in a format that can be used to facilitate transition planning. (p. 75)

There is a wealth of information in the general education, special education, rehabilitation, and career and technical education literature on methods and models of assessment that identify the vocational, educational, independent living, community functioning, and the personal/social strengths and needs of individuals with disabilities. New methods and models of assessment are not needed to identify postsecondary goals and facilitate transition planning. The task is to determine what methods of assessment are most appropriate at various transition points for individuals with disabilities to make decisions regarding their futures.

Analysis of Background Information

One of the first sources of information about the student should be existing records that contain observations of previous teachers, support staff, and staff from other agencies (e.g., mental health, juvenile justice, or youth and family services) who have worked with the individual. In addition to the cumulative folder, there are often other records kept by the teacher or other support staff who have worked with the student. These other records usually have more useful information than the "official" student files. Be sure that you also review past individualized education programs (IEPs), with particular emphasis on transition-related goals and activities contained in these IEPs. Also ask for any additional formal and informal assessments that have been conducted with the student. Although all of this information should be in the student's official files, this is often not the case. If other youth and adult service agencies have been working with the individual, ask if you may also review their information, after receiving appropriate releases of information from the family or the individual.

Student portfolios provide valuable information that has been selected by the student and staff as representative of the student's interests, goals, and finest work. In fact, a transition portfolio is an excellent means of organizing and summarizing all of the transition assessment and transition planning activities in which the student has participated. These and other existing records often contain a wealth of information on the strengths and interests of the individual, as well as the areas on which the individual needs to focus. This information might be in the form of comments of previous teachers, guidance counselors, and other support staff and adult service providers; formal and informal assessment results; and records of IEP meetings. These records might also contain information on the experiences the individual has had in the community related to living and employment, and the techniques and approaches that have worked (or not worked) with the individual in the past. Information on health-related issues can also be found. If transition planning activities have been conducted with the student in previous years, it is very helpful to review the trends in the student's expressed interests and preferences over these years.

It is important to remember in reviewing records, however, that individuals may react differently to new living or work environments and personnel. They may enter these environments with a changed attitude. Also, in the adolescent years, students often change behavior and attitudes almost overnight. Thus, although previous information should be considered, take some time to form opinions based on your own observations and experiences with the student as well as his or her self-reports.

Interviews/Questionnaires

Interviews with the student, family members, former teachers, friends, counselors, other support staff, and former employers may be one of the best sources of information on how the individual functions in the real world and what he or she would like to do as an adult. Frequently, brothers and sisters of students have more realistic and accurate information than their parents about their siblings' long-term goals, their social and personal aspirations, and their abilities. Siblings are major stakeholders in students' transitions, since they may one day assume responsibility for their brothers and sisters who have disabilities. Sitlington, Neubert, Begun, Lombard, and Leconte (1996) is a good resource for specific hints on conducting interviews. If face-to-face or phone interviews are not possible, some of the same information can be gathered through questionnaires that require short, written responses. Care must be taken, though, to make sure that those completing the questionnaire can understand the questions and are able to respond clearly in writing.

Psychometric Instruments

Psychometric instruments (sometimes called *paper-and-pencil instruments*) are often standardized tests and inventories that are available from commercial publishers. Psychometric instruments are farther removed from tasks required in the real world of employment and adult community living than most of the other techniques presented in this section, but they do relate to current academic goals and demands and may relate to choices or decisions for further education and training.

These instruments generally fall into two categories: norm referenced and objective referenced. In many instruments, objectives take the form of competencies. Salvia and Ysseldyke (2004) provided the following definitions for these terms:

> *Norm-referenced devices:* Tests that compare an individual's performance to the performance of his or her peers.

> *Objective-referenced assessment:* Tests referenced to specific instructional objectives rather than to the performance of a peer group or norm group. (p. 691)

Appendix 5A on the companion website offers a listing of selected commercially available assessment instruments for transition planning. This list was developed by Clark (2004) and includes instruments appropriate for students of varying ages. Kapes and Whitfield (2001) also provided information on the major psychometric tests related to the areas of transition. Although some of these instruments must be administered by individuals formally trained in test administration and interpretation, many can be administered by the classroom teacher or are completed by the student. Some are scales to guide observation of the student in a variety of environments or to rate the student in various competency areas.

One advantage of this approach is that it provides an "official-looking" score and a standardized method of gathering specific information. These instruments can also provide information on the functioning level of the student in a number of planning areas, including the areas of strength and the areas in need of improvement. Many professionals use these instruments as a starting point to plan other assessment activities or to engage in discussion with the student, especially in regard to planning and decision making about college or other postsecondary education expectations. Many people think of assessment only as administering these formal instruments. Like any of the techniques described in this chapter, however, psychometric tests should not be used as the *only* method of gathering the information you need to assist the student and his or her family in transition planning.

Psychometric tests can also provide information on the *knowledge* level of the student related to functional living areas (e.g., managing money, maintaining a home, and shopping) and to specific occupations or occupational clusters. These instruments, however, usually do *not* provide information on how well the individual applies this knowledge in real-life situations. In addition, the ability of the student to perform well on these instruments depends not only on knowledge but also on the amount of experience the student has had with the situations presented in the test.

Work Samples

Work sampling is defined as a "work activity involving tasks, materials, and tools which are identical or similar to those in an actual job or cluster of jobs" (Fry & Botterbusch, 1988, as cited in Dowd, 1993, p. 12). Work samples can be used to assess an individual's interests, abilities, work habits, and personal and social skills. The key to administering work samples is to observe and document information concerning level of interest, attention to task, and requests for assistance or clarification in addition to an individual's actual performance of the task. Work samples often provide a direct link to occupational information, since they simulate specific aspects of vocational training or employment. Daily living activities can also be simulated in a type of community living sample.

Generally, work samples fall into two categories: commercial and locally developed or homemade. Commercial work samples are generally found in vocational evaluation units in school systems or rehabilitation facilities. Information on commercial work samples and the advantages and disadvantages of using them with individuals with disabilities are presented in Brown, McDaniel, and Couch (1994). Locally developed or homemade work samples are generally developed by a teacher or vocational evaluator and are more often used in the transition assessment process. These work samples can be developed on the basis of local job analyses, on the premise of tasks in vocational training programs, or as part of the classroom career exploration process.

Work samples generally have a standard set of directions, tasks, materials, and key behaviors to observe. The Rehabilitation Resource at University of Wisconsin–Stout has developed a manual for practitioners to follow when developing and administering informal work samples. Homemade work samples can also be found within vocational evaluation units and tend to sample tasks found in vocational programs or jobs specific to the local community. These samples tend to have high face validity because individuals can see and think about actual work.

Curriculum-Based Assessment Techniques

One of the major thrusts in the field of education is toward curriculum-based assessment (CBA). This is assessment based on what is contained in the curriculum. Curriculum-based assessment is really an *approach* rather than one specific method. This approach is included here, however, because it is often viewed as a specific assessment technique and is being used increasingly in content-area classes, such as math and English, as well as in career and technical education programs. Curriculum-based assessment instruments can be developed by the teacher or other staff and should focus specifically on the content being taught. Examples of curriculum-based assessment techniques include criterion-referenced testing, curriculum-based measurement, portfolio assessment, performance-based assessment, and curriculum-based vocational assessment. Each of these approaches will be discussed in the following paragraphs. They can be used to gather information related to planning for future living, working, or educational environments.

Criterion-Referenced Testing. The criterion-referenced testing approach compares an individual's performance to a preestablished level of performance (e.g., 80 percent) rather than to the performance of others or to a set of norms. In this approach, the emphasis is on the knowledge or skills needed for a specific content area and whether the individual has demonstrated mastery of this knowledge. Results of the assessment would indicate that the student scored 70 percent on two-digit by one-digit multiplication problems and 40 percent on two-digit by two-digit multiplication. The criterion-referenced testing approach is used primarily in academic areas but can be used in any content area where skills can be broken down into specific subareas.

Curriculum-Based Measurement. Curriculum-based measurement (CBM) is an ongoing assessment approach that was developed by individuals at the University of Minnesota. It consists of a specific set of assessment techniques for the areas of reading, written expression, spelling, and math, using timed samples of the student's work. Norms are usually developed using scores from the local school or district. When using the CBM approach, you would administer probes of short duration to your students on a weekly basis and graph their performance each week. You would then use the graphic data to evaluate student performance and determine the success of the instructional interventions being used with the students. When students are not progressing, you would change instruction and then examine subsequent data to evaluate the effects of that change (Busch & Espin, 2003).

The majority of the studies on the use of CBM have been at the elementary level. A group of authors, however, has examined the reliability and validity of this approach at the secondary level—in the content areas of reading, written expression, mathematics, social studies, and science (Espin, Busch, Shin, & Kruschwitz, 2001; Espin & Foegen, 1996; Espin, Skare, Shin, Deno, Robinson, & Brenner, 2000; Espin & Tindal, 1998; Tindal & Nolet, 1995).

Portfolio Assessment.   The concept of portfolio assessment has been in use in the fine arts area for a number of years, as well as in vocational programs such as architecture, drafting, and graphic arts. As the emphasis in assessment moves toward the concept of *authentic assessment,* portfolios are being developed in a number of content areas and across content areas. The major steps in portfolio assessment are as follows:

1. Describe the curricular area.
2. Identify the overall goals of the portfolio.
3. Delineate the portfolio format and the type of materials to be included.
4. Describe the procedures for evaluating the work in the portfolio (e.g., student conferences and teacher review of material).
5. Describe how the contents of the portfolio will be summarized.

The following aspects of portfolio assessment are critical:

1. Criteria for selection of materials must be stated.
2. Students must participate in the development of these criteria and in the actual selection of the materials.
3. Criteria for evaluating the materials must be specified.
4. An opportunity for self-reflection on the part of the student must be provided.

The types of materials to be included in the portfolio can range from the results of vocational interest inventories to essays written by the student concerning his or her goals to samples of projects from social studies class or architectural drafting. This approach is an excellent method of compiling and summarizing all of the transition assessment activities of the student. In using this method, it is critical that the student have input into the types of materials to be included in the portfolio and that guidelines be established and followed for including materials in the portfolio. A portfolio with everything the student has completed will be difficult to evaluate and does not truly represent the student's abilities, interests, and preferences. It is also very important that the material in the portfolio be evaluated on an ongoing basis by the student and the teacher.

Performance-Based Assessment.   Performance-based assessment is related to the concept of *authentic assessment.* It lends itself to a variety of academic areas as well as nonacademic areas, such as music, art, dance, theater arts, speech, and physical education. Performance can be an observed performance (song, speech, dramatic monologue, etc.) or a product (musical composition, sculpture, painting, costume design, keyboard printout, etc.). In both types, observed performance or product, assessment is done through preestablished rubrics or criteria for evaluation.

Curriculum-Based Vocational Assessment.   One of the most recognized applications of the curriculum-based assessment approach is curriculum-based vocational assessment (CBVA). This is a process for determining the student's career development, vocational, and transition-related needs based on his or her ongoing performance within existing course content. For the specific application of CBVA, the target is usually performance in vocational education courses or on work experience sites in the school or community, although important information can also be gathered from performance in academic classes. This process not only allows you to collect information on the student's performance in a setting close to real life but it also allows you to determine the support that the student will need to succeed in vocational education classes or on the job. Albright and Cobb (1988b) identified three general phases in the CBVA process:

1. *Assessment during program placement and planning.* This includes activities prior to and during the first few weeks of student participation in a vocational program. Information gathered during this phase assists in program selection, program placement, and program planning.
2. *Assessment during participation in a vocational program.* These activities monitor the student's program, determine the appropriateness of the program and service delivery plan, and evaluate the success of the student's program.
3. *Assessment during program exiting.* Assessment activities in this phase occur near the end of the student's program and immediately following completion of the student's program. Information gathered in this phase assists the team in identifying the special services needed to help the student transition into employment and/or postsecondary education and the best program(s) for the student.

If the student is in career and technical education classes or work experiences in the community, information can be gathered on how well the individual actually performs tasks related to specific occupations. The student can also determine whether he or she is interested in the specific vocational area. Additionally, information can be gathered on how well the individual relates to others, including peers and supervisors, and in such areas as working independently, staying on task, and asking for assistance when needed. For more information on CBVA, consult Albright and Cobb (1988a, 1988b) and Stodden, Ianacone, Boone, and Bisconer (1987).

Summary. Curriculum-based assessment is becoming a major emphasis within content area courses. This presents an ideal opportunity to gather information on the individual across a variety of instructional settings. If data are gathered on the student's performance in academic classes, information can be gathered on basic academic skills and how the student learns best, as well as his or her work habits, preferences and values, and attitudes. The specific academic areas in which the student is interested and in which he or she excels can also be identified. The curriculum-based assessment approach can also provide information on the student's performance and/or knowledge of skills related to daily living, such as managing a checking account, negotiating with authority figures, doing laundry, and preparing meals. Finally, this approach can provide information on the student's interest and skills in leisure-time activities.

Situational Assessment

Situational assessment is the systematic observation process for evaluating behaviors in environments as close as possible to the individual's future living, working, or educational environment. Observing and recording individual behavior in different work and community settings over time provides the foundation for transition assessment. Dowd (1993) defined an *observation procedure* as "an organized method of observing and objectively recording the behavior of an individual for the purpose of documenting this behavior. The emphasis is usually upon productivity, behavior patterns, expressed interest, and interpersonal interaction" (p. 20).

For information to be useful, behavior observation should be systematic and should take place in a variety of settings. It is also helpful to have different team members observe the same individual in various situations to make sure the information gathered is valid and reliable. Many different techniques can be used by practitioners to observe and record behavior, including narrative recording, time sampling, event recording, and rating scales.

The demands of the environment (e.g., work tasks, independent living tasks, and community functioning skills) can be varied while recording behaviors such as interest, actual skill level, use of materials, and social interactions. Situational assessments can be a valid and reliable source of data if the sites are systematically developed (uniform tasks a student will do, amount of time, supervision responsibilities, etc.) and if practitioners systematically record behaviors during the assessment process. The data collected can then be used in planning and placement decisions concerning further situational assessment sites, types of programs to consider for placement, and instructional/social accommodations needed in specific situations. Situational assessments can be conducted in recreation sites, community sites (e.g., a bank facility), and simulated or real sites that require independent living skills (e.g., home economics lab, family home, or supervised apartment).

Situational assessment also can be used to collect data on students' interests, abilities, interpersonal and social skills, and accommodations and needs in school-based work sites, community-based work sites, and vocational training programs.

In arranging situational assessments in work sites, keep in mind that guidelines have been developed by the U.S. Departments of Labor and Education for the purpose of placing students in unpaid job sites while meeting the requirements of the Fair Labor Standards Act. For a complete listing of the guidelines, see Inge, Simon, Halloran, and Moon (1993) or Simon, Cobb, Halloran, Norman, and Bourexis (1994).

Summary

The focus of all the methods described on the previous pages was on gathering information on the strengths, needs, preferences, and interests of the individual. As you work with the student and other members of the IEP team to decide which method(s) to use, it will help to focus on the types of information you want to gather and the learning characteristics of the student. The portfolio approach offers an ideal vehicle for the student, family, and other members of the transition planning team to select and summarize the most relevant transition assessment information that has been collected. This transition assessment portfolio can then be used in making the match between the student's strengths, needs, interests, and preferences and the future environments in which the student will function as an adult.

When you are working with students with more severe disabilities, you may find that some of the approaches discussed in this section are not applicable. Hughes, Pitkin, and Lorden (1998), in particular, found that a technology has been developing for assessing preferences and choices for this group of students. In their cumulative review and analysis of studies that had focused on this topic, they found that preference and choice have been measured via one or two of the following responses:

- Activation of a microswitch
- Approach toward a stimulus
- Verbalizations, signing, gestures, vocalizations, or affect

- Physical selection of a stimulus
- Task performance
- Time engaged with a stimulus

In another approach, Lohrmann-O'Rourke and Gomez (2001) focused on integrating preference assessment throughout the transition process using person-centered planning. In this process (an application of the situational assessment approach discussed previously), possible options related to living, working, playing, and learning are selected, based on what the team knows about the student. The team then provides hands-on opportunities to sample these options (such as types of living arrangements and leisure opportunities in the community). Next, the student's response to each option is observed and these responses are interpreted as a relative indicator of preference or nonpreference. Such an approach clearly encompasses the analysis of future living, working, and educational environments discussed in the following section.

Methods of Assessing Potential Environments

The previous section presented information on a number of methods that you can use in gathering information on your students. In order to make a match between each student's needs, preferences, strengths, and interests and his or her future environments, however, you also need to have information on the demands of the living and working environments in which the individual may be functioning as an adult and the training programs in which the student will enroll on the path to adulthood. Analysis of these environments also involves examining circumstances and situations that occur within these environments.

To determine the training and support your student will need in order to succeed in the future living, working, and educational environments he or she has identified, it is critical that the student, the family, you, or someone in your program systematically look at the demands of these environments. In general, the lower functioning the student (or the bigger you feel the gap will be between the student's abilities and the demands of the environment), the more detailed the analysis should be. This will allow you to identify the training and supports that the individual will need to succeed. It is important to remember that the environment, situations, and circumstances can be adapted, adjusted, or realigned so that minimal supports will be needed. The following section will present basic information on analyzing community and employment settings and postsecondary training programs.

Analysis of Community Environments

The concept of environmental analysis, particularly related to community-based living settings, was first introduced by professionals working with individuals with severe disabilities. In terms of future living environments, it is important to identify the demands of both the home environment in which the individual will be living as well as the current living environment. The structure and demands of the broader community in which the individual will be shopping, banking, and pursuing leisure activities should also be considered. If the specific community-based environments are known, the task becomes one of analyzing the demands of these specific environments (e.g., the apartment, the grocery store, the bank, etc.). Often, however, educators do not always know the specific location in which the individual will live, so the analysis would focus on a number of possible environments. In addition, the individual will want to frequent a number of locations within a given community, such as a number of different restaurants.

Alper (2003) proposed the following steps in identifying curricular content using the ecological inventory approach developed by Brown and colleagues (1979):

- Select the domain of choice (e.g., domestic).
- Identify environments within the domain in which the student needs to learn to function (e.g., home).
- Identify subenvironments that are a priority for the student (e.g., kitchen, family room).
- Identify activities within each subenvironment in which the student is to be included (e.g., heating up leftovers, operating the DVD player).
- Task analyze the priority activities into their component skills.

Job Analysis

The process of analyzing the demands of working environments is called *job analysis*. In essence, it is a task analysis of the job and what it demands. This process involves systematically gathering information on what the worker does, how the work is done, and under what conditions the work is done. This also includes other areas, such as amount of supervision, production requirements, and more. Information should also be gathered on other demands of the workplace, including activities during breaks and transportation to and from work.

Rogan, Grossi, and Gajewski (2002) identified four major focal points for an ecological inventory and workplace analysis:

- Physical environment (accessibility, layout)
- Typical activities or work tasks (rate, sequence, quality, frequency, duration)
- People within the environment (age, gender, characteristics of supervisors and co-workers, nature of interactions)

■ Climate and culture (customs, traditions, rituals, routines, rules, expectations)

The job analysis process is time consuming and must be done on site to observe the "essential functions" of the job, as defined in the Americans with Disabilities Act. It is important to directly observe the worker and talk with the worker and direct supervisor. Also check to see if there is an existing job description that has been developed by the employer.

Sitlington and colleagues (1996) used steps identified by McDonnell, Wilcox, and Hardman (1991) to analyze the job of dental assistant:

1. Identify the specific responses that will be required to complete each job assigned. These responses should be both observable and measurable. (Identify the basic tasks that the dental assistant must complete. Be very specific. Identify the tasks you have observed and other tasks completed at a time you were not observing.)
2. Identify the environmental cues that will control the completion of the task. These will be cues to tell the individual to perform certain tasks or certain parts of the task. (Identify the commands of the dentist, the requests of the patient, and the requests of other office staff that prompt the specfic tasks.)
3. Identify the speed requirements of the job in terms of average time required to complete a response or task, or in terms of the number of products to be completed within a given time period. Identify how important this speed requirement is to the employer. (Identify how quickly the dental assistant must respond to the requests of the dentist, patient, and other staff. Identify how important speed is.)
4. Specify the quality requirements for each job task. The accuracy of the supervisor's expectations should be cross-checked by discussing them with co-workers who perform the same job. (Identify what criteria will be used to evaluate the quality of the dental assistant's performance.)
5. Identify exceptions to the normal routine. These exceptions may include changes in the job routine or unpredictable situations that may arise during the course of the workday. (Identify tasks the dental assistant does not perform daily but that are important to completion of the job, such as quality checks to be conducted on instruments.)

Analysis of Secondary and Postsecondary Training Environments

The "place and pray" system for putting students in academic environments at both the secondary and postsecondary level is alive and well! Just as a member of the IEP team should analyze students' current or targeted work environments, they should do the same for current (secondary) and targeted (post-secondary) academic environments. If one of the goals of the student is post-secondary education, the teacher, the student, and/or the family should visit the targeted educational program to determine the demands of specific courses and of the total educational environment. This involves gathering information on the specific courses in which the student will be enrolled and determining the demands of these courses, in terms of daily assignments, amount of reading and writing required, major tests, and the like. Information should also be gathered on the requirements of any field experiences or laboratories related to the class. Support services and available accommodations should also be identified.

Information for postsecondary education environments should be gathered on the following aspects of the training program:

1. Application procedures
2. Admission procedures
3. Support services
4. Willingness of individual faculty members to provide accommodations
5. Career/personal counseling services
6. Training programs, both academically and vocationally related
7. Existing fee structures
8. Availability of financial support

The supports available for all students and specifically for students with disabilities are critical. See Chapter 7 for more information on what to look for in postsecondary education and training programs.

As in the job analysis, it is important for someone on the IEP team to identify the types of information the team wants to gather on postsecondary programs, and adopt, adapt, or develop a program analysis form that will provide this information for you. The form should allow you to record information on a specific program and then refer to this information at a later date. The form should also be one that all staff or family members or the individual could use and that would allow the results of a specific program analysis to be shared with others, particularly the individual.

Summary

An analysis of the future living, working, and educational environments the individual has chosen will be a major help in determining the training he or she will need to succeed in these environments. This training could involve enrollment in general education courses in high school, participating in work experiences in the community, instruction in learning strategies or study skills, or training in self-determination. If the training involves enrolling in general education classes, such as career and technical education classes, math classes, or English courses, it will be helpful to conduct an analysis of the demands of these training environments so that you can determine the support the student will need in order to learn from these programs. The steps involved in this program analysis are identical to those discussed in analyzing postsecondary educational environments. The preceding sections have focused on gathering information about the demands of potential living, working, and educational environments. Analysis of each of these environments also requires analysis of the personal and social skills required.

Tying Assessment into Transition Planning

It is very important to have an organized approach for tying the information you gather through the assessment process into transition planning with your students. This involves developing an assessment plan; making the match between each student's strengths, needs, preferences, and interests and the demands of future environments; and using the assessment information properly.

Developing an Assessment Plan

To determine appropriate methods for the transition assessment process, an assessment plan should be developed and periodically updated with the individual and his or her family. The assessment plan should address the following questions (Sitlington et al., 1996):

- What do I already know about this student that would be helpful in developing postsecondary outcomes?
- What information do I need to know about this individual to determine postsecondary goals?
- What methods will provide this information?
- How will the assessment data be collected and used in the IEP process?

Using an assessment plan will ensure that the methods are varied and appropriate for the purposes of the assessment and for the individual's characteristics and stage in the career development and transition process. An existing transition skills assessment (see Appendix 5A for instruments listed under Transition/Community Adjustment) could be used initially to identify the areas where the IEP team needs more information.

Making the Match

Figure 5.3 presents the process of making the match between an individual's strengths, needs, preferences, and interests and the demands and culture of

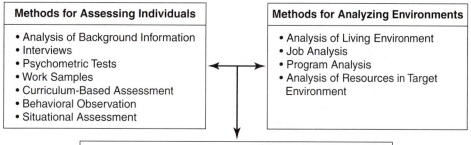

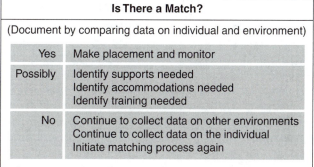

FIGURE 5.3   Making the Match

Source: From *Assess for Success: Handbook on Transition Assessment* (page 99) by P. L. Sitlington, D. A. Neubert, W. Begun, R. C. Lombard, and P. J. Leconte, 1996, Reston, VA: Council for Exceptional Children. Copyright 1996 by the Council for Exceptional Children. Reprinted by permission.

current and future environments (Sitlington et al., 1996). A variety of assessment methods in special education, rehabilitation, and vocational education can be used to facilitate this process. The upper left-hand box in this figure presents methods for gathering information about an individual's needs, preferences, and interests. The upper right-hand box lists methods for gathering information on the demands of future working, educational, and community environments. Such assessment requires not only looking at the specific tasks involved in these environments but also observing aspects of the "culture" of these environments with which the individual must interact. This assessment process also uses assistive technology, when appropriate, to enhance an individual's capabilities and adapt the characteristics of the environment prior to, during, and following assessment.

The lower box in Figure 5.3 focuses on the critical process of actually making the match between the individual and the environment. If a match is made, the professional would make the placement and provide the ongoing monitoring and support needed. If a match is possible, but not definite, it is essential that resources, supports, accommodations, and training needs are identified to make the match work. If a match does not seem feasible, based on the available information, then additional data need to be collected on the individual and other target environments, and the matching process must be continued until a viable match is made.

As mentioned previously, a transition profile may be the most useful means of summarizing assessment information and can be incorporated into a portfolio or transition assessment folder. This profile needs to be updated periodically by the student and personnel responsible for the assessment. The outcomes of transition assessment should focus on recommendations for appropriate placements, instructional strategies, accommodations in various environments that support an individual's strengths and abilities, and even recommendations for further needed assessment.

Appendix 5B on the companion website to this text provides sample questions for transition planning and assessment in the areas of employment, postsecondary education, community involvement, personal/social, and independent living. This appendix also provides suggested methods for collecting the information to assist in answering these questions.

Using Assessment Information

If no decisions are made after collecting assessment information, why collect it? In some cases, the answer to that question depends on whether the information collected is "real" information. In other words, data can be collected but later questioned as to their validity or reliability. Without some sense that the data are real (i.e., valid and reliable), it would be unprofessional and unethical to use the data to make decisions. Thus, the underlying assumption of collecting and then using assessment data is that the data are worthy of using.

The most critical use of transition assessment information is in the statement of the student's present levels of academic achievement and functional performance in his or her IEP. Transition goals, along with linkages with non-school agencies, should come directly from transition-referenced assessment and the information in the present level of performance. The data should have direct implications for instructional program decisions, including program design, program placement, curriculum planning, instructional procedures, and additional assessment requirements. If the concept of present level of academic achievement and functional performance at all age levels is to be broadened to include transition knowledge and skills and any needs for linkages to youth, postsecondary, or adult agency services, it is apparent that assessment practices must extend beyond traditional academic assessment.

It is especially important that everyone using information from the transition assessment process has access to resource persons outside the transition planning team for help with unique or complex concerns that come up with students and their families. It is also important to know when it is critical that a referral be made, rather than wasting time or compounding the problem by attempting to work in isolation or without assistance from referral sources. Confidentiality and appropriate referral procedures must be addressed from the beginning of the referral decision. If a student or family member requests specific confidentiality, then that must be honored, unless, of course, child abuse, suicidal behavior, or threats involving harm to others are involved. In other cases, general confidentiality and "need to know" criteria should be followed in any referral process or IEP linkages to nonschool agencies.

An important legal use for transition assessment information obtained in developing an IEP is the documentation that it provides. Clearly, documentation of assessment procedures for present level of educational performance for IEP planning, as well as evidence of secondary-level student participation in the IEP planning process, is important. The data may also provide crucial documentation in the event that a student's placement or program service delivery is challenged at a formal hearing or in litigation. Finally, the data may function for high school students as the legal documentation needed for students to be able to access postsecondary education student assistance services or adult services for people with disabilities. The types of information being requested by postsecondary education and training programs are discussed in more detail in Chapter 7.

The *Transition Planning Inventory* (Clark & Patton, 1997) and *Informal Assessments for Transition Planning* (Clark, Patton, & Moulton, 2000) present a process for transferring the results of the assessment process directly into knowledge and skills goals or linkage goals on the IEP, or into the identification of further assessment that is needed. Whether you and the planning team choose to use this specific instrument or not, the process itself is a concrete example of using the results of the transition assessment process to drive student's IEPs. See Appendix 5C on the companion website for an example of *Transition Planning Inventory* results.

In addition, Appendix 5D on the companion website contains case studies of four students with mild, moderate, or severe disabilities. Each case study first presents a brief student history, the assessment that was conducted, and the results of this assessment. The statement of needed transition services and annual goals and objectives emanating from the assessment are then presented. Although the specific format each district uses for reporting assessment results and transition planning may be slightly different, the process and relationship of assessment to the statement of needed transition services and the IEP goals should remain the same.

Issues to Consider When Conducting Assessments

A number of issues must be considered when planning and conducting any type of assessment of students, but this is particularly true for a transition assessment. These issues are presented in the following sections. A number of other publications related to transition assessment are listed in the Resources section of the companion website. These publications also address these and other issues.

Being Sensitive to Gender and Cultural Diversity

The number-one issue in gender and cultural sensitivity is fairness. The IDEA regulations specify procedures for guaranteeing nondiscriminatory assessment through the requirement that tests and other evaluation material should be administered in the student's native language or other mode of communication, unless it is clearly unfeasible to do so. This effort for fairness is commendable for non-English-speaking students, but it does not address issues of gender, ethnicity, or cultural variations due to geography or income.

A variety of proposals and efforts have been made to deal with the issue of fairness in testing and assessment practices. Some of these include developing culture/gender-fair tests, culture/gender-free tests, translation of existing tests in English to other languages, and using language interpreters during testing. So far, none of these approaches has been a resounding success. The efforts have probably improved testing practices, but they have not solved all the problems.

Commonsense sensitivity to gender and cultural factors in selecting standardized instruments, developing informal procedures, and interpreting and reporting assessment results will ordinarily not only conform to federal mandates for nondiscriminatory evaluation but also go beyond them. Clark (1998) stated some commonsense guidelines that are summarized here:

- Be aware of possible past discrimination in the assessment process.
- Be ready to respond positively to identified past discrimination experiences. This may involve assigning a same-gender, same-race, same-language, or same-ethnic group professional to conduct the assessments and provide appropriate interpretations and reports.
- When in doubt about the proper interpretations to be made from a student or family response in the assessment process, use selected members of their cultural community to verify impressions or clarify responses that are difficult to understand.
- When interviewing a student or family of a different cultural group for the first time, be careful about the use of names and titles. Attempting to

be friendly too quickly may be insulting and viewed as a violation of social etiquette.

- Talk with the student and family about the best way to communicate, then be sure that comprehension is working both ways in the process by summarizing what has been said or by asking the student or family member to summarize what has been said.
- If translators (for written materials) or interpreters (for oral interactions) are requested and used, spend time with them before their participation to acquaint them with the purpose and context of the assessment activity.

Planning for life transitions is a proactive level of thinking that is associated with middle-class people. These individuals often have education, economic security, and relatively high levels of success in their own life transitions. For many students with disabilities and their families, transition planning is an unfamiliar concept and beyond their current concerns for day-to-day survival. The language used in talking about transitions in assessment activities (e.g., *vision for the future, empowerment, independence/interdependence, self-determination*, etc.) may be difficult for them to understand. Even if they have no difficulty understanding the words, they might have different cultural values associated with the words. Be sensitive to communication barriers and work continuously to establish common understandings when performing student and parent assessments and use those common understandings when drafting IEP goals and objectives.

Organizing and Reporting Information

One of the oldest of criticisms of testing in schools is that the scores get filed somewhere and are never seen again. There is some truth in this criticism. Since most schools are not in the ideal world, a combination of reality and recommended practice suggest that there are alternatives for organizing and making assessment information available. Since the material in assessment files contains a considerable amount of very personal information about students, the issues of organizing and making the materials available must be handled with strict adherence to both ethical and legal standards of confidentiality and rights to access of personal information. The Family Educational Rights and Privacy Act (FERPA) (PL 93-380) states that any educational agency that accepts federal money must give parents the opportunity to inspect, challenge, and correct their children's records. Students of majority age (age 18 and older in most states) also have the same rights in regard to their own records. Also, FERPA specifies that a school cannot release identifiable data on any student without the parents' or student's (when age 18 and older) written consent. School administrators and school psychologists have specialized training on the responsibilities of the school in maintaining confidentiality in the storage, disposal, and sharing of information of assessment records. If you have questions about confidentiality procedures, consult your building principal or special education administrator.

Whatever organizational format is used with assessment information, it should be designed for a specific purpose. There might be multiple purposes for wanting assessment information organized in a certain way for retrieval and use, including student planning use, school district use, and use by other youth services and adult providers (Clark, 1998). It may be that the traditional cumulative folder is maintained primarily for the school district's need for legal documentation, institutional accountability, and curriculum planning. This does not mean that there cannot be more than one organizational file. Notice should be placed in all files, however, about the existence of information in the other files.

Whatever format or system is used for organizing, maintaining, and making available student assessment information, there are two primary considerations: (1) the protection of students' and parents' rights of privacy and (2) the legitimate need to know of the person or agency who is participating in decision making and service delivery with the student. Maintaining secure files in locked filing cabinets is a basic recommended practice. Further, the FERPA provisions listed previously must be followed to demonstrate commitment to a concern for privacy and legal access.

People Involved in the Transition Assessment Process

As Sitlington, Neubert, and Leconte (1997) stated, the roles and responsibilities of those involved in transition assessment continue to evolve and change as the focus on school-to-adult transition gains emphasis in the education process. The transition planning process is most effective when (1) assessment data are collected on an ongoing basis through an interdisciplinary team approach and (2) responsibility for using assessment results and coordinating collection of ongoing assessment information is assumed by one person, often called a *service coordinator* or a *case manager*.

Possible roles of key players in the transition assessment process are presented in Appendix 5E on the companion website. Of course, the student is the key player in this process. Although many people may be involved in assessment activities throughout the students' educational, vocational, and transition programming, the secondary special educator is a logical person to assume the major responsibility for coordinating and using assessment information in the decision-making and planning process. Of course, the people who will know students throughout their educational and transition processes are parents or other family members. Parents, guardians, and advocates are needed to provide their perspective on the student's needs, preferences, strengths, and interests. It may also be important to know the views of the parents, guardians, or advocates regarding what they prefer for the student. However, because some family members are not in a position to assume the service coordination role immediately, it is incumbent on certified secondary special educators to model that role for family members and the student, who should eventually assume this responsibility. If needed, others who could undertake this responsibility and role modeling include vocational special needs educators, counselors, and transition specialists.

Since transition assessment activities must be tailored to meet the needs of individual students in various placements, it is important that secondary special educators, or service coordinators, understand interdisciplinary roles and learn how service systems operate. Examples of personnel with whom collaboration must occur are general educators, related services personnel, vocational educators, supported employment specialists, vocational evaluators, assistive technology specialists, rehabilitation counselors, employers, employee co-workers, financial aid personnel, social security counselors, residential counselors, and housemates.

Transition assessment may also need to be coordinated with and conducted by assistive technology specialists in employment, educational, and residential settings. The IDEA mandates that such assessment be conducted prior to other assessments if accommodations or technology will enhance students' abilities to perform and learn. Assistive technology assessment involves accessing services, identifying financing for these services, coordinating assessment activities, incorporating results into individualized education programs, and determining how students can maintain or upgrade their accommodations or technology.

Most important, service coordinators must become skilled in fostering and facilitating self-advocacy and self-determination skills of students. To begin this process, students must be guided in understanding their strengths, needs, preferences, and interests and then instructed on how to verbalize this information to others in terms that are specific and understandable. Eventually, students should assume responsibility for coordinating their assessment and transition processes.

Competencies for personnel involved in transition assessment should focus on skills related to assessing the individual and assessing his or her current and potential environments. In addition, skills are needed to establish a match between the culture and demands of these environments and the strengths, needs, preferences, and interests of the individual, and then to use and communicate the assessment data to facilitate transition planning. We support the competencies identified by DCDT (Sitlington, Neubert, & Leconte, 1997), which built on competencies identified by the Interdisciplinary Council on Vocational Evaluation and Assessment Position Statement (Smith, Lombard, Neubert, Leconte, Rothenbacher, & Sitlington, 1994).

Recommendations for Transition Assessment

Assessment for planning transition services for students with disabilities need not be overwhelming or take on a life of its own. Assessment must be kept in perspective; it is a means to an end, and never an end in itself. However, because of the state of the field in assessment for transition planning, some initial time and effort in planning and implementation is necessary. Some summarizing suggestions for developing or expanding current transition planning assessment for students with disabilities may be in order. The following suggestions are presented for your thoughtful consideration in your situation.

1. Incorporate the transition assessment process into the ongoing assessment efforts of the district and state, including those related to standards-based reform efforts.

2. Select assessment instruments and procedures on the basis of how to answer key questions in a student's individual transition planning and the assessment plan.

3. Make transition assessment ongoing. Assessment activities should start as early as possible and continue through life. There may be specific times for intensive assessment activity, and there may be key points in a student's educational progress where certain types of assessment should be planned, but much of what is needed for week-to-week instructional planning is ongoing. If at any point a student is seen as "satisfactorily assessed" in any area (educational, vocational, or personal life skills), such that no more questions need to be asked for planning or instruction, then that student essentially has been declared a static, dehumanized object for the school to handle as it chooses. That is an unacceptable position to take.

4. Use multiple types and levels of assessments. No single assessment approach in transition planning is adequate. The variety of life demands on students for adjustment in school, at home, and in the community indicates the need for a variety of assessment approaches for planning how the students can best meet those demands. Standardized, nonstandardized, quantitative, qualitative, group, individual, educational, noneducational, professional, and nonprofessional approaches each have some value at certain points and for certain needs.

5. Think of assessment procedures in terms of efficiency as well as effectiveness. A few carefully selected assessment procedures may be more efficient and effective than an extensive array of instruments, forms, and scores based on a hit-or-miss approach. Batteries of tests or assessment procedures routinely administered to all students may be not only inappropriate but also inefficient. Assessments that cover a wide range of outcome areas are excellent for screening purposes, but whenever the results of such procedures are too general or not indicative of present level of performance, more specific choices of assessment must follow.

6. Develop a transition assessment approach that is gender/culture/language fair as well as gender/culture/language enhanced. Transition assessment that meets the challenges of multicultural populations requires careful thought, as evidenced by the cultural bias in traditional cognitive and academic assessment. A great risk of cultural bias also exists in assessing nonacademic knowledge and skills, as well as preferences and interests, when the process is approached from a white, middle-class orientation to life.

7. Organize assessment data for easy access in IEP planning and instructional programming. Good information that goes unrecorded and resides solely in the memory or inaccessible files of school personnel is not usable information. Current recommended practices of portfolio assessment for students and families and well-organized student assessment folders at school are relevant in transition assessment. Some redesign of a school's forms or portfolio formats will be required, in most cases, to accommodate the new sources of transition assessment data.

8. Broaden the focus of transition assessment to add an emphasis on assessing the ecology of future living, working, and educational environments, including the natural supports in these environments.

9. Move from dictating how to assess the individual and telling him or her what the results mean, to involving the individual and the family in the design and implementation of the assessment process and deciding together what implications the results have for the individual's future.

10. Move from a set assessment sequence involving the same assessment for all students to one that is individualized based on the future living, working, and educational environments identified by the individual and family.

11. Promote the belief that transition assessment is a responsibility of all special education professionals, not something done solely by the transition specialist or job placement personnel. Integrate competencies related to transition assessment into coursework for all personnel certified to work with secondary special education students. Specific transition assessment coursework must be included in preparation programs for those focusing specifically on the area of transition or vocational preparation. Those individuals preparing to serve as vocational assessment specialists or vocational evaluators should be certified by and meet the Knowledge and Performance Areas required by the Commission on Certification of Work Adjustment and Vocational Evaluation Specialists (CCWAVES).

12. Integrate efforts in transition assessment with those of adult service providers. This must include involving them in the transition assessment process and structuring the assessment conducted in school so that it provides the relevant information needed for adult providers to serve individuals with disabilities more effectively. This must also include summarizing the results of ongoing assessment and, with the individual's and family's permission, transferring these results to the adult providers who will be continuing the transition support.

13. View assessment as a critical component of the transition planning process. The assessment results must provide information on the decisions that need to be made. The assessment questions must flow from the information that is needed to assist the individual and his or her family in making the transition to the living, working, and educational environments they have identified.

Conclusion

The need for workable transition assessment procedures for students with disabilities is urgent. Even as professionals become more sophisticated about assessment, planning, and program and service delivery, new questions arise about how to do each task better and meet federal mandates. Still, the IDEA mandate for IEP planning did not necessarily call for novel kinds of assessment and planning. Common sense and using available assessment procedures and results would be an encouraging start. There is the need, however, to look at educational assessment and the boundaries of "present level of educational performance" more openly. Fortunately, some existing instruments, procedures, and guidelines do exist that can be used immediately while better systems are being developed. The challenge will be to accomplish quality transition-referenced assessment in the context of all the other demands on educators for better outcomes with students with disabilities across all age levels. The key to this challenge is determining the nature of "better outcomes" for each of those age levels. The way to do that is through sound assessment practices involving a variety of school personnel, with students and their families actively participating.

We firmly believe that transition assessment is not just vocational assessment or career assessment with a new name. It is also not a totally new way of conducting assessment. Transition assessment builds on the concepts of vocational evaluation and assessment as well as career assessment. It broadens the focus of assessment efforts to all aspects of adult life and to the shift from one stage of life to another. Assessment must be an integral part of the transition process. We must also coordinate our efforts closely with the overall assessment process for the student; we can no longer function as an island within the educational system. In particular, transition assessment must tie in directly to the standards-based reform efforts occurring nationally and in each state, district, and school building.

IDEA 2004 mandates that for students age 16 and older, the IEP must include appropriate, measurable, postsecondary goals that are based on age-appropriate transition assessments. The transition assessment process we have described in this chapter provides a framework for you to examine your current or future assessment practices and to focus on methods that will assist students in identifying appropriate employment, postsecondary education, independent living, community functioning, and personal and social outcomes for adult life. In addition, professionals must work with students and their families so that they are actively involved in the transition assessment process. In this way, goals and outcomes can periodically be updated and changed as life roles continue to emerge.

As Sitlington, Neubert, and Leconte (1997) stated, the transition assessment process must allow students, families, and professionals an opportunity to participate in assessment activities that are conducted in a variety of natural environments and that address the multiple outcomes associated with the transition process.

6 Transition to Employment

We cannot cross a bridge until we come to it; but I always like to lay down a pontoon ahead of time.

—Bernard M. Baruch

The transition of youths with disabilities to employment is a key component of all of the transition models presented in Chapter 1. At times, this transition occurs directly from high school; other times, it occurs after postsecondary education or training, or after a time as a full-time homemaker. The 2004 National Organization on Disability/Harris Survey of Americans with Disabilities found the following information on employment and closely related areas of adult life:

- Only 35 percent of people with disabilities reported being employed full or part time, compared to 78 percent of those who do not have disabilities.
- Three times as many live in poverty, with annual household incomes below $15,000 (26 percent vs. 9 percent of those without disabilities).
- People with disabilities are twice as likely to drop out of high school (21 percent vs. 10 percent).
- Individuals with disabilities are twice as likely to have inadequate transportation (31 percent vs. 13 percent), and a much higher percentage go without needed health care (18 percent vs. 7 percent).
- Life satisfaction for people with disabilities also trails, with only 34 percent indicating that they were very satisfied with their lives, compared to 61 percent of those without disabilities.

National and statewide follow-up studies of young adults with disabilities found that the individuals with disabilities were employed at rates ranging between 50 and 60 percent. A high percentage of those employed were employed in part-time, low-status jobs and received few fringe benefits. The encouraging news is that unemployment rates *do* decrease the longer the young adults are out of school. In addition, studies have found that transition education and services *do* decrease the unemployment rate for individuals with disabilities (Frank & Sitlington, 1997, 1998).

The transition to employment is closely intertwined with the transition to postsecondary education and training and life in the community. As Rogan, Grossi, and Gajewski (2002), stated: "Work is a central component of a quality adult life. Employment provides a source of income, enhances self-esteem, provides important social connections, and allows people to fulfill their duties as contributing, tax-paying citizens" (p. 104).

As you probably well know, where one lives often determines the boundaries of employment possibilities. Conversely, seeking a certain job often determines where one will live. In the same way, a certain job determines whether postsecondary education or training is needed. Conversely, the amount of education or training a person has determines the range of jobs open to him or her. Because of this, the knowledge and skills required for a successful transition to employment involve all nine of the knowledge and skills domains of the Comprehensive Transition Education Model presented in Chapter 1. In addition, the process of actual transition to employment settings involves all of the education and service delivery systems presented in the Comprehensive Transition Services Model, also discussed in that same chapter.

The focus of this chapter is on the preparation of youths with disabilities with the experiences and skills needed to make the transition to employment, whenever that transition occurs. The content of this chapter is closely coordinated with that of Chapter 11, which focuses specifically on the placement, training, and supervision of adolescents with disabilities on exploration, training, or employment sites. This chapter discusses the instructional content needed to prepare students for the transition to employment, the principles and approaches to delivering work-based learning, program models for delivering work-based learning, and issues in preparing students for the transition to employment. A list of resources and websites is provided on the companion website to help you in working with students transitioning to employment.

As you prepare individuals with disabilities to function effectively in the workplace, you will face a number of challenges: (1) the changing nature of the workplace and the increasing demand for employees who possess social, academic, and occupational skills; (2) the growing number of students leaving school without these skills; and (3) the failure of the general education high school curriculum to address these areas (Benz, Yovanoff, & Doren, 1997).

The nature of occupations has and will change dramatically. In the new economy, the number of high-paying, blue-collar jobs available to workers with high school diplomas is shrinking. New job creation has been concentrated on knowledge jobs rather than production or extraction jobs, such as farming and mining. Farm and factory jobs have actually suffered job loses

(Carneval & Desrochers, 2002). As Carnevale and Desrochers stated, the demand for specific vocational skills has been augmented with a growing need for general skills, including reasoning abilities, general problem-solving skills, and behavioral skills. Cognitive styles, such as how workers handle success and failure on the job, are also positively related to job success. Occupational and professional skills, however, are also still needed.

Content for Instruction

Preparing any student for the transition to employment requires instruction and hands-on experiences in all of the knowledge and skill domains of the Comprehensive Transition Education Model presented in Chapter 1. There are also a number of compentency lists that may help you focus on the content that you may want to address in preparing your current or future students. The other models presented in Chapter 1 often contain lists of competencies. In addition, Clark, Patton, and Moulton (2000) provided a detailed list of competencies organized by the same knowledge and skill domains used in the Comprehensive Transition Education Model. Appendix 4B on the companion website also presents a list of student competencies and indicators organized under the following areas: self-knowledge, educational and occupational exploration, and career planning. These were developed by the National Occupational Information Coordinating Committee (1996), and are divided into elementary, middle/junior high school, high school, and adult competencies.

We have found that one of the most effective methods of approaching the knowledge and skills needed by youths in preparation for employment is to focus on three major areas: (1) occupational awareness, (2) employment-related knowledge and skills, and (3) specific occupational knowledge and skills. We will discuss each of these in the following sections. The sources listed in the previous paragraph, and in the Resources section of the companion website, may be of help to you in identifying competencies to cover in each of these areas.

Occupational Awareness

Figure 6.1 presents a Career Development Checklist that highlights some of the competencies needed by students, organized by the major phases of career education discussed in Chapter 1. These phases are (1) career awareness, typically beginning at the elementary level; (2) career exploration, usually starting at the middle school/junior high level; (3) career preparation, commonly beginning in high school; and (4) career assimilation, focusing on the transition of the student into life as a young adult (Brolin & Loyd, 2004). The career awareness competencies contained in this figure illustrate many of the typical types of occupational awareness information. Part of the problem in specifying exactly

FIGURE 6.1   Career Development Checklist

Career Awareness

- Can identify parents' and other family members' jobs.
- Can describe what parents and others do on their jobs.
- Can name and describe at least 10 different occupations.
- Can describe how people get jobs.
- Can describe at least three jobs to investigate.
- Can discuss what happens if adults cannot or do not work.
- Can identify why people have to get along with each other to work.

Career Exploration

- Can discern the difference between a job and a career.
- Can identify three ways to find out about different occupations.
- Can state at least three things they want in a job.
- Can identify the steps in finding a job.
- Can identify at least three careers they want to explore.
- Can state preferences for indoor versus outdoor work, solitary work versus working with others, and working with their hands and tools/machines versus working strictly with their minds.
- Can identify how to get applications and how to complete them.
- Can discuss why interviews are important.
- Can identify their strengths, abilities, skills, learning styles, and special needs regarding work or specific jobs.

Career Preparation

- Can identify career/vocational courses they want to take in school.
- Can describe the educational and work requirements of specific careers and jobs.
- Can identify where education and training can be obtained.
- Can explain steps in acquiring the skills necessary to enter a chosen field or job.
- Can describe entry level skills, course or job requirements, and exit level competencies to succeed in courses.
- Can identify community and educational options and alternatives to gaining education and employment in a chosen field.
- Can identify the worker characteristics and skills in working with others that are required in a chosen field or job.

Career Assimilation

- Can identify steps to take if they want to advance in their place of employment.
- Can identify educational benefits and ways of gaining additional training through their employment.
- Can explain fields that are related to their current work in which they could transfer.
- Can identify ways to change jobs without losing benefits or salary.
- Can describe appropriate ways of leaving or changing jobs and companies.
- Can relate their skills to other occupations or avocations.
- Can explain retirement benefits.
- Can identify and participate in leisure activities that they can pursue after they retire.

Source: From *Assess for Success: Handbook on Transition Assessment* by Patricia L. Sitlington, Debra A. Neubert, Wynne Begun, Richard C. Lombard, and Pamela J. Leconte, 1996, Arlington, VA: The Council for Exceptional Children. Permission is granted to reproduce this page.

what information should be taught, and when, is the overall issue of scope and sequence in schools' curricula. Established scope and sequence for any instructional content area is rare. The area of occupational awareness is a good example of this. Chapter 4 discussed this area as part of elementary and middle school instruction. Clark, Carlson, Fisher, Cook, and D'Alonzo (1991) have detailed the kinds of information that children and youths with disabilities need to learn, beginning in the early childhood years: occupational roles, occupational vocabulary, occupational alternatives, and basic information related to some realities of the world of work. Each of these areas will be briefly covered in the following paragraphs.

Occupational Roles.   An occupational information program should provide learning experiences that result in new or expanded awareness of possible roles for students with disabilities. In producer/worker roles, the possibility of productive work, including paid and unpaid work, must be stressed. This includes awareness of roles such as the work of the student as a learner, the work as a volunteer, the work at home as an unpaid family worker, or the work activities or productivity in which one might be involved as a part of daily living (washing clothes, polishing shoes, repairing a leaky faucet, etc). In consumer roles, there needs to be a stress on the variety of roles one can experience as a consumer, such as customer, patient, client, renter, borrower, user, and so on.

Occupational Vocabulary.   Students who are learning about their present and future occupational roles must develop vocabularies to acquire information basic to such learning. This is not unlike a student entering law or medical school. The first few months emphasize the language of the profession. It is said that students in both these professions must acquire up to 20,000 new words during their preparation. Vocabulary development is not limited to a reading vocabulary; it may also include comprehension in hearing vocabulary and speaking vocabulary. From this perspective, it is obvious that occupational information must include purposefully taught occupational vocabulary. This includes general vocabulary necessary for understanding concepts about employability and employment. Suggested vocabulary words are available from Fisher, Clark, and Patton (2004).

Occupational Alternatives.   Before getting too involved in any type of special career-development programming for youths, educators of students with disabilities should have some general perspective on occupational choice theory as it relates to normal growth and development. From a number of theories, only one is mentioned in brief here to serve as an example; it is one of the original theories of occupational choice. Ginzberg, Ginsburg, Axelrad, and Herma (1951) studied the occupational choice process and concluded that it is a developmental process. They suggested that the occupational decision-making process occurs in three basic stages or periods: fantasy, tentative choice, and realistic choice. They further suggested that the process involves a series of decisions made over a period of years, and that each step is meaningfully related to what has been decided before. The entire process is characterized by a continuous compromise among many factors—abilities, education, social status, age, physical and mental characteristics, geography, and so on. Some people have to compromise little, others a great deal.

Career education content in the curriculum must include a component of occupational information that relates to occupational choice and awareness of occupational alternatives in a way that provides keen sensitivity to students' needs for self-esteem. It is not unusual for high school youths to say that they want to be professional basketball players, movie stars, or rock singers. Rather than be overly concerned with such verbal behaviors, teachers and counselors need to respond with occupational information that encourages any stated desire to want to work or be productive in a legitimate occupation. Teachers and parents should elicit from the students the reasons underlying their stated occupational choices and begin the process of providing information to the students that affirms or challenges their understanding of what they think they want and what the occupation demands. Sometimes the reasons students give for a fantasy choice are very helpful in suggesting other alternatives.

Basic Information on Realities of the World of Work. There is a point at which providing basic occupational information about the world of work to students with disabilities becomes problematic. On one hand, the goal is to encourage students to want to work; on the other hand, educators have to be forthright in pointing out some of the negative realities of work. This section presents some of the realities—both positive and negative—that are especially important for students with disabilities to know.

Reality 1. North American society in general, and the United States in particular, is a work-oriented society. It values work and those who are workers. No one can be directly compelled legally to work in U.S. society, except those few who are ordered by the courts to labor as a punishment for some crime. Even so, there are many formal and informal elements of society operating to make people into workers. For many, the system is so effective that unemployment produces high levels of anxiety, personal guilt, or feelings of worthlessness. For persons with disabilities, these feelings may be heightened, even though they may be able to reason that factors beyond their control are responsible for their unemployment.

Some argue that the leisure ethic has replaced the work ethic in U.S. society. Even though in the past several years the media have shown more evidence of worker alienation, an increase in leisure alternatives, and a heavy emphasis on leisure and recreation, the traditional meaning of work is still dictated by the power structure and is still espoused by major societal institutions. Moreover, the fact that most people cannot have any access to leisure or the necessities of life without some means of purchasing them leads people to seek employment. As long as these facts remain, this reality should be communicated to youths in school as part of their occupational information.

Reality 2.   Work, whether paid or unpaid, occurs in a particular locale: the factory, the store, the office, the construction site, the shop, the clinic, or the home. Work can occur in the home for an increasing number of occupations (cottage industries, artist, writer, telemarketer, etc.), but by and large a person must go outside the home to work. This fact has two important implications for individuals with disabilities. First, one must be mobile in order to get to work. This requires a set of competencies regarding travel that is critical for getting to the work setting. Choices of work alternatives may be influenced by this reality alone. A second implication is that work is most frequently performed in a public place. A place has limitations on privacy; it usually has a set of socially expected behaviors, and there are formal or informal standards for dress and social behaviors.

Whether these realities are positive or negative to an individual depends on whether the individual is attracted to or uninterested by the nature of work that deals with location. One person might want to work alone at home, whereas another works primarily for the social interaction or the status that might go with a particular locale and its status, behavioral expectations, uniforms, and the like. Choices by one individual may involve no compromises; for another, it might involve significant compromise.

Occupational information about these realities is necessary in preparing youths with disabilities for work. Information on mobility requirements, transportation alternatives, and skills needed for use of transportation options are important curriculum content. Occupational information about the expectations of different kinds of work environments in public places for appearance, dress, speech or language, interpersonal relations, and social etiquette provides additional knowledge for students in entering these new and unfamiliar settings.

Reality 3.   Paid work is largely impersonal work. Work for which there is no pay may or may not be impersonal, depending on its nature; the personalized relationships associated with play, recreation, or love are not expected on a job in most situations. In fact, they may be forbidden. This is one reality that youths may have already been exposed to indirectly at home when they detect a different kind or set of expectations by a parent when the parent tells the child to perform a household chore. The child learns that the parent becomes the "boss" and has expectations about *what* is accomplished, *how well* it is accomplished, and, in some instances, *in what way* it is accomplished. The parent temporarily becomes an impersonal work supervisor and acts out a role that is the norm in the work world.

The reality of working for relative strangers who are "all business" may be discouraging to those adolescents who have strong needs for more personal relationships. Although exposing them to this reality runs the risk of seeing them reject the notion of working, it is even more of an injustice to ignore the reality or, worse, distort reality so that they build up unrealistic expectations about the nature of work. Adult service providers have been critical of special educators who not only do not teach this reality but teach the students that they are special and do not have to measure up in performance. They assert that special education teachers tend to reward their students even when the students do not perform satisfactorily.

If students with disabilities have experienced overprotectiveness from teachers or parents, the impersonality of work may provide them with their first opportunity to produce and be judged honestly on the quality and quantity of their work. Even if the objective opinion of the employer is more negative than feedback from school or home, many young people find the honesty refreshing and motivating. In these cases, the reality of paid work relating to impersonality may prove a positive factor in their work experience. For some, it may be their first experience where the disability is less important than productivity. How many people have you known in your life who might have been voted "least likely to succeed" while they were in school but who blossomed and achieved when given a fair chance to perform in the work world?

Reality 4. Work has several reward systems. Paid work obviously has the reward of getting money, but unpaid work may provide the reward of saving money—that is, not having to pay someone else to do the work. There are other rewards of work, however, that should be mentioned. Some people see the value of work as offering them the opportunity to be of service, an opportunity to pursue interests and abilities, a means of meeting people, a way of avoiding boredom, or a chance to gain or maintain self-respect or self-esteem.

Youths need to know that people work for money but that they work for other things also. The question, What's in it for me? is not inappropriate as students begin to sort out their values and establish a basis for being able to verbalize, "I want to work because . . . ."

Reality 5. Work is bound by time. Most workers have starting times and ending times. Certain times are set aside for breaks, for eating, or for cleanup. Many jobs are based on payment for certain hours, with extra payment for overtime. Even when pay is based on piecework, the individual is racing against time to produce or complete as many pieces as possible. There are job benefits that relate to time off and there are penalties or sanctions against being late or slow. To waste time at work is always frowned upon, and if it is chronic behavior, it may be grounds for dismissal from the job.

An inability to discipline oneself to meet time demands or constraints is one of the most serious obstacles to adjustment to work. This is frequently an especially difficult area for some individuals who have trouble relating to time concepts. It may also be an obstacle to those youths who believe that people who are slaves to time schedules are irrationally compulsive. Nevertheless, although one might appreciate some students' resistance to the hectic, time-oriented pace of living in the United States, the reality exists, and their understanding of the system and possible alternatives to it must be taught as a part of occupational information.

Reality 6. Work is seldom performed in complete isolation or independence. Even with the increasing number of occupations that allow people to work at home, most work involves two or more people who interact in various ways. One of the most important of these interactions is the worker to the supervisor. Others are the interaction with fellow workers, customers, and subordinates. Depending on the size and complexity of the work setting, a number of interpersonal reactions are required that may be more critical to staying on that job than is the ability to perform the work tasks.

Expected behaviors in work interactions may not be formally communicated, but they are communicated nevertheless through modeling, the worker grapevine, and events that occur that illustrate the rewards or penalties meted out to workers. People need to learn these basic expectations so they can develop a response system that shows a balance between dependence and independence in job performance (worker-supervisor interactions) and between the intimate and the casual (employee-fellow worker and employee-customer interactions).

Although interpersonal and social interactions are a part of most work environments, the reality of having to work for or with other people is not always a demanding factor that sets up a person with disabilities for adjustment problems or failure. This aspect has the potential also for providing the support and positive reward of working that help an employee with disabilities keep a job. The personal rewards of an identity at least at one place outside the home can be significant. Many people, with and without disabilities, look for any possible social interactions on the job that compensate for the loneliness of nonwork hours.

Reality 7. Work settings, like individual workers, rarely exist in isolation. As societies have moved from agrarian work settings to modern, industrial work settings, there has been an increasing dependence and interdependence among workers and work groups. Producers of goods require the services of workers in raw materials, manufactured goods for tools and equipment, transportation services, marketing and distribution services, and business and office services. Periodically, they may need workers in the building trades, communication and media field, custodial and maintenance services, health services, and public services. Likewise, any one of these work groups will have dependent or interdependent relationships with one or more of the others.

Students should become aware of these relationships in order to understand the importance of all types of work groups and to combat some of the occupational stereotyping and status problems that inevitably arise in a study of the world of work and their own fantasies and plans about being a part of it.

Reality 8.   Not everyone who wants to work can obtain work, nor can everyone who obtains work be employed in the work of his or her choice. This reality particularly affects individuals with disabilities. As stated earlier, youths with disabilities should be allowed to have their fantasies about doing various kinds of work, and too much reality too soon can be not only inappropriate but also destructive. Those who work with the student should not set their goals too low. The availability of assistive technology and other supports on the job have opened many doors to occupations that were previously closed to individuals with disabilities. A balance between realism and optimism should be encouraged.

Reality 9.   The choice of an occupational area or a specific job is not a permanent or binding action. Choices, whether made with any compromises or not, can be reconsidered. Most people who make choices about job opportunities at the beginning of their careers do so with the view that most jobs will temporarily meet certain needs and preferences now, but movement up or out of the occupational situation is not only probable but also desirable. The emphasis that more or less self-actualized professionals in school and adult service agencies place on making the "right" occupational choice may send the "wrong" message. That is, young people with disabilities may get the message that because the world of work is so tough and that people with disabilities have to prove themselves even more convincingly than people without disabilities, it is absolutely imperative that they choose the right job the first time.

Students with disabilities should be given the facts about the desirability of exploring one's interests and preferences in several occupations and the assurance that most people in the workforce have worked at a number of different kinds of jobs. They also should be given some of the disadvantages of job hopping without any pattern of occupational development or responsibility in leaving jobs inappropriately. Educators and adult service providers need to remember that what is myth or reality to an adolescent regarding occupational choices and job selection is difficult to know without probing for beliefs and levels of understanding. Nothing can be assumed for any one student.

In summary, individuals must begin to come to grips as early as possible with the realities of the world of work so that coping with or challenging those realities will be easier later. These realities must be introduced gradually and must include encouragement as well as cautious, but realistic, optimism.

Employment-Related Knowledge and Skills

The area of employment-related knowledge and skills is often called *work habits and attitudes.* There is hardly an end to a description of all the employment-related information that one could use in choosing an occupation, seeking training or employment in that occupation, knowing what is required to maintain employment by performing the work routine adequately, and handling problems that may arise on the job.

The curriculum models covered in Chapter 1 and the other competency lists referred to at the beginning of this chapter all contain competencies related to this area. These competencies can be organized in a number of different ways, but by and large they relate to the general areas of finding and keeping a job. Of course, the area of keeping a job is one of the most challenging; it entails skills in relating to co-workers, supervisors, and customers, as well as being on time and staying on task.

Specific Occupational Knowledge and Skills

A number of sources of competencies and specific occupational skills are needed for the transition to employment. Perhaps one of the most widespread and organized efforts related to skills needed in the workplace was undertaken by the Secretary's Commission on Achieving Necessary Skills (SCANS). This group was established in February 1990 to examine the demands of the workplace and to provide suggestions on how to prepare the current and future workforce. Commission members included representatives from the nation's schools, businesses, unions, and government. Specifically, the commission was directed to advise the Secretary of Labor on the type and level of skills required to enter employment.

Figure 6.2 presents the three foundation skills areas and five basic competency areas identified by SCANS. The Resources section on the companion website lists a number of the SCANS documents. Refer to them for a more in-depth explanation of these areas, along with practical ideas on how to prepare your students with these skills. More detailed information on SCANS and SCANS documents is also available on their website (www.ttrc.doleta.gov/SCANS/).

Another source, the Vocational Technical Education Consortium of States (V-TECS), has published over 130 curriculum guides for approximately 250 different job titles. These guides have a standardized format for tasks, tools, performance standards, and support materials. They are organized into an easy-to-read outline format, with diagrams, vocabulary, and step-by-step directions. Each state in the consortium develops new guides and revises old guides as a function of their areas of established expertise. In return, they are then allowed to use guides developed by other members. The Mid-America Vocational Curriculum Consortium and the American Association of Voca-

FIGURE 6.2 **Foundation Skills and Basic Competency Areas Identified by the Secretary's Commission on Achieving Necessary Skills (SCANS)**

A Three-Part Foundation

Basic Skills: Reads, writes, performs arithmetic and mathematical operations, listens and speaks

A. *Reading*—Locates, understands, and interprets information in prose and in documents such as manuals, graphs, and schedules

B. *Writing*—Communicates thoughts, ideas, information, and messages in writing; and creates documents such as letters, directions, manuals, reports, graphs, and flow charts

C. *Arithmetic/Mathematics*—Performs basic computations and approaches practical problems by choosing appropriately from a variety of mathematical techniques

D. Listening—Receives, attends to, interprets, and responds to verbal messages and other cues

E. *Speaking*—Organizes ideas and communicates orally

Thinking Skills: Thinks creatively, makes decisions, solves problems, visualizes, knows how to learn, and reasons

A. *Creative Thinking*—Generates new ideas

B. *Decision Making*—Specifies goals and constraints, generates alternatives, considers risks, and evaluates and chooses best alternative

C. *Problem Solving*—Recognizes problems and devises and implements plan of action

D. *Seeing Things in the Mind's Eye*—Organizes, and processes symbols, pictures, graphs, objects, and other information

E. *Knowing How to Learn*—Uses efficient learning techniques to acquire and apply new knowledge and skills

F. *Reasoning*—Discovers a rule or principle underlying the relationship between two or more objects and applies it when solving a problem

Personal Qualities: Displays responsibility, self-esteem, sociability, self-management, and integrity and honesty

A. *Responsibility*—Exerts a high level of effort and perseveres towards goal attainment

B. *Self-Esteem*—Believes in own self-worth and maintains a positive view of self

C. *Sociability*—Demonstrates understanding, friendliness, adaptability, empathy, and politeness in group settings

D. *Self-Management*—Assesses self accurately, sets personal goals, monitors progress, and exhibits self-control

E. *Integrity/Honesty*—Chooses ethical courses of action

(continued)

tional Instructional Materials are other sources of jointly developed curricula (Evers & Elksnin, 1998).

Many states have developed lists of competencies associated with vocational areas. These are usually developed by committees of industry representatives and vocational teachers. Consult your state department to see what is available in your state. If you are currently teaching, also contact vocational education or other school-to-work staff in your school.

FIGURE 6.2   Continued

Five Competencies

Resources: Identifies, organizes, plans, and allocates resources

A. *Time*—Selects goal-relevant activities, ranks them, allocates time, and prepares and follows schedules
B. *Money*—Uses or prepares budgets, makes forecasts, keeps records, and makes adjustments to meet objectives
C. *Material and Facilities*—Acquires, stores, allocates, and uses materials or space efficiently
D. *Human Resources*—Assesses skills and distributes work accordingly, evaluates performance and provides feedback

Interpersonal: Works with others

A. *Participates as Member of a Team*—Contributes to group effort
B. *Teaches Others New Skills*
C. *Serves Clients/Customers*—Works to satisfy customer's expectations
D. *Exercises Leadership*—Communicates ideas to justify position, persuades and convinces others, responsibly challenges existing procedures and policies
E. *Negotiates*—Works toward agreements involving exchange of resources, resolves divergent interests
F. *Works with Diversity*—Works well with men and women from diverse backgrounds

Information: Acquires and uses information

A. *Acquires and Evaluates Information*
B. *Organizes and Maintains Information*
C. *Interprets and Communicates Information*
D. *Uses Computers to Process Information*

Systems: Understands complex interrelationships

A. *Understands Systems*—Knows how social, organizational, and technological systems work and operates effectively with them
B. *Monitors and Corrects Performance*—Distinguishes trends, predicts impacts on system operations, diagnoses systems' performance and corrects malfunctions
C. *Improves or Designs Systems*—Suggests modifications to existing systems and develops new or alternative systems to improve performance

Technology: Works with a variety of technologies

A. *Selects Technology*—Chooses procedures, tools, or equipment including computers and related technologies
B. *Applies Technology to Task*—Understands overall intent and proper procedures for setup and operation of equipment
C. *Maintains and Troubleshoots Equipment*—Prevents, identifies, or solves problems with equipment, including computers and other technologies

Source: From *What Work Requires of Schools: A SCANS Report for America 2000* (pages 12 and 16) by the Secretary's Commission on Achieving Necessary Skills, 1991, Springfield, VA: National Technical Information Service, Operations Division. NTIS Number: PB92-146711.

Delivering Instructional Content

Educators must determine for their school program what should be taught, to whom, and in what way. School personnel tend to approach such decisions in the easiest possible way. It is not uncommon to hear the expression, "We shouldn't reinvent the wheel." There is some truth to that. But if the result of that approach is to select the wheel that is the most fashionable, the least expensive, the most available, or the easiest to use, without consideration for size, durability, or appropriateness, it is better to choose a wheel that has not yet been invented.

There is considerable scope in the content described in the previous sections. It can be simplified and the tasks analyzed with priorities established for which content elements are the most critical for students with severe disabilities, or it can be open ended, reaching for the highest levels of cognitive acquisition for students with more mild disabilities. Ideally, schools should lay out a scope and sequence curriculum in this area for all students and ensure that all students have access to it. In many schools, hard decisions must be made about how students with disabilities can acquire this information.

If students with disabilities are being served primarily in the general education classroom, with support from special education personnel, you need to determine if content related to occupational awareness, employment-related knowledge and skills, and specific occupational knowledge and skills is available in one or more courses in the general education curriculum. If it is available, is it accessible to *every* student with disabilities, regardless of the level of disability? If the content is not accessible to your students, how can this content be made available to them? If some students in your program are being served outside of the general education classroom, the same questions need to be asked. You also need to examine how this content can best be delivered within the context of the special education delivery model or in conjunction with the general education program.

Unfortunately, these questions have not been asked as frequently as the basic question, Is occupational awareness and employment-related information so critical to include that one should sacrifice instructional time from basic academics? Many high school programs buy into the need for both academics and either career and technical education or community-based work experience options. The assumption is made that all the content just described will be included in the career and technical education classes or will be learned in on-the-job training, thus eliminating the need for occupational information being taught purposefully and systematically. We believe that this is a false assumption and that high schools must provide this content as professionally as possible, using all the pedagogy and technology at their disposal.

Principles and Approaches to Delivering Work-Based Learning

Work-based learning experiences are "activities at the high school level that involve actual work experience or connect classroom learning to work" (National School-to-Work Office, 1996, p. 64). A number of studies have found that the transition to employment can be positively affected by the work-based learning programs covered later in this section. Benz, Yovanoff, and Doren (1997) found that students with and without disabilities who had two or more work experiences during the last two years of high school, exited school with high social skills or high job search skills, or had no continuing vocational instruction needs one year out of school were two to three times more likely to be competitively employed one year out of school. Students with disabilities who possessed high reading, writing, or math skills were also two to three times more likely to be competitively employed than were students with low skills. The researchers also found that students with high career awareness skills and students who reported having no continuing instructional needs in vocational and personal social content areas were one and one-half times more likely to be productively engaged.

Phillips, Blustein, Jobin-Davis, and White (2002) found that opportunities for work-based learning and exploration greatly facilitated the development of work-related skills and knowledge. Hughes, Bailey, and Mechur (2001) discovered that programs funded under the school-to-work initiative had improved student attendance, academic achievement, and graduation rates, and had helped young people become prepared for employment in higher quality jobs with better wages. Kiser (1999) reported that students enrolled in school-to-work programs had higher grade-point averages and were more likely to graduate than their classmates who did not take part in these programs.

The National Longitudinal Study (NLTS; Wagner & Blackorby, 1996) found that students enrolled in any type of career and technical education were more likely to be competitvely employed and earning higher wages than students not enrolled in these programs. In addition, enrollment in career and technical education programs related to specific occupations resulted in lower dropout rates. Smith and Clark (1999) reported that youth apprenticeship programs contributed to improved student outcomes in two major areas: (1) students developed career goals that in most cases involved further education or advanced training and (2) students saw themselves as gaining a better sense of career paths and the steps along these paths. Griffith (2001) found that graduates who participated in work-based learning fared better than nonparticipants on a number of employment outcomes. In particular, career and technical education participants had higher earnings and reported greater relevance of their high school curriculum to their postsecondary education, training, and employment. In addition, career and technical education participants rated themselves better prepared in what to expect on the job and in knowing technical information about the job. Brown (2000) found that tenth- to twelfth-grade cohorts of Tech Prep participants had slightly higher annual attendance rates and lower annual dropout rates than those not involved in Tech Prep. In addition, Tech Prep students in their senior year had slightly higher graduation rates than nonparticipants, with increasing percentages completing college preparatory programs.

In the most recent study, the National Assessment of Vocational Education (U.S. Department of Education, 2004a) found that career and technical education had important short- and medium-term earning benefits for most students. In addition, NAVE found that over the last decade of academic reforms, secondary students who participated in CTE programs increased their academic course taking and achievement, making them better prepared for both college and careers than their peers were in the past. In fact, students who take both a strong academic curriculum and a CTE program of study may have better outcomes that those who pursue one or the other.

General Principles of Work-Based Learning Programs

Various principles, characteristics, and approaches should underlie any school program whose goal is to prepare youths to make the transition to employment. These will be presented first, before discussing some of the approaches to delivering work-based learning. Hamilton and Hamilton (1997) identified seven principles that make work a learning experience and provided the following recommendations related to implementing each principle:

1. Youths gain basic and high-level technical competence through work. Recommendations are to (a) identify work tasks that teach technical competence, (b) organize learning activities, and (c) design a multiyear learning plan that is increasingly challenging.
2. Youths gain broad technical competence and understand all aspects of the industry through rotation and projects. Recommendations are to (a) inform youths about all aspects of the industry, (b) rotate youths through several placements within the industry, and (c) design projects and activities that teach multiple skills and broad knowledge.
3. Youths gain personal and social competence in the workplace. Recommendations are to (a) recognize personal and social competencies as key learning objectives, (b) systematically teach personal and social competence in context, and (c) provide extra assistance to individual students as needed.
4. Workplace teachers convey clear expectations to youths and assess progress toward achieving them. Recommendations are to (a) state expectations for behavior and learning at the outset of the work experience; (b) regularly monitor and document the acquisition of competence; (c) provide feedback on progress to youths, school, families, and the business; (d) encourage youths to assemble a portfolio; and (e) use industry-wide standards to provide credentials that will go across different employment settings.
5. Youths learn from adults with formally assigned teaching roles. Recommendations are to (a) assign clear teaching roles and responsibilities

to personnel involved in the program; (b) specify teaching roles in job descriptions and performance assessments; and (c) orient, train, and support adults who teach.

6. Youths achieve high academic standards. Recommendations are to (a) set high academic standards, (b) specify courses and degrees related to the career area, and (c) open multiple options for postsecondary education.

7. Youths identify and follow career paths. Recommendations are to (a) provide opportunities for career exploration and information on related careers; (b) advise youths about career paths, coordinating planning with high school and college advisors and family members; and (c) pay particular attention to the transition to postsecondary.

Ascher (1994) identified a number of features of good cooperative education programs. Most, if not all, of the following features apply to all work-based learning programs:

■ Quality placements in which the student is allowed to perform work that both provides opportunities to develop new competencies and contributes to the productivity of the organization

■ Placement coordinators with appropriate occupational experience related to the specific industry, as well as professional preparation for operating a cooperative education program

■ Close supervision at the worksite by a training sponsor or supervisor, as well as a mechanism by which the training sponsor can share his or her professional experience with the student

■ An accurate and realistic description of the job for the student, as well as accurate expectations by the training sponsor

■ Strong links between job training and related instruction, including an individualized written training plan that is coordinated with the student's in-school curriculum

■ Frequent and specific informal and formal evaluations by the placement coordinator, with feedback and follow-up to improve performance

■ Involvement of parents or guardians

■ Placement of graduates in full-time positions or referrals for additional training, and follow-up of graduates after three and five years

■ Strong administrative support

Approaches to Delivering Work-Based Learning

Providing experience at the worksite is the core of all work-based learning programs. Whether you establish your own work-based learning program or work with an existing program, it will help if you understand the major approaches to providing work-based learning. These approaches may be found in programs with different titles. Focusing on the approach itself will help you better understand the goals and structure of the program, and whether it would be beneficial to your students.

One or more of the following approaches is typically used in programs providing work-based learning to students: (1) cooperative education, (2) student internships, (3) youth apprenticeships, and (4) school-based enterprises (National Center for Research in Vocational Education, 1995). The goal of these learning experiences is to allow learners to observe and perform hands-on work, develop work readiness skills, and learn to draw their own conclusions. Effective work-based learning is integrated with instruction (in school, on the job, or both), follows a training plan, and teaches all aspects of a particular industry or career. It is important that you have a general understanding of each of these approaches, so you can identify work-based learning programs that are already in existence in your current or future school. This will allow you to coordinate your efforts as much as possible with these programs, with the goal of integrating your students into programs that are appropriate to them. Your role can then be one of working with program staff and others to provide the necessary supports for your students to succeed.

Cooperative Education. Ascher (1994) defined *cooperative education* as "a program which combines academic study with paid, monitored and credit-bearing work" (p. 1). Cooperative education was established around the turn of the twentieth century as part of a movement to create experience-based education. This approach enhances traditional classroom or academic instruction by providing practical, work-based learning relevant to the learner's educational and career goals. Today, cooperative education is concentrated mainly in the vocational areas of marketing, trade and industry, and business (Ascher, 1994). A cooperative education placement generally lasts a year or less, with students working half a day and attending both traditional academic and vocational classes the remainder of the day.

Cooperative education typically has a classroom training component that is concurrent with or prerequisite to the off-campus training. In the off-campus component, the student is supervised by the on-site mentor or training sponsor, who is the primary source of instruction and feedback. The school program coordinator typically provides the on-campus instruction and monitors student progress via observations and conferences with the students and their mentors.

Student Internship Programs. The *School-to-Work Glossary of Terms* (National School-to-Work Office, 1996) defines *student internships* as "situations where students work for an employer for a specific period of time to learn about a particular industry or occupation. Students' workplace activities may include special projects, a sample of tasks from different jobs, or tasks from a single occupation. These may or may not include financial compensation" (p. 31). Internships provide structured work experience for students in a career field that is of interest to them (National Center for Research in Vocational Education, 1995). Although internships are usually short term, their duration varies along with the complexity of knowledge and skills the student is required to master.

Youth Apprenticeship Programs.   The National School-to-Work Office (1996) defined *registered apprenticeships* as

> those programs that meet specific federally approved standards designed to safeguard the welfare of apprentices. The programs are registered with the Bureau of Apprenticeship and Training (BAT), U.S. Department of Labor, or one of 27 State Apprenticeship Agencies or Councils approved by BAT. Apprenticeships are relationships between an employer and employee during which the worker, or apprentice, learns an occupation in a structured program sponsored jointly by employers and labor unions or operated by employers and employee associations. (p. 3)

Apprenticeship completers are perceived by their industry as having the highest level of craft, sometimes more than employees who have been graduated from college.

There was a movement in some states to develop and implement youth apprenticeship programs in order to meet the School-to-Work reform mandates (McKernan, 1994; Osterman & Iannozzi, 1993; Paris & Mason, 1995; Reisner et al., 1993). Often, however, these programs more closely resemble cooperative education programs than the traditional apprenticeship. *Youth apprenticeship* is defined by the *School-to-Work Glossary of Terms* (National School-to-Work Office, 1996) as "typically a multi-year program that combines school-and work-based learning in a specific occupational area or occupational cluster and is designed to lead directly into either a related postsecondary program, entry-level job, or registered apprenticeship program. Youth apprenticeships may or may not include financial compensation" (p. 65).

School-Based Enterprises.   A *school-based enterprise* is a school-sponsored, work-based learning opportunity in which a group of students (1) produce goods or services for sale or use by other people, (2) participate in multiple aspects of the enterprise, and (3) relate service and production activities to classroom learning. School-based enterprises must be student run. They give students real practice in entrepreneurship, accounting, budgeting, marketing, inventory control, and business-related skills. They also allow students to develop generic work skills in problem solving, communication, interpersonal relations, and learning how to learn in the context of work. A well-established example of a school-based enterprise program is the Junior Achievement model.

School-Based Approaches and Activities That Bridge across Classrooms and Workplaces

Most work-based learning programs include a special related class in which students are able to reflect on and integrate their job experiences, as well as obtain some of the employment-related and specific vocational skills needed for their vocational area. If the student is on the work site for the entire day, this instruction is provided by the supervisor on the job site. Some programs have a studio, which is a special kind of classroom. It provides students with a specific location in which they may work to complete a project or activity. Students have more space to work, enjoy greater freedom or movement, and bear more responsibility for the internal and external security and maintenance of the space. Teachers empower students through initial training and structuring work schedules and then act as roving floor supervisors, mentors, and technology troubleshooters. They become coaches, mentors, advisors, and supervisors in the learning process. Examples of programs in which students assume these roles are drafting and graphic arts.

In some work-based learning programs, the actual work site is operated by the school. Examples include construction programs that build a house and then sell it to someone in the community, as well as restaurants, automotive maintenance centers, and child-care centers operated by the school. Other examples would be school-based enterprises discussed in the previous section.

One major component of school-to-work programs is connecting activities. In addition, the National Center for Research in Vocational Education (1995) identified connecting activities that bridge classrooms and workplaces, including guidance and counseling, mentoring, job shadowing, guest speakers, and field trips. In the first type of activity, school counselors, teachers, and business representatives can work together to provide students with experiences early on in high school to determine their focus of study and later to assist with postsecondary decisions.

In most programs, the focus of mentoring is to guide the students who participate in work-based learning and to help structure their learning and contribution to the workplace. Mentors can provide a safe place for questions to be asked about life outside of school, in particular, work. Observing or shadowing a worker in an industry helps students understand the tasks performed in that industry, the knowledge and skills needed, and the work environment. Students have a chance to ask employees questions and reflect on their observations in the classroom. Both guest speakers and field trips tied to classroom learning can provide youths with exposure to a variety of industries, employers, and careers. This helps youths see the connections between what they are studying and the workplace and also helps with future planning.

Program Models for Delivering Work-Based Learning

A number of actual program models use one or more of the approaches presented in the previous section. Most of these models include both a classroom-based and a work-based component, along with activities that connect the two. All include the principles of work-based learning discussed in the previous section. These models may have specific names within your state or school district and may be funded by different funding streams. We will outline the basic components of each of the program models, but we encourage you to contact your state department of education and your local school-to-work and career and technical education staff to identify the specific program options available in your area. It is important that you determine the options available for all students, as well as those available solely for students with disabilities.

We would also encourage you to focus on integrating students with disabilities into the work-based learning programs available to all students in your district. As you do this, however, you will need to make sure that students are receiving the supports and accommodations they need to succeed in these programs. Mooney and Scholl (2004) found that half of the students with disabilities whom they interviewed in youth apprenticeship programs received far fewer supports and accommodations in their off-site classroom settings than they were used to receiving in their home schools. In addition, nearly three-quarters of the students did not receive any workplace accommodations. One of your roles as a special education professional should be to make sure that students with disabilities know how to advocate for the supports and accommodations they need in both the classroom and work-based components of these programs. The staff of these programs also need to be made aware of the best approach to providing these supports and accommodations. This is similar to the role you may play in working with academic programs.

Career and Technical Education (Formerly Vocational Education)

Vocational education is a term that traditionally has had very specific meaning. It has been a major part of the public education system since the Smith-Hughes Act of 1917. Evers and Elksnin (1998) provided an excellent history of vocational education in the United States; this history was also traced by Neubert (1997; see also Chapter 2 of this text).

The American Vocational Association (1998) defined *vocational education* as

> part of a program designed to prepare individuals for gainful employment as semiskilled or skilled workers, technicians, or subprofessionals in recognized

occupations and in new and emerging occupations, or to prepare individuals for enrollment in advanced technical education, but excluding any program to prepare individuals for employment in occupations generally considered professional or which require a baccalaureate or higher degree. (p. 73)

The focus of the field of vocational education is gradually shifting as it attempts to find its role within the standards-based reform movement and other systems change efforts occuring within the schools. The current title of career and technical education (CTE) builds on the previous title of vocational and technical education and the original title of vocational education.

Gray (2001) identified four main proposals that emerged from the literature related to the best role for high school CTE, within the current school reform initiatives:

1. *Integrated CTE:* A program of sequential occupational courses in a single labor market preparation area (e.g., business, health care) integrated with a program of sequential academic courses. The performance goal for this approach is general occupational competency and mastery of the traditional academic curriculum. The outcome goal is the transition from high school to postsecondary prebaccalaureate technical education or full-time employment.
2. *Traditional CTE:* A program of sequential occupational courses in a single labor market preparation area. The performance goal is entry-level occupational competence. The outcome goal is transition to full-time employment.
3. *Related Academics:* An instructional strategy of providing courses with broadened occupational content (clusters) related to traditional academic subjects, such as math and science. The performance goal is academic mastery. The outcome goal is transition to college.
4. *Common Academics:* Eliminating high school CTE altogether in favor of traditional academic course sequences. The performance goal is academic proficiency. The outcome goal is transition to college.

The National Assessment of Vocational Education (NAVE; U.S. Department of Education, 2004a) identified three types of courses offered by career and technical education: (1) specific labor market preparation (occupational education), which teaches skills and knowledge required in a particular occupation or set of related occupations; (2) general labor market preparation, which provides general employment skills that are not specific to any particular occupational area, such as courses in keyboarding; and (3) family and consumer sciences education, intended to prepare students for family and consumer roles outside the paid labor market, including consumer and home economics. Within the specific labor market preparation courses, the NAVE report identified 10 broad occupational program areas:

1. Agriculture (and Renewable Resources)
2. Business, including Business Services and Business Management
3. Marketing
4. Health Care
5. Protective Services (and Public Services)
6. Technology, including Computer Technology, Communication Technology, and Other Technology
7. Trade and Industry, including Construction, Mechanics and Repair, Precision Production, and Transportation
8. Food Service and Hospitality
9. Child Care and Education
10. Personal and Other Services

Career and Technical Education Program Options and Training Settings.
The three basic administrative arrangements for delivering the content of vocational education are (1) general high schools, (2) comprehensive high schools, and (3) vocational technical centers and career academies (Evers & Elksnin, 1998). General high schools provide programs in four or fewer vocational areas. Frequently, occupationally specific training is available in only two or three of the vocational training areas, along with some general industrial arts or homemaking. Comprehensive high schools house vocational programs in at least five of the vocational areas, along with traditional academic programs. Students typically attend vocational classes on campus for one to three periods (or up to half a day) each day. Classes are traditional lectures with reading assignments, homework, and tests. This training is alternated with actual hands-on instruction, supervised practice of skill development, and completion of projects in the relevant vocational laboratory or job site in the community. Examples of vocational laboratories range from a house built (and then sold on the market) by a construction program, to a restaurant run on or off the school grounds by the quantity foods program, to an auto service center run on campus by the auto mechanics program. If the hands-on experience is provided in community businesses, the program is usually called a *cooperative education program.*

Vocational-technical centers and career academies are stand-alone facilities, usually not located on the high school campus. These centers usually offer only vocational programs and academics associated with these programs. Students typically attend the center for half of each school day and then return to their home schools for traditional classes. Training options are usually limited to occupations that reflect local labor needs (Evers & Elksnin, 1998).

Cluster programs provide a way for vocational programs to deliver training that is not narrowly occupation specific. Cluster programs combine training in similar occupations in order for students to benefit from a broader knowledge and skills base—for example, a construction cluster may include carpentry, construction, plumbing, masonry, electrical technology, and air conditioning, heating, and refrigeration technology. Other clusters would include services, manufacturing, and transportation, or other areas of local need (Evers & Elksnin, 1998).

Tech Prep is another special model of CTE that is offered in many high schools. A key component of Tech Prep is a formal articulation agreement between high schools and postsecondary institutions that provides for a pathway from one to the other. The original Tech Prep design included a "2 + 2" approach, encompassing grades 11 and 12, plus two years of postsecondary education. Other models have also come into being, including "2 + 2 + 2," which incorporates an additional two years at a four-year college.

Instruction in career and technical education programs is the responsibility of career and technical education teachers. Support services to the student or the instructor may be provided by the special education professional, vocational resource teacher, or special needs vocational instructor. These services (sometimes called *vocational special needs services*) are available as a function of meeting the inclusion mandates in the Carl Perkins Vocational Education Act, as well as ongoing requirements of the Vocational Rehabilitation Amendments and the Americans with Disabilities Act. Individuals who staff these programs are usually either special educators who have skills and specialized training in vocational education, or vocational educators who have skills and training in working with students with disabilities. These instructors go by a number of job titles, such as *related vocational instructors, transition coordinators, job coaches,* and *vocational special needs instructors* (Evers & Elksnin, 1998). Special education professionals need to work alongside vocational instructors in integrated settings, just as they do in secondary academic classrooms. With this arrangement, students have the opportunity to be taught by instructors with training and experience in the specific vocational area and to work with peers who have no disabilities. They also have more vocational training options available to them, both in high school and postsecondary vocational training settings.

Support services to the student could include one or more of the following: audiotapes of readings, note-takers, interpreters, modifications of equipment, architectural accommodations, speech or communication assistance, instructional aids or equipment, peer tutoring, individualized contracts, support personnel, or transportation. Some students might also need additional support outside the classroom or shop in reading or math instruction in order to be successful in the regular program.

Characteristics of Career and Technical Education Programs That Need to Be Considered.   Career and technical education, then, is an established discipline, just as special education is its own discipline. Individuals who teach CTE courses are certified in that area, just as special educators are certified for their specific roles. Special educators can provide work-based learning, such as work experience or vocational training, but they are not providing CTE.

The content expertise and connections in the community that CTE educators have developed are invaluable to the transition of individuals with disabilities into adult life. As IDEA and other legislation encourages more cooperative efforts with general education, CTE is a natural partner for special education. There are, however, a few characteristics of CTE personnel and programs that require careful consideration as efforts are merged (Evers & Elksnin, 1998). First, CTE instructors are as diverse as the programs they support, especially at the postsecondary level. Business, agriculture, and consumer and home economics instructors are usually trained at the baccalaureate level, where one can major in that academic area. Most trade and industry instructors, however, acquire their expertise by working in their specialty field, and they are often not four-year college graduates. The background of CTE educators usually results in individuals who have broad content-area expertise but who have limited, if any, training in instructional methods (Office of Educational Research and Improvements, U.S. Department of Education, 1994).

Second, the goal of CTE is to train high-wage, highly skilled, technically oriented individuals. However, vocational teachers continually fight the perception that their programs are easier and of lower status than academic programs, and that they are the default track for students who cannot succeed in academic programs. In addition, the measure of a successful vocational program and its subsequent funding support is the number of students who become employed in their content area within a specific period of time. Because of these factors, some vocational educators are hesitant to accept students with disabilities into their programs.

Although youths with disabilities have learning characteristics that may hinder them in acquiring the more traditional aspects of CTE, there are also aspects of CTE that tend to enhance the acquisition of skills and knowledge. Vocational education tends to be tangible as well as goal and outcome oriented, and schooling is made relevant within the context of the world of work. In addition, a portion of the curriculum requires hands-on learning and site-based learning experiences that free students from the confines of the academic environment (Evers & Elksnin, 1998).

Vocational Student Organizations.   Vocational student organizations are an integral part of the vocational curriculum and should not be confused with social clubs. Vocational student organizations have as their primary focus the development of leadership skills. Many vocational programs have mandatory attendance requirements for these organizations. These groups also emphasize working on community projects, which helps facilitate the development of social and leadership skills and civic responsibility. The 10 vocational student organizations recognized by the United States Department of Education (Evers & Elksnin, 1998) are as follows:

1. National FFA Organization (FFA) (formerly Future Farmers of America)
2. National Young Farmers Education Association (NYFEA)
3. National Future Homemakers of America—Home Economics Related Occupations (HERO)
4. Future Business Leaders of America (FBLA)
5. Distributive Education Clubs of America (DECA)
6. Vocational Industrial Clubs of America (VICA)
7. Technology Student Association (TSA)
8. Business Professionals of America (BPA)
9. Health Occupations Students of America (HOSA)
10. National Postsecondary Agriculture Student Organization (NPASO)

School-to-Work Programs

The School-to-Work Opportunities Act of 1994 provided a major thrust for school-to-work (STW) programs in general education. The overall purpose of school-to-work transition programs is to prepare *all* students for work and further education and to increase their opportunities to enter first jobs in high-skill, high-wage careers. The federal School-to-Work Opportunities Act of 1994 defined *all students* to include disadvantaged students; students from diverse racial, ethnic, or cultural backgrounds; students with disabilities; school dropouts; and academically talented students (U.S. Department of Education, 1994). Although this Act sunset in 2002, there are still a number of programs in existence that were initially funded by this initiative.

The school-to-work transition systems in place in local districts offer a great deal of opportunity for individuals with disabilities. These students can be included in ongoing STW programs, although they may need additional support for some of the STW activities. This inclusion of students with disabilities in ongoing programs is in keeping with the local, areawide, and state initiatives to blend the special education and general education systems to serve *all* students.

School-to-work programs should include a variety of school-based and work-based learning opportunities through high school, including (1) career exploration and counseling; (2) academic and occupational instruction that is integrated and focused on high standards of achievement; and (3) a variety of structured work experiences that teach broad, transferable workplace skills (Benz, Yovanoff, & Doren, 1997).

The purpose of this section is to provide an overview of the STW programs found in many schools and the new components they added to the concept of work-based learning. We will organize our comments around the three major components of this system: (1) the school-based learning component; (2) the work-based learning component; and (3) connecting activities. Benz and Kochhar (1996) and Benz and Lindstrom (1997) cover these topics in much more detail. The National School-to-Work Learning and Information Center also has an Internet homepage (www.stw.ed.gov). You are encouraged to consult these sources for more information on this topic.

School-Based Learning.   As with all students, the school-based learning component of STW programs is one of the most critical for students with disabilities. Many students will have received some type of background through the classroom instruction that is often associated with experience-based career education programs or work experience programs offered through special education. These programs, however, often do not serve students with disabilities who are receiving most of their education in the general education classroom.

The National Center for Research in Vocational Education (1995) identified four alternative organizational approaches to work-oriented education in the school setting: (1) courses, (2) programs consisting of a number of courses, (3) schools within schools, and (4) commitment (restructuring) of an entire school. Courses are integrated curricula related to education for work. These courses are offered within a single classroom by a single teacher. Teachers within an academic or vocational discipline may work together to implement a program with coordinated or integrated coursework and special activities and services for students. Teachers might be organized within one academic area or across several academic or vocational courses. Schools within a school (SWS) are often called *career majors, clusters, houses,* or *academies.* They are designed as structured programs that are administratively distinct from other school programs. One of the ways in which SWS differs from other school programs is that teachers often have greater autonomy in designing courses, scheduling courses and students, and staffing their teams. The final option, school restructuring, occurs on a much larger scale than the organization of a single program or school within a school. School restructuring might involve setting up multiple programs or SWSs (i.e., forming clusters, pathways, or career majors).

The National Center for Research in Vocational Education (1995) provided information on two approaches to developing curriculum that focuses on learner outcomes, integrates academic and vocational curriculum, and blends the best instructional practices from both disciplines. These two approaches are (1) curriculum focused on specific industry and other work-related themes and (2) projects integrated into the ongoing academic curriculum. A *thematic curriculum* usually involves a single course or teacher and a new team that has usually not worked together before. In this approach, team members want to coordinate their curriculum, but not necessarily participate in joint projects. Often, however, they have the same students. In thematic curriculum units, the process begins with learner outcomes for each course where each course is integrated around the same theme. The team selects an industry theme and then aligns its course material. Team members work on learning activities (in their own courses) that integrate with one common theme. A common project may or may not result.

In the *integrated projects approach,* the instructional team has usually previously worked together on the curriculum. The team must consist of the same students, and team members must share the goal of wanting to move toward eliminating discipline boundaries and focus on joint projects and products. In integrated project units, the process begins with learner outcomes for the project or product and aims to incorporate them from each course. Learning activities that support the end project or product are designed for each course. Discipline boundaries may disappear, and a common project results.

The concept of a career major or a career pathway is central to the school-based learning component. The career pathway component of STW programs also offers a great opportunity to include students of all ability levels in exploring the same career area. This component allows lower-functioning students as well as higher-functioning students to work in the same career area. Sources of support for students with disabilities in regular STW programs are special education teachers, work experience coordinators, and other special education support staff, such as consultants. These professionals can work closely with general education staff to provide the support needed by students with disabilities to gain the most from regular STW programs.

Work-Based Learning Component. The second component of STW programs, work-based learning, consists of structured learning experiences for students, based in employment settings, that develop broad, transferable skills. This component emphasizes the importance of work and community environments as the context in which students with disabilities can learn and apply the academic and occupational knowledge and skills that they learn in the school-based component. Students with disabilities need real-world experiences in order to be more successful in the transition from school to the world of work. Providing students with these learning experiences will require the participation of students, parents, administrators, teachers, employers, and other school staff.

Connecting Activities. Connecting schools and the world of work does not occur naturally, so connecting activities are the third component in a STW program. Programs must build strong partnerships among secondary schools, postsecondary education institutions, employers, and community agencies. The student can no longer be the only thread to the world of work. All participants must be bound together to enhance outcomes for all students, especially students with disabilities. These connecting activities are focused on individual students, administrative personnel, and those activities that focus on both.

Individual students should be matched with a workplace mentor who will develop a relationship and give the student supports in the workplace to assist with the successful transition into the world of work. Students with disabilities must be matched with work-based learning opportunities that match their interests, abilities, and future goals. School-to-work programs do not end with graduation. Students must be provided with postprogram assistance to secure employment, continue their educational training, and link them with other community services that may be necessary to assure successful transitions.

Benz, Yovanoff, and Doren (1997) stated that special educators should work with their counterparts in the school-to-work movement to ensure the following:

1. Local programs should include (a) options for multiple pathways and time frames, (b) reasonable accommodations and support services, (c) relevant performance indicators, and (d) adequate training and technical assistance for all personnel.
2. Career exploration and planning should provide the foundation and framework for the school-based and work-based activities in which students participate.
3. Emphasis must be on integrating academic and occupational instruction, teaching this content in contextual settings, and holding students accountable for high standards of achievement in these areas.
4. Support services must be available to address the individual needs of students, especially students who are vulnerable to failure in postschool settings, and must be available to students not only during high school but also during the early transition years.

Specially Designed Work-Based Learning Programs

There are still a number of programs that are provided mainly to students with disabilities—to supplement the work-based learning programs in the general education curriculum. Evers and Elksnin (1998) listed a number of these "specially designed" vocational programs:

1. Career exploration
2. Cooperative work training
3. Student or school-based businesses
4. Job shadowing
5. Volunteer service learning experiences in the community
6. Classroom and school as the workplace

The wider the choice of school-to-work, career and technical education, and other work-based learning programs available in general education, the less need there should be for specially designed work-based learning programs. Students with disabilities are often placed in specially designed programs for one of two reasons: (1) no similar programs are available in general education or (2) even with supports, the student cannot succeed in the general education program.

The focus of programming for students with disabilities should be on including these students in general education programs related to training in occupational awareness, employment-related knowledge and skills, and specific occupational knowledge and skills, as well as providing them the needed supports to succeed in these programs. In establishing a specially designed program, one should incorporate the principles of work-based learning offered in the beginning of this chapter. In addition, it is probable that one would offer a modified or exact version of the approaches and program options discussed earlier. We encourage you to work closely with the school-to-work staff in your school who are offering these programs so that you can build on their expertise and coordinate your efforts with theirs. Use your principal to establish the logic of a single program, rather than segregated programs that duplicate efforts in the general education curriculum.

Supported Employment

Supported employment is a specific example of a specially designed program in which you may be involved if you are working with individuals with more significant disabilities. It incorporates all of the principles of other work-based learning programs, but it is specific enough in its approach that we believe it should be covered in more detail. In supported employment, you will be part of a team of vocational rehabilitation counselors, job coaches, case managers, other school support staff (e.g., occupational therapists, physical therapists, work experience coordinators, assistive technology specialists) and adult service provider staff.

As Wehman, Revell, and Brooke (2003) pointed out, the use of supported employment, "when intertwined with the philosophical depth of self-determination, effectively marries supports as a programmatic strategy with self-determination as a philosophical foundation" (p. 163). These authors outlined 9 basic supported employment values (see Figure 6.3). In addition, they identified 10 quality indicators for supported employment programs (see Figure 6.4). As can be seen from the list in Figure 6.4, the focus of supported employment is on community integrated jobs with commensurate wages and benefits. Supported employment's philosophical foundation and implementation strategies challenge the practice of providing services that remove people with disabilities from the mainstream of community activity.

The evolution of supported employment services has required families, educators, adult providers, employers, policy makers, and individuals with

FIGURE 6.3   **Supported Employment Values**

Value	Value Clarification
Presumption of employment	Everyone, regardless of the level or the type of disability, has the capability to do a job and the right to have a job.
Competitive employment	Employment occurs within the local labor market in regular community businesses.
Self-determination & control	When people with disabilities choose and regulate their own employment supports and services, career satisfaction will result.
Commensurate wages & benefits	People with disabilities should earn wages and benefits equal to that of co-workers performing the same or similar jobs.
Focus on capacity & capabilities	People with disabilities should be viewed in terms of their abilities, strengths, and interests rather than their disabilities.
Importance of relationships	Community relationships both at and away from work lead to mutual respect and acceptance.
Power of supports	People with disabilities need to determine their personal goals and receive assistance in assembling the supports for achieving their ambitions.
Systems change	Traditional systems must be changed to ensure customer control, which is vital to the integrity of supported employment.
Importance of community	People need to be connected to the formal and informal networks of a community for acceptance, growth, and development.

Source: From "Competitive Employment: Has It Become the First Choice Yet?" by P. Wehman, W. G. Revell, & V. Brooke, 2003, *Journal of Disability Policy Studies, 14*(3), p. 165. Copyright 2003 by PRO-ED, Inc. Reprinted with permission.

disabilities to examine their values (Wehman et al., 1998). Before the availability of supported employment, sheltered employment programs were valued as an alternative to staying home. The emphasis was on providing a reliable routine and a safe, well-supervised environment. As Wehman and colleagues (2003) pointed out, there are clear indicators of the progress achieved in developing the supports used by many individuals with significant disabilities to live and work more fully integrated within their home communities. Some sheltered workshops have downsized or closed, with an accompanying

FIGURE 6.4   Quality Indicators for Supported Employment Programs

Indicator	Example of Functional Measures
Meaningful competitive employment in integrated work settings	Employee with a disability is hired, supervised, and paid directly by business where job setting is located; receives wages/benefits commensurate with those of nondisabled co-workers.
Informed choice, control, and satisfaction	Employee selects own service provider and job coach, selects jobs and work conditions, and is satisfied with job and supports.
Level and nature of supports	Program is skilled in identifying workplace support options and developing those options.
Employment of individuals with significant disabilities	Program is serving individuals whose intermittent competitive work history, disability profile, functional capabilities, and other barriers to employment are truly reflective of people who need ongoing workplace supports to retain employment.
Amount of hours worked weekly	Program is achieving employment outcomes at 30 or more hours per week consistently; individuals receiving support are satisfied with their hours of competitive employment.
Number of persons from program working regularly	Program currently has a majority of its participants working in competitive employment; individuals receiving support are satisfied with their program of services.
Well-coordinated job retention system	Program maintains regular contact with its employed customers to monitor job stability and can respond effectively to both planned and unplanned job retention support needs; program replaces individuals who do not retain employment.
Employment outcome monitoring and tracking system	Program maintains an information system that readily provides information to its customers on employment status, longevity, wages, benefits, hours of employment, and jobs.
Integration and community participation	Employees with a disability work in jobs where the work environment facilitates physical and social interaction with co-workers; employees are satisfied with the quality of their work and community integration.
Employer satisfaction	Program viewed as an employment service agency rather than a human service provider; employers are seen as a customer of the service, and the program designs policies and procedures that are responsive to the business community.

Source: From "Competitive Employment: Has It Become the First Choice Yet?" by P. Wehman, W. G. Revell, & V. Brooke, 2003, *Journal of Disability Policy Studies, 14*(3), p. 166. Copyright 2003 by PRO-ED, Inc. Reprinted with permission.

selective reallocation of funds from segregated programs to programs focusing on integration in the community (Murphy, Rogan, Handley, Kincaid, & Royce-Davis, 2002).

For many years, nonintegrated or sheltered employment was approved as a potential employment outcome for individuals with a disability who received vocational rehabilitation services. However, on January 22, 2001, the Rehabilitation Service Administration of the U.S. Department of Education amended the regulations governing the State Vocational Rehabilitation Program to redefine the term *employment outcome* to mean "an individual with a disability working in an integrated setting" (State Vocational Rehabilitation Services Program, Final Rule, January 22, 2001). This is another step forward in focusing specifically on employment in integrated community-based settings.

Even with all of this progress, competitive employment is not always readily available to people with significant disabilities (Wehman et al., 2003). As the authors reported, there are still a much higher percentage of individuals with significant disabilities in day, work, and sheltered programs that are not competitive or work oriented, compared to those being served in supported employment.

Issues in Preparing Students for Transition to Employment

The companion website to this text contains a number of resources and websites that may be of help to you and your students as you work with them in making the transition to employment, regardless of their level of disability. We would urge you to work with exisiting programs in your building to provide work-based learning experiences to your students. As you design these experiences, you will need to address the issues that are presented in the following paragraphs.

Parental Values

Parents of adolescents with disabilities have a wide range of perspectives on the value of vocational training. The traditional view that a high school diploma represents basic academic competence persists, and some parents have a difficult time seeing vocational education or training as a major thrust of a high school course of study. Another variable is the degree to which parents will allow their child to make, or even believe that their child can make, independent occupational choices. Socioeconomic backgrounds, concern for status, and basic views about what a high school education should be about all have an effect on parents' aspirations for their children and the degree to which they can or will accept vocational training in high school, and, if so, what type of training is acceptable.

Postsecondary Vocational Training Opportunities in the Community

Educators as well as parents have a tendency to postpone vocational training as long as possible. One way that educators do this is to use the argument that the school does not need to provide any vocational offerings, or, at best, only a minimum of vocational offerings is needed because the community has strong postsecondary offerings available. Parents may use these same arguments with their sons and daughters, drawing on their own perceptions of the importance of academics at the high school level. The lack of postsecondary vocational programs, on the other hand, forces school boards and educators to look at vocational programming as an important component of secondary education. The number and kinds of students who might need or want such programs then have an effect on the range of program options in a vocational training continuum.

Philosophical Differences in the Field

The philosophical differences between advocates of academic versus vocational programming are not limited to regular and special educators. Some special educators view career and technical education and other vocational training alternatives as having lower status for students and possibly for themselves. This is found in all categories of teachers but is more common among special education personnel and families involved with students with disabilities. Philosophical differences over the value of academic versus employment preparation are probably the most challenging factors in getting training related to occupational awareness, employment, and specific occupational knowledge and skills into the curriculum.

These philosophical differences have been evident for a number of years in the ranks of those involved with students with mild disabilities. This debate has now entered circles of professionals and family members involved with students with more significant disabilities. As Browder, Fallin, Davis, and Karvonen (2003) stated, two major influences have occurred in planning curriculum for students with severe disabilities in the last three decades. The first has been to identify curriculum that relates to real life—a functional or life-skills curriculum approach. The second influence has been the inclusion of students with severe disabilities in general education settings. This inclusion has led to the development of a parallel curriculum in which students learn either adaptations of the general curriculum or ways to participate in class activities using their life skills.

What Makes a Program Effective?

Regardless of what the program is called or what program model is used, it is important for you to be aware of what makes a program effective. Benz, Lindstrom, Unruh, and Waintrup (2004) identified seven transition practices that researchers have associated with greater student retention and better employment and education outcomes. We have summarized them here:

1. Direct, individualized tutoring and support in such areas as completing homework, attending class, and staying focused on school
2. Participation in career and technical education classes during the last two years of high school, especially classes that offer instruction in specific occupational areas
3. Participation in community-based work experience during the last two years of high school
4. Competence in academic areas (e.g., reading, math, problem solving) and functional skills (e.g., personal-social, career awareness, self-advocacy)
5. Participation in a transition planning process that promotes self-determination
6. Direct assistance in understanding and connecting with adult services related to postschool goals (e.g., postsecondary institutions, vocational rehabilitation)
7. Graduation from high school

It is also important to identfy the factors that contribute to program longevity. Benz and colleagues (2004) identified three factors from case studies of a number of programs:

1. The program has credible, stable staff and the support of at least one key administrator over the time period.
2. The school and community view the program as having a positive impact on student outcomes. This includes the fact that the program documented its impact on students and had specific strategies for communicating this information to school staff and administrators, parents, and the community.
3. The program has a clear role and presence in the district. It has found a unique niche and created a fit between the needs of the district and the features of the program.

Conclusion

This chapter has discussed the principles and approaches of work-based learning, as well as the content for instruction and program models for delivering this content. We also reviewed a number of issues related to preparing students for employment. The emphasis on academically oriented standards-based education has put work-based learning in a precarious position. It is important that educators mount an effort at the district and state levels to include competencies related to work-based learning in district- and state-level standards. It is also important that work-based learning activities be built on each student's strengths, preferences, and interests (identified as part of the assessment process discussed in Chapter 5) and that appropriate accommodations and supports be provided as needed.

7 Transition to Postsecondary Education

I am still learning.
            —Michelangelo

Two of the transition outcomes identified by the Individuals with Disabilities Education Improvement Act of 2004 (IDEA 2004) and its amendments are postsecondary education and vocational training. Participation in postsecondary education is perhaps the most common alternative to direct employment, at least within the general population (Halpern, Yovanoff, Doren, & Benz, 1995). This postsecondary education and training can be provided in a number of settings, including four-year colleges and universities; community and junior colleges; private vocational schools that offer certificates in a particular job area, such as hairdressing or truck driving; apprenticeship programs; on-the-job training programs; adult education programs; the military; and others. Community colleges are themselves rather complex, offering a range of programs, including liberal arts preparation for transfer to a four-year college or for an associate's degree, specific vocational training accompanied by an associate's degree or a certificate, and many adult education courses that are not degree oriented. These adult education courses can address either vocational or avocational content. The military also serves as a vehicle for postsecondary education, both in terms of specific leadership and vocational skills and in terms of funding for future formal education.

This chapter focuses on a number of topics: (1) general information on postsecondary education, (2) the skills needed by students in postsecondary education programs, (3) suggested strategies and services at the secondary level and postsecondary level to assist the student with the transition process, (4) the information and documentation required by postsecondary programs in order to determine eligibility and to provide the needed accommodations to your students, and (5) approaches for gathering the information needed. The term *postsecondary education* will be used to include programs whose emphasis is further education or institution-based vocational and technical training. Educational institutions may also be involved in some way in apprenticeship and on-the-job training programs, which are covered in Chapter 6.

General Information on Postsecondary Education for Individuals with Disabilities

There are a number of findings related to postsecondary education. In 1996, 6 to 9 percent of all undergraduate students reported having a disability (Henderson, 1998; National Center for Education Statistics, 1996), with learning disability the most prevalent disability reported (29 to 35 percent of those reporting a disability). In 2000, the National Council on Disability reported that 17 percent of all students attending higher education programs in the United States had a disability. In that same year, 40 percent of freshmen with disabilities reported having a learning disability, making it still the most common disability reported (Henderson, 2001).

Although the number of students with learning disabilities attending college has increased, they are still less likely than their nondisabled peers to attend college (Blackorby & Wagner, 1996; Greenbaum, Graham, & Scales, 1995; Murray, Goldstein, Nourse, & Edgar, 2000; Vogel & Adelman, 1993). In 1994 (and again in 1999), the National Joint Committee on Learning Disabilities (NJCLD) expressed concern that many students with disabilities do not consider postsecondary options. This has been supported by a number of adult adjustment studies (Blackorby & Wagner, 1996; Frank & Sitlington, 1997; Levine & Nourse, 1998; National Center for Education Statistics, 1996; Sitlington, Frank, & Carson, 1992; Wagner, D'Amico, Marder, Newman, & Blackorby, 1992).

Of those who graduate from high school, 14 to 19 percent of students with disabilities, as opposed to 56 percent of students without disabilities, attend a postsecondary school within the first two years of exiting high school (Blackorby & Wagner, 1996; Wagner et al., 1992). Individuals with physical or sensory disabilities had higher participation rates (28 to 36 percent) than did those with cognitive, emotional, or severe disabilities (4 to 17 percent). Of this group, students with mental retardation had the second lowest rate of participation (6 percent) and students with multiple disabilities had the lowest rate (4 percent). There are, however, an increasing number of postsecondary education programs for individuals with more significant disabilities (Neubert, Moon, & Grigal, 2002; Page & Chadsey-Rusch, 1995).

Three to five years after high school, 27 percent of students with disabilities, as opposed to 68 percent of students without disabilities, attend some form of postsecondary education (Blackorby & Wagner, 1996; Stodden, 2001). A positive relationship between disability, level of education, and adult employment has been clearly established (Benz, Doren, & Yovanoff, 1998; Blackorby & Wagner, 1996; Reis, Neu, & McGuire, 1997). Thus, this gap significantly affects long-term career and employment prospects (Stodden, 2001).

In addition, there is evidence suggesting that many students with disabilities who enroll in postsecondary institutions have difficulty completing their postsecondary programs. Murray and associates (2000) found that of the students with learning disabilities who had attended postsecondary education institutions, 80 percent had not graduated five years after high school, compared to 56 percent of youths without disabilities. Ten years after graduating from high school, 56 percent of youths with learning disabilities had not been graduated from postsecondary education, compared to 32 percent of individuals without disabilities.

Transition to Postsecondary Education as a General Goal

For all individuals, the choice of what path to take after high school should depend on their life goals. In the case of individuals with disabilities, the choice of postsecondary paths should be made more clear through a transition planning process that includes students and families. The discussion of postsecondary education options needs to be framed within the context of admission requirements, performance demands, and expected outcomes of these options. Discussions related to options should also include the availability and quality of support systems for assisting individuals with disabilities in meeting their transition goals. The reality is that some institutions are more "student friendly" than others.

The decision of whether participation in postsecondary education is a desired transition outcome for a specific student should be made as early as possible in the transition planning process. In the following sections of this chapter, we discuss the skills that your students will need to pursue postsecondary education and suggest some strategies for making a successful transition to postsecondary education programs. Preparing your students for a successful transition specifically to college and university programs will require that they carefully plan their high school coursework to include the needed college preparatory coursework.

We feel that it is critical, however, that training in functional skills also be addressed for all students, including those pursuing postsecondary education. Clark (1994) defined a *functional curriculum approach* as

> a way of delivering instructional content that focuses on the concepts and skills needed by all students with disabilities in the areas of personal-social, daily living, and occupational adjustment. What is considered a functional curriculum

of any one student would be the content (concepts and skills) included in that student's curriculum or course of study that targets his or her current and future needs. These needs are based on a nondiscriminatory, functional assessment approach. (p. 37)

The functional curriculum approach described by Clark suggests that functional content be addressed in the individualized education program (IEP), but that it has no restrictions regarding the type or location of instructional delivery.

Skills Needed in Postsecondary Education Programs

Numerous authors have written on the skills needed by all individuals, but particularly individuals with disabilities, to succeed in postsecondary programs (Brinckerhoff, McGuire, & Shaw, 2002; Gajar, 1998; Getzel, Stodden, & Briel, 2001; Sitlington et al., 2000; Vogel & Adelman, 1992; Webb, 2000). Webb (2000) talked about three domains of planning and preparation: (1) academic, including determining required college preparation classes and identifying appropriate learning strategies; (2) career, including identifying job shadowing opportunities and determining appropriate employment opportunities; and (3) personal-social, including self-determination and extracurricular activities. We have chosen to present information from a number of these authors, even though there is some overlapping of ideas, to provide specific input for preparing your students for the transition to these programs. Although many of these sources focus primarily on students with learning disabilities, their recommendations also apply to other disability areas.

Scott (1991) highlighted the fact that there is a change in legal status for students with disabilities as they make the transition to postsecondary education. While in high school, IDEA 2004 and legislation that preceded it ensure individuals with disabilities the right to participate in publicly supported education programs; education in the least restrictive environment; nondiscriminatory testing, evaluation, and placement; procedural due process of law; and appropriate educational services as delineated in a written IEP. In postsecondary programs, Section 504 of the Rehabilitation Act (1973; PL 93-112) and the Americans with Disabilities Act (ADA) are basic civil rights provisions. (We will present information on these laws and the requirements they place on postsecondary education institutions in a later section of this chapter.)

DuChossois and Michaels (1994) commented that for any college-bound student, the process of selecting a college is an emotional as well as an academic decision. They also stated that secondary education must be a process of moving students with disabilities from a state of dependency to independence.

They identified a number of nonacademic areas that are often problematic for all students making the transition to postsecondary education, but that frequently become overwhelming for the student with learning disabilities: problem solving, organizing, prioritizing multiple task completion, studying, self-monitoring, attacking and following through on tasks, managing time, and interacting socially in a variety of new situations.

In their position paper on transition to postsecondary education, the National Joint Committee on Learning Disabilities (NJCLD, 1994) stated that success in postsecondary educational settings depends on the student's level of motivation, independence, self-direction, self-advocacy, and academic abilities developed in high school. The NJCLD also identified roles and responsibilities for the student, parents, secondary personnel, and postsecondary personnel in the transition process. Although these roles and responsibilities were written specifically for those with learning disabilities, they apply to all individuals with disabilities. The roles and responsibilities proposed for the student translate into skills that the student will need in postsecondary settings. A number of them are listed here:

1. Understanding his or her disability, including its effect on work and learning
2. Establishing realistic goals
3. Stressing strengths, while understanding the influence of the disability
4. Knowing how, when, and where to discuss and request needed accommodations
5. Developing and using social skills
6. Seeking instructors and learning environments that are supportive
7. Developing and applying effective studying, test-preparation, test-taking, time-management, and note-taking strategies
8. Maintaining an ongoing personal file that includes school and medical records, the IEP, a resumé, and samples of academic work
9. Knowing the rights and responsibilities necessary to prepare for and access postsecondary education
10. Identifying and accessing resources needed for support
11. Selecting courses that meet postsecondary requirements
12. Preparing for and actively participating in the postsecondary application process

The NJCLD also identified a number of ways secondary school personnel could assist students in developing the needed skills. Some of these were the following:

1. Include the student and parents in the entire transition planning process.
2. Demonstrate sensitivity to the culture and values of the student and family.

3. Develop an appropriate packet of materials to document the student's secondary school program and to facilitate service delivery in the post-secondary setting.

4. Inform the student about statutes, rules, and regulations that ensure his or her rights.

5. Ensure competency in literacy and mathematics.

6. Help the student use a range of academic accommodations and techno-logical aids, such as electronic date books, texts on tape, and grammar and spell checkers.

7. Provide appropriate course selection, counseling, and academic support services.

8. Ensure that the student learns effective studying, time-management, test-preparation, and test-taking strategies.

9. Help the student evaluate his or her dependence on external supports and adjust the level of assistance when appropriate.

10. Help the student develop self-advocacy skills, including a realistic under-standing of the disability.

11. Foster independence through increased responsibility and opportunity for self-management.

12. Encourage the student to develop extracurricular interests and to partici-pate in community activities.

13. Inform the student and parents about admission requirements and demands of diverse postsecondary settings.

14. Inform the student and parents about support services that postsec-ondary settings provide.

15. Help the student and parents select and apply to postsecondary institu-tions that will offer both the competitive curriculum and the necessary level of support services.

16. Develop ongoing communication with postsecondary personnel.

In addition, Brinckerhoff (1994) stated that high school teachers need to give students with disabilities a more realistic picture of what to expect in col-lege by describing the different roles assumed by campus support staff and faculty. Many students will anticipate that the support staff on campus will perform the same tasks and provide the same support as the high school resource room teacher. They may also erroneously expect that all postsec-ondary institutions will have a specialist on campus who can be a content tutor who will assist with homework, monitor progress in completing class assign-ments, and, if necessary, talk to teachers on their behalf. Brinckerhoff (1994) also pointed out that students with disabilities need to be forewarned that col-lege classes are typically larger, interactions with faculty are less frequent, and opportunities for extra help are more limited. He identified *organization, time management,* and *communication skills* as critical for transition to postsecondary education.

Gartin, Rumrill, and Serebreni (1996) identified four difficulties commonly experienced by students with disabilities when they make the transition from high school to postsecondary education: (1) a decrease in teacher/student contact, (2) an increase in academic competition, (3) a change in personal support networks, and (4) a loss of the protective public school environment. They proposed the Higher Education Transition Model, which utilizes a three-part framework.

The first part of this framework is *psychosocial adjustment.* Instructional objectives related to this area would include self-advocacy skill development, handling frustration, social problem solving, college-level social skills, and mentor relationships. Among the recommendations the authors provided for promoting psychosocial development were including college settings and situations as discussion scenarios to aid in the transfer and generalization of communication and social skills, and using cooperative learning and peer tutoring.

The second component of the Higher Education Transition Model is *academic development.* Tasks the secondary teacher can perform related to this area include the following:

- Monitor the students' performance in their college preparatory courses.
- Teach study strategies and technology skills.
- Assess the students' academic histories, abilities, and potential for college success.
- Provide technical assistance to college disability services personnel.
- Provide information concerning standardized college entrance examinations, such as the American College Test (ACT) or the Scholastic Aptitude Test (SAT).
- Provide information on procedures for requesting in-class accommodations.
- Assist in the evaluation of the appropriateness of career goals by providing opportunities for participation in occupational information groups, vocational assessment, and career exploration programs.
- Routinely use in-class accommodations similar to those used in postsecondary institutions.
- Review transcripts yearly to determine if students are enrolled in coursework appropriate for admission to postsecondary programs.

Exposure to postsecondary settings provides many benefits. In the third component of their model, *college and community orientation,* Gartin and colleagues (1996) suggested the following:

- Encourage students to link with the postsecondary institution as early as possible through such activities as science fairs, band camps, sports camps, and other special events.

- Acquaint students with postsecondary campuses by arranging for tours.
- Prepare students to participate fully in campus life.
- Teach strategies for accessing community services, such as how to provide for medical needs, banking, and shopping.

The family should be included in all of these education components. It is important to involve the student, family, and secondary personnel with post-secondary personnel and environments.

Finally, Brinckerhoff (1996) categorized the major differences between high school and college requirements under seven basic categories: (1) time in class, (2) class size, (3) time required to prepare for each class, (4) frequency of tests, (5) minimum grades required to remain in school, (6) teaching practices, and (7) amount of freedom allowed the student. The major differences in each of these categories pose significant problems for students with disabilities (and all students) as they make the transition from the secondary to the post-secondary learning environment. He stated that secondary school personnel can help prepare students with disabilities for the challenges of higher education by beginning to replicate some of the demands of postsecondary education while the student is still in high school. Postsecondary providers can help by collaborating with their secondary-level colleagues and by realistically foreshadowing the higher education experience for applicants with disabilities. Parents can assist their sons and daughters by validating their dreams and nurturing their social development and academic growth. The students themselves, however, hold the key to success in higher education and ultimately in their adult lives.

Use of Assistive Technology

Technology is a term that encompasses a continuum of low-tech to high-tech approaches. These approaches can assist students in compensating for their difficulties in areas such as mathematics, reading, organization, memory, written language, and listening. Technology has important implications for students attending postsecondary education institutions. The IEP team is obligated to consider whether the student needs assistive technology services and devices, regardless of the age or disability category, in order to receive an appropriate public education. As a transition plan is developed, the need for revision of technology needs should be included as part of a student's short and long-term goals. Interagency responsibility in relation to assistive technology must be clear if a student is to have technological supports often essential for postschool success (Brinkerhoff et al., 2002).

Specifically, Mull and Sitlington (2003) made four recommendations related to assistive technology and the transition to postsecondary education: (1) the transition process must include an identification of funding sources for the assistive technology needed by the student in postsecondary education, (2) selection of the specific assistive technology approach should be based on an assessment of the student's needs and the demands of the postsecondary education environment, (3) students must be trained in the proper use of the assistive technology device, and (4) professionals working with the student at the secondary level must carefully consider the impact of removing the student from eligibility for special education services—especially in terms of the services the student will need at the postsecondary level.

In a survey of members of the Association for Higher Education and Disabilities (AHEAD), Michaels, Prezant, Morabito, and Jackson (2002) found that the actual achievement of assistive technology access at postsecondary education institutions is not up to the level consistent with its perceived importance by disability service providers. They found the most frequently cited technologies were: scanners, telecommunication devices, screen or text readers, screen magnification devices, specialized tape recorders, voice recognition/dictation software, adapted work stations, and assistive listening devices. These were still only available at approximately three-fourths of the campuses. Devices available at approximately one-half of the campuses included speakerphones, screen review software, mouse and switch access options, recorded textbooks, adapted keyboards and keyguards, laptop computers, and reading and writing software. A number of authors (Day & Edwards, 1996; Higgins & Zvi, 1995; Raskind & Higgins, 1998) provide actual examples of the use of assistive technology to support students with disabilities in postsecondary education programs.

Suggested Instructional Strategies and Services at the Secondary and Postsecondary Levels

A number of strategies or approaches have been suggested to assist youths with disabilities in making the transition from high school to postsecondary education programs. Some of these strategies may be used at the secondary level; others are helpful to teachers, students, and their families as they work with postsecondary institutions. It is important that those students who are interested in postsecondary education include this interest in their vision statement as early as possible. The student's IEP then needs to address postsecondary education in terms of the student's present levels of academic achievement and functional performance and goals.

Secondary Level

Durlak, Rose, and Bursuck (1994) summarized the self-determination skills that a number of researchers had related to students making a successful transition to postsecondary education, including some of the skills described in the preceding section. Those skills included (1) an awareness of academic and social strength and weaknesses as well as compensatory strategies, (2) the ability to express such an awareness to faculty and staff, (3) an awareness of service needs and appropriate accommodations, and (4) the ability to request information, assistance, and accommodations when appropriate and necessary.

Van Reusen, Bos, Schumaker, and Deshler (1994) developed a motivation strategy entitled *The Self-Advocacy Strategy for Education and Transition Planning.* Students may use this strategy when preparing for and participating in any type of education or transition planning conference. The Self-Advocacy Strategy is taught using a modified version of the acquisition and generalization stages that have been developed and expanded as part of the Strategies Intervention Model (Ellis, Deshler, Lenz, Schumaker, & Clark, 1991). The five steps involved in the strategy form the acronym *I PLAN:*

- Inventory: Involves students in identifying and listing their perceived education and/or transition strengths, areas to improve or learn, goals, needed accommodations, and choices for learning
- Provide your inventory information: Focuses on providing input during the conference
- Listen and respond: Relates to effectively listening to others' statements or questions and responding to them
- Ask questions: Involves asking appropriate questions to gather needed information
- Name your goals: Involves communicating personal goals and ideas on actions to be taken

Webb (2000) proposed the OPEN model (Opportunities in Postsecondary Education through Networking). This model has the following steps: (1) decide to attend a postsecondary education institution, (2) explore your options, (3) select, (4) apply, and (5) enroll. This model also includes planning and preparation, which are divided into three domains: academic, career, and personal/social.

Brinckerhoff, McGuire, and Shaw (2002) provided a timetable for transition planning, beginning in grade 8. Planning may need to begin even earlier in subjects such as math, because of the sequential nature of courses. The timetable focuses on individuals with learning disabilities and ADHD. We have broadened the focus to include all individuals with disabilities, and have chosen major components of this timetable to summarize. Goals for each grade include continuing to practice goals from the previous grades. Even if students miss planning activities in the earlier grades, they should still go through the steps, even if at a more rapid and intensive pace. Consult the original source for a more complete listing.

Grade 8
1. Take academically challenging courses.
2. Consult teachers on how to become independent learners.
3. Actively participate in IEP meetings.
4. Seek opportunities to become more independent at home and in school.
5. Begin to identify preferences and interests.

Grades 9 and 10
1. Develop an understanding of your disability.
2. Learn about your rights and the legal responsibilities of high school and postsecondary education institutions.
3. Use support and accommodations in math or foreign language classes, rather than seeking a waiver, if possible.
4. Focus on strategy-based learning.
5. Try out accommodations and auxiliary aids in high school classes.
6. Form a realistic assessment of your potential for college and vocational school.
7. Consider a part-time summer job or volunteer position.

Grade 11
1. Review the IEP for needed modifications.
2. Keep grades up.
3. Match vocational interests and academic abilities with appropriate post-secondary education institutions.
4. Finalize arrangements for appropriate college entrance examinations.
5. Start with a broad list of postsecondary education institutions and narrow listing based on competitiveness, location, curriculum, level of support, and so forth.
6. With parent and teacher assistance, develop a file including current diagnostic information, IEPs, grades, letters of recommendations, and student activity chart or resumé.

Grade 12
1. Retake college entrance examinations, if needed, to improve scores.
2. Select colleges from your list and rank as safe bets, possibilities, and long shots.
3. Pick up financial aid forms from guidance counselor.
4. Explore services/funding available from adult agencies.

Postsecondary Level

Higher education programs have developed a number of support services, including counseling, tutoring, peer mentoring, and instructional support (Brinckerhoff et al., 2002). Black, Smith, Chang, Harding, and Stodden (2002) found that the following were the most commonly provided supports in two-year postsecondary education programs: (1) common generic supports, such as testing accommodations, personal counseling, advocacy, and tutors; (2) educational/personal strategies instruction, including developmental/remedial instruction, learning center laboratory, and study skills; (3) career/vocational assessment and counseling; (4) notetakers/scribes/readers and interpreters; and (5) priority registration/course scheduling. They also found that two-year postsecondary education institutions offered significantly more support in these areas than four-year postsecondary education institutions. Two-year institutions also offered more outreach and linkage supports for working with high schools and other agencies than did their four-year counterparts.

Mull, Sitlington, and Alper (2001) conducted a systematic analysis and synthesis of published research from 1985 to 2000 related to postsecondary education services for students with learning disabilities. They found that (1) the majority of the articles described services such as readers or qualified notetakers, but did not address providing program modifications, or substitutions or waivers of courses or degree requirements; (2) changes that did not affect program requirements were emphasized more frequently than accommodations that could alter program requirements; (3) 65 percent of the articles discussed test accommodations and 77 percent addressed the use of assistive technology devices; (4) the majority of assessment service recommendations emphasized the need to establish documentation of a learning disability and the student's present level of performance; (5) although all of the articles recommended a variety of support services, few addressed the need to evaluate the effectiveness of those services; and (6) two-thirds of the articles did not discuss direct service personnel or instructional staff training.

McGuire and Shaw (1996) proposed a continuum of postsecondary support services for students with learning diabilties. This continuum, presented in Figure 7.1, applies to all students with disabilities. It is important that individuals with disabilities and their families actually interview postsecondary institutions to identify where each postsecondary institution stands on this continuum, and the specific supports it provides. This is best done by carefully reading all of the information sent by the institution and then conducting an on-campus visit and interview of staff, particularly those who will be providing the support services. Richard (1995) suggested a list of questions to ask during college visits. These questions include:

1. What are the regular criteria considered in the application for admission process (ACT/SAT scores, class rank)?
2. Are there special considerations for admission of students who have documented disabilities?
3. Is the student's current diagnosis from high school accepted? Are there guidelines regarding the recency of the test scores used for the current documentation?

FIGURE 7.1   Continuum of Postsecondary LD Support Services

1	2	3	4
Decentralized and Limited Services	*Loosely Coordinated Services*	*Centrally Coordinated Services*	*Data-Based Services*
→ No formal contact person	→ Contact person available	→ Full-time learning disability coordinator	→ Full-time learning disability director
→ Limited services	→ Generic support services available	→ Services often housed in disability student services office	→ Learning disability assistant coordinator
→ Few established policies	→ Peer tutors available to help at-risk students	→ Accommodations provided for testing and coursework	→ Full range of accommodations provided
→ Students dependent on sympathetic faculty	→ Students referred to other on-campus services	→ Established policies on admissions and service delivery	→ Policies and procedures in place
		→ Strong emphasis on student self-advocacy	→ Strong emphasis on student self-advocacy
		→ Peer support groups sometimes available	→ Development of individualized support plans based upon current documentation
		→ Specially trained LD tutors may be available	→ Tutoring in learning strategies available from trained staff and graduate-level interns
		→ Student required to provide current documentation of learning disability	→ Data-based contact records and service use profiles generated for annual report

Source: Resource Guide of Support Services for Students with Learning Disabilities in Connecticut Colleges and Universities by J. M. McGuire and S. F. Shaw (Eds.), 1989 (revised 1996), Storrs, CT: A. J. Pappanikou Center on Special Education and Rehabilitation: A University Affiliated Program, University of Connecticut. Reprinted by permission.

4. How many credit hours must be taken to be a full-time student? Are individuals with disabilities permitted to take reduced course loads and still be considered full-time students?
5. Is there an office of student disability services at the school? If so, what are qualifications and size of the staff? What are the student's responsibilities for obtaining services?
6. How willing are faculty members to provide appropriate accommodations?

The concept of universal design is also being used more frequently at the postsecondary education level. A Universal Design (UD) Think Tank, hosted by the Association on Higher Education and Disability (AHEAD; Scott, Loewen, Funckes, & Kroeger, 2003) generated the following list in response to the question, "How will we know when we have achieved our vision on infusing principles of UD in all campus environments?":

1. People with disabilities do not need to constantly advocate for access.
2. The criterion of a "reasonable" accommodation becomes moot.
3. Curriculum materials and resources are available in alternative formats as a de facto standard and are provided through a broad range of offices across campus.
4. Every student takes advantage of a universally designed product, classroom, or feature. Students with and without disabilities use the same design, and no one is stigmatized as having "special" needs.
5. Students with disabilities are included in instruction and learning beginning on the first day of class, instead of having to wait for accommodations before being able to fully participate.
6. Each campus has facilities and support to make materials available in alternative formats as a proactive part of preparation and dissemination.
7. Higher education environments have significant numbers of faculty, staff, and students with disabilities.
8. No one wastes time and energy negotiating physical and virtual access or navigating the campus environment.
9. The focus of the campus community is on effective teaching and learning for all students instead of on the provision of legally mandated accommodations. (p. 80–81)

Dual enrollment programs are another example of how to link high school and college. The concept of dual enrollment allows students (with and without disabilities) to complete high school while attending a postsecondary education institution. Although these programs have existed for over 30 years, their enrollments have increased rapidly in recent years (Bailey, Hughes, & Karp, 2002). These programs have a number of advantages. First, they are a way to offer high school students access to coursework (academic and vocationally related) not available at the high school. The increased emphasis on academics and standards has led to a deemphasis on vocational coursework in the high school, particularly those that are lab-intensive. The presence of well-developed vocational courses and labs at the community and technical colleges means that dual enrollment can provide such options (Bailey et al., 2002). Second, dual enrollment programs can also facilitate the psychological transition to postsecondary education, providing access to on-campus activities and support centers, allowing students to learn about these services before they begin postsecondary education. Third, the ability of students to accumulate college credit allows them to shorten the time it takes to earn a postsecondary degree and to save significantly on the overall cost of their education. Finally, this approach provides a funding mechanism for students who may not be eligible for federal aid programs at the postsecondary level (Hart, Pasternack, Mele-McCarthy, Zimbrich, & Parker, 2004). If you are interested in determining whether dual enrollment is an option in your state, consult the Education Commission of the States report (2001), which provides specific information on how and if dual enrollment is implemented in each state.

Postsecondary Students with Significant Disabilities.   Providing opportunities for individuals with severe disabilities to participate in educational, vocational, and recreational activities on college campuses has been a topic of interest among educators for over 30 years (Gaumer, Morningstar, & Clark, 2004; Neubert, Moon, Grigal, & Redd, 2001). Initial research has shown that completion of any type of postsecondary education (e.g., one college course or a certificate program) significantly improves the chance of an individual with significant disabilities securing meaningful employment (Zafft, Hart, & Zimbrich, 2004). As Gilson (1996) pointed out, reasonable access and accommodations need to include opportunities for full participation in nonclassroom events and nonclassroom spaces (i.e., physical education facilities, student common areas) as well as in the classroom. In addition to employment, student interactions with peers and instructors without disabilities, participation in social and recreational activites, and connections with adult agencies and services must also be addressed (Neubert, Moon, & Grigal, 2004).

In a review of the literature in this area, Neubert and colleagues (2001) found that the literature from the 1970s to 1990s provided descriptions of programs or advocated for the inclusion of this population mainly in position papers. Although located on college campuses, the programs were segregated from other college classes, and often focused on vocational training, functional skill development, and work adjustment skills. The literature during the 1990s shifted to providing postsecondary programs or individual supports to students with significant disabilities, ages 18 to 22, who were still enrolled in public schools.

This concept of dual enrollment, discussed in the previous section, allows students with disabilities to complete high school while attending a postsecondary education institution with same-aged peers and pursuing an academic or vocational curriculum in an inclusive setting. This approach also provides a funding mechanism for students who may not be eligible for federal aid programs at the postsecondary level (Hart et al., 2004).

Hart and associates (2004) surveyed 25 such dual enrollment programs across the United States and found three different models being followed: (1) substantially separate, (2) mixed, and (3) inclusive. The first category of programs focuses on life skills, community-based instruction, and rotation through a limited number of employment slots, either on or off campus. In the mixed programs, students have the option of being supported in college courses and having some interaction with college students in such settings as the cafeteria and sporting events. Most of the curriculum, however, is focused on life skills, community-based instruction, and rotation through a limited number of work experience slots. In the inclusive individual support model, students are provided with individualized services (e.g., educational coach) that are needed to ensure access to and progress in college courses, certificate programs, internships, and/or degree programs. All services are student centered, based on student choices and preferences, and inclusive of those available to the general student body. Some programs also offer internships and employment-related supports.

Neubert and colleagues (2002) found that postsecondary programs had been developed on college campuses (two- and four-year institutions) and in the community. The advantages of four-year institutions were that they are usually larger than communty colleges and often provide housing for students. Generally, they also have departments in education, the social sciences, and medical fields, whose students often need experiences, formal and informal, with students who have disabilities. Students also have access to other students during the day, evenings, and weekends. Advantages of community colleges include the fact that they often have open-door policies that may facilitate access to nontraditional students. Also, they are often more prevalent and closer to the student's home. In addition, community colleges are often the first postsecondary experience for many students exiting high school and provide a natural setting for integrated experiences with students without disabilities. Students in community college settings, however, often come to campus to attend their classes and then leave after class has ended. This may impact the opportunities to access college students to serve as peer buddies or tutors, and may limit social interactions and participation in organizations on campus.

Neubert and colleagues (2002) urged planning committees not to overlook the benefits of locating a program in a community site other than a college, such as a community building, local mall, or office building. Programs in the community often are not faced with the space or isolation concerns of programs on college campuses. In addition, locating a program in the community does not preclude students from enrolling in classes or recreational and social activities on college campuses. This approach benefits students who need jobs close to their homes. If one of the major goals of the program is to promote integrated employment, the community site approach may facilitate key partnerships with business and industry. Such a location may also provide greater access to transportation. Programs serving larger numbers of students may provide multiple options; college-based and community-based options are not mutually exclusive.

It should be pointed out that the location of a program on a college campus does not automatically result in participation in college courses or social integration of students with significant disabilities. In the programs they surveyed, Neubert and associates (2004) found that although students with significant disabilities were successfully engaged in employment training, access to college courses and extracurricular activities was limited.

These findings lend credence to using an individual support model, which has received a great deal of emphasis in the recent literature. As Weir (2004) indicated, in this model students are not part of a specially designed program for students with disabilities, but are individuals who access existing supports available through the college, the local school district, vocational rehabilitation, and other relevant support agencies. Collaboration and person-centered planning are key features of this approach. Weir noted three factors that differentiate individual supports from supports provided by programs: (1) there is a difference in the number of colleges a student can attend, since a college does not have to have a specific support program in place; (2) the student plays a different role—that of independent student versus program participant or "special" student; and (3) the student is empowered to continue a college education on his or her own timetable, rather than only during the transition years. If you are interested in utilizing this model, consult Weir (2001, 2004) for a detailed explanation of this concept and a listing of steps that have been effective in establishing such programs.

As a result of their review of literature, Neubert and associates (2001) stated that the location of postsecondary programs or support on college campuses deserves exploration and documentation. Neubert and colleagues (2004) suggested that as school systems consider the option of providing services to students with significant disabilities outside of the high school, they must clearly identify the priorities for instruction and inclusion and then determine if these priorities would be met on a college campus. Equally important is for the school and community personnel to engage in person-centered planning processes with students and their families to identify their goals and dreams for college and community participation. Doyle (2003) pointed out that three aspects of postsecondary education need to be understood: the culture, the cost, and the curriculum. She identified a series of steps for those interested in a postsecondary education program for students with significant disabilities.

Grigal, Neubert, and Moon (in press) have developed a handbook that presents a process and sample forms for designing, implementing, and evaluating such programs.

Regardless of the approach taken in providing access to postsecondary education for students with significant disabilities, it is critical that information be collected on the extent to which students have achieved the specific goals of the program. Studies have found that such information is currently missing from such programs (Hart et al., 2004; Grigal et al., 2001; Neubert et al., 2004).

Information and Documentation Required by Postsecondary Programs

The *Guckenberger v. Boston University* case (1997) brought to the forefront the legal requirements of responding to requests for reasonable accommodations on the part of postsecondary institutions (Elswit, Geetter, & Goldberg, 1999; Wolinsky & Whelan, 1999). In 1977, the Department of Health, Education, and Welfare (now the Department of Education) established guidelines for implementing Section 504 of the Rehabilitation Act. Individuals with disabilities must be afforded "equal opportunity to gain the same result, to gain the same benefit, or to reach the same level of achievement, in the most integrated setting appropriate to the person's needs" (104.4(b)(2)). Section 504 mandated that "no otherwise qualified handicapped individual . . . shall, solely by reason of his/her handicap, be denied the benefits of, or be subjected to discrimination, under any program or activity receiving Federal financial assistance" (Rehabilitation Act of 1973 s 504, 29 U.S.C. § 794).

Subpart A of the regulations delineated general provisions of the law. It stipulated that an individual with a disability is one who has a "physical or mental impairment which substantially limits one or more major life activities" (Subpart A, 104.3(j)(1)(i)), including learning. The regulations qualify that, in addition to individuals currently manifesting a disability, an individual who has a record of such an impairment or who is regarded as having such a disability is also covered under Section 504.

Subpart E of the federal regulations for the Rehabilitation Act pertains specifically to postsecondary education. The regulations established that institutions of higher education must modify academic requirements and methods of evaluation that are discriminatory. Postsecondary institutions, however, are not required to compromise on requirements that are essential to the program or course of instruction, that are directly related to licensing requirements, or that alter content or process that is essential to the evaluation (Section 104.44(c)). In addition, institutions of higher education also may not impose rules that have the effect of limiting the participation of students with disabilities, such as prohibiting tape recording in the classroom (Section 104.44(b)). In 1990, the Americans with Disabilities Act (ADA; PL 101-336) reinforced the mandates of Section 504 and expanded its coverage to all programs and services regardless of whether or not they receive federal financial assistance (Linthicum, Cole, & D'Alonzo, 1991).

Understanding that nonessential methods or criteria may be accommodated without changing the essence of the course is critical to understanding the rights to higher education of students with disabilities. Protections offered to postsecondary students under Section 504 and the ADA differ greatly from those provided to secondary students by IDEA. Students wishing to gain entry to and services in a postsecondary setting will need to be prepared to document their disability and to work with officials of the postsecondary setting to identify the accommodations they need.

The primary decision makers regarding accommodations are the student and responsible institutional officials. Students are required to initiate the process by identifying and documenting their disability and by requesting specific accommodations in a timely manner. Responsible institution officials must then decide on a case-by-case basis whether and how to provide effective accommodations within the context of (1) academic and nonacademic standards, (2) the essential nature of the course of study in question, and (3) the unique abilities of the student (Frank & Wade, 1993).

The Association of Higher Education and Disability (AHEAD) is the main professional group for individuals providing support services for individuals with disabilities at the postsecondary level. They have published program and professional standards and a code of ethics in the area of postsecondary education for individuals with disabilities, as well as guidelines for documentation of a learning disability (AHEAD, 1997; Dukes, 2001; Dukes & Shaw, 1998, 1999; Price, 1997; Shaw & Dukes, 2001; Shaw, McGuire, & Madaus, 1997).

Documenting a Disability

Two points need to be addressed in documenting a disability. First, students need to provide evidence that their disability "substantially limits" a major life activity (e.g., their learning). Second, students need to demonstrate that they are "otherwise qualified"—that they are able to meet the essential requirements of the course or program when provided reasonable accommodations (*Davis v. Southeastern Community College,* 1979; Frank & Wade, 1993; Gregg & Scott, 2000; Scott, 1994; Thomas, 2000).

According to recent case law, at least four options exist in interpreting whether the student's disability "substantially limits" his or her learning: (1) in comparison to most people in the general population; (2) in comparison to the average person having comparable training, skills, and abilities; (3) in comparison to the average unimpaired student; and (4) in terms of the disparity between inherent capacity and performance (Thomas, 2000).

When determining if a student is "otherwise qualified" Scott (1991) proposed three questions: (1) What are the program or course requirements? (2) What nonessential criteria can be accommodated without changing the essence of the course or program? and (3) What are the specific abilities and disabilities of the student within this context?

McGuire, Madaus, Litt, and Ramirez (1996) stated that documentation serves several important purposes. First, it may be used to decide if a student is "otherwise qualified" to meet the technical demands of the institution, in spite of his or her disability, when provided with reasonable accommodations. Second, documentation is essential for determining appropriate academic adjustment and auxiliary aids on a case-by-case basis. Finally, clear and complete documentation is important to help the adult student with a learning disability recognize his or her learning strengths and weaknesses, and to establish clear and realistic goals.

The Association of Higher Education and Disability (1997) has published guidelines for documentation of a learning disability in adolescents and adults in four areas: (1) qualifications of the evaluator, (2) recency of documentation, (3) appropriate clinical documentation to substantiate the learning disability, and (4) evidence to establish a rationale supporting the need for accommodations. Although this document relates specifically to those with learning disabilities, it establishes a precedent for evaluating the need for accommodations for students with any disability. This would be particularly helpful for students who received accommodations at the secondary level under Section 504 of the Rehabilitation Act, rather than through special education under IDEA. In such cases, adequate documentation of the disability might not exist in the school records.

The guidelines by AHEAD indicate that professionals conducting assessments, rendering diagnoses, and making recommendations for appropriate accommodations must be qualified to do so in terms of comprehensive training and direct experience with an adolescent and adult LD population. The following professionals are considered qualified by AHEAD, provided they have additional training and experience in the assessment of learning problems in adolescents and adults: clinical or educational psychologists, school psychologists, neuropsychologists, learning disabilities specialists, medical doctors, and other professionals.

According to the guidelines, the provision of all reasonable accommodations and services must be based on assessment of the impact of the student's disability on his or her academic performance at a given time in the student's life. The Association of Higher Education and Disability urges flexibility in accepting documentation, but states that outdated or inadequate documentation may not address the student's current level of functioning or need for accommodations.

The guidelines are very specific when addressing the substantiation of a learning disability. They state that documentation should validate the need for services based on the individual's current level of functioning in the educational setting. Although an IEP or a 504 Plan can be included as part of a more comprehensive battery, they are not sufficient documentation by themselves. The guidelines state that a comprehensive assessment battery and the resulting diagnostic report should include the following:

1. A diagnostic interview
2. A comprehensive assessment battery that addresses at least the domains of aptitude, academic achievement (in relevant areas such as reading, mathematics, and oral and written language), and information processing
3. A specific diagnosis of LD
4. Standard scores and/or percentiles for all normed measures, including a profile of the student's strengths and weaknesses
5. A diagnostic summary based on the comprehensive evaluation process

It is our interpretation of these guidelines that the emphasis is on standardized assessment instruments. In fact, the document provides a list of commonly used standardized tests in its appendix. The guidelines indicate that other assessment measures, such as nonstandard measures and informal assessment procedures or observation, may be helpful and may be used in tandem with formal tests.

Hatzes, Reiff, and Bramel (2002) found that 14 percent of the postsecondary institutions that responded to their survey indicated that they adopted, without modification, the AHEAD guidelines. In addition, the authors found that the responses of the remaining institutions regarding ability and achievement tests accepted indicated specifications consistent with the AHEAD guidelines. The majority (67 percent) of the institutions responding also followed AHEAD's guidelines regarding documentation being current.

The Association of Higher Education and Disability also recommended "recent and appropriate" documentation, although specifics as to number of years are not provided. In *Guckenberger v. Boston University* (1997), a precedent was established that postsecondary settings can require students to provide documentation of a disability that is current and has been conducted by a qualified professional. However, postsecondary settings must also demonstrate that requirements for the acceptable documentation of a disability are necessary. For example, in the *Boston University* case, the judge ruled that the specific requirement that documentation be no more than three years old was not necessary. While the AHEAD guidelines indicated only that it is best to provide recent and appropriate documentation, the requirement of major testing agencies regarding the date of testing is more specific. For example, the

Educational Testing Service (1999) defined *recency* to be within the past three years for high school students and within the past five years for adults.

Determining Accommodations

The second type of information needed by postsecondary institutions relates to determining appropriate accommodations and supports for the student. Accommodations may take place at the program level and commonly include part-time schedules, longer time to complete the program, and priority registration. Accommodations may also be directly related to instruction and commonly include changes to the testing or evaluation procedures, the use of assistive technology, recorded books or a reader, tape-recorded lectures, and notetaking modifications (Mull & Sitlington, 2003; Mull, Sitlington, & Alper, 2001). Lewis and Farris (1999) found that 98 percent of the postsecondary institutions that enrolled students with disabilities in 1996–1997 or 1997–1998 had provided at least one support service or accommodation to a student with disabilities.

In the area of determining accommodations, the AHEAD guidelines stated that it is important to recognize that accommodation needs can change over time and are not always identified through the initial diagnostic process. Also, a prior history of accommodation does not, in and of itself, warrant the provision of a similar accommodation. In fact, 86 percent of the respondents to the survey by Hatzes and colleagues (2002) indicated that a previous diagnosis of learning disability does not automatically qualify a student for an accommodation. The diagnostic report should include specific recommendations for accommodations as well as an explanation as to when each accommodation is recommended. The evaluator should describe the impact the diagnosed learning disability has on a specific major life activity as well as the degree of significance of this impact. The recommendation should be supported with specific test results or clinical observations.

Once a student has sufficiently documented that he or she has a qualifying disability, a postsecondary institution is responsible for providing reasonable accommodations that "do not result in unfair advantage, require significant alteration to the program or activity, result in the lowering of academic or technical standards, or cause the college to incur undue financial hardship" (Thomas, 2000, p. 254). Federal law has required that an "otherwise qualified" student with a disability shall not be discriminated against, but offers little guidance in determining how to weigh accommodation requests for students with disabilities (Scott, 1994). The AHEAD guidelines provide some direction in this area, suggesting that a qualified person, serving as the evaluator, list specific accommodations and a rationale for those specific accommodations.

Case law is also establishing precedents in this area. Scott (1994) analyzed related court cases and provided recommendations for postsecondary settings. She suggested that postsecondary settings should consider the essential requirements of their programs proactively, so that standards are set prior to requests for accommodations. Scott recommended establishing essential requirements both at the institutional level and at the program and course levels. Once these essential requirements have been established, postsecondary officials can look at an individual student's request based on these preestablished standards. Scott also recommended asking four specific questions as postsecondary officials attempt to weigh requests for accommodations: (1) Does the student have a learning disability? (2) Has the student provided adequate documentation? (3) Is the student qualified? and (4) Is the accommodation reasonable?

This last question gets to the heart of the matter. What makes an accommodation reasonable? Reasonable accommodations, as established in case law, are determined on an individual basis, do not compromise essential requirements of the program, and will not put the public or the student at risk (Scott, 1994). Additionally, as Scott pointed out, reasonable accommodations do not place undue financial burden on the postsecondary setting, although this alone may not be used to refuse an accommodation request.

Certainly, determining appropriate, reasonable accommodations on a case-by-case basis will continue to be an issue of contention. Scott (1991) referred to the attainment of accommodations as a "two-way street" (p. 462). She placed the burden on the school to provide reasonable accommodations and on the student to request and use accommodations appropriately.

Gathering the Information Needed by Postsecondary Programs

Gathering Documentation to Assist in the Transition to Postsecondary Education

As indicated in the previous section, specific information is required by postsecondary programs related to documenting a disability and determining the accommodations that are needed. As more and more students with disabilities are attempting to access postsecondary education, changes that are occurring in special education pose challenges and hold promise for providing the information that is required by postsecondary education to document a disability.

Changes Posing Challenges.   Three specific innovations in special education have created some challenges in the transition of students with disabilities to postsecondary education (Kincaid, 1997; Sitlington, 2003). First, under IDEA 2004, a district is required only to provide the student exiting high school with a summary of his or her academic achievment and functional performance, which shall include recommendations on how to assist the student in meeting his or her postsecondary goals. The last formal evaluation data collected on the student may be a number of years old when the student graduates from high school. It does not mean, however, that ongoing data have not been collected, although possibly of a more informal nature.

Second, special educators in many states are moving away from an emphasis on standardized assessments and toward the use of curriculum-based assessments. These assessments may provide a great deal of information to postsecondary institutions in terms of the student's performance in specific content areas and comparing the student's performance to students with and without disabilities in the district. However, the student's performance is usually not compared to a statewide or national sample.

Finally, many states are moving away from specific disability labels and toward the concept of "individual with a disability" or a "noncategorical" label. Although a specific disability label may not be applied to the student, documentation should have been provided that the student's disability does "substantially limit" his or her learning. Thus, although these innovations pose challenges to the smooth transition of adolescents with disabilities into postsecondary education, they also promise data that may be more recent and more relevant. The challenge is to identify how to convert the data that are currently being gathered at the secondary level into information that is needed by postsecondary institutions.

Changes Holding Promise.   Other changes within secondary education have the potential for providing information that may be helpful to postsecondary institutions. Specifically, IDEA 2004 requires that all students with disabilities be included in testing required of other students. In addition, the IEP must include a statement that addresses the issue of participation in state- or districtwide assessments. IDEA 2004 requires that the IEP must include:

- A statement of any appropriate accommodations that are necessary to measure the academic achievement and functional performance of the Child on State and districtwide assessments . . . and
- If the IEP Team determines that the Child shall take an alternate assessment on a particular State or districtwide assessment of student achievement, a statement of why (aa) the Child cannot participate in the regular assessment; and (bb) the particular alternate assessment selected is appropriate for the Child. (IDEA, Sec. 614, H.R. 1350)

The IDEA 2004 also requires that the student's IEP reflect a statement of the student's present levels of academic achievement and functional performance, including how the student's disability affects his or her involvement and progress in the general curriculum. The IEP must also include a statement of measurable annual goals focused on meeting the student's needs related to involvement and progress in the general curriculum.

State and local districts are also increasing their graduation requirements to include more rigorous coursework and tests to demonstrate knowledge and skills needed after high school (Kochhar-Bryant & Bassett, 2002b). Many states and districts now set benchmarks to ensure that students are at appropriate points along the pathway to receiving a standard high school diploma (National Center on Educational Outcomes, 2002). As stated in Chapter 2, the No Child Left Behind Act (2002) requires that by 2005–2006 all states have in place tests in reading and mathematics in grades 3 to 8, and at least once between grades 10 and 12. By 2007–2008, states must assess students in science at least once in elementary, middle, and high school. Since IDEA 2004 requires that students with disabilities be included in these tests, this should provide information on how students with disabilities compare to those without disabilities in their district and state. Thurlow, Thompson, and Johnson (2002) attempted to tie together the transition and standards-based education process in the following statement: "Since state assessments primarily assess progress toward standards, and since progress toward standards is addressed on IEPs, and since IEPs for older students become transition plans, it all fits together" (pp. 96–97).

Elliott, Braden, and White (2001) defined *assessment* as "the process of gathering information about a student's abilities or behavior for the purpose of making decisions about the student" (p. 3). They then defined *testing* as "one simple procedure through which we obtain evidence about a student's learning or behavior" (p. 3). We would propose that the focus should be on *assessing* students with disabilities, rather than *testing* them, as they make the transition to postsecondary education. We would also propose that the student and his or her family be active participants in the assessment process, as well as in the entire transition process. This will require providing specific training in the area of self-determination, and providing opportunities for the student to apply the skills he or she has learned (Field, Martin, Miller, Ward, & Wehmeyer, 1998a, 1998b).

Recommendations for Documenting a Disability. We support the six recommendations made by Sitlington and Payne (2004), as alternatives to the formal test results recommended by AHEAD.

1. Summarize information from the IEP that documents why the student is "in need of special education services," including why the student's disability "substantially limits" his or her learning.
2. Report the results of any curriculum-based measurements in which the student is compared to a district or school norm group.

3. Include the results of the statewide and districtwide assessments that compare how the student performed in comparison to all students in the state or district.
4. Summarize information from the student's IEP that compares the student's performance to the standards and benchmarks of the district.
5. Include the results of any applicable formal psychometric tests that may have been given as part of the transition assessment process.
6. Arrange to have a certified or licensed professional from a local educational agency provide a review and evaluation of previous disability documentation and current data on the impact of the disability on the academic achievement and functional performance. This review would include recommendations on how to assist the student in meeting his or her postsecondary goals (S. Shaw, personal communication, February 17, 2004).

Determining Accommodations Needed

The focus of assessment in this area is to determine whether accommodations are needed and, if so, what accommodations are the most effective. There are a number of challenges to gathering valid information in this area. First, the accommodations that have been provided in high school are seldom evaluated in terms of their effectiveness. Most of the data on the use of accommodations is from assessments, usually state-level tests (Tindal & Fuchs, 2000). In addition, the grades in which students with disabilities are involved in transition planning are the same grades in which researchers see declining numbers of students using accommodations. If accommodations are not built in during transition planning, it is difficult for students to know which accommodations are needed (Thurlow, Thompson, & Johnson, 2002). Finally, the need for specific accommodations may vary from the high school to the postsecondary education environment.

Acknowledging these challenges, we would still recommend the following approaches to gathering the information needed to determine accommodations for each student. This information could be summarized in a transition portfolio (Neubert & Moon, 2000) that would go with the student to the postsecondary program. Again, we support recommendations made by Sitlington and Payne (2004) that the assessment process and resulting findings focus on the use of accommodations to support the student's strengths and we endorse the following specific approaches they outline to achieve this:

1. Include information related to accommodations that have been found effective.
2. Conduct an interview with the student, since he or she should be in the best position to identify the accommodations needed and those that have been effective in the past.

3. Interview family members, secondary instructional and support staff, and any adult service providers who have worked with the student.
4. Summarize information from the student's IEP and other records regarding how the accommodations were used and their effectiveness.
5. Work with the student to assist him or her in conducting a systematic analysis of the specific postsecondary program and possible related employment situations—to determine the essential requirements of these environments and the accommodations that will be needed. Summarize this information in a format useful to postsecondary institutions.
6. Conduct a situational assessment of the student within the postsecondary course and/or future employment situation—to determine if the student can meet the demands of these environments following appropriate instruction and effective accommodations.

Integrating the Information Gathered into the Transition Assessment Process

It is important that this process of gathering information be integrated into the ongoing assessment and planning process discussed in Chapter 5. It should not be a process of gathering isolated information for the use of the postsecondary institution. In order to accomplish this, we recommend the following:

- With the student, develop a process for determining what accommodations are most effective for the individual student at the secondary level, and include only those accommodations in the student's IEP. In examining accommodations for testing, Tindal and Fuchs (2000) referred to the concept of "differential effectiveness"—that is, when students with disabilities perform better with the accommodation *and* the accommodation does not benefit students without disabilities. Although this concept is often not currently applied when selecting accommodations, it may yield accommodations that are truly effective when used by the student.
- Work with the postsecondary institutions in the surrounding area (those most often attended) to identify the format for providing the information they need. Hopefully this can be done as part of the activities of the local or regional transition advisory board, which includes representatives of key adult providers (Blalock & Benz, 1999).
- If possible, involve a representative of the postsecondary institution in the IEP meetings in which transition to postsecondary education is being discussed.

On a national level, we also recommend that the Council for Exceptional Children (CEC) and its relevant divisions establish ongoing communication with AHEAD to identify strategies for enhancing the transition of students with learning and other disabilities to postsecondary education. In the newsletter from Disability Access Information and Support, Jarrow (2003) issued a call to postsecondary disability service providers to focus on the accommodations that have been requested by the student *before* they review the documentation the student has provided related to his or her disability. We view this as a positive indication that the issues that have been presented in this chapter may be open for discussion.

Conclusion

This chapter has provided general information on postsecondary education and the participation of individuals with disabilities in this option. It also outlined the skills your students will need in postsecondary programs and some strategies that you can use at the secondary level to assist your students with this important transition. In addition, some strategies were identified for you, the individual, and the family to use in evaluating and accessing postsecondary education options. This chapter also discussed the information and documentation that many postsecondary institutions are requiring in order to determine eligibility and to provide the needed accommodations to students. The final section focused on gathering the information needed through the transition assessment process.

We identified two major issues related to postsecondary education that you and the IEP team need to consider. Key players on this IEP team must be the student and the family. First, Is postsecondary education a transition goal for the student? If so, How will you balance the need for training in individually determined functional skills with preparation in the skills needed to succeed in postsecondary education, particularly at the college or university level? Second, How will you ensure that your student will have the documentation required by the postsecondary institution to determine eligibility and obtain the needed accommodations? Kincaid (1997) recommended that the informed family, as part of the student's transition planning, will "know to demand that the district update the youngster's documentation so that it is acceptable in a postsecondary or employment setting" (p. 6).

There are no quick answers to these questions. We feel that it is imperative, however, that they be asked as part of the transition planning process, which is fully integrated into the IEP process. We also believe that it is critical that you work closely with those individuals and institutions who are providing postsecondary education in your geographic area.

Finally, we urge that you consider *all* of the postsecondary education options that were presented at the beginning of this chapter. Each of these options provides specific training and experience that can benefit all individu-als, including individuals with disabilities. Much of the literature addresses four-year colleges and universities, but junior colleges, community colleges, private vocational schools, and adult education programs also offer a number of programs that may assist your students in meeting their postsecondary education transition goals.

8 Transition to Adult Independent and Interdependent Living

Be not simply good—be good for something.

—Henry David Thoreau

In Chapter 1, we affirmed the notion that school-to-adult living transition is not only a results-oriented *process* (as stated in the IDEA definition) but also a multidimensional *service delivery system.* Halpern (1994) laid out five outcome goal areas requiring multiple delivery approaches: (1) employment, (2) participation in postsecondary education, (3) maintaining a home (independent living), (4) community involvement, and (5) personal and social relationships. Independent functioning in each of these areas is usually a stated goal, but realistically we recognize that no person is truly independent. This is especially true for those individuals with severe disabilities. Interdependence is more realistic and can actually have a positive value in terms of mutually supportive functioning in life. This idea is discussed further in this chapter.

One way of explaining transition from school-to-adult independent and interdependent living is to describe the major components of independent and interdependent living and then present some of the features of good school and community support systems. The components and features presented in this chapter incorporate Halpern's five areas. They reflect what we believe are currently recommended concepts and practices in the transition process and needed service delivery systems. We will focus on all the content areas of transition planning presented in Figure 1.1, with the exception of *employment* and *further education and training,* since these were covered in Chapters 6 and 7.

Training in Independent and Interdependent Daily Living Skills

The theme of the transition education and services models presented in Chapter 1 is the goal of systematic, quality training in life career and transition skills. It bears repeating here that it is our basic assumption in writing this book that training for community living for every age period and the transition stages between age periods must occur well before transition from school-to-adult living. This assumption is supported by the Council for Exceptional Children Division on Career Development and Transition (Clark, Carlson, Fisher, Cook, & D'Alonzo, 1991); they concluded that all transition models should contain features that focus on systematic, quality training. This training should be provided at home and in the schools as early as possible.

One of the problems with general program models in education is that they typically stop short of describing the instructional procedures that lead to effective implementation of the programs. This frustrating characteristic of models is not solely the failure of their authors, though. Users of a model must adapt the concepts of the general model to their own situations. If a model is too specific, it does not generalize well to other situations. Hence, the development of specific systematic instructional procedures has to occur at the local level. Guidelines from the model's authors or state guidelines can be extremely helpful, but the local ownership is critical. A good example of this is trying to follow a standards-based educational model and make instruction functional and applicable for community skill outcomes.

A systematic approach to training students with disabilities for life demands and life transitions begins with the development of a locally referenced scope and sequence curriculum. This curriculum should address life-centered career competencies and transition skills in community living, social and interpersonal interactions, and employment. The content of the curriculum should stem from the outcomes for education that teachers and parents have determined jointly. This set of outcomes should serve as a basis for developing IEPs. Even with such a set of outcomes, however, unless there is a systematic approach to the generation of annual goals and short-term objectives, a student could end up with a set of objectives that are skewed toward only one area, such as academics, vocational outcomes, social skills, or leisure.

Most of the existing school transition models call for quality programming in terms of age-appropriate, integrated, functional, and community-based instruction. The implication here is that instruction should be increasingly functional rather than increasingly academic, but at the same time should be provided in integrated settings. These common features of quality programs come out of the literature on vocational transition programming for students with severe disabilities (McDonnell, Mathot-Buckner, & Ferguson, 1996; Wehman, 1996). Most parents and educators affirm a strong functional component for students with severe disabilities. However, there is a point at which this is a real problem for students classified as having mild disabilities who may need instruction in this area (i.e., learning disabilities, mild behavior disorders, or mild mental retardation). The current instructional options available to this population in schools are increasingly academic rather than increasingly functional. The one avenue where some meaningful functionality exists within general education for some students is at the high school level in career and technical education (Evers & Elksnin, 1998) and some electives.

Where the curriculum and instruction problem most often occurs is in the areas of daily living skills and personal-social skills. Only so much can be taught through incidental learning in integrated academic classes; the rest must be taught systematically and with direct accountability of outcomes to objectives. Money management and consumer math are good examples of where a general education math textbook includes one or two application examples or presents several word problems involving consumer math. These are good for students who make the connection easily between a math concept or skill and its practical application, but they do not provide nearly enough detail or opportunity to practice and demonstrate achievement in concrete, generalizable tasks for students who need that.

The literature for special education is full of proposals for and support of functional curriculum models (see Chapter 10). What is functional and what is nonfunctional continues to be in the eye of the beholder, however. The student or parent who insists on an academic high school curriculum may view it as highly functional for achieving the goal of participating with peers who are nondisabled or the goal of going on to higher education. It is because of this personalizing of values, and the goals that emerge from those values, that individual choice in determining what is functional must be honored. The policy implications of this for a school district make it imperative that each special education program in the district provide both an option for a regular, integrated course of study with functional content as well as a functional, life-skills course of study. Each is legitimate for the school to address. Each is worthy of the school's official approval. The challenge in this is to prevent the two courses of study from being so mutually exclusive and inclusive for one type of student that the two courses of study become educational "tracks." Persistent attention to functional outcomes *and* the issues of instructional delivery are marks of any quality program.

Communication Skills and Academic Performance for Independent Living

Reading and writing are communication skills that are essential for success in most academic tasks. Communication and academic skills are both developmental outcomes that are the means to an end for goals of further education and training and adult living after high school. Specific attention to academic performance outcome goals is given in Chapters 7 and 10. This section presents only the more functional uses in daily living for communication and academic skills.

Communication Skills.   Basic skills of listening and speaking are the foundations of people's interactions at home, in the neighborhood, at work, and in the community. For those individuals who have hearing or speech problems, alternative methods of language reception and expression are critical. It is important that transition education includes as much instruction and/or related services as needed for each individual to ensure that he or she can communicate satisfactorily and independently in as many settings and situations as possible.

If a student is uncomfortable with his or her ability to listen to or receive information in getting and following directions, participating in a social conversation, being an active listener to a friend or family member, or understanding information given by a nurse, attorney, judge, or salesperson, then the student's IEP should include some type of instructional plan to help him or her improve. Whether the listening skills are limited because of primary language differences, cultural patterns of limited language interaction between adults and children, psychosocial factors, or any other reason, it makes no difference. If a student's present level of performance in listening skills is limited, but he or she has goals and preferences for the future that involves better auditory, manual, or augmentative/alternative receptive language skills, then there is a transition need for the student to move from one level of communication performance to another.

The same case can be made for speaking, signing, or augmentative/alternative means of expressing information. If you have ever been required to simulate a communication disability by going into a store to purchase an item or by trying to get bus or subway information from a stranger in the street, you know that it is not only a frustrating task to communicate, but also a socially stressful situation because of the personal and social reactions to you. One needs to be sensitive to students who stutter, who have limited English proficiency, who have labored and difficult speech due to cerebral palsy, who sign but cannot speak, who use a communication device, or who have any other expressive language problems.

If it is true that language disorders can persist across the lifetime of an individual, it is also true that the symptoms, manifestations, effects, and severity of those disorders change over time. Too often, people assume that expressive communication skills are established early or are stabilized by the time a student reaches adolescence. The consequence of that assumption leads students, their families, and professionals to give up on any continuing instruction, therapies, or related services.

Articulation problems in speech are the most common among speech disorders and involve problems with phonology and speech production. It is important to remember that some invisible expressive language problems also exist. Nippold (1993) discussed three important elements of normal language development that may need attention with some children and youth: syntax, semantics, and pragmatics.

- *Syntax* is the grammatical structure and complexity of language. This element of language can be a problem for students with language disorders or for those who grew up in a nonstandard English language environment, a non-English-speaking environment, or a socioeconomic environment that does not value standard English language structure.
- *Semantics* involves the meaning of words and sentences as well as the combinations of certain words in special contexts. Examples of semantics are in the various meanings of single words, depending on context and/or inflection of the voice when speaking the word, as well as combinations of words or phrases that have two or more meanings.
- *Pragmatics* refers to the functional use of both verbal and nonverbal language. This means that using socially appropriate language is important in communication, and sometimes more important than the use of proper syntax and semantics. Pragmatics presents difficulties for many children and youths with learning, behavioral, and communication disorders. These difficulties emerge in job interviews, interacting with salespersons, social interactions with peers, social interactions at work, and in many other life situations.

In planning for communication skill needs for students in the transition planning process, it is important to know as much about these needs as possible. Without knowledge of the specific communication difficulties a student has, and how those difficulties contribute to performance in school, interactions with friends and adults, and communication in the community, it is difficult to know whether to write goals that will be delivered via instruction, related services, or both. Assessment of the nature and frequency of communication problems is critical for being able to focus on the real skill problems and determine how best to address them in the IEP. Adequate direct instruction in these areas in typical language arts, English, and speech classes cannot be assumed.

Academic Skills.   Functional academic skills for independent living involve reading, writing, and computation. Just as an inability to read, write, or solve math problems is not an insurmountable handicap for getting and keeping a job, it is not an insurmountable handicap for independent or interdependent living. No one would argue that the more skilled an individual is in functional academics, the more options he or she has in community participation and the more independent he or she can be. Reading street signs, traffic signs, product labels, written instructions, personal notes or letters, public notices, and the like are common adult daily living reading tasks. Completing forms and writing personal notes or letters are written communication tasks requiring some academic skills in handwriting, spelling, and basic sentence construction. These also are common adult activities, especially in employment and fulfilling the role of a parent. Finally, counting, addition, subtraction, multiplication, division, and use of fractions and decimals are common task demands in managing money, consumer problems, measuring, and job requirements. Academic achievement is also a functional skill for meeting adequate yearly progress (AYP) and for anyone hoping to attend a postsecondary education or training program.

One of the most common forms of assistance in an interdependent living relationship is assistance with reading, writing, and math. Parents, siblings, spouses, and sometimes even the children of persons with limited abilities in functional academics provide support for reading, writing, or math tasks. Some individuals can accept this help without loss of self-esteem, but others find accepting help of this kind more difficult. It is important to identify in the IEP transition planning process (1) a student's present level of functioning in functional academics; (2) instructional goals for reading, writing, and math; and (3) the family's preferences regarding instructional content and instructional delivery priorities. Parent preference decisions and informed consent to a course of study plan must be based on what a student will actually receive in one type of instructional setting versus another with regard to traditional or functional academics.

Self-Determination Skills for Independent Living

Self-determination might be defined by students as "making our own decisions." Some high school students have developed a mature level of self-determination in making their own choices and acting on those choices, but most students (with or without disabilities) are still at an emerging level of self-determination. Those students are making some choices and decisions, but are still dependent on parents for most major decisions.

Going back to the definition of *self-determination:* Is making one's own decisions all that is involved in self-determination? Although there are a number of formal definitions of self-determination offered by individuals who have a professional interest in self-determination (Field, Martin, Miller, Ward, & Wehmeyer, 1998a), we present the definition and self-determination model of Field and Hoffman (1994). Their definition states that *self-determination* is "one's ability to define and achieve goals based on a foundation of knowing and valuing oneself" (p. 164). Their model, presented in Figure 8.1, shows how the self-determination process involves affective, cognitive, and behavioral

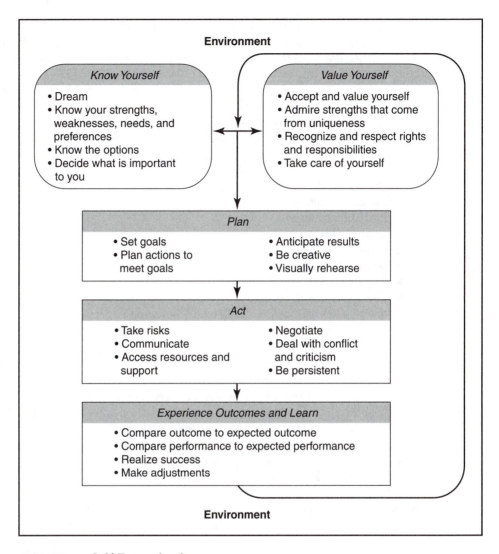

FIGURE 8.1   Self-Determination

Source: From "Development of a Model for Self-Determination" by S. Field and A. Hoffman, 1994, *Career Development for Exceptional Individuals, 17* (2). Copyright 1994 by CDEI. Reprinted by permission.

activity by a person, each of which affects the extent of self-determination that that person will achieve. As you can see in the model, there are five major components: (1) know yourself, (2) value yourself, (3) plan, (4) act, and (5) experience outcomes and learn. These involve much more than mere decision making. Field, Hoffman, and Spezia (1998) laid out a set of practical strategies for teachers to use in teaching self-determination skills following this model.

Self-determination skills in an individual are reflected in some of the characteristics of that individual. Using the Field and Hoffman (1994) model of self-determination, one would look for the extent to which a student knows himself or herself, values himself or herself, plans for the future, acts on his or her plans and goals, and experiences the outcomes of the planning and action and learns from that experience. More specifically, Wehmeyer (1997) suggested the following characteristics of self-determined individuals:

- Choice making
- Decision making
- Problem solving
- Goal setting and attainment
- Self-observation skills
- Self-evaluation skills
- Self-reinforcement skills
- Internal locus of control
- Positive attribution of efficacy and outcome expectancy
- Self-awareness
- Self-knowledge

Some children seem to have inherited an ability to know their own minds and be decisive; many others learned these characteristics. Even someone with a natural ability to solve problems and be internally motivated can improve those abilities with opportunities to learn new skills related to self-determination. Learning self-determination skills, then, comes out of learning environments that encourage, nurture, and support self-determination values, thinking, and behavior. Field and associates (1998) stated their belief that schools can and should be providing supportive environments for students in learning self-determination skills. Among these school environmental characteristics, which include both classroom and schoolwide factors, are the following:

- Availability of self-determined role models
- Curriculum variables
- Patterns of response to student behaviors
- Availability of student supports (p. 4)

Self-determination skills are generic, but, to be useful, they have to be applied to real problems, interests, preferences, and needs. The transition planning process through the IEP is an ideal way to help students focus their learning of self-determination skills on their own transition planning. Some students may resist planning for the real world after high school because they are very happy with their roles as children who do not have to take full responsibility for their food, clothing, or a place to live. Their parents might even provide them with a means of transportation and some spending money. If, at the same time, these same students are enjoying some of the privileges of adulthood (choosing their friends, choosing life-style activities, determining their own curfews, etc.), it is no surprise to see some of them show resistance to moving out of this phase of life into real independence and personal responsibility. They do not really want to think about that aspect of their futures, especially at the elementary, middle school, or even early high school years.

Another type of student who might resist specific planning for life demands in the future are those who have been sheltered and protected by families and schools. These students have no real information about the possibilities and demands of adulthood nor do they know themselves well enough to know what they want for themselves and whether they have the knowledge and skills to make it in adult life. Some of these students are overly dependent on parents because of parent behavior. Others are dependent because of cultural traditions in the family with regard to ethnic identity and gender roles.

Another type of student is the student with severe disabilities. The nature of the disability and the specific limitations a student has cognitively are important factors in how much self-determined behavior is appropriate in terms of maintaining health, safety, and actual life decisions. Even for those considered to have the most severe disabilities, though, some self-determination is possible. Many with little or no verbal communication are still able to know their preferences for certain foods, activities, and settings, and communicate those preferences in a variety of ways. Teachers and paraprofessionals need to learn to interpret their behavior as communication and to work continuously to give choices and encourage self-help behavior. Interdependent living depends on good communication between these students and those in their environments who are in a position to teach self-determined behavior and assist students in developing in this area (Wehmeyer, Agran, & Hughes, 1998).

Fortunately, there also are students who are eager to become independent. They want to make choices about vocations, further education and training, type of residence after leaving home, and how they will get involved in the community as citizens, consumers, and participants in leisure and recreation. They find the transition planning process a challenging and enjoyable opportunity. They thrive on assessments of their interests, preferences, and skills that relate to what they see as "real" adult demands, as opposed to current school or home environment demands.

The perspective of self-determination that we encourage in this book is an understanding that individual students have a variety of backgrounds and influences on them. They are not necessarily going to be at the same place as other students in developing self-determination skills simply because they are of a certain age or grade level. Self-determination skills can be taught, but they must be taught with a high degree of individualization, guidance, and support. Students must begin the process of learning and practicing self-determination skills where they are in their own lives, and the earlier the better. They may or may not be ready for the hard questions that are imposed sometimes in the IEP transition planning process. A careful, thoughtful approach to each student's current and near future goals for himself or herself is necessary. As with other instructional need areas for transition education, parental preferences are key here. Parents must be willing to let go of some decision making and encourage self-determined behavior. Some parents have difficulty with this, whereas others welcome the school's initiative and efforts.

Interpersonal Relationship Skills for Independent Living

Interpersonal relationship skills, as an outcome domain in the Comprehensive Transition Education model (Figure 1.1), incorporates much of the thinking of the two components of the original School-Based Career Development and Transition Education model (Clark & Kolstoe, 1990, 1995), which were referred to as *attitudes, values, and habits* and *human relationships.* The broader term of *interpersonal relationships* necessarily draws on personal values, social attitudes, and interpersonal interactions. We believe the school cannot take full responsibility for these areas because the family's role remains absolutely critical. Still, the school simply cannot ignore the importance of knowledge and skills in interpersonal relationships and leave all instruction in this area to the family and community institutions.

Values, Attitudes, and Habits in Interpersonal Relationships. People's values are the basis for what they find worthy in other people and in themselves. Values undergird personal conduct, preferences leading to choices, and ideas leading to social judgments. The current calls for reform from both liberal and conservative elements of society send schools different messages. Many school administrators and even some teachers see a problem in the school becoming involved in the process of developing and fostering values, because that raises the question of determining *which* values should be included. Values can be associated with any number of things—money, religious beliefs, race, education, sexuality, length of hair or hemlines, the right to carry a gun, civic responsibility, patriotism, work, leisure, and so on. Some of these raise issues that are controversial or sensitive to certain students and their families.

In the early days of U.S. education, there was absolutely no problem about teaching moral values in schools. The McGuffey readers explicitly taught reading and moral values in the stories that were included. Over the years, values education became less direct, but schools still persisted in teaching respect for the flag, patriotism and loyalty and responsibility to country, and, in many areas of the country, certain Christian religious beliefs through school prayer, religious music, and observances of various holidays. The national racial and human rights demonstrations of the 1960s, coupled with the debates over U.S. involvement in the Vietnam war, led the general public and many schools to rethink the school's role in social values issues.

Raths, Merrill, and Sidney (1966) offered a workable compromise during this turbulent period, though not a solution, to the dilemma of to teach or not to teach values when they suggested in the mid-1960s that educators should not be concerned with the *content* of people's values, but rather with the *process* of valuing. From this viewpoint, the focus changes from thinking about whether to teach students certain value-laden concepts to how to teach students to select, defend, and act on their values. The term *values clarification* became a part of this movement. Advocates of this approach believed that school-aged children and youths should be able to know *what* they think or believe, *why* they think or believe in that way, and *how* their actions are related to those beliefs. This approach encourages students to decide for themselves what are positive values and what are not. Obviously, some parents who want their children to adopt specific family values and not make value decisions on their own at school strongly object to this approach.

The values-clarification compromise approach in values education is not completely acceptable to many who believe the school has a responsibility to maintain and preserve traditional moral and social values. We believe that the valuing process is very important in learning self-determination and in developing interpersonal relationships. They are very important in being able to participate actively in one's own transition planning and education. However, we believe also that the valuing process should not be taught to the exclusion of or apart from certain specific values that are known to be positive and beneficial for individual and group success in life.

Some examples of positive values for all students are those included in the Eanes Elementary School (Eanes School District, Austin, Texas) curriculum (Eeanes School District, 2004):

- *Respect:* To foster pride in all endeavors with people, places, and things
- *Friendship:* To make and keep a friend through mutual trust and caring
- *Cooperation:* To work together toward a common goal or purpose
- *Organization:* To plan, arrange and implement in an orderly way; to keep things orderly and ready to use
- *Responsibility:* To respond when appropriate, to be accountable for your actions
- *Integrity:* To act according to a sense of what's right and wrong
- *Effort:* To try your hardest
- *Sense of humor:* To laugh and be playful without hurting others
- *Problem solving:* To seek solutions in difficult situations and everyday problems
- *Caring:* To feel and show concern for others
- *Curiosity:* To have a desire to investigate and seek understanding of one's world
- *Common sense:* To use good judgment
- *Flexibilty:* To be willing to alter plans when necessary

- *Initiative:* To do something because it needs to be done
- *Patience:* To wait calmly for someone or something
- *Perseverance:* To keep at it (p. 3)

The Eanes Elementary School credits Kovalik and Olsen (1994) as the inspiration for what they refer to as their Life Skills program. *Life skills,* as defined by the Eanes program, refers to citizenship and courtesy. On the first day of the school week, a new life skill is presented and elaborated on during the morning announcements. All classroom teachers and staff are expected to reinforce the topic, such as flexibility or patience, throughout the week in every setting of the school building or campus. Each homeroom teacher gives a Life Skill Citizenship Award each week to one student who demonstrated the skill of the week. Names of students receiving the award are listed each week in the parent newsletter.

The focus on values thus far has not directly related to attitudes and habits. The reason for this is that values, attitudes, and habits are so interdependent that a rationale for one is a rationale for the other two. Values lead people to assume attitudes or positions that are relatively consistent, which then result in relatively predictable behaviors or habits. For example, if a student values respect and wants others to respect him or her to say or do the right thing, then that student should extend respect to others. Respect, friendship, cooperation, integrity, sense of humor, and caring are all values that contribute to positive interpersonal relationships in most situations.

Will a program like the Eanes program (or some variation of it) work in any socioeconomic setting? Will it work at the middle school or high school levels? Are these character or citizenship values idealistic middle-class values only? Would a few students (maybe more than a few) so resist some type of effort to work on these values that you would be unwilling to participate in a school effort or even try some strategies on your own? These are important questions to answer as you grapple with the issue of values.

Human Relationships.   Historically, schools have not taught human relationships directly. Indirectly, however, they have used classroom discipline, behavior management, and strategies for meeting students' emotional needs through the instructional process. However, these have been taught almost exclusively through rules of behavior and incidental methods rather than through clearcut, purposeful objectives and procedures. The family has been rightfully viewed as the primary unit responsible for children's basic personal-social development, including interpersonal relationship skills. Carter (1998) presented an eloquent case for better human relationships—what he calls *civility.* In his view, civility is lacking in U.S. society and parents need to respond to the problem. These days of school violence, gang activity, sexual harassment, and the sale and use of addictive substances on school property make it imperative for schools to respond in a positive, responsible way with parent and family support.

Aggressive, acting-out behavior is important, whether it is seen among students with disabilities or students without disabilities. The vast majority of students with disabilities do not engage in such extreme, antisocial behavior. However, there are instances of such behavior among students receiving special education services, both as aggressors and as victims; thus, the issue cannot be ignored. This is one of the reasons the topic of bullying is appearing more frequently in professional literature for educators (Braun, 2001; Dake, 2003; Espelage & Swearer, 2003; Sampson, 2002; Smith, Morita, Junger-Tas, Olweus, Catalano, & Slee, 1999).

Children and youths with disabilities are frequently concerned about peer acceptance, making and keeping a circle of friends, dating, and engaging in the same kinds of social interactions as do most other persons their ages. Most all teenagers without disabilities are concerned about these same things, but there is one major difference between teenagers with and without disabilities that makes interpersonal relationships more difficult. That difference is the social stigma that is attached to being identified or labeled as a person with a disability. Most children and youths with disabilities have far too many memories of emotional pain, social embarrassment, or even anger at the reactions of peers, teachers, counselors, principals, and others toward them. Reactions range from avoidance or outright rejection to poorly concealed curiosity when the disabilities are highly visible. For the more hidden disabilities (deafness, mild mental retardation, learning disabilities, etc.), the reactions may range from disguised rejection to teasing or laughter at situations when their problems in performing various tasks become obvious.

It is commonly accepted that the criteria for acceptance or rejection in social situations are generally classified as pertaining either to personality and social skills or to ability to perform valued skills. Body size, muscular strength, maturational development, and athletic ability also appear to be important to youths in sizing someone up for acceptance or rejection into their circle. If this practice is accepted, it is clear that a number of students with disabilities are not going to "make the cut" among their peers without disabilities. If the notion is accepted that instruction, training, and modification of behavior can impact one's manifested personality, social skills, physical appearance, or performance skills, then it is clear that many students need assistance to deal with those aspects of human relationships that affect their acceptance. Such assistance can come from direct instruction (social skill training), modeling (mentors, peer tutors, friendship groups, etc.), skill training (sports, fitness training, recreational skill training, etc.), and related services (school counselor, school social worker, school psychologist, school nurse, physical therapy, occupational therapy, or speech therapy).

Many teachers and parents express concern about current school and neighborhood social environments for all children and adolescents, not just for individuals with disabilities. School violence at one extreme to excessive social isolation at the other cause tensions and psychological stress for students, teachers, administrators, and parents. Somewhere in between there are students who are bothered by typical peer interactions related to everyday competitions for teacher favor, peer favor and acceptance, students seeking social dominance over others (benign bullying), cliques and in-groups, and the like. Among the majority of students at school there is a general desire for, at best, some basic civility and respect as a person. At the least, they hope for being left alone to make their way without fear of teasing, unkind comments, or outright rejection.

Interpersonal relationships, or "getting along with others," is difficult in large school environments where students know few classmates by name. Anonymity at school, like in the larger community, does nothing to encourage knowing someone well enough to recognize common traits or those human qualities that could be admired, accepted, or even tolerated. We all remember individuals in our own experience at school that were easy targets for teasing or gossip, simply because no one really knew them. There were students with old or out-of-style clothes, students on free lunches, students with body odor, students with physical appearance differences, students who "talked funny" because of accents or patterns associated with uneducated families, students with no social graces, students from markedly different religious backgrounds, students who deliberately sought attention or identity by hair coloring or style and clothes, and students who tried too hard to be accepted and made things worse by their behaviors.

The case of Craig Turner (page 87) illustrates the last example of students with interpersonal relationship issues. Craig was described as a student who is in frequent trouble at school due to his truancy, bringing alcoholic drinks and drugs onto the school campus, and his "in-your-face" beligerance toward many students and authority. He was described as a manipulator of his parents and teachers, and peers found him difficult to trust as he showed two very different interpersonal styles. It is very possible that Craig's reading difficulties and general school achievement problems contribute to his interpersonal relationship difficulties. What should Craig's IEP look like, given his case scenario? Will his IEP goals focus only on his academic deficits because that is his parents' primary concern and clearly a school concern in relation to test scores?

Interdependent living outcomes are highly related to interpersonal relationships. Does Craig need some instructional IEP goals related to better interpersonal skills or does he need a linkage goal to a mentor, a stable and well-adjusted peer (or peer group), or a specially selected guidance counselor or teacher who relates well to students like Craig? Results-oriented goals are as appropriate in the area of interpersonal relationships as they are for academic, vocational, or independent living skills. Is it reasonable to predict that Craig will "make it" someday in a job, a social group, and a marriage or loving relationship? Some students do mature and move out of negative patterns as they get out of school, but many do not. Even for those that do, the task is painful and difficult.

Good interpersonal relationship skills affect every area of life. Students in transitions through the school years to the adult world deserve to have programs and services that will assist them in reaching their potentials in this skill area as much as programs and services in academics, physical education, and music or art. Quality of life at home, at school, at work, and in neighborhoods and communities is often judged by a general sense of happiness and well-being. These indicators of quality of life are often the result of successful interpersonal relationships. It is no surprise that parents of graduates or dropouts who have been in special education programs frequently rank satisfactory psychosocial adjustment as the number-one problem for their sons or daughters after leaving school.

Some people with disabilities find social acceptance in work settings that was missing at school, even though they make no changes in their social behavior. Others, if they continue some of the social behaviors that were typical at school, continue to find social rejection in the workplace. At the extreme, such individuals may even lose their jobs. More people with disabilities, in fact, lose jobs because of socially related problems than they do for skill deficiencies. Elksnin and Elksnin (1998) presented an excellent case for the need to teach occupational social skills for many students, particularly those with disabilities.

Integrated Community Participation Skills for Independent Living

Life skills needed for integrated community participation overlap considerably with communication skills, self-determination skills, independent living skills, employment skills, and leisure and recreation skills. We acknowledge that overlap but separate them for emphasis on certain areas that may be overlooked or ignored otherwise. Inclusive education practices have allowed many students with disabilities to experience integration in the school community in new ways. However, many of the inclusive activities or strategies at school are organized and orchestrated by professionals or peer groups. Preparing students with the skills to integrate themselves without integration programs or advocacy in the adult community is a major challenge.

Just as there are individuals who would prefer not to be integrated with nondisabled peers at school, there are those who will feel the same way about certain settings in the community. Most people, in fact, pick and choose what they want to do in the community based on who they will be doing it with and their abilities. Let us assume, though, that a majority of individuals with disabilities want to be a part of their neighborhoods and community. How can they make that happen? How can you, as an educator, help them make that happen, especially when their choices for certain kinds of participation are very individualized?

One community participation issue is a common one across many different types of disabilities, even though it may play out a little differently for certain types of disabilities. That is the issue of being able to get out into the community. Mobility may be part of the problem for students who are blind or who have physical disabilities affecting movement. It is often difficult for these students to have quick and independent access to the community, which may limit their participation in community activities. Training and guidance on obtaining and using mobility strategies for getting around in the community, including assistive technology, is the responsibility of educators or orientation and mobility specialists.

Similarly, students with orientation problems in relation to travel experience limitations in getting where they want to go because of difficulties in knowing where they are and how to reach locations outside their familiar surroundings. This may include students who are blind as well as those who have spatial orientation problems (left-right, north-south, east-west, etc.). Mobility and orientation instruction is not typically taught in general education; therefore, special planning on the IEP may be required for a student to get the specific kinds of instruction and support he or she needs to be able to have the skills and confidence to move out of familiar and comfortable surroundings into the community.

Transportation alternatives are related to mobility and accessing the community. Transportation options vary with communities so much that it is difficult to generalize. On the other hand, all students and their parents need to be guided in thinking about the students' future needs in terms of finding, accessing, and using transportation alternatives. Learning to drive, use public transportation, or use carpools may be as important, if not more important, as any employment skill. Having an employment skill without the knowledge or skill to plan for and use transportation options to get to work is meaningless. General issues in available and accessible public transportation and individual issues in having enough money to own a car or use public transportation are common barriers, but one should never fail to give students the opportunity to learn travel and transportation skills so that they are prepared for the future.

Some generic integration opportunities require certain skills, either in accessing the opportunities or in participating in them. Among these are residential alternatives, citizenship alternatives, personal development and fulfillment alternatives, and leisure/recreation alternatives. Since leisure and recreation will be discussed in a later section, we will discuss only the first three of these in this section.

Residential Alternatives.   One of the most discouraging barriers to successful transition for students as they move from school to adult living is the lack of satisfactory or satisfying residential alternatives. Persons with physical disabilities find the inadequacy mostly related to architectural accessibility (see the companion website for an accessibility checklist). Individuals with mild disabling conditions—such as those with learning disabilities, low vision, or who are hard of hearing—may have more alternatives because of their independent functioning levels. Even so, the high cost of housing makes living away from home prohibitive for many. As a consequence, young adults with disabilities often live at home with parents. This is not uncommon even for single young adults who are nondisabled. The practice of living at home or returning home during transition periods among young people decreases some of the negative values attributed by professionals to living at home. Still, the important thing to remember in addressing the issue of residential alternatives is that if there is a need or desire for greater independence in living arrangements, there need to be alternatives.

Areas of skill for being able to access and use residential alternatives include the following:

1. *Skills for living alone or without adult supervision.* These skills begin with (a) knowing how to find a place to live; (b) making comparisons on price, locality, convenience, accessibility; and (c) negotiating a purchase, rental, or lease. The skill domain expands from there considerably into the areas establishing and maintaining a residence, such as securing connections for gas, electricity, water, and telephone; purchasing and knowing how to use needed furniture, applicances, and household goods; and ensuring security with locks and/or security alarms. Individuals who are blind or deaf need to have additional skill in securing necessary electrical devices for audio or visual alarms.

2. *Skills for living semi-independently (alone or with someone else).* These skills may involve some of the same skills as for living alone but will include the critical skills of knowing how and when to call for assistance from the police and the fire department, how to access information for community resources, how to access and use a transportation system, and how to be a responsible roommate, housemate, or neighbor.

3. *Skills for living at home.* Home living skills with parents will vary, but as young people work to establish their identities as adults while living at home, certain adult skill expectations are important for them to have. Among these include a greater concern for parents' privacy; skills for being able to manage one's own time, belongings, and space; skills permitting much more sharing in performing household tasks (laundry, cooking, housecleaning, snow/leaf removal, etc.); and skills in personal money management.

4. *Skills for living in a group home.* Group living skills are similar to skills for living at home except that there will need to be some preparation for moving out of the family home into a group home, and individuals need to learn the social skills required for sharing a room or house with non-family members. Among these are respect for personal privacy and property, awareness of social problems and how to resolve them, knowing

how to participate in group solving and decision making, and making sure to show responsibility for sharing in group home maintenance. Having social communication and leisure skills to pass time and share with others in the group is also an important skill for making and keeping friends.

Citizenship Alternatives.   Citizenship duties and opportunities stem from three sources: what people must do or must not do under the law, what people are permitted to do under the law, and what people are encouraged to do as responsible citizens to improve their communities. Adolescents with disabilities probably have some knowledge about what certain laws require citizens to do—such as pay taxes, obey traffic and driving laws, register for marriage licenses, register certain firearms, and the like. They also may have some varying degrees of knowledge about certain laws that prohibit citizens from doing certain things—such as assault, murder, robbery, burglary, theft, vandalism, drinking under age, selling or possessing drugs, rape, sexual assault, sexual relations with a minor, driving under the influence of alcohol, breaking curfew, and others. Students are likely to be less informed about their rights—what the law permits people to do in terms of their civil rights or how they, as citizens, can contribute to a better community. In all cases, however, students, with and without disabilities, have a greater chance of successful community integration if they are more knowledgeable and skilled in all aspects of community participation. The following knowledge and skill areas should be offered in social studies electives or approved as part of the content of high school graduation requirements for government or civics classes:

- Specific information on laws directly related to good conduct as citizens, including information addressing misconceptions and misinformation the students might have learned from the media, family members, or peers who are not well informed
- Specific information on accessing assistance from law-enforcement officers, reporting crimes, what it means to testify in court, and some understanding of penalties that are commonly associated with criminal behavior
- Specific information on civil rights for privacy; freedom of speech; trial by judge versus trial by jury; the right to be represented by counsel; Miranda rights; rights related to nondiscriminatory treatment in relation to race, ethnic background, or disabilities; rights (under the IDEA) upon turning age 18 (or majority age in their state); and the right to vote
- Specific knowledge and skills for obtaining information through accessing public records, public meetings, public services (e.g., libraries, museums, parks and recreation, etc.) and public and private assistance agencies (e.g., legal aid, public health, mental health, Planned Parenthood, and hotlines for suicide, substance abuse, and child abuse)

- Specific information on alternatives for community contributions, including volunteering for organizations and agencies, self-initiated activities for the welfare of the neighborhood and others (e.g., recycling, neighborhood safety watch, neighborhood clean-up, etc.), and charitable giving

Personal Development and Fulfillment Alternatives. Knowledge and skills for personal development and fulfillment are those that relate to being a successful, confident member of the community in those parts of the community where one can engage in personal development and growth activities. Knowing how to access religious group activities, civic organization activities and events, and public agency services as a means of continuing education and personal improvement is important. It is important, first of all, because integrated participation in the community requires some level of knowledge and skill. To be able to join and participate in a community activity, one must have some level of knowledge or skill in order to be accepted. Participation in religious worship, for example, requires some basic knowledge of the nature and purpose of certain rituals, understanding of the personal or social behavior that is expected in a particular synagogue, church, mosque, or meeting place, as well as some expectation of the personal benefits for attending and participating. Or if an individual decides to participate in a different religious group setting, old knowledge or skills might not be sufficient to participate successfully.

Another example of an alternative for personal development in the community is an organization or group that addresses personal problems or concerns. These groups are composed of people who have concerns about their health, weight, addictions (e.g., smoking, alcohol, drugs, gambling, etc.), money management, shyness, fear of public speaking, personal safety, discrimination, or any one of many other problem or concern areas. Will graduates with disabilities be able to access and participate in groups of this type? Will they even know about them? Will they know how to find out when and where they meet and what is expected of them to gain admission? Once admitted to a group, will they have the skills to be able to gain acceptance and maintain themselves in the group?

Integrated community participation is valued by everyone. Where knowledge and skills are the primary keys for young adults to participate in the community independently, educators need to respond by providing appropriate educational experiences. When an individual reaches his or her potential for learning certain participation skills, but still needs supports in the community in order to participate, one needs to respond just as one would for a person who needs support systems for accessing and maintaining employment or residential living. In other words, personal development and fulfillment is no less important as a transition planning and education commitment than employability and life skills.

Health and Fitness for Independent Living

The large amount of information on health and fitness issues today is stagger-
ing. It is difficult to pick up any newspaper or magazine or watch television
without seeing some article or program on health. Fitness magazines and commercial advertisements for fitness programs, centers, or equipment are numerous also. Concerns for good health (wellness) and fitness are common in adult
populations, as are concerns about the cost of health care, both preventive care
and treatment. Children and adolescents with or without disabilities typically
do not have these concerns. Those students whose disabilities are related to
chronic health problems, frequent or extended hospitalizations, persistent
pain, or even a terminal illness are exceptions, and undoubtedly think about
their current health conditions as well as their futures. We believe it is important that health and fitness be addressed individually in transition planning,
and that *all* students have access to physical education and health classes.
Knowing how important it may be for many students with disabilities to
improve their weight, endurance, flexibility, strength, and stamina, physical
education classes are important, both as required and elective credit classes.
Health classes are typically offered less frequently, but should be considered as
good sources of information on nutrition, common illnesses and how to treat
them, preventive measures for diseases, sex education, mental health problems
and treatment alternatives, and some of the advantages and disadvantages of
medications.

The obvious advantage to more knowledge about good nutrition, rest,
and exercise is that individuals can become more self-determined about their
physical status. One advantage children and youths do not always recognize
in knowing about and following through with health information and fitness
is the positive effects on mental health. Exercise has highly beneficial effects in
reducing stress, changing self-image, and increasing self-confidence. Consider
the example of Paul, who was in a high school self-contained class in Kansas
when he started lifting weights and bodybuilding. He was somewhat over-
weight but not obese. He developed a very muscular body with powerful
arms, legs, and broad shoulders and lost his soft, pudgy look. He continued
this activity as a young adult in the community at a fitness center and was
known as one of the "regulars." He maintained his integrated employment
and integrated fitness program in such a way that only a few people knew or
remembered that he had ever been in a special education program.

Health and safety concerns naturally overlap with daily living skills in
independent living environments (e.g., home security, fire prevention, using
toxic chemicals for cleaning in the kitchen or bathrooms, etc.). However, some
are health and safety concerns for which some students with disabilities might
need instruction, such as the following:

- Preventing colds and other contagious conditions
- Preventing infections

- Preventing sexually transmitted diseases
- Prenatal nutrition and avoidance of tobacco, alcohol, and harmful drugs
- First aid
- Immunizations
- Food handling and storage
- Nutrition
- Healthy sleep patterns
- Personal hygiene
- Substance abuse
- Use of over-the-counter and prescription medications

Independent/Interdependent Daily Living Skills

The need for schools to provide instruction in life skills for students with mild to moderate disabilities has been well documented (Brolin & Loyd, 2004; Cronin, Patton, & Wood, in press; Grigal & Neubert, 2004; Patton & Trainor, 2002; Pierangelo & Giuliani, 2004). Still, it is easy to become focused on employment skill training or postsecondary education and training preparation in transition programs and forget the importance of direct instruction in daily living or life skills. Keep in mind that the degree to which a person knows about and can perform daily living tasks is directly tied to how independent he or she is. Teachers owe it to their students and their students' families to provide the instruction and learning experiences for students to prepare them to be as independent as possible.

Daily living skills are important as they affect independence, but they also are important for the positive emotional and social supports they provide. There are certain social "penalties" that persons with disabilities have to pay if they cannot perform these competencies. Stares, comments by observers, embarrassing interactions, and questions from well-meaning but ignorant persons are typical. Competence in as many skills as possible helps individuals with disabilities present themselves as confident and capable people.

The Life-Centered Career Education Mild/Moderate curriculum programs (Brolin, 2003; Brolin & Loyd, 2004) specify nine daily living-skill or competency areas:

1. Managing family finances
2. Selecting, managing, and maintaining a home
3. Caring for personal needs
4. Raising children and living as a family
5. Buying and preparing food
6. Buying and caring for clothes
7. Engaging in civic activities
8. Using recreation and leisure
9. Getting around the community (mobility)

This list includes some areas of overlap with several transition competency areas that we have chosen to discuss separately (e.g., engaging in civic activities, using recreation and leisure, and, to some extent, caring for personal needs). The overlap or the different ways of organizing the content of life skills should not be important. What is important is that there is a great deal of agreement on what the basic life skills needed for independence are. The nine broad competency areas, and the numerous subcompetencies that come under each of them, reflect not only a logical, commonsense view of what daily living skills are critical but they also represent validated research results, demonstrating agreement on them.

Most life skills associated with independent living are rarely accomplished solely by an individual. In today's society, no one is truly independent of others and completely self-reliant. It is for that reason that we include the concept of *interdependent living*. Husbands and wives, couples living together, or roommates or housemates typically divide up responsibilities and depend on one another for certain tasks to be completed. People also yield their independence when they employ someone to do what they do not know how to do, do not have time to do, or are unable to do (e.g., repair their cars, prepare their income tax returns, dry clean their clothes, care for their sick pets, etc.). These are examples of interdependence. Interdependence has its own set of skills and subskills, and needs to be considered when looking at the transition planning and instruction needs of students with disabilities.

An example of skills needed for interdependent living is caring for personal needs. One of the most private and independent set of skills that most independent functioning people engage in is personal hygiene. The vast majority of people brush their own teeth, toilet themselves, shampoo their own hair, and perform other personal hygiene tasks. If a person is unable to perform these tasks because of a physical disability, someone else must do them. Individuals who grow up with such disabilities typically had parents or siblings to perform these tasks for them from the beginning, and there was little to learn about how these tasks were done and few or no personal adjustments to make in terms of embarrassment or self-esteem. These same individuals moving into independent living situations, or those who acquire a physical disability later in life, have a lot to learn about how to employ, supervise, and evaluate a personal care attendant. Knowledge and skills are needed in finding resource agencies with approved personal care attendants, interviewing and selecting an attendant, dealing with the psychological aspects of personal identity and vulnerability, and managing the payment, supervision, and evaluation roles as an employer.

Another example of interdependent living skills is child rearing and living as a family. Of all life skills, child rearing and living as a family must be among the most interdependent. Mutual reliance on one another is at the core of having and raising children. Knowledge and skills in making decisions about division of responsibilities, finding and using family resources, supporting and assisting the efforts of others, dealing with conflicts and disagreements, knowing when demands are beyond one's ability, and intimate interpersonal relationships are only a few of the subcompetencies under this general competency area. Individualized education program teams must remember adult-oriented outcomes such as these when considering individual transition service needs of school-aged students.

For students with more severe disabilities, a community-based approach to learning life skills is critical (Wehman & Kregel, 2004). This implies more than group field trips, however. Wehman and Kregel believe strongly in a curriculum design that is (1) individualized and person centered in terms of content, (2) highly functional in terms of application, (3) adaptive to the student's learning styles, and (4) ecologically oriented to the student's current and desired future environments. A good curriculum design for this population will try to build on strengths for independent activity whenever possible and consider what interdependent living skills need to be taught with supports.

Leisure and Recreation Skills in Independent Living

Barriers to leisure alternatives parallel those of residential options in spite of the recent trends in the United States for leisure and recreational pursuits and the popularization of fitness (Maynard & Chadderdon, n.d.). Leisure alternatives, like residential alternatives, are limited primarily by attitudes. Attitudinal barriers to leisure-time participation, for example, are often reflected in a person's feelings of fear and lack of confidence in skills for participation in community activities. Also, both public and commercial recreational facility managers may have some degree of uneasiness about persons with disabling conditions using the same facilities as their clientele who are nondisabled. Sadly, this even includes church memberships, community social groups, and political action groups. Environmentally, there are still numerous barriers preventing participation because of a lack of accessibility to theaters, public buildings, auditoriums, churches, and natural sites such as parks, plazas, and gardens. This is despite the provisions of Americans with Disabilities Act of 1990 (PL 101-336). Reasonable accommodation, undue hardship, and exemption of historical sites are provisions of this law that maintain some recreation and leisure participation barriers. Socioeconomic factors limit experiences primarily because of the high cost of participation in so many of the more popular leisure-time alternatives. Again, the low-income status of the vast majority of persons with disabilities restricts their choices considerably.

Planning and providing for leisure-time alternatives should focus on normalized settings and nonspecialized leisure activity options for persons with mild to moderately severe disabilities. To accomplish this, however, the emphasis has to be on preparation of individuals with disabilities to be able to use and enjoy the leisure and recreational alternatives that are available. Pierangelo and Giuliani (2004) suggested that there are some advantages of special leisure programs (nonintegrated), such as Special Olympics, summer camps, coffeehouses, community parks and recreation programs, and the like. Although these programs obviously provide recreational or leisure experiences, they may not be the best preparation for persons with disabilities for participation in leisure activities in a community of people without disabilities.

Transition services in the area of recreation and leisure alternatives are the primary responsibility of adult service agencies and the community. Training for recreation and leisure skills is the responsibility of parents, public schools, postsecondary education programs, advocacy groups, and adult service agencies. Availability and accessibility to both services and the skills for using them should be planned with the assumption that recreation and leisure activities usually are more an expression of life-style and personality than work, and that a person's life-style has consequences for his or her development and well-being.

Communication with Students and Their Families

In contrast to a community independent living center's philosophy, which focuses on direct communication with an adult client or "consumer," school transition programs must include parents or guardians in the planning process and, in effect, consider them, as well as the students, to be "consumers" in transition. The informed cooperation and collaboration of parents or guardians in the transition process is considered a very important component. Informed parents and guardians are those who have sought and found or have been provided information that they needed.

Parent and guardian input on IEPs is a starting point for determining their concerns for the future. Sometimes these concerns are justifiable, and the IEPs should reflect goals that speak to these concerns. At other times, the concerns expressed by parents or guardians are viewed as unrealistic or even inappropriate by professionals. When this occurs, it provides a natural opportunity for talking about those concerns and sharing new information. A common example of this is when a parent or guardian insists that his or her child should be placed in regular academic classes so that graduation requirements and university admission requirements can both be met. If the student is a nonreader and functioning in the mild to moderate levels of adaptive behavior, the parent or guardian is clearly uninformed and needs information based on valid assessment data and admission criteria. On the other hand, information regarding possibilities for some type of college experience should also be introduced, since participation in various kinds of programs for persons with cognitive or developmental disabilities is increasingly available on college campuses.

Students were expressly encouraged to be participants in their own transition planning in the regulations for the IDEA (PL 105-17) and this did not change in the 2004 IDEA reauthorization. It makes good instructional sense to include students along with their families in their high school program planning and long-range goal setting for connecting with adult service agencies. Students may present different preferences than their parents in joint planning, but even that is preferable as a starting point for effective planning than only a one-sided perspective of just the parents' or teachers' views.

It is highly desirable to train parents and guardians, along with their sons and daughters, to be effective advocates and self-advocates for and consumers of services. Some activities toward this end include the following:

1. Orient students and families to local and regional agencies that provide postsecondary services.
2. Assist students and families in understanding the specific responsibilities of the public schools (regular, special, and vocational education), vocational rehabilitation, and other adult service programs and some of the differences in policies.
3. Prepare students and families to work with various agencies in the transition process, including information on how to apply for services.
4. Train students in self-advocacy, beginning with participating actively in their own IEP meetings.

Expecting all low socioeconomic, uneducated students and their families to seek out information or to choose to be active participants in the transition process is unrealistic. On the other hand, failure to try to involve and inform them in a positive way is unprofessional and counterproductive. To assume that students and families do not care or are incapable of positive contributions simply because they do not play by the "rules" is unethical for someone in a helping profession. To assume that it is better to leave the student or family out of the process because of those same reasons is counterproductive because they can passively or actively undermine the efforts of professionals when they sense or actually experience that they are being excluded from the process.

It is not defensible in this multicultural, multilingual society for teachers or adult service agency providers to impose only one dominant culture's ideas or values on any group. One must take the initiative in collaboration with parents in planning and executing transition planning and programming, expecting in this process to gain insight into the concerns, fears, and limitations perceived by culturally different or impoverished families. Transition planning must reflect a culturally and economically feasible set of life and work alternatives, and professionals rarely can do this independent of families and individuals involved.

The professional's role in encouraging self-determination and self-advocacy for students and parents might include some of the following:

- Realize that all people have the right to make choices.
- Get to know the students and parents as individuals.
- Ask questions and listen carefully to be sure that you understand not only what the student and family are saying but also what they are feeling.
- Encourage students to set goals for themselves.
- Propose options for decision making rather than give personal opinions.

Communication between Schools and Service Providers

It may seem that communication that deals with conflicting policy goals between schools and adult service delivery agencies is not the best place to start. This is probably an accurate assessment of the situation for the local level, but it may not be for the state and federal levels. How can there be any hope for consistent, systematic interagency cooperation at the local level, however, without some consistent, systematic policy at the state and federal levels? Many federal and state policies work at cross-purposes and create serious disincentives to appropriate service delivery, employment, and community integration. It is no wonder that one frequently sees at the local level either nothing happening at all in the way of collaborative effort or a service system that is piecemeal, fragmented, and characterized by gaps in or duplication of services.

Still, on the basis of demonstrated working relationships at the local level, even without state or federal support for doing so, communication between transition team participants can happen. When it does, it is usually characterized by a focus on the needs of an individual or individuals and a sharing of information about those needs, the service alternatives available or needed, and existing barriers for getting those services.

Those who work best under informal arrangements find ways to communicate regularly through electronic mail, telephone calls, drop-in visits, sharing information from their respective discipline newsletters or journals, and follow-up contacts to evaluate actions taken. Those who need more of these kinds of activities find regular, planned, goal-oriented staff meetings helpful to keep momentum in the dialogue and collaborative process. The more formal, regular schedule approach has the advantages of facilitating more systematic information exchange between transition personnel and being a mechanism for staff development activities, program evaluation, and joint planning for the future.

As discussed in the next chapter, the emergence of the local community transition council as a vehicle for targeting ways and means of improving transition services for a community is an exciting step forward. The interaction a local council provides for school personnel, adult service professionals, parents, and all other stakeholders in the transition process is valuable. The notion of pooling financial resources, energy, and commitment to work together toward mutually determined goals is catching on and the rapid development of local councils across the county is a welcome sign for the 4 Cs: cooperation, coordination, collaboration, and communication.

Generic Community Services

It is out of the school's realm of responsibility to provide certain generic services after a student graduates or exits the school system. (Transportation and housing are the best examples of such services.) But it is important for educators to understand that generic community support services are critical in successful transitions from school-to-adult living. Full access to community resources is absolutely necessary for anyone to approach full citizenship. Generic services that persons with disabilities need include housing, community transportation, legal services, medical services, financial guidance, and mental health services. The school has a stake in making sure that as many of these are available as possible so that transition services can continue when the handoff is made to community services.

Housing

Residential settings that are most frequently considered as alternatives include the following:

1. Independent living (alone or with a spouse, significant other, or roommates) in a house, mobile home, dormitory, or apartment
2. Supported living (alone or with someone else) in a house, mobile home, or apartment with periodic supervision
3. Living at home with one or both parents or other relatives with minimal to no supervision
4. Group home living with 6 to 10 other residents under minimal but continuous supervision
5. Family care or foster home living with close and continuous supervision

How do young people with disabilities choose their residential settings? Do they really have much choice? Many do not. The vast majority of adults with disabilities can be classified as low-income persons. This poses an immediate barrier to certain kinds of residential alternatives. Because developers are investing in condominiums and other residential options, rental properties are becoming more scarce and expensive. Rental properties that have been especially designed or adapted for architectural accessibility are even more expensive, and many persons with disabilities have to depend on subsidy assistance from the Department of Housing and Urban Development (HUD). Federal rent subsidies, frequently referred to as Section 8 housing subsidies, are available to low-income people whose incomes do not exceed 80 percent of the area average. A tenant typically pays 25 percent of his or her income toward the rent, and the federal government subsidizes the remainder. This has been a major development for adults with disabilities in providing some choice in independent residential living.

In summary, the barriers that exist for providing residential options for adults with disabilities are basically attitudinal, environmental, and financial. Negative to skeptical attitudes about young persons with disabilities living independently come not only from community neighborhoods, landlords, or apartment managers but also from parents, professionals, and sometimes the individuals with disabilities themselves. Prime concerns usually focus on fears of exploitation, social discrimination, and health and safety. Environmental barriers result from a lack of accessibility to available residential alternatives, lack of accessible transportation, and dangerous or stressful neighborhoods that pose threats to a person's sense of well-being. Financial barriers include not only exclusive costs for accessing residential options but also the prevention of the development of housing facilities in certain neighborhoods under the fear or expectation of property value loss.

Transportation

Transportation systems have had to accommodate to the demands for mobility in the United States. Large cities have developed their public transportation systems with taxis, buses, trains, and subways. Many smaller cities and more rural areas have used privately owned vehicles as the primary transportation source. Available and accessible transportation for adults with disabilities becomes, then, both a practical necessity and a symbol of independence. For many persons with disabilities, it is the key to independent living in the sense that without transportation to educational, vocational, cultural, recreational, and commercial opportunities, one might as well live in an institutionalized environment where everything is provided under one roof. Symbolically, transportation sustains the philosophy of independent living and some sense of control in life, as it gives persons with disabilities the feeling that they have access to the same resources at the same price at which they are available to everyone else. The reality, however, is that transportation is not available for many persons with physical disabilities, particularly in rural areas. Even when it is available in a community, the complexity of using it or certain safety factors may inhibit many who have emotional or intellectual disabilities.

Advocacy for better transportation systems by consumers who are disabled, families, advocacy groups, adult service agencies, and schools will eventually result in improvements. Until then, individual arrangements have to be made using creative approaches that provide dependable, affordable transportation, such as car pools, volunteers, bicycles, negotiated discounts with taxi companies, and subsidies from the city or county. School and adult service agency personnel need to elicit the collaboration of community leaders and employers in the transportation field to address local, long-term transportation problems that affect the total population of persons who are disabled, are elderly, and of low income, in addition to their assistance in individual arrangements.

Legal Services

Legal problems are difficult to sort out for most people. Adults with disabilities find themselves needing assistance more than ever now that as a group they are more involved in the process of independent living. They experience rental or lease agreement disputes; civil rights violations; exploitation by high-pressure salespersons, repair and service workers, and personal care attendants; sexual harassment; divorce proceedings; writing wills; filing small-claims suits; and sometimes felonies and misdemeanors. People with disabilities, like everyone else, sometimes need legal assistance. One man who had epilepsy was evicted from a low-cost housing apartment complex (HUD Section 8 housing) for doing some computer work in his apartment. This computer work at home violated Section 8 regulations that specify that living facilities cannot be used for self-employment activities. Legal assistance over an extended period of time finally resulted in an interpretation in his favor. Without it, he was extremely vulnerable and might have lost his source of income or his residence.

Local independent living centers can be helpful in providing some basic legal information and referral assistance. States are also required to have a "protection and advocacy" office for persons with disabilities to provide legal information, advocacy, and support in legal issues.

There is a void in the private sector for legal advocacy in cases involving persons with disabilities. The American Bar Association went so far as to create a Commission on the Mentally Disabled in the 1970s. This grew into several separate efforts, including publication of what is now called the *Mental and Physical Disability Law Reporter*, the establishment of a legislative reform section of the American Bar Association to assist in drafting model legislation, and the funding of various demonstration advocacy projects. Local attorneys may take on *pro bono* legal counsel through court appointments or effective referrals. Still, not enough affordable individual case advocacy and assistance is available for people with disabilities.

Medical Services

Health care and medical services are needed by everyone these days, but adults with disabilities have proportionately more need. Chronic health problems, poor nutrition, weight and stress control, physical fitness needs, susceptibility to respiratory infections, dental problems, vision and hearing problems, and preventive medicine needs occur with greater frequency among persons with disabilities. These needs interfere with daily living routines and affect quality of life by adding to existing problems. The availability and accessibility of a variety of health services to address these needs cannot be taken for granted. Without medical insurance, a Social and Rehabilitation Services card, or Medicaid, access to hospitalization or medical care is routinely denied. Lack of transportation and little or no information or knowledge about health-care needs can contribute to inaccessibility. The difficulties in negotiating complex managed health-care programs is an increasingly difficult task for people with disabilities. For those adults with disabilities who are trying to live independently but who find it difficult to cope with the health-care system, a client-management system may need to be instituted to assist them in finding and using community health-care resources.

Financial Guidance

Somewhat related to legal questions and problems is information about consumer issues. Not all financial problems or decisions require an attorney, however; parents or legal guardians might need to provide both real and consultive assistance in the financial affairs of an adult with disabilities. The assistance needs that are highlighted here include the following:

- Assistance in financial planning for a limited, and sometimes fixed, income
- Assistance in obtaining financial guidance for planning major purchases, such as cars, lift vans, home or apartment modifications, and the like
- Guidance in obtaining and retaining entitlements from state and private agencies
- Assistance in money management in general consumer decisions, credit buying, budgeting, consolidating loans, and investment of inheritance or trust funds

Mental Health Services

Mental health services should provide an array of options for adults with disabilities to help them in adjusting to their disabilities, adapting to personal and social barriers to daily living and employment, dealing with concerns about sexuality, coping with stress, dealing with death or separation from family members, or accepting intensive therapeutic interventions for severe psychological or behavioral disorders. These service options can be provided individually, in groups, or by both means. They can be provided professionally through mental health centers, psychiatric services in hospitals, and individual therapists, or by nonlicensed personnel in postsecondary training programs, independent living centers, religious organizations, vocational rehabilitation services, and various adult service systems.

The availability and accessibility of mental health services to families of persons with disabilities is equally important when their lives are closely involved. Spouses, children, parents, and siblings have many personal and emotional issues to face as they support and advocate for their family members who have disabilities. Many parents of young adults have to adjust to some harsh realities of inadequate adult services after having become accustomed to a wide variety of services from schools. Feelings of anger, frustration, disappointment, confusion, and uncertainty are common, and parents need to have some support for dealing with their concerns.

Two types of adult service agencies provide various social, interpersonal, and mental health services that can assist individuals with disabilities during the school years or after they leave school: independent living centers and mental health centers. Each is described briefly.

Mental Health Centers.   Two groups that appear to need mental health services more than some other groups classified as having disabilities are those who are classified as students with emotional or behavioral disorders and students who have mild mental retardation. The latter group is frequently referred to under these circumstances as those with a dual diagnosis, because mental health centers generally do not serve persons with mental retardation as a single diagnosis, but rather only those who have some type of severe personal, social, or adjustment difficulty in addition to another disability. Community mental health centers or similar agencies typically offer individual and group counseling to these and other persons in need of assistance in emotional, social, and behavioral problem areas. Some centers use community-based therapeutic activities with the goal of training for functional interpersonal and social skills at home, at school, and in the community.

Independent Living Centers.   The whole purpose of independent living centers is to address personal-social adjustment and independent living problems. Counseling, whether peer counseling or professional, is at the heart of the services of agencies like this and continually focuses on learning to take control over one's life—emotionally, socially, occupationally, and functionally at home and in the community. Even the assistance given in transportation, housing, legal problems, interpreting (for the deaf), attendant care, reading, and training in independent living is designed to increase self-confidence and minimize dependence on others. For information on the location of independent living centers, direct an Internet search through www.rahul.net/designlink/centers.htm.

Independent living centers are consumer controlled and operated and have strong ties to the communities they serve. They usually offer their services at no cost to the consumers. They are funded primarily by the Rehabilitation Services Administration, state funding, and local funding. They offer a variety of services designed to assist prsons with disabilities to be more independent in the community (Pierangelo & Giuliani, 2004). Among these are the following:

- Independent living skills training
- Peer counseling (consumers counseling consumers)
- Individual advocacy for dealing with community barriers
- Services related to obtaining housing or shelter
- Assistive technology loans
- Life skills training
- Computer literacy training
- Interpreter services
- Assistance in finding personal attendants
- Transportation assistance
- Mobility training

For information on the location of independent living centers, direct an Internet search through www.rahul.net/designlink/centers.htm.

Conclusion

We hope it is clear to you by now that the transition process for students with disabilities as they prepare at school for adult life and then move into adult roles is complex. The student needs to be involved and self-determined. Families must be involved and supportive, letting go when appropriate. Schools need to take the transition services mandate seriously and look at adult-oriented outcomes in the transition planning process, making instruction, related services, and transition programs available to students. Communities need to be involved and supportive, with community-based support systems in place for students who leave school.

The outcomes of the transition process from school to adult living for individuals with disabilities depend largely on the effectiveness of all the stakeholders and participants in the process. There is no doubt that good programs and services in schools and in the community can contribute to positive outcomes. On the other hand, programs and services may be available and accessible in school and in the community and the individuals and/or their families do not take advantage of the programs. As a transition educator, you must assume from the beginning that your students and their families want good outcomes. If they appear to be passive or even reluctant to be involved, it could be a lack of trust in schools and community agencies, a lack of information about predictable outcomes without planning and intervention, or a lack of knowledge and skill in doing what needs to be done. This chapter presented some of the information that all participants in the transition process need to know and some of the implications for how to apply that information to successful transition efforts.

9 School-Based and Community-Based Resources

Linkages and Referrals

You cannot hope to build a better world without improving the individuals. To that end, each of us must work for his own improvement, and at the same time, share a general responsibility for all humanity.

—Marie Curie

The well-known anthropologist, Margaret Mead, once said, "Never doubt that a small group of thoughtful, committed citizens can change the world. Indeed, it's the only thing that ever has." One only has to look at any major movement in any society to see some evidence of Mead's view. Governments, religious groups, labor unions, political action/social justice groups (e.g., Green Party, NAACP, Urban League, La Raza, Sierra Club), youth groups (Scouting, 4-H, Boys and Girls Clubs of America, etc.), and international aid agencies such as the International Red Cross are examples of the vision of a few, committed people who banded together to solve problems.

The transition movement in the United States is a systems change movement that may never change the world or even have a major impact beyond North America. Still, the broader notion of looking beyond ourselves as individuals or families for ways to support individuals with disabilities is almost universal. Although each individual or each family can contribute a great deal to the quality of life of persons who have disabilities, there are some things the average person does not have the training, skills, or experience to do. At these points, it is critical to be able to turn to school and community resources for help. This chapter is designed to help you know some of the ways resource persons at school or in your community can be used as referral sources and as participating partners in transition education and services.

The promise of the American Dream—the freedom and opportunity to work and live and lead a satisfying life—is difficult enough for anyone to achieve. For those who have disabilities, it can be a major challenge. Futurists, whose job it is to chart the trends of the world, point to the pressures faced by children growing up in U.S. society. More than half live or will live in single-parent families. Even in two-parent families, both parents may be working. Children in these situations have a burden of self-management that is, for some, simply too much with which to cope. At school, children have the added problem of facing school reforms that emphasize academic curricula with increasingly demanding standards for success. For many students, this additional pressure to succeed results in failure and stress.

When the problems of disability are coupled with the difficulties of life in today's world, it is apparent that the obstacles to fulfilling the American promise are substantial. Students who have their other problems compounded by disabilities may need all the help they can get to have any chance at all of achieving even a modest measure of success. To a large degree, their chances for adult adjustment may be determined by the referral resources available. Since the difference between dependency and relative independence could be determined by resources support, this chapter examines linkage and referral needs, linkage and referral sources, referral strategies, and the interdisciplinary collaboration that can make more possible the realization of the American Dream.

Referral Needs of High School Students in Special Programs

Although the term *referral* may sound innocuous enough, most high school teachers will have a number of dramatic stories to tell about students who ultimately had to be referred for help from persons more qualified. The reason for the referral may have been a suicide attempt or a student who needed only a straightforward medical referral initially but somehow slipped through the cracks of the system, resulting in the problem reaching crisis proportions. Both types of experiences can prove disheartening and shocking to the teacher who has never encountered such situations. The fact is, most referrals are not emergencies; rather, they surface from persisting student needs that just do not seem to go away.

It is not possible to list and discuss here all the possible needs that students with disabilities might have during their school years. The examples provided in the following lists will give you an idea of the range and variety of situations that the education teacher, work experience coordinator, or transition specialist might encounter. When a "statement of transition needs" or "statement of needed transition services" indicates certain needs, the IEP team has a responsibility to determine whether those needs can be met through transition education (instruction), transition services, or a combination of the two. Although some of the needs listed here were mentioned in Chapter 3, the following needs are much more specific and tend to be those that do require school-based or community services consideration.

Physical Needs

1. Poor dental health, resulting in problems of appearance, eating difficulties, bad breath, and absenteeism
2. Obesity, resulting in social problems, health problems, and practical problems such as fitting into school furniture, using toilets, and finding clothes to fit
3. Malnutrition, resulting in frequent illnesses and absenteeism, inability to participate in rigorous activities at school or on job training, and fatigue in classes
4. Recurring bruises, scratches, abrasions, or swollen body parts, suggesting physical abuse
5. Signs of alcohol or drug abuse, affecting performance at school as well as personal-social relationships

Personal-Social Needs

1. Sudden and extreme changes in personal behavior
2. Changes in patterns of school attendance
3. Juvenile court or police involvement
4. Signs or direct evidence of illegal conduct
5. Complaints from student about being subjected to gang intimidation, bullying, or physical violence, including assault and rape
6. Complaints from student about being subjected to sexual harassment at school or at a job site
7. Inappropriate public sexual behavior
8. Evidence of exploitation by real or foster parents, guardians, or welfare agencies

Physical and personal-social needs tend to get the most attention in any discussion of referral needs, but high school teachers and support personnel should remember that referrals can also be made for enrichment of students' positive attributes and special interests. Interest in the positive characteristics that students show at school should receive attention equal to the problem areas, and referrals to appropriate school or community sources can pay dividends in student attitude and performance. Some of these positive characteristics or strengths include:

- Superior academic achievement in one or more academic areas
- Superior leadership ability
- Superior talent performance in the visual or performing arts
- Superior talent in mechanical/technical tasks
- Creative abilities in the visual or performing arts
- Superior talent in creative problem solving (e.g., inventive)
- Superior talent in sports, dance, or other motor activity

School-Based Linkage and Referral Sources

As simplistic a statement as it may seem, to benefit from the resources furnished by individuals and agencies, a student must first be connected with the resources. This is what is meant by a *referral* in traditional programming and *linkages* in transition services. Referrals or linkages are mainly for services of two kinds: related services within a local education agency and generic services associated with the community.

General Education Referrals

The school reform movements of the past two decades have increased pressure on students to achieve academically. For some students with disabilities, the new opportunities to be included in general education and to be challenged academically have promoted new and satisfying results. Finding teachers or community mentors who respond to students with superior skills, talent, or creativity is usually not a difficult task. The fact that a student with learning disabilities or a severe emotional disorder is also academically gifted may be an interesting challenge for general education teachers. Having a student IEP meeting with this type of focus presents a needed balance to the perceptions of many general education teachers.

For other students, though, academic skills are very difficult and get more difficult through each grade. When academic achievement is a precondition for being able to get into more appropriate career or vocational education classes, some of these students are able to muster the effort to master the required courses. Brolin (1995) initially developed his Life-Centered Career Education (LCCE) model around the premise that regular teachers can and should be involved in helping students with learning difficulties acquire various career and transition competencies. He specified how various secondary school staff can contribute in meeting the 22 basic competencies by infusing instructional activities into academic subjects that relate to the various LCCE competencies. Table 9.1 is an adaptation of his listing of possible competency instructional responsibilities for both junior and senior high school personnel.

The most common strategy to assure some success in basic academic classes has been to seek out general education teachers who understand the

TABLE 9.1   Proposed Competency Instructional Settings for Personnel for Secondary Special Education Students

Competencies	Instructional Setting/Instructional Personnel
Daily Living Skills	
1. Managing personal finances	General business, consumer education, math, home economics
2. Selecting, managing, and maintaining a household	Home economics, home and family living
3. Caring for personal needs	Health, home and family living, home economics
4. Raising children and meeting marriage responsibilities	Home and family living, home economics
5. Buying, preparing, and consuming food	Home economics, home and family living, health, consumer education
6. Buying and caring for clothing	Home economics, consumer education, home and family living
7. Exhibiting responsible citizenship	Social studies (government, history), home room/guidance period, community-based experiences
8. Utilizing recreational facilities and engaging in leisure	Physical education, art, music, theater arts
9. Getting around the community	Driver's education, orientation and mobility (for blind students)
Personal-Social Skills	
10. Achieving self-awareness	All instructional areas; counseling and guidance staff, self-determination/futures planning curricula
11. Acquiring self-confidence	Selected instructional areas of student strengths, selected extracurricular activities, music, speech, theater arts, social and inter-personal skills curricula, counseling and guidance staff
12. Achieving socially responsible behavior	All instructional areas; counseling and guidance staff
13. Maintaining good interpersonal skills	Selected instructional areas of student strengths, selected extracurricular activities, music, speech, theater arts, social and inter-personal skills curricula, counseling and guidance staff

TABLE 9.1   Continued

Competencies	Instructional Setting/Instructional Personnel
Personal-Social Skills (continued)	
14. Achieving independence	Self-determination curricula, community-based instruction, counseling and guidance staff
15. Making adequate decisions	Self-determination curricula, community-based instruction, counseling and guidance staff
16. Communicating with others	Selected extracurricular activities, English, speech, social and interpersonal skills curricula, foreign languages, English as a second language (ESL)
Occupational Skills	
17. Knowing and exploring occupational possibilities	Selected instructional areas, vocational education, home economics, counseling and guidance staff, technology systems for career exploration, community-based experiences (mentoring, job shadowing, job samples, field trips, internships)
18. Selecting and planning occupational choices	Counseling and guidance staff, technology systems for career decision making, mentors
19. Exhibiting appropriate work habits and behaviors	Vocational education, home economics, community-based experiences, community work-based learning programs, art, music, theater arts, computer centers, library, study hall
20. Seeking, securing, and maintaining employment	Counseling and guidance staff, vocational education teachers, community work-based learning staff, job coaches, transition coordinators/specialists
21. Exhibiting sufficient physical-manual skills	Vocational education, home economics, community work-based learning programs, physical education
22. Obtaining specific occupational skills	Vocational education, home economics, community work-based learning programs

Source: Adapted from Brolin (1995).

needs of students with disabilities and who adjust their class activities. Referral of selected students to these carefully identified teachers is the best way to guarantee any degree of success in placing students with disabilities in high school academic courses. This is an example of enhancing inclusion by referrals to teachers who are most likely to respond cooperatively.

Guidance and Counseling Services in Schools

Any consideration of career or transition programming must speak to the role of guidance and counseling. What are the elements of guidance and counseling that function in school programs? What are the goals of guidance and counseling activities? Who should provide guidance and counseling services to students with special needs?

The terms *guidance* and *counseling* are frequently used as two independent concepts, but most school personnel in this field view *guidance* as an umbrella term that includes a number of techniques or approaches, with *counseling* being the heart of the guidance program. Guidance, according to Shertzer and Stone's (1981) classic text, is "the process of helping individuals to understand themselves and their world" (p. 40). They presented counseling in school settings as a technique "to assist students to explore and understand themselves so that they can become self-directing individuals" (p. 172). Since these definitions do not clearly differentiate between the two terms, other than one being viewed as a process and the other as a technique, each will be discussed in greater detail.

Guidance Services

The school guidance counselor is responsible for providing guidance services and a comprehensive counseling and guidance program to all students, including special education students (Allen & LaTorre, 1998). The American School Counselor Association's *National Standards for School Counselors* (Dahir, Sheldon, & Valiga, 1998) laid out the framework for a comprehensive counseling and guidance program. The standards include three major domains of responsibility for the school guidance counselor: academic, personal-social, and career. The intent is clear in the standards that guidance and counseling programs should help ensure that all students have an equal opportunity to participate fully in the educational process.

Allen (2001, 2004), Fabish (2004), and Synatschk (1999) have addressed the challenges for school counselors in responding to the career development and transition needs of students with disabilities very specifically. The positive implications of a comprehensive guidance services model for students with disabilities are that they are much more likely to receive some needed instruction and programming within the mainstream of a school if that school has a guidance curriculum and if counselors are committed to individual planning for *all* students.

Until comprehensive guidance program models are in place everywhere, advocates for students with disabilities must look at any existing guidance and counseling program in terms of the services that are offered and how these services can be accessed. It may be that all of the services that students with disabilities need will not be accessed via the guidance counselor(s) in a given school. In those cases, some of the services may have to be provided by others with the support of the guidance counselors. Special education teachers have long served in the areas of guidance and counseling either by default or for convenience. Performing these roles, when appropriate and with the support of guidance counselors, is the ideal. The "ours" and "theirs" problem between regular and special education is a barrier in accomplishing this ideal. In a study of high school programs for youths with disabilities (Clark, Knowlton, & Dorsey, 1989), one high school counselor spoke openly about special education students, IEP students, and "our" students. An interesting distinction was made between "special students" (in this case, students with mild mental retardation) and "IEP students" (students who have learning disabilities and behavior disorders). However, the more telling attitude was the "ours" and "theirs" when referring to identified students with disabilities versus students without such an identification.

Counseling Services

Counseling in public schools is usually viewed as one part of a guidance program. Any one counselor may approach the counseling relationship from a unique perspective, ranging from an intention to deal primarily with practical information giving for one counselor to working through intense psychological stress with another. The American School Counselor Association (1997) adopted a definition of *school counseling:*

> Counseling is a process of helping people by assisting them in making decisions and changing behavior. School counselors work with all students, school staff, families, and members of the community as an integral part of the education program. School counseling programs promote school success through a focus on academic achievement, prevention and intervention activities, advocacy and social/emotional and career development. (p. 8)

This definition does not limit counseling only to a trained counselor. Counseling at some level can take place in a relationship between a counselee and a professional, paraprofessional, or nonprofessional counselor. This opens up the counseling role to transition specialists, teachers, teacher aides, parents, employers, school staff, and even peers.

Although the definition of counseling remains difficult (especially when differentiating it from psychotherapy), the nature of the counseling process can be described. For our purposes in discussing the counseling process with students with disabilities who need and/or request counseling, the following statements reflect the nature of counseling:

- The counseling process, whether successful or not in terms of outcomes, is characterized by a unique, helping relationship between the person performing the counselor role and the student(s).
- The counseling interaction process includes both verbal and nonverbal communication.
- Counseling may be a service used more by students who are well adjusted and whose mental health is stable than those who exhibit extreme modes of behavior or emotional instability.
- Counseling stresses rational planning, problem solving, and support in the face of situational pressures.
- Counseling approaches, whether selected strategically or naturally and spontaneously, are based more on focusing on everyday reality and conscious observations than unconscious motivations, past events, dreams, or symbolic material.
- Counseling tends to rely on the counselee's positive individual strengths for problem solving or decision making rather than stressing the diagnosis and remediation of personality defects.

Counseling is ordinarily viewed as a short-term process in which specific problems are identified and outcomes are achieved over a relatively short period of time.

The American School Counselor Association (ASCA, 2001–2002), in a position statement entitled "The Professional School Counselor and the Special Needs Student," recommended the following school counseling service roles in working with special needs students:

- Multidisciplinary team member
- Collaborator with other pupil personnel specialists
- Instructor of social skills training
- Coordinator of group guidance activities to improve self-esteem
- Counselor—individual, group, and family
- Advocate for students in both school and community
- Observer and facilitator of behavior modification plans
- Coordinator of career planning and transition
- Facilitator—in the understanding of special needs students
- Referral agent to other specialists in the school and community

Goals of Guidance and Counseling Activities

Professionals responsible for guidance and counseling with children and youths approach their own professional activity goals with a variety of assumptions about career and transition development in the abstract (or ideal) and for career and transition development for youths with disabilities in particular. One way of putting goals into perspective is to challenge the notion that guidance and counseling is highly cerebral and can work only with those who have the intelligence and verbal communication skills to deal with problems, information, and decision making at a self-actualization level. Very few people operate at that level in all areas of their lives. Maslow's (1954) need hierarchy was related to counseling and guidance goals for persons with severe disabilities by both Lassiter (1981) and Jageman and Myers (1986) some years ago. These authors suggested possible goal alternatives in guidance and counseling activities with students with special needs that are practical and on target for a range of strengths as well as needs. Examples are provided for each of Maslow's need levels in Table 9.2.

Key Providers of Counseling Services

Writers in the field of guidance and counseling (Dahir, 2004; Gysbers & Henderson, 2001; Herr, Cramer, & Niles, 2004) generally maintain that, although there are a number of important contributors to a guidance and counseling program, the key person is the professionally prepared and personally committed counselor. This position is not a difficult one to defend from a logical and practical point of view, even though some people argue that the teacher is the key person because of day-to-day interactions and knowledge of each student's needs. The main differences between teaching and guidance are inferred from a clear difference between the functions of teaching and the functions of guidance. Since counseling is such an important role in guidance, the differences frequently focus on the dissimilarities between teaching and counseling.

Those who argue in favor of the teacher role being the most important may have an idealized elementary, middle, or high school teacher in mind, but it is becoming increasingly clear that teachers are being asked to do many more things, few of which are related to guidance and counseling. The typical teacher is—by training, by inclination, and by the requirements of a teaching position—a specialist in teaching subject matter. It is in the teacher role that the teacher expects to develop a career and meet the expectations of students and their parents. The counselor, on the other hand, is specifically assigned guidance and counseling responsibilities and has some type of training and credentials supporting competency in those responsibilities. All of this may seem too obvious for discussion. However, the reality of schools and their hierarchical bureaucracies (Skrtic, 1991) breaks through the professional logic and

TABLE 9.2   Examples of Career Guidance and Counseling Goals and Activities Based on Maslow's Hierarchy of Needs

Need	Prevention Goals	Intervention Goals
Physiological Survival Needs	Assist students in learning effects of good eating and drinking habits. Assist students in planning exercise and rest schedules. Assist students in understanding sources of pain and pain-reduction alternatives. Assist students in understanding sexual needs and appropriate responses. Assist students in acquiring knowledge on health and hygiene requirements of a job.	Assist students in dealing with problems of overeating, alcohol or substance abuse, or eating disorders. Provide student support and reinforcement for efforts in accomplishing plans. Assist students with stress-management techniques or making medication schedules work. Provide students assertiveness training. Confront students with inappropriate sexual behavior and modifying behaviors.
Safety/Security Needs	Assist students in understanding stress in life changes. Assist students in planning for risk events. Assist students in organizing their behavior and environments to establish order and routine.	Counsel students to assist in coping with stress and adjustment to new settings, new people, new demands. Assist students in coping with risk events. Assist students in adjusting to disorganized or chaotic life environments and teaching organizational skills/strategies.
Belonging/Love Needs	Assist students in learning about needing to belong. Assist students in learning appropriate ways of seeking acceptance and love.	Provide accepting support system in a counseling relationship. Provide therapeutic environment and assistance in coping with rejection/loneliness.
Esteem Needs	Assist students in learning ways of behaving that are seen as successful and confidence building. Assist students in finding places to work, groups to join, or places to live that foster self-esteem. Assist students in understanding conflicts within themselves relative to their disabilities.	Assist students in coping with low self-esteem or mild depression. Assist students in self-evaluation of self-defeating and self-derogatory behavior. Assist students in coping with continuing adjustment demands to their disabilities.
Self-Actualization Needs	Assist students in learning ways of personal growth and self-improvement. Assist students in learning ways of using their strengths to move beyond their present levels of functioning.	Provide students with support and encouragement for efforts in personal growth. Assist students in coping with routine, boredom, and malaise.

presents a disturbing view of the actual achievement of guidance and counseling goals via this system, especially in high schools.

All types of students in today's schools are falling through the cracks of the guidance system. Our view is that this is especially the case for students receiving special services under IDEA. This is not the fault of school guidance counselors, but rather a symptom of some of the issues confronting school guidance programs today. Some of the more common issues include the following:

- Guidance counselors are assigned responsibility for providing guidance services to large numbers of students, making significant individual contact difficult and forcing students to be aggressive and persistent if they want to receive assistance.
- Guidance counselors have been assigned administrative support roles over the years (such as scheduling) that have consumed much of their time that could have been used more effectively.
- Guidance counselors have traditionally spent much of their time helping students select and apply to colleges. This will continue, if not increase, in response to educational reform policies being implemented and will require more planning for academic course of study decisions.
- Guidance counselors rarely are required to have any preservice training in even the basic needs of exceptional students, much less training in career development or transition guidance for them.
- High school special education teachers are becoming increasingly involved in course selection and scheduling for students on IEPs. This requires more academic planning and guidance in light of new and changing graduation policies.
- Vocational assessment and career/transitional guidance are not available in any systematic form in most high schools. High school guidance counselors claim lack of time or expertise for these services for students in special education services.
- High school special education programs have responded to the guidance and counseling service void for their students by assigning or reassigning teachers to function in similar roles, either on a part- or full-time basis, such as vocational counselors, work experience coordinators, vocational-adjustment coordinators, and so forth. For the most part, these individuals have little or no preservice training for these roles, and only a few states recognize such a role with a certificate or endorsement credential.

In light of the issues reflecting the reality of school organizations, what should be expected of school guidance counselors? Consider the following as a proposal for what should be exemplary program practice:

- Help with social adjustment problems in general education classes or all-inclusive activities in the school.

- Help with problems that may occur with teachers in general education classes, the resource room, or the special class.
- Provide assistance with questions or decision-making needs about educational goals beyond high school.
- Give help when students find it difficult to establish friendships and communication with peers.
- Provide support when students' interests and goals appear to conflict with those of their parents.
- Help with decision making on appropriate courses in school that are appropriate for students' interests and needs.
- Encourage students to search for meaning and values in their lives.
- Give assistance when students need information about their abilities, aptitudes, and interests.
- Help with the development of self-advocacy skills.

It is unrealistic to believe that school guidance counselors can do all the tasks they know need to be done on an individual basis. Typically, caseloads are high and counselors are assigned too many inappropriate noncounseling program tasks. When counselors have a tangible linkage to student planning and instruction for all students, it is easier for them to focus on critical counseling tasks and reach more students. Synatschk (1999) presented a comprehensive developmental counseling model implemented by the Austin (Texas) Independent School District that shows a commitment by the school district to both individual planning and a guidance curriculum. The commitment to individual planning is indicated in the requirement for all students in grades 6 through 12 to have an *Individual Academic-Career Plan (IACP)* completed annually. The states of Utah and Washington use a similar document called the *Student Educational and Occupational Plan (SEOP)* and the *Education Plan (EP)*, respectively. The commitment to guidance information and teaching self-determination skills is evident in the comprehensive developmental guidance curriculum (Austin Independent School District, 1996). Figure 9.1 shows the strands of the Austin Independent School District Guidance Curriculum and reflects the efforts of a school district to take seriously its role in addressing some of the major adult outcome-oriented goals for all students. When this kind of programming is available and accessible for all students, with and without disabilities, the goal of inclusive education as well as adequate guidance and counseling in public schools is much more realistic.

Specialized Related Services in Schools

School Psychology Services

School psychologists frequently serve primarily in assessment. Assessment for initial identification and placement, periodic reevaluations, and some diagnos-

FIGURE 9.1 Strands of the Guidance Curriculum

A.	Self-Knowledge and Acceptance	This domain helps students learn more about their abilities, interests, and personal characteristics. Students learn to identify their strengths and the areas in which they need to improve so that true self-acceptance is possible.
B.	Interpersonal and Communication Skills	This domain emphasizes the value of developing positive interpersonal relationships and how communication skills affect the ways in which people interact with each other. They also learn to value differences and uniqueness among people.
C.	Responsible Behavior	This domain assists students in developing a sense of personal responsibility for their behavior. It gives attention to how attitudes and perceptions can affect behavior, how feelings and behaviors are related to goals and consequences, and how behavior can be changed, if desired.
D.	Conflict Resolution	The focus of this domain is nonviolent solutions to conflict situations. Students will also deal with styles of cooperative behavior, prejudice, and healthy expressions of anger.
E.	Decision Making/ Problem Solving	This domain involves learning the steps for making effective decisions and solving problems. It also involves an increased awareness of the factors that influence change and decision making as well as helpful procedures for problem solving. There is an emphasis on responsibility and individual choice.
F.	Motivation to Achieve	This area is designed to assist students to achieve success in school and their adult lives. It will help them develop positive attitudes and habits which will enable them to get the most out of schooling. They will also focus on the connections between what they are learning in school and what their futures will be like.
G.	Goal Setting	This domain is designed to help students understand the importance of setting goals for themselves and monitoring their own progress toward their goals. They will also learn to differentiate between realistic and unrealistic goals.
H.	Career Planning	This domain helps students understand more about the world of work, increase their career awareness, and do in-depth career exploration related to personal interests, values, and abilities. It also includes how to make effective educational plans so that students may achieve their career goals.

Source: From "Counseling" by K. O. Synatschk in *Transition and School-Based Services: Interdisciplinary Perspectives for Enhancing the Transition Process* by S. H. deFur and J. R. Patton (Eds.), 1999, Austin, TX: PRO-ED. Reprinted by permission.

tic assessment for educational or personal-social adjustment consume much of their time. Training, background, or personal preference may move some school psychologists out of the psychometric role into consultation with teachers about learning or behavior problems, personal adjustment difficulties, interpersonal relationships, and adolescent psychology. Some even seek out opportunities to do some individual or group counseling when their training has included such an emphasis and their school district values that type of service.

For the past two decades, a small but committed group of school psychologists and school psychology educators has gradually moved the field of school psychology to acknowledge the significance of vocational programming as an appropriate role for practitioners (Levinson & Murphy, 1999). The National Association of School Psychologists provided early support for this group by approving a special-interest group organization for vocational school psychology and included both vocational assessment and intervention into its *Standards for the Provision of School Psychological Services* (Thomas & Grimes, 1995).

Despite these encouraging developments, school psychologists are not significantly involved in vocational assessment or transition planning. Carey (1995) reported that in his national study of school psychologists, less than 1 percent of their time was spent in vocational assessment. Staab (1996) found in her national random sample of 602 school psychologists working with secondary schools that school psychologists were interested in transition planning activities and perceived these activities to be important, but believed generally that they were unprepared to conduct transition activities.

The nature of life-span transitions (discussed in Chapter 1) and the scope of transition planning assessment (discussed in Chapter 5) clearly indicate an overlap between the interests of transition services advocates and school psychologists. These interests converge most obviously in assessment of students' strengths, needs, preferences, and interests; the mutual concern for collaborative planning with students and their families; the need for encouraging school sensitivity to cultural, ethnic, experiential, and language backgrounds; and the promotion of self-determined, satisfying involvement at school, in the workplace, and in the community.

Special educators should cultivate good working relationships with school psychologists. Requests for assistance in interpreting tests already given, requests for testing in specialized areas (adaptive behavior, learning styles, emotional/behavioral adjustment, etc.), professional opinions on student or family characteristics, ideas on strategies for teaming and collaboration, support in making school-based services referrals as well as community-based referrals, and crisis counseling are just a few of the ways school psychologists may be enticed into the transition planning and transition education process.

School Nurse Services

Students having chronic health impairments often seek out the school nurse for assistance on their own, or referrals are made to the school nurse by attending physicians. High school special education staff, however, should be aware of the needs of all students with disabilities and be ready to bring the school nurse into emergency or consultation situations. Students who do not have any chronic health conditions can benefit from the nurse's services in a variety of ways.

School nurses serve all students in public schools, but they have been actively involved with students with chronic conditions since the passage of PL 94-142 in 1975. *Students with chronic conditions* refers to those students with special health needs who may or may not receive special education services. The National Association of School Nurses (NASN) identified the importance of this group by making one of its 10 standards to practice specifically related to students with special health care needs (Proctor, Lordi, & Zaiger, 1993). More recently, the NASN developed an issue brief that outlined the specific roles and responsibilities of the school nurse for students with disabilities and called for the inclusion of the professional school nurse as a related services provider under the IDEA (NASN, 1996).

The health-care community recognized the need to think about the transition of children and youths from pediatric to adult health-care services in 1985 when the National Center for Youth with Disabilities (NCYD) began operating with a goal to improve services for youths through the second decade of life as they transition to adult living, health care, and vocations (Blum, 1995). The NYCD (1996) completed a survey of adolescent health transition programs in the United States. The organization identified 277 programs that support the transition of youths with chronic illness or disabilities from pediatric to adult health care. Responses from 129 of these programs indicated that services are both formal as well as informal and that health education, case management, and individual planning for transition to an independent life-style were the three services offered most often. The vast majority of these programs were direct service health-care programs in clinics or community agencies and followed an acute care medical model of health-care delivery. Few programs included vocational counselors as part of the team, and even fewer actively engaged in educational transition planning or transition services delivery through collaboration.

In most settings, the school nurse works individually with students and their families. The nurse focuses on training for good health and competence and responsibility for independence in self-management and care of the health condition. The practice of school nursing is accomplished through the development of an individualized health care plan (IHP), which is either incorporated into a student's IEP or is a separate document for health services (Cox &

Sawin, 1999). The IHP includes information about the student's needs, nursing interventions designed to meet those needs, and a description of how the care supports the education process of the school.

The National Association of School Nurses (1996) listed the following general roles and responsibilities of nurses working with students with special health-care needs:

- Assists in screening and identifying students who may need health-related services
- Assesses the identified child's sensory and physical health status in collaboration with the student, parent(s), and health-care providers
- Develops individualized health and emergency care plans
- Assists the IEP team in developing the IEP when it relates to health needs of the student
- Assists the parent(s) and teachers to find and use community resources
- Provides in-service training for teachers and staff regarding the individual health needs of the student
- Provides and/or supervises assistive personnel to provide specialized health-care services in the school setting
- Evaluates the effectiveness of the health-related parts of the IEP with the student, parent(s), and other team members, and makes revisions to the plan as needed

Some specific contributions of nursing to transition programming and service delivery commonly include the following:

- Teaching self-care skills needed to manage specific health conditions
- Coordinating and communicating with school and health providers in implementing IHPs or health-related goals on the IEP
- Providing sexuality education instruction
- Addressing the prevention of secondary conditions
- Focusing counseling on psychological adjustment to special health conditions, long-term treatment, and terminal illnesses
- Providing instruction and guidance in nutrition, weight control, substance abuse, and child abuse
- Providing attendant or personal care provider training

Not all secondary schools have school nurses readily available, and frequently health management caseloads for school nurses are unrealistically high. Still, the obvious relevance of school health and school nurse professionals to transition planning and service delivery for many students with disabilities is clear. We believe that the health component—health decision making and self-management, prevention of secondary disabilities, and health services—

must be addressed by school-based transition teams. The school nurse can be an important participant on those transition teams.

School Social Work Services

When influences outside the school setting interfere with the success of the student, school social services workers can become an important transition services partner. Functioning as a bridge between the home and the school, school social workers can evaluate the variables of the home and community setting that could be having an influence on the performance of the young person who has a disability. Although school social workers often can deal directly with a problem, they also broker services, calling on other persons or agencies to supply specific services to the student, the family, or related school personnel.

The actual monitoring of referral sources and services may fall to any of a variety of professionals in the school, such as the guidance counselor, school psychologist, or social worker. The school social worker's role is most frequently described as coordinating and integrating services between school and families, between families and community agencies, and between schools and community agencies. Social work training, in fact, focuses a great deal of attention on social worker skills in understanding and conceptualizing relationships between individuals and multiple services. Networks and linkages outside of school are relatively new to special education teachers, but are routine to school social workers.

Other than the linkage and coordination of services roles of social workers, Markward and Kurtz (1999) cited several additional roles that school social workers can assume in a school's transition services: parent involvement, collaborative teaming, assessment, and organizational work.

Parent Involvement. Parent involvement is seen by many teachers as one of their greatest challenges, especially at the secondary level. For any number of reasons, parents of adolescents with disabilities are less involved with their students' lives at secondary school than they were during the elementary and middle school years. School social workers can help remove some of the barriers that keep parents from being involved in their children's school planning and progress. Cultural misunderstandings, current or past communication difficulties, personal histories involving school failure or alienation, intimidation by school personnel, or even adolescents' preferences that their parents not be involved at school are a few of the many barriers that social workers can address through individual or group assistance.

Collaborative Teaming. Collaborative teaming is an attractive alternative for cost effectiveness during times of budget restrictions, but one of the elements of current school reform and restructuring for effective schools is the notion of transdisciplinary teaming and collaborative work. School social work personnel must work closely and collaboratively with other support service personnel, especially school counselors, school psychologists, and school nurses. School social workers' knowledge of family systems and mental and public health resources, family consumer education, teen pregnancies, drug and alcohol abuse, domestic violence and child abuse, and dropout prevention support even more their potential for collaborative teaming with teachers on curriculum, program development, and actual instruction. Further, in cases where school social workers are intensely involved with students and families related to serious emotional or behavioral problems, they may need to do collaborative planning and coordination with community work-placement supervisors, job coaches, or job supervisors.

Assessment.   In some states, school social workers are part of formal diagnostic and assessment teams for the school. The common formal assessments that social workers might provide are social development and adaptive behavior assessments. These two areas change over time and could provide helpful information for transition services planning with students 14 years of age and older. Informal assessments are also conducted upon request, including social histories, ecological or environmental assessments of the home, observations of parents' understanding of technical or unfamiliar terms related to their children's schooling, and interviews of parents' long-term dreams and fears for their children's futures.

Organizational Work.   The interactive, connective nature of school social work gives school social workers a unique perspective of the school, the community, and families. They frequently participate on committees and task forces in various organizations to address systems changes in schools or in the community. They can be valuable members of local transition teams or councils as well as community interagency councils because of their knowledge and skills in group dynamics, policy development, and advocacy.

Speech and Language Pathology Services

The speech and language pathologist (SLP) is the school-based services professional primarily responsible for speech and language programs for students with communication disorders. Traditionally, the role of the SLP in schools has been as a service provider who worked independent of, rather than collaboratively with, other school staff. Speech and language services were also traditionally concentrated on elementary-aged schoolchildren. In recent years, however, there has been a growing awareness of the needs of adolescent students with communication disorders as they make transition plans for the future. Communication skills in self-determination, self-advocacy, successful socialization with peers at school and in work settings, and integrated community participation are increasingly seen as critical for successful adjustments and quality of life.

Communication skills assessments are an important beginning point in taking advantage of the school-based services of a speech and language pathologist. Actually, all students with communication disorders as a primary or secondary disability should have "present level of performance" data on their communication skills. It is important to find out how or whether a student's communication problems might interfere with environmental tasks and demands. Assessment of students is useful only to the extent that the assessment results provide information of how an individual functions within his or her natural environments—home, school, work, and in the community. This approach demands functional versus formal or standardized assessments and moves the SLP from traditional clinical practices and techniques to what is referred to as *pragmatics,* a functional approach to communication disorders intervention.

Speech and language intervention that is functional fits in at various points in the transition planning and services delivery process. Helping students articulate their interests, preferences, hopes, dreams, and fears in a safe, accepting communication relationship is a direct transition education intervention. Helping students learn new vocabulary related to adult living in the community is a functional language intervention that may be supplemental to their academic instruction, but, in some cases, it may be the only direct instruction they get in that area (Fisher, Clark, & Patton, 2004). Giving students practical tips on how to control their speech production (voice sounds and fluency) when asking for a date or participating in an interview is much more relevant to an older adolescent than clinical exercises in a small room with a two-way mirror.

Many adolescents with communication disorders are declassified at their own request as needing speech or language interventions because they do not choose to be singled out by an SLP in front of their adolescent peers or they feel that the basic techniques or procedures are not suitable for their age and grade. Would secondary students be as likely to complain about speech therapy or ask to terminate their therapy if the focus of the interventions were more practical?

The pressure on SLPs to serve large numbers of students results in a concentration at the elementary school level where the children are more compliant and concentrated in greater numbers. It is important to reevaluate the communication needs of students in middle and high schools and provide them with functional, goal-directed interventions to help them get through the difficulties of social relationships and communication problems with adults. Secondary special education personnel should look for those SLPs in the school district who are willing to work with middle and high school students and who are flexible in their assessment and intervention approaches to allow for a functional approach.

Occupational and Physical Therapy Services

Students with disabilities requiring occupational or physical therapy services are usually among the low-incidence groups served in special education and related services. Special education teachers and transition services personnel need to know about occupational and physical therapy services so that those services can be accessed quickly and effectively when needed. Transition services personnel particularly need to know the kinds of services that occupational and physical therapists provide, because they will discover a support system group that embraces many of the same values for functional adult outcomes, independence, and self-determination. This is especially true for occupational therapy.

Unfortunately, many special education professionals have had little contact with occupational or physical therapists. Infrequent contact results in sparse information about what the therapists' primary professional roles are and how compatible those roles are with transition services goals. For example, current roles and functions for each of these two related services are described here.

Occupational Therapy.   Occupational therapy aims to enhance a person's development, increase or restore independence, and prevent disability. Therapy focuses on how individuals spend their time to fulfill life roles within various environments (home, school, work, and community at large). Self-care, work or school, and play or recreational activities are evaluated and used to increase an individual's ability to participate meaningfully (Shepherd & Inge, 1999). Specifically, the occupational therapist (OT) may adapt tasks or environments according to an individual's age and social role. In school settings, therapists may address sensory-motor, cognitive, and psychosocial skills and behavior so that students can perform self-care and school work or play tasks in multiple environments (e.g., classrooms, cafeteria, restrooms, gym, school grounds, etc.). In work and community settings, OTs may assist in vocational exploration, job acquisition, and enhancing job performance (e.g., effective and efficient performance of job tasks, appropriate use of time, mobility management, self-care skills, social interaction skills, and compensatory techniques needed in work or community settings) (American Occupational Therapy Association, 1994).

Physical Therapy.   Physical therapy assists individuals of all ages with disabilities resulting from disease or injury in promoting fitness, health, and quality of life (American Physical Therapy Association, 1995). After assessing a person's strength and ability to move and endure physical activities, a physical therapist (PT) plans, designs, and conducts therapeutic interventions to decrease or prevent pain, injury, or further limitations. In school settings, for example, a PT may work with a student's ability to (1) move in organized patterns (e.g., gross motor skills), (2) assume and maintain sitting and standing postures, and (3) perform functional mobility tasks (e.g., getting to and from classes, carrying books, climbing stairs, opening doors, etc.). In work settings, the PT may address some of these same task demands, with specific attention to specific job environments and job demands, such as strength, coordination, or stamina.

Occupational therapy and physical therapy are two of the related services that were specified in 1975 under the Education for All Handicapped Children Act (PL 94-142). The use of OTs and PTs in school settings increased significantly after this legislation. According to the American Occupational Therapy Association's (AOTA) 1996 member survey, 18 percent of the occupational therapists employed in the United States work in public schools (AOTA, 1996). The American Physical Therapy Association reports that 8 percent of its members work in schools (Shepherd & Inge, 1998). Still, the numbers remain relatively small and are concentrated on children in the elementary and middle school levels.

Shepherd and Inge (1999) laid out some possible roles for the OT and the PT that may inform special educators and transition personnel of possible linkages that can be made and thus increase the future participation of these therapists. Figures 9.2 and 9.3 show some of the possible specific roles Shepherd and Inge proposed for the OT and PT. As is apparent, both OTs and PTs assess and evaluate students, teach functional tasks, evaluate students' environments, adapt tasks, use assistive technology, and promote self-advocacy, prevention of further impairment, and health/fitness maintenance. They also are trained and able to educate others (e.g., school personnel, family members, peers, volunteers, employers, etc.) about how persons outside the field can support and enhance the occupational or physical therapy process.

Rising costs for special education and related services in schools is resulting in decreased employment opportunities in schools and more restricted availability of related services personnel, such as school occupational therapists, school physical therapists, and school nurses. Dole (2004) cited eight influential court decisions at the state superior court, federal district court, and U.S. Supreme Court levels that show that students who need unique related services must receive them. Schools appear to be operating under the assumption that they can avoid the costs of related services, such as occupational or physical therapy and nursing services, by not offering the services as options with parents, by telling IEP case managers to commit the school to academic goals and objectives exclusively, or by claiming that no professionals are available to provide such services. Too often, only those informed and persistent parents who insist on services with threats of due process or litigation are the ones whose children receive the services.

FIGURE 9.2   Possible Roles for the Occupational Therapist in the Evaluation, Service Planning, or Delivery of Transition Services

1. **Teach functional tasks related to temporal aspects (age, maturation, ability/ disability, and life stage):**
   - Activities of daily living:
     —self-care (e.g., dressing, feeding, hygiene, toileting)
     —communication
     —socialization
     —mobility within home, school and community
   - Home management (e.g., cooking, cleaning, money management)
   - Work and health habits
   - Work skills
   - Leisure

2. **Evaluate environmental supports and barriers and recommend adaptations if needed:**
   - Physical characteristics
     —accessibility (e.g., terrain, furniture, objects)
     —sensory stimulation (e.g., tactile, visual, or auditory cues or distractions)
     —types of objects, tools, equipment
     —temporal cues (e.g., watches with alarms; toothpaste left on sinktop)
   - Social characteristics
     —activities (e.g., individual or group)
     —people
     —role expectations
   - Cultural characteristics
     —customs, expectations
     —values
     —beliefs

3. **Adapt tasks:**
   - Changing the physical characteristics of the task (e.g., sit instead of stand)
   - Changing the social characteristics of the task (e.g., increase or decrease the number of people involved)
   - Changing the demands (e.g., do part of task; checklists)
   - Work simplification (e.g., get all items together before shower; reorganize kitchen so able to find objects)
   - Use instructional techniques: (e.g., task analysis, forward and backward chaining, partial participation, positive supports, systematic instruction, natural cues)
   - Teach compensatory techniques

4. **Adapt materials and/or recommend assistive technology:**
   - Increase or decrease the size, shape, length, or sensory characteristics of materials/ objects being used
   - Adaptive aids (e.g., button hook, reacher, lapboard, talking watch, book holder; memory aids; talking calculators)
   - Switches, computers, appliances, augmentative communication devices, telephones, wheelchairs, environmental control units, positioning devices, alerting systems

FIGURE 9.2   Continued

5· **Develop interpersonal and social skills to support participation in the school, community, home, or work environment:**
   - Awareness of interests
   - Stress management
   - Time management
   - Self-management/coping techniques
   - Leisure activities to promote socialization and develop friendships
   - Assertiveness training
   - Decision making/problem-solving skills

6. **Educate others and learn from others in the home, classroom, community, or workplace:**
   - Student training
   - Family training
   - Staff training
   - Peer training

7. **Promote self-advocacy, prevention, and health maintenance:**
   - Legal rights and responsibilities
   - Disability and health awareness
   - Talking to others about disability and needs
   - Promote habits to maintain health (e.g., hygiene, medications, pressure reliefs, birth control; equipment maintenance, etc.)

Source: From "Occupational and Physical Therapy" by J. Shepherd and K. J. Inge in *Transition and School-Based Services: Interdisciplinary Perspectives for Enhancing the Transition Process* by S. H. deFur and J. R. Patton (Eds.), 1999, Austin, TX: PRO-ED. Reprinted by permission.

Assistive Technology Services

The National Council on Disabilities concluded that "with the assistance of technology, almost three-quarters of school-age children were able to remain in a regular classroom . . . and 45 percent of school-age children were able to reduce school-related services" (Morris, 1992, p. 5). Connecting these results with a common transition services goal, high school graduation, and spending a greater percentage of the school day in general education (with special education support) is associated with higher graduation rates (United States Department of Education, 1995; Malian & Love, 1998). Thus, it appears that with the assistance of technology, positive outcomes can be achieved.

Educational technology, in the popular sense, brings to mind for most people accessing and using computers. It is much more than that, just as assistive technology is much more than using computers and computer devices for people with disabilities. Today, the computer literacy of high school students is well beyond the expectations of even the early enthusiasts. Rapid development of instructional software programs incorporating universal design, inter-

FIGURE 9.3   Possible Roles for the Physical Therapist in the Evaluation, Service Planning, or Delivery of Transition Services

1. **Develop or compensate for skills that support participation in the school, community, or work environment.**
   - Strength
   - Endurance
   - Movement patterns
   - Assume and maintain postures

2. **Improve the student's mobility within the home, school, work, and the community setting.**
   - Ambulation
   - Wheelchair mobility
   - Climbing stairs
   - Opening doors
   - Transfers
   - Carrying items
   - Public and private transportation

3. **Promote self-advocacy, prevention, and health maintenance.**
   - Exercise
   - Nutrition
   - Body mechanics/positioning
   - Disability knowledge and precautions
   - Legal fights

4. **Adapt tasks and environments so the student can participate.**
   - Accessibility
   - Position of student and activity
   - Job site analysis

5. **Recommend or adapt assistive technology.**
   - Mobility aids (e.g., walkers, canes, wheelchairs, standing tables)
   - Computer access and positioning
   - Augmentative communication device
   - Exercise equipment
   - Accessibility

6. **Educate others and consult in the home, classroom, community, or workplace.**
   - Student training
   - Family training
   - Staff training
   - Peer training

Source: From "Occupational and Physical Therapy" by J. Shepherd and K. J. Inge in *Transition and School-Based Services: Interdisciplinary Perspectives for Enhancing the Transition Process* by S. H. deFur and J. R. Patton (Eds.), 1999, Austin, TX: PRO-ED. Reprinted by permission.

active guidance systems, technology software for students to develop their own electronic resumés, and the like make educational technology for students with disabilities a significant equalizer. Take computer-based occupational information systems as an example. These systems are rapidly becoming part of the common technology of secondary school guidance programs and allow students with disabilities to be a part of the general education program in new ways. Chapters 7 and 11 suggest references for occupational information, employment trends, legislation, and services available on the Internet. Clearly, there are some definite advantages in using computer-based information systems. Among these are the following:

1. Computers reduce the time counselors and career information personnel must spend in repetitive and routine dissemination tasks.
2. Computers provide almost instantaneous information.
3. Computer technology is still motivational and has moved from merely information storage to some creative interactive, decision-making systems.
4. Information can be updated more easily and more quickly than can print information.
5. Information can be made available in rural and remote areas with Internet access.
6. Audio attachments for students with visual impairments or nonreaders open up the systems to new populations.
7. Special switches and voice commands for students with visual or physical disabilities make it possible to use computers more independently.
8. Computers can provide data to teachers and counselors on what information students have obtained and how they have used the system.

Assistive technology includes any device or product that helps people with disabilities live, learn, work, and play more independently (Fisher, 1999). It can range from products as simple as reaching sticks, Velcro fasteners, or enlarged print to more technical devices such as hearing aids, Opticons, or sophisticated augmentative speech devices. But there is more to assistive technology than products or devices. Under the related services provision of the IDEA, assistive technology services goes beyond devices to those services required to make assistive technology work, such as evaluation of need for assistive technology, training for all involved persons in an assistive technology service, maintenance and repair of assistive technology devices, customization of an assistive technology device, ongoing assessment and monitoring of assessment device use, developing applications of assistive technology to new situations and environments, and coordinating therapies and services with assistive technology. The Technology Related Assistance for Individuals with Disabilities Act of 1988 (PL 100-497), known as the Tech Act, laid the groundwork for defining and furnishing guidelines for assistive technology and services in the lives of people with disabilities (Judith Fein National Institute on Disability and Rehabilitation Research, 1996). The Tech Act also provided the legal basis for later provisions of the IDEA and a framework for local and state education agencies to operate in establishing assistive technology services.

The language of the assistive technology requirements of the IDEA came out of the Tech Act, with only minor modifications. It states that the IDEA

> provides that if a child with a disability requires assistive technology devices or services, or both, in order to receive a free appropriate education, the public agency shall ensure that the assistive technology devices or services are made available to that child, either as special education, related services, or as supplementary aids and services that enable a child with a disability to be educated in regular classes. Determinations of whether a child with a disability requires assistive technology devices or services under this program must be made on an individual basis through applicable individualized education program and placement procedures. (*Federal Register,* 1991, p. 41272)

The 1997 IDEA Amendments emphasized the importance of assistance technology by including a provision requiring the IEP team to consider the specific needs of each child in the general education curriculum, as appropriate, including such needs as assistive technology (*Federal Register,* 1997, p. 55028).

As a related service for local schools to deliver, there is still a great deal of concern about costs and compliance guidelines for delivering assistive technology services. General guidelines are in place in all states, but specific guidelines and policies are in varying stages of development and clarification (Fisher, 1999). Secondary special educators and transition services personnel need to know the person(s) responsible for assisting in accessing assistive technology services. This assistance should be available at the assessment/evaluation stage of planning, the IEP planning stage, and the implementation and evaluation stage. Unfortunately, many school districts have no single qualified individual designated as responsible for providing assistive technology services. It remains the responsibility of the IEP team to know the student's rights in regard to assistive technology and to press for assistance or action in implementing an assistive technology provision in the IEP.

According to Chambers (1997), there are four basic questions to ask to determine whether a student really needs assistive technology:

1. Is assistive technology necessary to receive a free, appropriate education?
2. Is assistive technology necessary to receive services in the least restrictive environment?
3. Are the devices and services a necessary related service?

4. Will the student have access to school programs and activities with the assistive device or assistive technology services that he or she would not have access to without such devices or services?

From a transition services point of view, these questions might not be explicit enough. Fisher (1999) noted that another reasonable question to ask is: Is assistive technology necessary for a student to achieve employment, independent living, and social and community participation? The school setting is only *one* of the environments that needs to be considered for assistive technology. Especially for students in one or more types of community-based instruction, the environments or activity areas of employment, transportation, mobility, recreation and leisure, and home living warrant consideration for a student's need for assistive technology.

Community-Based Linkage and Referral Sources

A community services directory usually provides information for four kinds of assistance: emergency, financial, health, and program. *Emergency assistance* should identify sources for food, housing, legal, and any other general kinds of help. *Financial assistance* might include bail bonding, supplementary security income, aid to dependent children, food stamps, mortgages, auto loans, banking and credit unions, tax preparation, and financial planning. *Health problems assistance* would include mental health, dental health, visual assistance, and the subspecialties of physical health, preventive as well as corrective. *Program assistance* lists vocational rehabilitation, the state employment service, state and local advocacy groups, rehabilitation facilities, residential programs, and community agencies such as the chamber of commerce, city commissions, business and industrial councils, trade unions, and associations and human services agencies. In addition, some persons might wish to include sources for recreation and other leisure activities. The preceding is only a partial list of referral agency services and will certainly differ from community to community. (See the companion website for a listing of national resource agencies.)

Guidelines for Making Referrals

Most school districts have an established policy or procedure for making community referrals. This policy frequently includes a standard referral form. Consequently, the following guidelines are general in nature and are basically reminders for commonsense practice:

1. *Involve the administrator responsible for your program in the decision to make or recommend a referral.* Some administrators want only to be informed on routine cases but insist on involvement for certain kinds of problems or for certain parents.

2. *Involve the parents from the beginning.* Some schools and school personnel have had lawsuits brought against them for providing services without parental permission. By involving the parents in all decisions regarding the referral and obtaining their permission for specific referrals, special education staff will not only protect themselves from lawsuits but also may get helpful information and support from the parents. It is a fact, however, that parental involvement might lead to a refusal to cooperate and a denial of permission to refer. Still, parents are the ones with responsibility for their children, and school personnel must involve them.

3. *Provide all important information to the referral resource.* Referral resource personnel need as much relevant information as possible to be able to respond to the needs of the referred student. The important information should be written down and organized so that it can be used more easily. Whenever possible, discuss the information with the resource person to ensure that nothing is misunderstood and that there are no gaps in the information that the person needs.

4. *Inform key people on all stages of the referral.* Key people include the student who is being referred, his or her parents or guardians, other teachers or school personnel who have a need to know, the immediate supervisor, and the referral resource person. Each of these key participants in the referral process have information or a perspective that might be important as the process moves along. Having access to that information or those perspectives requires that these people be kept informed.

5. *Prompt referral resources into action.* Frequently, referral resource persons are overworked and have many other things to do besides respond immediately to a referral form or even to your personal request. Since one cannot ignore a student's needs, it is important to follow up the initial referral after a courteous time period to inquire as to the status of the referral. A referral situation is not always an emergency situation, so there is no rule as to how long to wait before prompting. There comes a point, however, in any referral that is based on need—either the need disappears or is heightened as time goes on. Prompting, on behalf of a student in need, is a professional expectation, and the referral resource person will understand a cheerful but persistent follow-up.

6. *Reinforce referral resources.* The referring professional should not forget to show appreciation personally and to give recognition to all those people who assist with their services. A short letter or memo of thanks with a copy to the person's supervisor or administrator is one simple way to show both appreciation and give recognition at the same time. Over time, one would need to be creative to keep the reinforcement process genuine and spontaneous.

Interagency Cooperation

Interagency and Community Linkages

Interagency and community linkages have developed over the years in some states and local communities. School programs characterized by "recommended practice" or "exemplary programming" have usually included some sort of interagency and community collaboration, usually in the form of an interagency agreement. IDEA 2004 omitted previous requirements for schools to include in the IEP, when appropriate, a statement of interagency responsibilities or any needed linkages. It did retain, however, the provision: "If a participating agency, other than the local education agency fails to provide the transition services described in the IEP in accordance with paragraph (I)(A)(i)(VIII), the local educational agency shall reconvene the IEP Team to identify alternative strategies to meet the transition objectives for the child set out in that program" (Sec. 614).

The IDEA clearly establishes the expectation that the delivery of transition services is not solely a school responsibility (Cozzens, Dowdy, & Smith, 1999). Recommended practice is that the school should ensure that linkages with nonschool agencies occur, rather than waiting for agencies to initiate something. Although not exclusively responsible for providing all services, the school is clearly responsible for ensuring that needed educational services are provided and that other needed services are addressed in the planning process. Schools have no authority to compel nonschool agencies to participate in the IEP transition planning process. The only exception would be if the school has a service contract with the agency. In that situation, the state education agency will hold the local school accountable for failing to ensure participation by the nonschool agency under contract. The regulations are clear, however. There is nothing in the provisions of the IDEA that relieves any participating agency, including a state vocational rehabilitation agency, of the responsibility to provide or pay for any transition service that the agency would otherwise provide to students with disabilities who meet the eligibility criteria of that agency.

Systematic Planning

Systematic planning for movement of youths with disabilities from school to adult community alternatives can and should occur at the state, local, and individual levels. Ideally, systematic planning should begin with a state plan.

This plan may be based on the federal mandate for transition planning among schools and adult service agencies, the legislative mandate for coordinating transition services, or a voluntary planning policy in the form of an interagency agreement or a "memorandum of understanding."

A multiagency policy or interagency agreement between senders (schools) and receivers (adult service agencies) can also provide a basis for statewide planning. The agencies ordinarily involved in these agreements are the State Department of Education (including the divisions of special and vocational education), the State Division of Vocational Rehabilitation, and other specific state agencies responsible for services to persons with disabilities, such as the Division of Vocational Rehabilitation for the Blind, state mental health and mental retardation services, developmental disabilities services, social welfare, and, sometimes, state corrections services. These policy-planning documents or planning agreements specify who does what, when, and how. Most states have interagency agreements or "memoranda of understanding" on transition in place, even though it is apparent that some agreements are real working agreements and others are concept agreements. Overlapping areas from law or regulatory authority have to be addressed, and assurances on "turf" issues have to be included for both the state and local levels before local impact can be felt.

Even if there is no state-level planning, senders and receivers at the local level can join together in planning how to make transition work better for its youth and adult population with disabilities. A written local interagency agreement or plan can be developed. Frequently, this is much less formalized than planning at the state level. These participants know one another, and planning can come out of daily operations of transition skill training, referral for individual planning, and service delivery. Blalock and Benz (1999) suggested very practical procedures for local collaboration through transition councils or community transition teams.

The transition process of an individual student with disabilities leaving school and entering the community can take place without benefit of a state or local transition plan. The odds against that individual making it these days without an individual transition plan as a component of his or her IEP and a support team are great, however. There is sufficient evidence from experience with individualized education programs to recognize that having transition goals and objectives on the IEP does not guarantee successful outcomes. On the other hand, not having those goals and objectives is not only noncompliance with the law but is flouting the spirit and logic of purposeful intervention.

Areas of Responsibility

The primary purpose of a local transition council is to develop a clear statement of the services that can be expected from each community agency and some system of collaboration. Any ambiguity concerning who takes responsibility for various tasks inevitably leads to issues that can become barriers to cooperation.

The most common disciplines involved in school career and transition program linkages are special education, career and technical education, and vocational rehabilitation. As each discipline or agency contributes its services to a given student, the effectiveness of the services is multiplied. Although special education and career and technical education services have been described elsewhere in a different context, they will be reviewed here in summary form. Vocational rehabilitation services will be described in more detail because they are the most frequent nonschool, external participants in the interagency linkage.

Special Education. Special education provides the usual educational programs and materials as a part of its ongoing responsibilities to school youth with disabilities. However, it also can be expected to provide for physical education, driver education, career awareness and exploration, employment training, and remedial classes when appropriate. In addition, special education can furnish readers, Braillers, and note-takers for students who have visual impairments, interpreters for students who are hearing impaired, and aids for those students with physical disabilities while they are in school. Occupational, physical, and speech therapy may also be furnished by special education. Motor development, mobility training, assistive technology services, and audiological evaluations are also paid for by special education. In some cases, special psychological, medical, and psychiatric evaluations can be furnished, and special transportation costs can be covered. Finally, special education can provide counseling and provide or arrange for prevocational and vocational evaluations, work-adjustment training, and job placement and follow-up. Comprehensive assessment and evaluation data are especially helpful to vocational education and vocational rehabilitation personnel since they are required to have evaluation data and because duplication of assessment procedures is extremely costly.

Career and Technical Education. Career and technical educators are responsible for assuring access to all regular career and technical education programs whenever possible. However, they must go beyond that to provide programs making accommodations for students with disabilities when needed. When called for, career and technical education specialists must make modifications to ensure access to the program or must adapt or modify the curriculum, materials, instructional methods, sequence, duration, content, and type of instructional units. Career and technical educators must ensure that appropriate vocational tools and equipment are available and adapt or modify those tools that are inappropriate. Career and technical education must also assure a barrier-free environment for the vocational education programs. Any vocationally related goals on the IEP must be based on a vocational assessment, including interests, abilities, and special needs with respect to completing the vocational education program successfully. Special education personnel are to be involved with career and technical educators in planning for youths with disabilities or special needs, and their parents must be notified—before the students enter the ninth grade—of the different career and technical education programs and services offered.

Career and technical education, as part of the comprehensive high school, is not the vital, visible program that it once was. Beginning in the 1980s, high school students took increasing numbers of academic subjects and the decline in vocational education enrollments continued until a leveling off in the mid-1990s. Despite the intensive emphasis placed on academic reforms of the past decade, high school students still earn more credits in vocational education (4 credits is average) than they do in math (3.4) or science (3.1) (Silverberg et al., 2002).

Career and technical education still organizes programs around the seven major occupational concentrations: agriculture, business and office, health occupations, marketing, family and consumer sciences, trade and industry, and technology and technical education. School districts select one or more of these, depending on their local labor needs and school enrollment (Evers & Elksnin, 1998). The educational reform movement and legislation of the past two decades (see Chapter 2) have impacted career and technical education programs in several ways. First, schools have had to drop programs that did not have enough students enrolling and finding employment in the training areas. Second, the high cost of maintaining expensive equipment and keeping up with changing technology caused schools to phase programs out and look to other program options. Third, school districts have found it more cost effective to develop partnerships with area or regional postsecondary vocational and technical schools. Finally, there has been an effort to change focus at the high school level by combining basic occupational instruction with academic instruction in Tech-Prep programs and career path programs as part of school-to-work or school-to-career programs.

Career and technical educational and school guidance and counseling services are taking the lead in implementing school-to-work or school-to-career programs in a number of states. Most states with such programs follow recommended components: school-based programs, work-based programs, and connecting activities. The *school-based component* must use career counseling and assessment to help all students select career majors by the eleventh grade and develop programs of study to pursue their major goals. The *work-based component* is a program designed by the school to complement the students' career major selections and includes instruction in specific occupational competencies as well as competencies related to business or industry gained through paid or unpaid work and on-the-job mentoring. *Connecting activities* are activities and programs designed by the school to ensure active and continuing participation of employers with the school in making the school-based and work-based components successful.

Inclusion of students with disabilities in some school-to-work programs is not easily achieved; neither is it in on-campus or vocational-technical center programs. Programs are often selective and use prerequisites that are difficult to meet. You will have to be involved in your local program and be assertive in helping your students gain access to vocational or technical courses or the school-to-work or school-to-career programs. Cooperative education programs, on-the-job training, and apprenticeship programs are more accessible, but not always available in rural areas.

Vocational Rehabilitation Services. The Vocational Rehabilitation Act Amendments of 1992 (see Chapter 2) and implementing regulations complemented the IDEA language by ensuring that all students who need vocational rehabilitation services receive these services in a timely manner. The intent of the language in the Act was to establish a policy that stated that there should be no gap in services between the education system and the vocational rehabilitation system. It was very clear in the Act that the provisions related to transition services were not intended in any way to shift the responsibility of service delivery from education to vocational rehabiitation. The primary role of the vocational rehabilitation system is one of planning for a student's years after leaving school.

Although each state has its own organizational structure for its vocational rehabilitation agency, the substantial federal support to states for the program has resulted in a basic sequence of steps that describe the expectations one could have in any state for seeking and obtaining vocational rehabilitation services. Most states do have separate vocational rehabilitation services for persons disabled by visual impairment and those disabled by all other physical, sensory, or mental impairments. The sequence of service delivery of both, however, is parallel. The steps in vocational rehabilitation generally include the following:

Step 1: Referral. Students in school programs will ordinarily be referred by someone in secondary special education. The initial contact, however, can be self-referral; students and their parents may contact the local or area vocational rehabilitation counselor on their own. Occasionally, referrals are made by physicians, psychologists, ministers, social workers, or caseworkers in social welfare programs. In any case, contact is made and an initial interview is scheduled or conducted at the point of initial contact.

Step 2: Initial Interview. In the initial interview, the counselor talks with the student and begins developing case management information. The student's own perceptions of his or her disability and how it relates to employment is an important part of this interview. Because most special education students are still minors at the time of referral, it is also important to obtain parent views on the disability. Initial probes into short- and long-term goals are usually made, but no decisions are made at this point. The counselor will begin arrangements for obtaining any new assessment and evaluation information that is needed. This will usually include a general medical examination, as well as specialist medical examinations, psychological evaluations, and vocational assessment and evaluations, when necessary. If schools have current psychological or assessment data, the counselor may request such data with the student's or parent's permission.

Step 3: Diagnosis. A vocational rehabilitation counselor must have an authoritative diagnosis of the presence of a physical or mental disability. In addition, there must be some statement or obvious implication relative to the effect of the disability on employability. Thus, examinations and evaluations are scheduled as needed to obtain this type of information and establish official eligibility for services. In this context, it is obvious that vocational rehabilitation insists on current diagnostic data and cannot always use what schools have available. The possibilities are the greatest for sharing of current test data for intellectual functioning, adaptive behavior, and personal-social adjustment.

Step 4: Assessment. Once eligibility is established through medical, psychiatric, or psychological diagnoses, additional assessment and evaluation are conducted to determine feasibility. Vocational rehabilitation has maintained the concept of feasibility as one criterion for acceptance for services for many years. *Feasibility* is a presumptive judgment based on all available diagnostic and evaluation data that the services rendered by vocational rehabilitation are likely to benefit the individual in employment or independent living outcomes. School personnel need to know about this aspect of the process of accepting students for services, so that data that speak to feasibility and eligibility are provided during the assessment and evaluation process.

Many special educators assume that vocational rehabilitation services are automatically available to their students and graduates, simply because of the school's determination that the students have disabilities. As mentioned in Chapter 2, educators need to understand and help families understand that rehabilitation services are not automatic and that services are frequently based on availability of federal and state funds and the state's "order of selection" policy. This policy is to be used to ensure fair and consistent eligibility determination practices as well as to provide a basis for acceptance of eligible clients during periods of limited funding.

Step 5: Preparation for Placement. Once a student is accepted for services by vocational rehabilitation, an individualized plan for employment (IPE) is developed. The plan states what the vocation objective is, what services are required, and how long the service will be needed. Although vocational rehabilitation counselors can provide a variety of services to persons with disabilities, they are required to make use of services offered by other agencies before using their own funds and to stay within the guidelines of the IPE. When a person is eligible for services, vocational rehabilitation can provide or buy a number of services. This may include medical treatment, surgery, therapy, prosthetic fitting, crutches, wheelchairs, glasses, hearing aids, dental work, and cosmetic enhancement. In the area of training, vocational rehabilitation can pay for tuition, on-the-job training fees to employers, books, supplies, transportation, readers for clients who are blind, interpreters for clients who are deaf, and aids for clients who are orthopedically handicapped. At the conclusion of training, it can pay for job development, engineering and redesign, and job-seeking skills. Vocational rehabilitation can also pay for licenses, tools, equipment, and supplies, and handle maintenance and transportation during the rehabilitation process.

Step 6: Placement. Vocational rehabilitation counselors have a professional stake in the successful culmination of the rehabilitation process, and the placement process is the step in which the counselor may become more active. Large caseloads frequently prevent personal involvement in every placement, however, so placement personnel in public schools, postsecondary training programs, other adult rehabilitation agencies, and the state employment offices are used.

Step 7: Follow-Up. Most state vocational rehabilitation agencies, whether official or unofficial, establish quotas for counselors in achieving successful closures, or *26s*, as the counselors call them (referring to the code number for "successfully closed in rehabilitated status" in their quarterly and annual reports). Counselors are encouraged to follow up on their clients for up to a year before closing the case, but a case could be closed within 90 days. Pressure to meet quotas probably has some influence on the length of time a counselor will spend on follow-up.

Altogether, vocational rehabilitation is an agency that can bring powerful resources to bear on behalf of eligible clients. However, since vocational rehabilitation must use the resources of other agencies first, it will often be unable or unwilling to provide some of its services while the person is a student and therefore the responsibility of the school. (This practice is often referred to as *first dollar.*) Since each special education student must have an individualized education program, the school can request the attendance of a vocational education representative and a vocational rehabilitation counselor at the IEP meeting. If the situation for an individual case permits working together, they can develop the IEP for the school and for vocational rehabilitation. Clearly, such coordinated efforts can do much to focus agency services on common goals. It is no coincidence that this type of joint planning presents such a powerful demonstration of what can be accomplished through linkages.

Multiple Partners in Transition Services.   Cozzens and colleagues (1999) described a growing list of transition services partners from among the increasing number of adult service programs and agencies that are now becoming more available. Federal programs (such as Medicaid, Social Security, and employment programs) are available in any location, although accessing the programs may require travel into a regional office. In many cases, other adult programs are found in larger communities and metropolitan areas. There are not enough of these programs and services, but it is encouraging to see the need recognized and efforts being made to address those needs. Figure 9.4 presents a list of examples of other multiple partners in the process of achieving satisfactory adult life outcomes.

Conclusion

A host of school and community agencies have been developed to provide various kinds of support efforts to persons with disabilities to enable them to live and work successfully. However, these resources are often fragmented and inadequate by themselves. School and agency collaborative efforts, often called *interagency linkages,* have been formed to provide more effective services to people who have disabilities.

The linkages may be between school discipline areas, community agencies, or combinations, but they share the common goal of improved support services. The heart of the collaborative effort is a transition council or committee made up of representatives from the various agencies that has full knowledge of all the resources that can be furnished to people with disabilities to help them become successful citizens. Cooperation in furnishing these resources requires a clear understanding of the capabilities and the limitations of each agency, plus a willingness to sacrifice some autonomy, jurisdiction, or ownership for the good of the linkage effort.

FIGURE 9.4 Major Adult Service Programs and Services Used in Transition Services

Employment Services

Workforce Investment Act (WIA) Programs	Designed to serve all individuals, but emphasizes under-served populations such as low-income individuals, out-of-school youth, and individuals with disabilities. Federally funded projects implementing youth councils, one-stop delivery services, youth activities, Job Corps, etc., by the Department of Labor and locally administered by local workforce investment boards.
Transitional Employment Services	Time-limited, facility or community-based employment for individuals with a range of disabilities. Provided as individual or group placements and includes the Projects with Industry (PWI) model. Funded by state and federal rehabilitation funds and authorized by the Rehabilitation Act, as amended.
Work Opportunity Tax Credit	Replaced the previous Targeted Jobs Tax Credit. Available on an elective basis for employers hiring individuals from one or more of several targeted groups, including vocational rehabilitation referrals, qualified summer youth employees, high-risk youth, and qualified food stamp recipients. Credit generally would be equal to 35 percent of qualified wages.

Social Security and Health Care Services

Social Security Disability Insurance (SSDI)	Provides disability insurance in the form of monthly payments to individuals with disabilities who have a work history and thus have paid into the Social Security system. Minors or children with disabilities are also eligible. Does not require a financial needs test. Funded and authorized by the Social Security Act, as amended.
Supplemental Security Income (SSI)	Provides monthly cash assistance to individuals who are needy, elderly, or have disabilities and who have little or no work history. Requires a financial needs test. Funded and authorized by the Social Security Act.
Medicaid	Hospital and health care insurance for eligible poor and persons with disabilities. Federally regulated and state administered under the Social Security Act, as amended. Typically accompanies SSI benefits.
Medicare	Hospital and health care insurance for eligible elderly persons and persons with disabilities. Federally regulated and state administered by the Social Security Act, as amended. Typically accompanies SSDI benefits.
Plan for Achieving Self Success (PASS)	Provides for the purchase of equipment, services, training, or education needed for work to be excluded from earnings or set aside income or resources for a work goal.

(continued)

FIGURE 9.4   Continued

**Community Living and
Support Services**

Housing and Urban Development Programs	Federally administered and state-authorized housing assistance program that provides low-cost loans (Section 202) to finance construction or rehabilitation of residential facilities for persons who are elderly or who have disabilities. This section also provides funding for the development of apartment complexes, known as *independent living complexes (ILCs)*, of up to 24 units per site and for group homes of up to 15 clients. Section 8 provides for rental aid to low-income families and individuals and to persons with disabilities but not elderly.
Community Developmental Disabilities Agencies Authorized under the Developmental Disabilities Act (CDDOs)	(42 CFR 435.1009) Coordinates all adult services in an area for persons with developmental disabilities. Under this program, the Developmental Disabilities Waiver program provides funding alternatives to state developmental disabilities divisions.
Group Homes/ Supported Apartments	Community-based residences of two or more individuals with disabilities and support staff. May or may not be regulated by Intermediate Care Facility-Mental Retardation (ICF-MR) funds. Also known as *supported homes, community care homes*, and *community living alternatives (CLAS)*.
Adult Board and Care Homes	Community-based homes of various sizes that provide room and board for adults with disabilities. Typically, they provide minimal supervision and resident programming.
Food Stamps	Provides stamps that may be exchanged for food at grocery stores. Families, individuals, and groups of individuals (e.g., group home residents) are eligible, depending on income and financial need. Typically, SSI recipients are eligible. Federally funded through the Department of Agriculture and state and locally administered by social service agencies.
Public Health Services	Health care and treatment for persons not covered by health insurance. State funded and locally administered.
Mental Health Services	Outpatient mental health evaluations and treatment for individuals and groups with a range of mental health problems. State and locally funded and locally administered.
Independent Living Centers	Independent living assistance for employment, housing, personal attendant registers, legal assistance, accessibility consultations, personal counseling, and ADA consultations. State and local funding and locally administered.

10 Instructional Strategies for Transition Education

MARY E. CRONIN

SASSY C. WHEELER

MELANIE FORSTALL LEMOINE

To teach a man how he may learn to grow independently, and for himself, is perhaps the greatest service that one person can do for another.

—Benjamin Jowett

This chapter overviews instructional strategies that will assist you in teaching students the needed skills for transition to their next subsequent environment. The topics covered include integration of the transition goals in the student's individualized education plan (IEP) along with techniques for enhancing the involvement of students from culturally and linguistically diverse backgrounds in the IEP process; teaching techniques in inclusive settings; teaching learning strategies and study skills; incorporating technology in the curriculum; exploring strategies to assist with the application of academic content to real-life situations; discussing various options to enhance learning experiences in the community; and presenting methods for empowering families in the transition planning and instructional process. A resource list is also provided in the Appendix which can be found on the Allyn and Bacon companion website.

Integrating Transition Goals and the IEP

The IEP is the guiding force when anticipating the course for a student's future. Wehman (2002) identified a sound school program, a written plan, and realistic options for students and their families to choose as the three essential elements for effective transition. In addition to these elements, much has been written about the necessity of the student's active involvement in planning his or her future (Bassett & Lehmann, 2002; Everson & Reid, 1999; Miner & Bates, 1997; Thoma, Rogan, & Baker, 2001; Wehman, 2002; Wehman, Everson, & Reid, 2001; Wehmeyer & Lawrence, 1995).

In preparation for the development of an IEP with a focus on the future transition needs of students, many steps must be taken to ensure the creation of a quality plan. The following concepts are crucial to ensuring that every aspect of transition planning is addressed in respect to the student's eventual postschool outcome. These concepts are based on the work of Everson and Reid (1999), Mount (1997), Wehman (2002), Wehman and associates (2001), Wehmeyer and Lawrence (1995), and Wehmeyer and Ward (1993).

1. *Person-centered planning session(s).* Person-centered planning (PCP) models and approaches were discussed in Chapter 5. Unquestionably, students with moderate to severe disabilities or multiple transition service needs benefit most from PCP. The extended time required for most PCP sessions raises the issue of efficiency planning for the large number of students in the mild to moderate disability group. The concept of PCP, though, can be implemented in a variety of forms. Strategies for PCP can be used in one-on-one interviews with the student, family members, or other stakeholders. Participants include individuals who provide a support system and who are significant to the student, such as the student's parents, siblings, extended family, current and past teachers, adult service providers, friends, and the like. Session topics discussed include the likes, dislikes, and fears of the student, in addition to the student's visions and dreams of his or her future. These discussions could all happen in one formal PCP session or in a number of formal or informal sessions over time.

An emphasis of PCP are the supports, specialized services, and contacts/connections needed by individual students, especially those with more significant disabilities (Wehman et al., 2001). The benefits of the student receiving these supports and services is "to engineer changes in the environments and apply all of the supports needed to ensure success in those environments" (Wehman et al., 2001, p. 95). Although time consuming, PCP is useful for assisting the student in planning his or her future and developing an appropriate IEP, as well as ensuring that the student's wishes, needs, and desires are heard.

2. *Responsibilities of the stakeholders.* By agreeing to assist the student with a disability in planning his or her future, a stakeholder also shares responsibility in assisting the student in investigating or carrying out steps that bring the student closer to his or her goals. This could take the form of making calls and inquiries regarding services available, writing letters of support or recommen-

dations to work-training sites or postsecondary education training sites, assisting in problem-solving transportation barriers, or other related assistance.

3. *Student-led meetings.* One of the most powerful steps toward assisting students in planning their futures is to train them in leading their own IEP meetings. Bassett and Lehmann (2002) identified six advantages of student-directed IEP meetings: "Students (1) develop self advocacy skills; (2) actively plan for their present and future goals; (3) practice their communication and negotiation skills; (4) take responsibility for and ownership of their decisions; (5) acquire self-evaluation and self-management skills; and (6) participate in a team approach to problem solving" (p. 68). The preparation to lead a meeting begins with watching a real or mock student-led IEP meeting (Allen, Smith, Test, Flowers, & Wood, 2001), then roleplaying in the classroom. Students need to participate at a more substantive level than merely presiding over their IEP meetings whenever possible. They need to concentrate on advocating for themselves through a clear presentation of their needs, preferences, and interests; some proposed goals; and some requests for specific programs and services. Knowledge to be able to do this can come from brainstorming ideas or scenarios of the future; reading materials on various living, working, and postsecondary situations; interviewing adults about their jobs and living situations; talking to former students; observing existing school programs and services; observing individuals in various jobs and work situations; and exploring various postsecondary educational options.

4. *Integrating transition goals into the overall goals of the IEP.* This is a significant step in the development of an IEP. A link needs to be made from the transition goals to identification of what skills and knowledge the student needs, in addition to recognizing the student's ability to apply concepts to real-life situations. Success in achieving these goals comes when the student can also identify the skills and knowledge he or she currently possesses. The goals and benchmarks on the IEP therefore need to reflect programming to meet any gaps detected.

5. *Respecting cultural diversity.* Given the number of students from culturally and linguistically diverse backgrounds who receive special education services, it is essential to be attentive to each student's individual culture. When planning transition goals, cultural heritage, family traditions, and cultural norms should be included in the final goals or benchmarks. By including these aspects of the student's heritage in the transition planning process a greater sense of connectedness can be established between the student's school and home life.

In this day and age of accountability, teachers of students with special needs must address the issues impacting curricula of this population. An educational system suggested by Kochhar-Bryant and Bassett (2002a) combines standard-based and opportunities-based systems. These systems would address increased standards in general education for all students; blending of curriculum options; academic, career-technical, and community-based learning curriculum options; multiple measures of the outcomes for all students on multiple domains; and identifying opportunities that help students with disabilities to participate in secondary general curriculum (Kochhar-Bryant & Bassett, 2002a).

Making the educational connection for students with disabilities while aligning with the system as described by Kochhar-Bryant and Bassett (2002a) and with the various mandates and standards of federal, state, and local education systems can be difficult at best. It is clear that academic skills must also be tied to real-life applications (Patton & Trainor, 2002) and life-skill instruction is still vitally important for all students with disabilities. Every teacher needs to make every attempt to comply with federal mandates and meet the needs of all students.

Teaching in Inclusive Settings

Over the years, many terms have been used to describe the experiences and time students with disabilities spend in the general education classroom. *Deinstitutionalization, normalization, mainstreaming, integration,* and *inclusion* have all appeared in the literature during the past 35 years (Hallahan & Kauffman, 2004; Friend & Cook, 2003; Smith, 2004). *Inclusion* is the most current term that has evolved and has probably been the most closely scrutinized concept, especially by general education administrators and teachers.

Various definitions of *inclusive education* have been generated (Bos & Vaughn, 2002; Bradley, King-Sears, & Tessier-Switlick, 1997; Friend & Bursuck, 2002; Friend & Cook, 2003; Salend, 2005) with common themes emerging from them. In this text, inclusive education (learning in inclusive settings) is the "participation by all in a supportive general education environment that includes appropriate educational and social supports and services" (Bradley et al., 1997, p. 6). In the context of this book on transition education and services, we support Wehman's (1997) statement: "The goal of inclusion is to prepare students to participate as fully contributing members of society" (p. 18).

Unfortunately, there are variables that contribute to the difficult task that special education teachers face with their students who have disabilities in the general education classroom. First, many general education teachers are not familiar with the characteristics of the various disabilities. Second, general educators are often unfamiliar with methods or strategies used to enhance instruction for students with disabilities. For example, a number of general educators often feel that the only strategy they need to employ in teaching students with disabilities is to provide extended time on tests and assignments, feeling that all students can successfully complete the assignments if they are not rushed. In-service or support programs provided by school systems for general educators cannot happen fast enough. Third, updating the curriculum of teacher education programs in higher education to reflect changes in how general and special educators should be trained is occurring at too slow a pace. Six areas in need of training include (1) collaborative teaching, (2) differentiated instruction, (3) teaching learning strategies and study skills, (4) integration of technology, (5) application of academic content to real-life situations, and (6) teaching community skills. Fourth, standards-based reform and, in spite of current practice, accountability systems put schools in positions that result in making academics the overriding task for teachers of all students.

Students with significant disabilities pose different challenges for teachers in schools and employers/co-workers in community settings. Understanding the functioning level, unique communication needs, and social capabilities of students with significant disabilities is a major hurdle for both teachers and employers/co-workers. Knowledge about the disabilities and understanding of the supports needed by a student with severe disabilities to function in a class or community setting is the key to the general education teacher's, employer's, and student's success in the inclusive setting. Smith, Polloway, Patton, and Dowdy (2001) identified several variables contributing to student success in inclusive classrooms. Some of the variables include the existence of a sense of community, social accceptance, appreciation of student diversity, attention to a student's curricular needs, evidence of management and instructional practices, and appropriate supports in classrooms. In Figure 10.1, Wehman (2001) offers tips for working with students with severe disabilities to assist teachers in inclusive settings.

Inclusive settings are not found only in school buildings. Inclusive settings are as unique and varied as the students who occupy them. Any setting that is a natural learning environment for all students is an inclusive educa-

FIGURE 10.1   Tips for Inclusion

1. Identify one or more students without disabilities who can help the student with severe disabilities at lunch, during art class, or on the playground.
2. Design general classroom activities in such a way that the student with severe disabilities can participate through use of volunteers, student teachers, or other classroom helpers.
3. Individualize curricula for students with severe disabilities by providing learning objectives consistent with life/functional needs.
4. Provide for necessary adaptations, assists, and supports in teaching techniques to minimize the severity of the student's disability.

Source: From *Life Beyond the Classroom: Transition Strategies of Young People with Disabilities* (3rd ed.) (p. 323) by Paul Wehman, 2001, Baltimore, MD: Paul H. Brookes Publishing Co. Reprinted by permission.

tional setting. As students matriculate in school, their inclusive educational settings increase in number and in scope. This occurs to such an extent that as students with disabilities prepare to exit their formal school programs, it is logical that more of their instructional time should be spent outside the traditional classroom and school buildings and in the numerous inclusive community settings to which they are moving. These types of community settings include work sites, general community sites (e.g., grocery stores, banks, gas stations, parks and gardens, public transportation, etc.), apartments or group homes, and community college or university campuses to name a few.

Collaborative Teaching

Friend and Cook (2003) defined *collaboration* as a style professionals choose to use in order to accomplish a goal they share. Being together as a team does not mean actually working together to accomplish a goal. True collaboration exists when all members of the team feel their contributions are valued, the team goals are clear, each member takes part in the decision-making efforts, and respect is shown for all team members (Blalock, 2005; Friend & Cook, 2003; Heron & Harris, 2001; Idol, 2002). Friend and Cook further clarified collaboration by identifying several key attributes, including voluntary participation, parity in the relationship, shared goals, shared accountability, trust and respect, shared resources, and shared responsibility for decision making.

Collaborative teaching occurs at all educational levels: elementary, middle, and high school and with all populations (students without disabilities and students with disabilities [mild/moderate, severe/multiple disabilities, sensory impairments]). The day-to-day work of a collaborative team can include, but is not limited to, shared problem solving, co-teaching, teaming, and consulting. Each of these identified tasks are described here.

Shared Problem Solving.   Shared problem solving can occur in several different forms in a school situation (Blalock, 2005). Examples include brainstorming options for community instruction or assisting a student in a person-centered planning meeting; both may require the problem-solving skills of a team. Friend and Bursuck (2002) offered a model for shared problem solving. Within their model, once a shared need is discovered, the next step is problem identification. Generating or brainstorming a list of solutions for the problem identified is next, keeping in mind that judgment is deferred, and the more ideas generated to select a solution, the better. Generated ideas are then evaluated as to their feasibility and contribution to the resolution of the problem. After one or two ideas are selected, the specific details needed to employ that option should be outlined. The implementation of the solution should then be followed by an evaluation of its effectiveness by the collaborative team after a predetermined amount of time has passed (a few days to a month or two).

Shared problem solving is a necessary skill for all teachers and can also be taught to students at the middle and high school levels when working in cooperative groups.

Co-Teaching. Hourcade and Bauwens (2002) stated that co-teaching occurs when two or more teachers share the instruction for a single group of students. Friend and Cook (2003) identified five of the more common co-teaching approaches: one teaches, one supports; station teaching; parallel teaching; alternative teaching; and team teaching. In the first delivery example, one teacher leads the lesson while the other supports or assists the educator who is teaching. In station teaching, Friend and Cook explained that the curricular content is divided into parts. Part of the content is taught by one teacher to a group of students, then the teachers switch and another part is then taught by the other teacher. When two teachers teach the same information to two different groups in one class, this is considered parallel teaching. This method affords individual teachers the opportunity to teach the same content using different teaching techniques, allowing them to divide the class by students who can benefit the most from one technique or the other (e.g., one teacher might use a hands-on approach while the other would use the discovery method).

Alternative teaching is used when one class is divided into one small group and one large group. Friend and Cook (2003) have observed that this method has been traditionally used to instruct a smaller group of students who need remediation. In recent times, the focus of this subgroup could be enrichment for students interested in a specific topic or preteaching concepts, such as specialized vocabulary, in preparation for a lesson the next day.

Team teaching consists of two teachers who share leadership in the classroom. Friend and Cook (2003) suggested that teachers can use the team teaching opportunity to roleplay situations or model behaviors, such as one teacher outlining on the board as the other teacher teaches the content.

Friend and Cook (2003) offered tips for successful co-teaching experiences. These include advanced planning, discussing differing views on teaching and learning before co-teaching begins, attending to details such as class rules and routines, explaining the co-teaching plan to parents, avoiding one of the teachers becoming the "helping teacher" or taking on tasks of a paraprofessional, talking out disagreements as they happen, and beginning co-teaching slowly.

Teaming. Teams in secondary special education have long assisted in planning the educational programs of students since the mid-1970s. The purpose of those planning teams has evolved since the 1970s to their current focus of assisting the students in planning their futures, with the student as an active member of the team. However, a greater emphasis has begun to be placed on middle school planning teams, as well as an attempt to better prepare students for their subsequent transition, and to begin the process of thinking about long-term future goals for middle school students. The success of a team depends on the commitment of every member of the team to the predetermined goals of the team (Blalock, 2005; Friend & Cook, 2003; Heron & Harris, 2001; Idol, 2002).

Consulting.   Consultation is a specialized type of problem-solving process in which a professional with specialized expertise assists another professional who requires the knowledge of that expertise (Idol, 2002). During the transition planning process, teachers frequently seek consultation with adult service providers (e.g., a vocational rehabilitation counselor or a specialist in positive behavioral support) to assist the transition team in planning postsecondary options for students with disabilities. Once a need or problem has been resolved, the services of the consultant are usually no longer needed.

Differentiated Instruction

The importance of differentiating instruction for students with multiple ability levels cannot be understated when discussing recommended practices or promising practices used in inclusive educational settings. *Differentiation* has been defined in a number of ways (Moll, 2003; Reis, Kaplan, Tomlinson, Westberg, Callahan, & Cooper, 1998; Tomlinson, 1999, 2001, 2003; Tomlinson & Cunningham-Eidson, 2003; Tomlinson & Kalbfleisch, 1998). It is usually regarded as accommodating learning differences. This is done by identifying students' strengths and using appropriate strategies to meet the needs of students' various ability levels, personal preferences, and learning styles. As these factors are determined, all students can then engage in a variety of educational experiences (Reis et al., 1998). Differentiated curricula and instruction can respond to students' varying readiness levels, interests, and learning profiles.

As early as middle school, students can be taught to identify their own learning styles (Heacox, 2002). By administering learning styles inventories to students in the middle grades, teachers can assist their students in recognizing the methods from which they learn best, as well as the ways in which they can best express their knowledge (Gregory & Chapman, 2002). Once students possess a firm understanding of their individual learning styles, they can then inform their teachers at each subusquent grade of their personal preferences (Tomlinson, 2003).

In addition to these issues, the concept of universal design for learning must also be addressed. Universal design for learning (UDL) is a concept that originated in architectural contexts but has since been modified to include educational practices as well. Central to the concept of UDL is the idea that all curriulum materials should be modified from the outset of instruction in order to teach all students effectively (Pisha & Coyne, 2001; Rose, 2001; Rose &

Meyer, 2002). Male (2003) identified four fundamental themes that UDL addresses: (1) students with disabilities fall along a continuum of learner differences, just as other students do; (2) teachers should make adjustments for all students, not just those with disabilities; (3) curriculum materials should be as varied and diverse as the learning styles and needs in the classroom, rather than textbook centered; and (4) rather than trying to adjust the students to learn from a set curriculum, the curriculum should be flexible to accommodate a range of student differences. If teachers are to make a concerted effort to accommodate the needs of all students in their classrooms, there should be a plethora of materials available and accessible in their classrooms.

Reis and colleagues (1998) suggested that after students' various instructional levels, interests, and profiles are identified, whole groups, small groups, and individual students can equally engage in a variety of curriculum enrichment and acceleration experiences. In addition, Reis and colleagues observed that teachers who offer differentiated curricula and instruction view students as individuals with their own skills, interests, styles, and talents.

Tomlinson (1999, 2001) offered nine principles of differentiated instruction. These principles offer a framework by which to analyze or identify when differentiated instruction is being used in an educational setting. By analyzing an educational setting for the existence of differentiation of curriculum and instruction, teachers will be more conscious of implementing a differentiated approach. Tomlinson's (1999) nine principles are as follows:

1. Learning experiences are based on student readiness for the task, his or her individual interests, and learning profiles.
2. Assessment of student needs is ongoing, and all tasks are adapted to meet a student's need based on assessment information.
3. Active and respected participation is required of all students in activities.
4. The role of the teacher is coordinator of instruction and learning variables rather than provider of information.
5. Various and flexible work group configurations are used.
6. Student needs determine the flexibility in time use.
7. Various instructional strategies are used to meet student needs.
8. Specific criteria are determined to ensure student success.
9. Emphasis is on student strengths.

Tomlinson (2003) suggested differentiating content, activities, and products to increase differentiated instruction in classrooms. Sample strategies for achieving this differentiation for students of varying ability levels include curriculum compacting, independent study, interest centers or interest groups, tiered assignments, flexible grouping, learning centers, adjusting questions, mentorships/apprenticeships, varied rubrics, reading buddies, multiple texts, interest-based mini-lessons, independent study projects, and learning contracts.

Teaching Learning Strategies and Study Skills

Instruction in learning strategies and study skills has been implemented most extensively at the secondary level with students with learning disabilities. Given the inclusive education movements currently present in the country, middle school students are also being introduced to these essential skills. This instruction is being broadened now to include students with all disabilities and even students without disabilities. Deshler, Ellis, and Lenz (1996) and Lenz and Deshler with Kissam (2004) identified three approaches to teaching learning strategies: the reductionist approach, the constructivist approach, and the functionalist approach.

The *reductionist approach* is based on the idea that to understand or explain something complex, it must be analyzed and divided into simpler, smaller, or more understandable components. Cognitive behavior modification is an example of such an approach. It combines behavior management techniques with self-training methods such as monitoring instruction, evaluation, and verbalization. The reductionist approach focuses on thinking about one's thinking. Much of the research on this strategy and its use with adolescents with disabilities has been conducted at the University of Virginia (Hallahan & Kauffman, 2004). They found the approach useful because it stresses self-initiative and helps the student overcome passivity in learning. This ties directly to the concept of self-determination.

The *constructivist approach* argues that learning is too complex to reduce to simple constructs and that learners construct knowledge in their own ways. This construction is based on the student's active involvement with new experiences in the context of previous experiences, values, needs, beliefs, and other factors that remain unknown to observers (Deshler, Ellis, & Lenz, 1996; Lenz & Deshler with Kissam, 2004; Sabornie & deBettencourt, 2004).

The *functionalist approach* to understanding learning is based on the idea that learning and the approaches used to promote learning depend on the individual, the place, and the time; it blends the principles of the reductionist and constructivist approaches. Probably the most fully developed practices representing the functionalist approach are embodied in the strategies instruction approach, which has served as the basis for the Strategies Instruction Model developed at the University of Kansas. Deshler, Ellis, and Lenz (1996) provided in-depth coverage of the learning strategies approach, with emphasis on the Strategies Instruction Model.

Regardless of the approach used in the teaching of learning strategies, nine steps have been identified that should be followed in the systematic teaching of any strategy to students:

1. *Present and obtain a commitment to learn.* Obtain a measure(s) of current student functioning in the area and discuss with the student how the strategy will improve performance. Make the student aware of ineffective or inefficient learning habits.

2. *Describe the strategy.* Give a rationale and situations in which the strategy could be used. Help the student set goals for the strategy's use.
3. *Model the strategy.* Talk out loud and model each of the steps of the strategy using a real-life example.
4. *Verbally rehearse each of the steps of the strategy.* Use consistent verbal rehearsal of all the steps until the student acquires mastery.
5. *Provide controlled practice.* Provide feedback to the student while supervising practice in easy material. Require mastery.
6. *Provide advanced practice and feedback.* Provide feedback to the student while practice occurs in general education courses or the workplace. Require mastery.
7. *Confirm acquisition of the strategy.* Document the student's mastery of the strategy. Make the student aware of the progress.
8. *Provide opportunities for and monitor generalization.* Obtain the student's commitment to generalize to other classrooms and community situations. Make the student aware of situations in which he or she can apply the strategy, and discuss cues that may signal the need to use the strategy. Discuss adaptations that can be made to the strategy and make periodic checks to be sure the student is using it.
9. *Conduct ongoing evaluation of the strategy instruction process.* Collect ongoing data on the effectiveness of the process used in working with the student.

Many people use the terms *learning strategies* and *basic study skills* synonymously. Deshler, Ellis, and Lenz (1996) and Lenz and Deshler with Kissam (2004) distinguished between the two by stating that both are forms of a plan, but that study skills contain little guidance with regard to facilitating effective thinking behaviors, such as decision making, self-motivation, or monitoring. Study skills usually involve just a listing of steps, rather than cues for planning, executing, and evaluating performance. Study skills need to be systematically taught, and we recommend that you use the steps listed previously in teaching a specific study skill. Hoover and Patton (2005) and Hoover (2004) provided extensive coverage of the concept of study skills, with examples of application of these skills in school and community settings.

Direct Instruction

One of the most popular teaching methods used today is direct instruction. Olson and Platt (2004) described direct instruction as a structured, teacher-directed program that includes a well-designed curriculum (sequential order, positive and negative examples, well-constructed formats, prompts, independent practice activities and mastery learning) and detailed instructional procedures (cueing, modeling, eliciting student responding, providing feedback, testing individual students, and teaching to mastery).

Polloway, Patton, and Serna (2005) suggested using a direct instruction procedure called PURPOSE. This is a systematic instructional approach that provides teachers seven steps to assist students in generalizing skills learned in the classroom to situations outside the classroom or school environment. The seven steps of PURPOSE are:

- Prepare the student to learn a skill.
- Understand the skill steps.
- Rehearse the skill.
- Perform a self-check.
- Overcome any performance barrier.
- Select other situations where the skill can be performed.
- Evaluate skill performance. (pp. 95–97)

The direct instruction approach can be used in several instructional situations. It can be especially effective when generalizing life skills and community skills from a classroom teaching situation to community environments.

Integration of Technology

The use of technological tools to function on a day-to-day basis has become an essential skill for all adults. Lewis (1993) suggested using the ABC model of technology when integrating technology into everyday classroom experiences (Male, 1997):

Augment abilities (use a speech synthesizer or magnifier).

Bypass disabilities (use switches, voice command, e-mail, etc.).

Compensate for disabilities (use talking word processors, grammar- or spell-checker, mapping or networking ideas, etc.).

Integrating technology in inclusive settings has become a priority. In addressing this priority, several variables must be examined (Male, 2003): integrating technology with individual educational programs, assisting in the acquisition of basic skills, improving quality of life and life skills, and utilizing the Internet and World Wide Web.

Integrating Technology into IEPs

For several years, technology has been used to assist with assessing students' needs and documenting their progress. In addition to using technology in a more traditional sense, such as data collection and record keeping, some unique and creative techniques using technology can equalize a student's participation within a general education setting by presenting projects or reports in a technology format (Bryant & Bryant, 2003; Lindsey, 2002; Male, 2003). Using electronic or multimedia portfolios as a means of documenting a student's progress can highlight a student's depth and breadth of knowledge and do it in a unique way (Lever-Duffy, McDonald, & Mizell, 2003; Lindsey, 2000; Male, 2003).

Acquiring Basic Skills

Lewis (1993) suggested six types of software appropriate for increasing a student's skills in content areas: tutorials, drill and practice, educational games, discovery, simulations, and problem solving. These various types of software packages allow for multiple academic and learning needs.

Male (2003) believes a teacher's level of expertise, skill, comfort, and curricular emphasis in the class contributes to his or her use of technology with students. Movement toward more thematic or unit teaching will help increase software use. Male also offers two suggestions to teachers when deciding to use a software program: Try to think of as many ways as possible to use one flexible piece of software, and think of ways of using different pieces of software that approach the same skills from different models or styles of presentation.

Establishing criteria when selecting software for classroom use is important. Dollars are limited and versatility and flexibility are essential. The Alliance for Technology Access (1994) has suggested 13 criteria when selecting any software for any population:

1. Easy-to-read screens
2. Consistency
3. Intuitive characteristics
4. Logical labels
5. Instructional choices
6. Friendly documentation
7. On-screen instructions
8. Auditory cues
9. Video cues
10. Built-in access
11. Alternatives to a mouse
12. Optional cursors
13. Creation of custom programs

Improving Quality of Life and Life Skills

Technology can play a significant role in enhancing a student's options beyond school experiences, such as social contacts, business and consumer resources, recreation and leisure, art and music, and career exploration (Bryant & Bryant,

2003; Male, 2003). Software is available in many of the core academic content areas, in addition to many of the fine arts. Simulations also offer a game format to learn more about the world. Software is available to gather information on a variety of topics important to daily life (e.g., plan a vacation, research various car and homeowner policy options with different insurance companies, research new cars, do comparison shopping, etc.).

Male (2003) suggested five principles when incorporating technology into everyday life:

1. There is no minimum age limit.
2. There is no maximum age limit.
3. Computer skills are not developmental and prerequisites should not apply.
4. Computer skills are expandable.
5. Computer skills can be adapted to any situation and can benefit people of varying ability levels, interests, and ages.

Utilizing the Internet and World Wide Web (WWW)

The use of the World Wide Web (WWW) and the Internet provides a valuable tool for all students. The way people communicate, advertise, teach, shop, learn, work, or just have fun has been permanently changed. With this in mind, each student's background and abilities must always be considered when the Internet or the Web is used in classrooms (Bryant & Bryant, 2003; Cunningham & Billingsley, 2003). A variety of resources are listed on the Allyn and Bacon companion website to assist you in maneuvering and accessing resources on the Web.

In addition to using the Web as a resource, creating a webpage has become a frequent activity in schools. Bryant and Bryant (2003), Cunningham and Billingsley (2003), Lever-Dufy, McDonald, and Mizell (2003), Lindsey (2002), and Male (2003) have provided resources for educators who are embarking on the Internet/WWW journey. These resources provide basic information and excellent instructional ideas.

Application of Academic Content to Real-Life Situations

Special educators have been advocating the benefits of relating the application of academics to real life for several decades (Brolin, 1989, 1997; Brolin & Loyd, 2004; Clark, 1979, 1994; Clark, Carlson, Fisher, Cook, & D'Alonzo, 1991; Clark, Field, Patton, Brolin, & Sitlington, 1994; Cronin & Patton, 1993; Cronin, Patton, & Wood, 2005; Kokaska & Brolin, 1985; Patton, Cronin, & Wood, 1999; Sitlington, 1996a, 1996b). The necessity to engage students actively in learning basic life skills needed for success in adulthood has become more important (Sitlington, 1996).

While the more recent National Longitudinal Transition Study (NLTS2) adult outcome database has some encouraging gains, too many students are still experiencing unemployment and/or underemployment, low pay, part-time work, frequent job changes, little engagement with the community, limitations in independent functioning, little postsecondary education, and limited social lives for individuals with disabilities. In addition, special educators have been urged for a long time to reexamine the curriculum used with special populations and now, more than ever, are working toward aligning it with the curriculum used in general education programs. This information, coupled with the nationwide mandate that has been handed to all educators to "leave no child behind," creates a charge for educators to relate academic knowledge to real-life applications. In assisting educators to meet this charge, a discussion addressing how to teach real-life content is warranted.

Although many terms or phrases exist to refer to those skills needed to function successfully in adulthood (Cronin, 1996; Cronin et al., 2005), the terms *real-life content* and *life skills* are used interchangeably in this chapter. *Real-life content,* or *life skills,* means specific competencies to include knowledge, skills, and the application of life skills of local and cultural relevance needed to perform everyday activities across a variety of settings (Cronin et al., 2005). Knowledge acquistion and skill performance of life skills have been discussed in the literature for many years. Cronin and associates (2005) have contended that neither of these components alone is sufficient enough to demonstrate an individual's life skills competency in many situations. It is imperative that an individual must also demonstrate the *appropriate application* of the knowledge and skills. Greenspan, Switzky, and Granfield's (1996) promotion of the concept of everyday intelligence supports the implication that the individual must be able to reason well enough to make key decisions on when to use the knowledge and skills (e.g., decide on whether a situation is an emergency) and how to use the information obtained appropriately (e.g., calling 911).

As noted in the preceding definition, the nature of life skills can vary from one setting to another. For example, a number of life skills are involved in grocery shopping; however, the details of shopping in a grocery store are a function of the city or locale where one lives (Cronin et al., 2005). Although the similarities of grocery stores are vast, the uniqueness of each store poses difficulties to many special needs populations.

Sitlington (1996b) outlined a variety of life-skills curricular models currently available (see Appendix 10A, Career Education and Life Skills, on the Allyn and Bacon companion website). The similarities of these models are numerous, such as the suggested materials to use, the content to be taught, suggested classroom and community activities, and the like. The primary differences can be found in the various curriculum designs (Patton et al., 1999). Every curriculum format or design establishes a similar yet different set of priorities in response to a set of needs considered important by various professionals and consumers (students, parents, teachers, administrators, community leaders, etc.). Given any one of the curriculum designs outlined in Appendix 10A, a discussion of the various options of how to teach life skills can begin. For illustrative purposes, the Cronin and Patton (1993) and Cronin and associates (2005) Domains of Adulthood will be used.

Functionality is an important concept to discuss when talking about life skills or functional curriculum. For many years, the concept of a functional or life-skills curriculum was aligned with students who have mental retardation. This way of thinking must be changed, as everyone needs functional skills. The need for functional skills is as different as each individual. A high school senior who will be attending Massachusetts Institute of Technology (MIT) in the fall has many skills she will need to function independently in that particular environment, just like the student attending the local vocational training institute has many skills he will need to function independently in that situation. Your job, as an educator, is to make sure each of these students is prepared to function independently in his or her next subsequent environment, whatever it might be.

A note should be made at this point regarding life-skills instruction for different types of students. The eventual outcome or vision a student has for himself or herself determines the path of life-skills acquisition, whether it is in a formal or informal instructional situation. A student who sees himself or herself pursuing a degree in higher education must have a solid foundation in all the academic subject areas. Yet the student also needs to have and apply learning strategies plus various organizational, research, and study skills, in addition to skills needed to do his or her laundry and balance a checkbook. Some of these students will also need employment-related skills; part-time employment, for example, is often necessary to support themselves during their college years.

Another group of students, on the other hand, sees high school as the termination point of their formal schooling. These students will need more intense life-skills and vocational instruction prior to their high school exit. Still another group of students might need extended education through age 21 and need intensive community-based instruction, communication skills training, self-help skills training and supported employment. All of these scenarios are a challenge for curriculum developers, administrators, and all teachers in the application of course content to real-life situations.

Concern is often voiced by teachers, school administrators, and parents that teaching within a life-skills format ignores teaching basic subjects. Nothing could be farther from the truth. The ability to read, write, compute, problem solve, and converse, as well as academic life skills to include social skills, school survival skills, and study skills are all extremely important for every educator to teach, no matter the age of the student or the content of the material taught. Figure 10.2 (Cronin et al., 2005) clearly illustrates through a matrix the interrelationship of scholastic and social skills to life-skills areas. The

FIGURE 10.2 Secondary Matrix: Relationship of Scholastic/Social Skills to Adult Domains

	Employment/ Education	Home and Family	Leisure Pursuits	Community Involvement	Emotional/ Physical Health	Personal Responsibility/ Relationships
Reading	Reading classified ads for jobs	Interpreting bills	Locating and understanding movie information in newspaper	Following directions on tax forms	Comprehending directions on medication	Reading letters from friends
Writing	Writing a letter of application for a job	Writing checks	Writing for information on a city to visit	Filling in a voter registration form	Filling in your medical history on forms	Sending thank-you notes
Listening	Understanding oral directions of a procedure change	Comprehending oral directions about making dinner	Listening for forecast to plan outdoor activity	Understanding campaign ads	Attending lectures for stress	Taking turns in a conversation
Speaking	Asking your boss for a raise	Discussing morning routines with family	Inquiring about tickets for a concert	Stating your opinion at a school board meeting	Describing symptoms to a doctor	Giving feedback to a friend about the purchase of a compact disk
Math Applications	Understanding difference between net and gross pay	Computing the cost of doing laundry in a laundromat versus at home	Calculating the cost of a dinner out versus eating at home	Obtaining information for a building permit	Using a thermometer	Planning the costs of a date
Problem-Solving	Settling a dispute with a co-worker	Deciding how much to budget for rent	Role-playing appropriate behaviors for various places	Knowing what to do if you are the victim of fraud	Selecting a doctor	Deciding how to ask someone for a date
Survival Skills	Using a prepared career planning packet	Listing emergency phone numbers	Using a shopping center directory	Marking a calendar for important dates (e.g., recycling, garbage collection)	Using a system to remember to take vitamins	Developing a system to remember birthdays
Personal/Social	Applying appropriate interview skills	Helping a child with homework	Knowing the rules of a neighborhood pool	Locating self-improvement classes	Getting a yearly physical exam	Discussing how to negotiate a price at a flea market

Source: From *Life Skills Instruction for All Students with Special Needs: A Practical Guide for Integrating Real-Life Content into the Curriculum* (2nd ed.) by M. E. Cronin, J. R. Patton, and S. J. Wood, 2005, Austin, TX: Pro-Ed. Reprinted by permission.

sample activities in each of the cells clearly demonstrate that life skills and basic skills can be taught simultaneously.

Figure 10.3 shows a continuum of options for teaching life skills. The five options for teaching life skills suggested by Cronin and colleagues (2005) fall into three types: coursework, augmentation, and infusion. All options are dependent on establishing a comprehensive set of competencies identified at the local level.

Coursework

Three options are available for teaching life skills via coursework that can be credit or noncredit courses, elective or required. The first is to develop a comprehensive sequence of life-skills courses that can lead to a diploma (Cronin et al., 2005). The purpose is to offer coursework that relates to traditional content courses with a life-skills orientation. Usually, this is done when a specific course of study is essential for those high school students who will not be attending a college or university, but who still need a curriculum that teaches basic skills within a life-skills context (Helmke, Havekost, Patton, & Polloway, 1994). Helmke and colleagues described a comprehensive course approach developed by the Dubuque (Iowa) Community Schools. The Dubuque Schools wanted a set of courses/curriculum that would better prepare their students for successful functioning as adults in the Dubuque community.

The second option is developing one course in a topical content area, such as "Math in the Real World," "Health and First Aid," or "Ready to Work." The content of these courses is very focused, yet they are typically thought of in many high schools as electives (as opposed to required courses). An example of how to develop this type of course is described in Helmke and associates (1994).

The third course option, which also has a single-course format, covers introductory life-skills information in a number of areas. "Independent Living

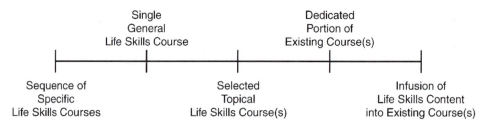

FIGURE 10.3 Options for Organizing Life-Skills Content for Formal Instruction

Source: From *Life Skills Instruction for All Students with Special Needs: A Practical Guide for Integrating Real-Life Content into the Curriculum* (2nd ed.) by M. E. Cronin, J. R. Patton, and S. J. Wood, 2005, Austin, TX: Pro-Ed. Reprinted by permission.

Skills," "Living on Your Own," and "Life 101" are examples of the third course option. Again, like the other single-course option, these courses can typically be found in high schools and are usually electives.

Augmentation

The fourth option, augmentation, involves supplementing existing content courses with additional life-skills information. This option is appropriate in settings where there is no opportunity for the development of separate life-skills coursework. Augmentation is also one of the best methods to use when relating content taught in any of the general education classes at any grade level to real-life application.

Augmentation can occur in several different formats (Cronin et al., 2005). Some schools have used a schoolwide focus with the entire school devoting every Friday, the last week of every month, or one month of the year (January or May) to applying the content learned in their courses to real-life situations. Still others have focused specific projects, such as service learning projects, to apply what they have learned in the content class to the real world. Individual teachers will use homework assignments or group projects to accomplish this goal.

One of the most popular augmentation techniques is the unit approach. Learning by doing is the basic theory in using the unit approach. Polloway and associates (2005) suggested that the inclusion of a variety of activities lends itself to individualization of instruction. Units are usually motivational because of the individual interests of the students plus their natural curiosity, prior experiences, and cultural backgrounds.

The unit approach relates instruction to a specific topic, problem, theme, or area of interest (Lenz & Deshler with Kissam, 2004; Olson & Platt, 2004; Polloway et al., 2005; Sabornie & deBettencourt, 2004). Polloway and colleagues (2005) suggested integrating a variety of content areas and activities when developing units. Units can be organized several ways. Within content courses, themes related to content topics can be the organizational structure for a unit. Thematic interest of the class can also provide a direction for the development of a unit—for example, students approaching driving age develop an interest in cars, trucks, sports utility vehicles, and other motor vehicles, which makes a natural match of high interest of students with an area that academic skills can be taught and reinforced. Periodically surveying interests of students will provide a valuable database of information.

Infusion

The structure of the infusion approach is through existing course content. Table 10.1 (Patton, Cronin, Bassett, & Koppel, 1997) provides examples of both the augmentation and infusion techniques. The objective of the infusion approach is to capitalize on opportunities presented in the content of the

TABLE 10.1   Augmentation and Infusion Examples

Source	Topic Covered	A/I	Sample Activities
Practical math textbook (Secondary level)	"Budgeting for Recreation"	A	Add coverage on the "economics" of dating
		I	Identify best time and cost for going to a movie
	"Credit Card Math"	A	Add coverage of how to get the best deal on a credit card (e.g., low APR, no annual fee)
		I	Present ways to get lower APR or waiver of annual fee
	"Maintaining a Vehicle"	A	Add coverage of the realities of being involved in an accident and what one needs to do
		I	Discuss the importance of keeping tires inflated at the proper levels
Basal math textbook (Elementary level)	"Using Decimals: Adding & Subtracting Money" —buying a sleeping bag	A	Add coverage of costs of purchasing or renting camping gear
		I	Discuss where one can buy or rent a sleeping bag
	"Using Tables to Solve Problems"	A	Add coverage on how to use the weather map from the newspaper
		I	Identify other tables that have numbers

Note: A=augmentation; I=infusion

Source: From "A Life Skills Approach to Mathematics Instruction: Preparing Students with Learning Disabilities for the Real-Life Math Demands of Instruction" by J. R. Patton, M. E. Cronin, D. S. Bassett, and A. E. Koppel, 1997, *Journal of Learning Disabilities, 30,* page 185. Reprinted by permission.

lesson of the day that addresses important material related to life skills (Patton et al., 1999). An example of the infusion approach can be found in Appendix 10B, *Most Loved Classics Series, Moby Dick* by Herman Melville (see the Allyn and Bacon companion website). Patton and colleagues feel it is important to take advantage of as many opportunities as possible to touch on topics that have life-skills implications.

Patton and associates (1999) outlined a four-step procedure. The main aspects of each step are crucial to infuse real-life content successfully into courses. The steps are as follows:

1. Familiarity with the comprehensive set of knowledge and skills needed in adulthood (i.e., life skills)

2. Identification of places in the existing [course or] curriculum that can be associated with real-life topics
3. Planning life skills infusion activities
4. Actual instruction of life skills during ongoing lessons (p. 10)

It should be noted that the types of activities for infusion are usually limited due to the short amount of time that can be devoted to the infusion process. The likely selection of activities might include asking a short, to-the-point question that requires a limited response; listing or brainstorming ideas or examples; describing examples or activities; identifying a sequence of tasks that needs to occur; and citing personal examples from the teacher or students. Teachers who use the infusion approach should keep a systematic inventory of infusion activities. Keeping notes on the effectiveness of the activities tried and ideas that might be helpful for the next year is recommended.

Classroom instruction is important in preparing students to apply basic academic skills to real-life situations in natural environments (Cronin et al., 2005). Classroom instruction gives students the opportunity to be introduced to and practice skills prior to encountering them in the natural environment. This might include activities such as filling out forms, roleplaying sales interactions, practicing interview skills, using a laundromat, and the like. The classroom can also be the place where people from the community can visit to meet students and share information on their chosen career prior to the students visiting their place of business.

Teaching Community Skills

Educators have been charged with multiple tasks from the 1997 and 2004 Amendments of IDEA. Two of those tasks are not in areas most teachers have received training—yet, they are two of the most important sets of activities for *all* students in the transition process. Independent living and community participation are critical for success in adulthood (Sitlington, 1996b). Many of the skills needed for successful day-to-day functioning can be taught within the classroom using any of the options listed in the continuum in Figure 10.3. An important extension of teaching life skills, no matter what option you use, is that the specific life skill is learned or at least practiced often by all students, regardless of the student's exceptionality, in the natural setting (e.g., the community) (Brolin & Loyd, 2004; Cronin et al., 2005; Kaye, 2004).

Many terms can be found in the professional literature that have been confused with the terminology used to describe community experiences that take place both on and off campus. Wehman and Kregel (2004) outlined some examples to help discriminate among *community-based instruction (CBI)*, *community-referenced instruction (CRI)*, and *community simulations (CS)* in Table 10.2.

TABLE 10.2   Differences among Community-Based Instruction (CBI), Community-Referenced Instruction (CRI), and Community Simulation (CS)

Skill	Community-Based Instruction	Community-Referenced Instruction	Simulation
Dressing	Putting on a coat to go into the community; taking off a coat when you arrive at the community location (if appropriate); trying on clothes in a department store; changing clothes at the YMCA to participate in swimming or aerobic dance	Changing clothes for gym; putting on/taking off a coat during school arrival/departure; changing shirts after lunch (if the current one becomes soiled); putting on a painting smock in art class	Five trials of putting on and taking off a shirt in the classroom during a dressing program; tying shoelaces on a dressing board; buttoning clothes on a doll
Purchasing	Purchasing items at the drug store; paying for a game of bowling; purchasing a soda at a restaurant; buying stamps at the post office	Purchasing lunch in the cafeteria; buying a drink from the soda machine; purchasing a ticket to a school basketball game; buying school buttons/ribbons to wear on color day	Counting money in the classroom (e.g., "Show me $6.25"); pretending to shop and pay for items in a classroom grocery store; sorting coins (nickels, dimes, and quarters)
Communicating/ Understanding Pictures	Locating items in the store from a picture grocery list; ordering in a restaurant using a picture menu; presenting a picture to a store clerk to determine location of a bathroom	Reviewing the school lunch choices and selecting pictures of the items desired; choosing a leisure activity from a series of picture choices; using a picture schedule throughout the school day	Matching pictures of various foods with their plastic replicas; identifying a picture by pointing to it when the teacher verbally requests "Show me the _____"

Source: From "Community Participation" by S. Dymond in *Functional Curriculum for Elementary, Middle, and Secondary Age Students with Special Needs* (2nd ed.) (p. 269) by P. Wehman and J. Kregel, 2004, Austin, TX: Pro-Ed. Reprinted by permission.

Cronin and colleagues' (2005) definition of *community based* will be used throughout the discussions in this chapter. *Community-based instruction (CBI)* is the aquisition of life-skill knowledge, performance of life skills, and the appropriate application of knowledge and skills in the community.

Students must become aware of the constant need in day-to-day living to know a wide range and number of life skills. Students could do a structured observation in and around the school building, at home, or on the bus, or use a community field experience. Students would complete a form, either with assistance or independently, and count the number and kind of tasks the person they are observing is doing. These tasks could be classified by skill area (reading, writing, listening, speaking, problem solving, mathematics, etc.) and place where the tasks occur (kitchen, office, garage, yard, cafeteria, etc.). The purpose of this activity is to bring an awareness to the students of the sheer number of tasks that people perform and where they happen. This will further emphasize and document the need to teach life skills in the natural environment.

Students with significant disabilities need additional supports with many tasks and activities to ensure increased success in any "natural environment" in the community (Wehman, 2001). Use of an ecological inventory approach to assess the environments in which the student will be working will assist in the curricular content and the determination of the supports and needed tools for the individual in a particular situation. The use of individualized "tools" to asssist the student in the completion of a task in the community, whether it is purchasing an item in the grocery store or performing a work task in an employment situation, is warranted. Some options for the "tools" that might be needed include photographs, picture prompts, verbal cues, augmentative communication systems, a checklist of picture tasks, side-by-side demonstrations by a peer or co-worker, or a job coach. Additional tips for the development of curriculum suggested by Wehman (2001) can be found in Figure 10.4.

There is an expanding literature base that supports community-based instruction for students with disabilities (Agran, Snow, & Swaner, 1999; Brolin & Loyd, 2004) as well as for all students (disabled and nondisabled) regardless of the student's disability, age, grade level, or functioning ability level (Beakley, Yoder, & West, 2003; Cronin, 1996; Cronin et al., 2005; Dymond, 2004; Sabornie & deBettencourt, 2004; Wehman, 2001). Cronin and associates advocate for authentic learning in the natural environment being a richer, more meaningful, learning experience.

Connecting the Classroom with the Community

One of the first connections that you, as a teacher, need to make in your community is to identify the available resources in the community. In doing so, the contacts made are potential resources for many aspects of your community skills program. They could fall into several categories. For example, a visitor to

FIGURE 10.4   **Curriculum Development for Young Adults with Significant Cognitive Disabilities**

Suggestions

1. Spend increasing amounts of time in vocational training placement.
2. Teach skills that are likely to be used regularly by students.
3. Focus on developing community functioning skills that allow for greater competence in shopping malls, recreational events, and so on.
4. Select vocational skills that have marketability in the local community.

Cautions

1. Don't use preschool materials and activities. Use real materials.
2. Don't confuse once-a-month field trips with the intensity of effective community-based training.
3. Don't teach from behavior checklists, developmental tests, or commercial curricula that have little relationship to comunity needs.
4. Don't provide instruction primarily in the school.

Source: From *Life Beyond the Classroom: Transition Strategies ofr Young People with Disabilities* (3rd ed.) (p. 324) by Paul Wehman, 2001, Baltimore, MD: Paul H. Brookes Publishing Co. Reprinted by permission.

your class could give an orientation to a specific topic, such as how to apply for a job or the various services offered by a bank. Other contacts might be better suited for site visits of a business, such as a grocery or a discount department store to use for comparison shopping. Still others might be excellent job-training sites. No matter the purpose of the contacts, the important factor is developing colloborative activities with community businesses and the schools in the surrounding neighborhood. Appendix 10C (Relationship of Community Resources to Adult Domains) and Appendix 10D (Community Field Experiences by Adult Domains) both offer options of the types of resources and field experiences available in most communities. (Both Appendices C and D can be found on the Allyn and Bacon companion website.)

Teaching students in the natural environment entails, in most cases, leaving the school campus. When teachers plan to leave school campuses for instructional purposes, many issues must be addressed prior to going into the community. One of these issues is that permission from the administration is imperative and guidelines of the school system must be followed. Some teachers have found they must choose their words wisely when trying to arrange off-campus activities. After being denied a request to go off campus, one teacher found that by simply changing her vocabulary from *field trip* to *field experience,* her request was granted (Cronin, Lord, & Wendling, 1991). In addition to changing vocabulary, some teachers have discovered that by submitting a detailed plan of their proposed excursion off campus to their school administrator documents the emphasis of the academic purpose of the outing and the individual IEP goals that would be addressed by teaching the activity in its natural environment activity (Cronin et al., 2005). Appendix 10E (Contacts/ Community Sites: Preparation Worksheet as found on the Allyn and Bacon companion website) offers an example of a detailed form that can be used for such a purpose.

The teacher should organize the community participation activity prior to going, as well as compiles important information for others in the school (school secretary, principal, paraprofessionals, etc.) and students' parents. Information could include the following: who is going, where and when they are going, what activities will be done, and how they will get to the activity location and return. A form such as this also provides a structure to ensure an evaluation component is addressed, outlines any follow-up activities, and provides ongoing documentation plus a history of places and activities for both individuals and groups of students (Cronin et al., 2005).

In addition to compiling this type of information, several other important components need to be addressed when implementing a community participation instruction program. The following partial list identifies some of the major items (Cronin et al., 2005; Wehman & Kregel, 2004):

1. Provide a detailed emergency information form with a current photograph of each student containing the following information: name, date of birth, Social Security number, height, weight, hair color, eye color, skin tone, nationality, communication mode(s), student's current schedule, name of school with school contact, school phone, parent/guardian name, home address, home phone, emergency information, and relevant medical information (Falvey, 1989, p. 104).
2. Prepare individual identification cards for each student with pertinent information.
3. Formally contact the manager of the location you are going to visit. Identify yourself, school, purpose of the trip, and when you will be visiting.
4. Establish a realistic adult-student ratio for the size and nature of your group. Discuss this with your school administrators.
5. Use additional adult volunteers (college students, foster grandparents, service organizations, etc.) for additional supervision.
6. Work with general educators to explore the community cooperatively within the inclusive content class setting or as an augmentation activity.
7. Use support personnel (speech-language pathologists, psychologists, social workers, etc.) to accompany you in the community.
8. Verify with your school system that adequate insurance coverage is in place for this type of activity.

Develop an emergency plan for off-campus activities if one does not exist.

1. Train all staff and volunteers in emergency, CPR, and first-aid procedures.
2. Review and practice community safety procedures with all students who go into the community.
3. Identify all the possible transportation options (public transportation, walking, taxi, etc.).
4. Obtain parental permission for every excursion off campus.

Components of Community-Based Instruction

There are four techniques that incorporate community-based instruction in most school systems in the United States: in-school learning opportunities (Beakley et al., 2003; Cronin et al., 2005; Wehman & Kregel, 2004); community-based opportunities (Beakley et al., 2003; Cronin et al., 2005; Wehman & Kregel, 2004); volunteerism (Beakley et al., 2003; Cronin et al., 2005; Kaye, 2004); and service learning (Kaye, 2004; Kinsley & McPherson, 1995; Lewis, 1995). Each of these options offers access to all students and can be incorporated into the general curriculum, thereby giving each student opportunities to apply what they learn in school to a variety of community activities.

In-School Learning Opportunities. Teachers might want to begin brainstorming to generate a list of the in-school learning opportunities available on their campus. Appendix 10F (In-School Job Opportunities—Brainstorming Activity), found on the Allyn and Bacon companion website, provides a form to assist with this activity. On-campus experiences provide the "best" first experiences to prepare students for future off-campus experiences (Cronin et al., 2005). Experiences such as working with the librarians, cooks and cafeteria workers, coaches, or school secretatry will give teachers and students an idea for the students' strengths and challenges that might occur in the community (Cronin et al., 2005). Appendix 10G (In-School Learning Opportunities), found on the Allyn and Bacon companion website), outlines examples of in-school options.

In some situations, teachers are unable to take their students into the community for instruction or are restricted as to how often they can go out. In these situations, bring the community into the school or class. Some businesses are mobile, such as auto-related businesses (mobile auto mechanics will change the oil in your car at your place of business or home). Parents of students often will be willing to visit schools or help find specific career-related individuals who will visit. Teachers or staff members at your school are also a willing group to assist in these endeavors.

Community-Based Opportunities. Community-based opportunities are those experiences in which students are able to apply the academic content to real-life situations. This includes such experiences as comparison shopping, purchasing items for a recipe to prepare for lunch, visiting the voter's registration office to register to vote, or any other experience that teaches independent living skills. A form can be found in Appendix 10H (see the Allyn and Bacon companion website) to assist schools in brainstorming the available community-based opportunities in local communities. Community opportunities also include career or job exploration, short-term job shadowing or job sampling, or a longer-term job placement toward the end of their community-based experiences. Table 10.3 outlines several community-based options typical in many communities.

Volunteerism.   For many students, their first experience in which they make an agreement to show up a certain number of hours per week or month is through a volunteer opportunity. Volunteerism is a viable alternative to apply what students learn in school to real-life situations (Cronin et al., 2005). Volunteer experiences are a prelude to adolescents' first paid jobs and can be either group or individual oriented. Schools, churches, scouting groups, and others frequently provide group volunteer opportunities that in many situations lead to individual volunteer experiences. Appendix 10I (Potential Volunteer Opportunities by Adult Domains), found on the Allyn and Bacon companion website, lists various volunteer options in most communities.

TABLE 10.3   Community Learning Opportunities by Adult Domains

Employment & Education	Home & Family	Leisure Pursuits	Community Involvement	Physical & Emotional Health	Personal Responsibility & Relationships
Assisting in a day care center	Grocery shopping	Sports store	Recycling center	Drug store	Stress workshops at community center
Read to younger children at school or the public library	Assist at a lawn & garden center	Bowling alley	Food pantry	Fitness center	Counseling services
Office worker	Day care center	Movie theater	Library	Hospital	Crisis center
Graphic designer	Automotive repair center	Museum	Red Cross	Doctor's office	Mental health center
	Bakery	Outdoor concerts	Humane Society	Hair salon/ barber shop	
		Swimming pool		Nursing home	
		Local zoo		Dentist's office	

Source: From *Life Skills Instruction for All Students with Special Needs: A Practical Guide for Integrating Real-Life Content into the Curriculum* (2nd ed.) by M. E. Cronin, J. R. Patton, and S. J. Wood, 2005, Austin, TX: Pro-Ed. Reprinted by permission.

Service Learning.   Service learning is a method by which young people learn and develop skills through active participation in thoughtfully organized service experiences (Kaye, 2004; Kinsley & McPherson, 1995). Beisser (1996) described service learning as the integration of the curriculum with a community- or school-based need. Many professionals believe that in participating in a service learning project, students experience authentic learning, learn to understand the meaning of community beyond self, and develop a sense of responsibility and respect for others (Beisser, 1996; Kinsley & McPherson, 1995; Lewis, 1995). Service learning is also a way of meeting actual needs in a community that are coordinated with the school and community.

In many states, service learning has become a graduation or exit requirement from high school. It has also been designated as a federal priority with the National Community Service Act of 1990 (PL 101-610) and the National Community Service Trust Act of 1993 (Americorps). Both initiatives provided funds to encourage the young people of this country to serve their communities and schools.

Activities of service learning are integrated into each student's academic curriculum. Service activities provide students with opportunities to use newly acquired academic skills and knowledge in real-life situations in their own communities. Service learning also provides opportunities for students with disabilities to be givers instead of takers (Council for Exceptional Children, 1998). In addition, they learn through hands-on experience in problem solving, conflict resolution, self-esteem, as well as academic and social skills that take place in inclusive settings. A student's involvement in service learning also gives him or her the opportunity to think about his or her role in the community as a citizen, to experience volunteerism, and to explore job exploration opportunities for the future.

Family Involvement in CBI

Family involvement in community-based programs is extremely important and family participation is crucial on several levels. First, the family is essential to the collaborative planning process along with the student, school-based personnel, agency representatives, and community representatives. During meetings families become part of the problem-solving and brainstorming process when identifying CBI activities, community sites, transportation issues, and supervising follow-up activities that complement CBI activities done in the community (Cronin et al., 2005). As a result of the planning process, they become active participants in the learning process for their sons or daughters through their follow-through on goals at home. The follow-up at home and in additional community environments assists with maintenance, generalization, and, in some situations, data collection of skills learned in school community placements. Table 10.4 provides examples of home-based life skill activities.

TABLE 10.4   Home-Based Life Skills Opportunities as Related to Adult Domains

Employment & Education	Home & Family	Leisure Pursuits	Community Involvement	Physical & Emotional Health	Personal Responsibility & Relationships
Calling the homework hotline when needed	Change a light bulb	Locating and reading the movie section of the news-	Gathering recycle materials for pick-up	Preparing a healthy lunch	Settle a dispute with a sibling
Check the want ads for a summer job	Clip coupons from the Sun-day paper	paper to select a movie and time	Decide on what Little League sport	Identifying the appropri-ate clothing for the	Write a thank you note to a relative for a gift
Completing an applica-tion for employment	Make a list of items needed from the grocery store	Using a map to locate the nearest park with a swim-	to play each season	weather	Take turns in a conversation
Practice interview skills	Make a list of emergency phone numbers	ming pool	Role play the possible situations	Decide how many hours of sleep you need per night	Send a get well card to a friend who is ill
Understand-ing the difference between net and gross pay	Discussing morning routines with family members	Search the Internet for information on a city to visit	you would call 911	Negotiate an appropriate bedtime	Develop a system to remember birthdays
		Using a shopping center directory	Read road signs and discuss what they mean	Compre-hending directions on medications	Read e-mail from a friend or relative
		Checking the Internet or TV for forecast to plan an out-door activity	Obtaining information for a build-ing permit	Describe symptoms to a doctor	Planning the cost of a date

Source: From *Life Skills Instruction for All Students with Special Needs: A Practical Guide for Integrating Real-Life Content into the Curriculum* (2nd ed.) by M. E. Cronin, J. R. Patton, and S. J. Wood, 2005, Austin, TX: Pro-Ed. Reprinted by permission.

Conclusion

This chapter has discussed instructional strategies to assist teachers in teaching students the skills needed to make a successful transition to the next environment. The approaches chosen should be based on the individual needs of each student and on the future living, working, and educational environments that each has identified through the IEP process. Once the approaches have been identified to use with each student, you may need to enlist the support of your building administrator. It is crucial to have a sound rationale for the approaches chosen and to present this rationale to the student, the family, and the staff who are in charge of determining program options and approaches. This task may not be an easy one, but it will result in more satisfying outcomes for students.

11 Job Placement, Training, and Supervision

Experience is the best of schoolmasters, only the school fees are heavy.
—Thomas Carlyle

This chapter will deal with the work-based learning component of the training needed to make the most effective transition from school to work. As mentioned in previous chapters, this component must be closely tied to school-based instruction and must be seen as part of the entire instructional process. The work-based learning activities must also be closely tied to the goals of the IEP and the transition planning process.

Job placement, training, and supervision tasks may be assumed by a professional who does this as a full-time job or by a classroom teacher who teaches for a portion of the day and serves as placement coordinator for the remainder of the day. Professionals who place and supervise students in the workplace are assigned different titles, such as *work-study coordinators, work experience coordinators, vocational adjustment coordinators, vocational special needs coordinators, school-to-work coordinators, cooperative education coordinators, job placement specialists,* and *job coaches.* The term *coordinator* will be used in this chapter to refer to any of these professionals who are involved in the placement, training, and supervision of individuals on job sites.

Four main issues are related to who will conduct placement activities. First, should the coordinator do this as a full-time position or as a teacher and coordinator (called a *teacher-coordinator*)? The advantages of full-time coordinators are (1) they can focus full time on the placement and supervision of students on the job and (2) they can be on call for the training sponsor at all times. The advantages of a position where the coordinator teaches half days and works with students in the workplace the other half are (1) they work daily with students in class, so they know them better; (2) they know the other teachers and staff in the school; and (3) they can more easily infuse the skills needed by each student into the student's other coursework. Full-time coordinators often teach one class, where they relate the in-school work with the demands of the workplace (often called a *related class*). This allows coordinators to become familiar with the students they will be placing and allows them to connect the school-based and work-based learning components.

The second issue concerns whether the placement and supervision activities should be done by a coordinator who is primarily working with general education students. The argument for this approach centers on the fact that this professional already has ties with work sites in the community and may have stronger preparation and experience in job placement and supervision than someone trained in special education. The argument against this approach centers on the preparation of someone in general education to work with students with disabilities, particularly in terms of placement, training, and supervision demands that may exceed those of students in general education. Whatever decision is made, it is critical that all professionals involved in coordination activities in the school work closely together in obtaining and maintaining training sites.

The third issue relates to the role of paraprofessionals in work-based learning. This is particularly important in working with individuals with more severe disabilities, who often require ongoing supervision on the work site. We recommend that the policies related to the use of paraprofessionals that have been developed for other components of the instructional program, such as community-based experiences, be followed in work placements. It is critical that a certified professional always be responsible for the program of the student. It is also critical that a coordinator be involved in the initial job placement and design of the work-based learning component.

The final issue concerns a philosophical debate as to whether the school should take responsibility for job placement or whether students with disabilities in a school-to-work program should secure their own jobs. Those who believe that the school is responsible have based their arguments on the belief that the school is responsible not only for the student's learning but also for program integrity. They maintain that placement should be based on a match between a student's strengths, preferences, and interests and a specific job situation, and that schools are more able to arrange that match. The advocates of students finding their own jobs believe that the students must learn the skills of job finding while in school and the best way to teach these skills is to provide them with training in job finding and then let them demonstrate their ability to apply these skills. The approach that we will take in this chapter is that the process of making the match between the student and the work-based experience is an intricate one and that the school is more likely to be able to carry out this process.

The district's response to each of these issues depends largely on the structure of the schools, the number of existing work-based learning programs offered by the district for students with and without disabilities, the number of schools and communities served by the coordinator, and the ongoing policies of the school related to students with disabilities and to community-based instruction.

This chapter discusses gathering information on the work environment, job development and selection (including matching the student with the job), what you need to know related to the legal aspects of work-based learning, and steps in the placement and supervision of students in these work-based learning sites. The chapter then concludes with a discussion of individualizing the planning for the transition to employment. Resources that may help you in placing, training, and supervising your students are available on the companion website.

Information on the Work Environment

The process of placing students with or without disabilities on work sites that will be the most beneficial for them is complicated. Before you begin to place students (or as you refine what you are currently doing), you will need to have knowledge of where to find information on possible occupations and the labor market, knowledge of what to look for in work environments, and an awareness of the legal considerations involved in placing students on the work site. It will also be helpful to know some strategies for finding appropriate work sites for your students and placing them on these work sites.

Sources of Occupational and Labor Market Information

It is important to be aware of the range of occupations that currently exist in the world of work and which of these occupations hold the greatest potential for employment for your students. This information will help in all phases of the transition from school to work—from in-school instruction to experiences on the work site. The information that is gained from the various sources of labor market information should be carefully matched with the information you have gained on each student's strengths, needs, interests, and preferences through the assessment process. Knowing where to go to find this information will be helpful to you, your students, and their families in a number of ways. First, you can assist your students and their families in exploring broad groupings of occupations or specific occupations. If you are working with students with mild disabilities, they can be taught to use these resources themselves. Regardless of the functioning level of your students, knowing the variety of occupations that are available to them opens up a whole new world. This is particularly important if you are teaching in a small community, where the range of jobs students can directly explore is limited.

The second use of this information is to identify occupational areas that offer the highest potential for employment. Although you should always encourage students to pursue occupations in which they are most interested, it is also important to add the element of reality to their choices. Identification of these occupational areas will also allow you to share with your students work sites with the most potential for future employment. The third use of these sources of information is to secure information about specific jobs. Such information will allow students to refine their career choices and to determine for themselves how much training is needed, what skills are desired, and the basic tasks involved in the job. Again, this information will help in securing specific job placements for your students.

A number of sources of labor market information are available at the national, state, and local levels. It is important to tap all of these sources, particularly if some of your students will seek employment outside their current community or state.

National Sources.   Sources of information at the national level tend to be in written form. Most of these sources are now also on the Internet. One of the most useful sources of information is the Occupational Information Network (O*NET; www.doleta.gov/programs/onet/). Other major sources of such information include *Dictionary of Occupational Titles* (*DOT*; 204.245.136.2/libdot.htm); *Occupational Outlook Handbook* (stats.bls.gov/ocohome.htm); and *North American Industry Classification System* (*NAICS:* www.census.gov/epcd/www/naics.html).

The Occupational Information Network (O*NET) is sponsored by the U.S. Department of Labor, in cooperation with firms from the private sector. O*NET provides a comprehensive database system for collecting, organizing, describing, and disseminating data on job characteristics and worker characteristics. It is designed to replace the *DOT,* but also to go beyond the types of information that the *DOT* provides. One of the goals of O*NET is to link with other sources of information, such as statistical labor market information, from national, state, and local sources. The framework that organizes O*NET is a skills-based structure called the *Content Model.* This model classifies information into six domains, or categories, that look into all aspects of the workplace, from the characteristics of occupations to the characteristics of the workers who do the job. The six domains and their subdomains of information are as follows:

1. Worker Characteristics (abilities, interests, work styles)
2. Worker Requirements (basic skills, cross-functional skills, general knowledge, education)
3. Experience Requirements (training, experience, and licensing)
4. Occupation Requirements (generalized work activities, work context, and organizational context)
5. Occupation Specifics (occupational knowledge, occupational skills, tasks, and machines, tools, and equipment)

6. Occupation Characteristics (labor market information, occupational out-look, and wages)

Before O*NET, the *Dictionary of Occupational Titles* was one of the major sources of organizing the world of work into basic occupational categories and of providing detailed information on occupations within these categories. The information provided on each occupation includes the following: (1) nine-digit occupational code for the occupation, (2) official occupational title, (3) industry designation, (4) alternate occupational titles, (5) basic tasks associated with the occupation, (6) additional tasks the job may entail, and (7) undefined related occupational titles. In addition, each *DOT* occupational definition includes a *Guide to Occupational Exploration (GOE)* number for the occupation, if one exists, and information on estimated minimum strength and academic functioning requirements for the occupation. (*Note:* We have found through personal experience that the academic functioning requirements often overestimate the academic skills that are needed.)

The occupational classification number from the *DOT* is often used by adult providers in identifying occupational areas or specific occupations that the individual may want to pursue. This number is also often referenced in occupational recommendations from commercial assessment systems. Each occupation in the *DOT* is assigned a nine-digit occupational code or number. The first three digits identify a particular occupational group. All occupations are clustered into one of nine broad categories, such as clerical, sales, and machine trades occupations. This category is the first digit in the code (e.g., 6 is machine trades occupations). These categories are then broken down into 83 divisions. These divisions form the first two digits of the code (e.g., 66 is wood machining occupations). The third digit defines the occupational group (e.g., 660 is cabinetmakers).

The next three digits (after the decimal) represent the worker function ratings of the tasks performed in the occupation. The fourth digit represents the worker's relationship with data, the fifth digit represents the relationship with people, and the sixth digit represents the relationship with things. One confusing aspect of this data-people-things classification is that the worker functions involving more complex responsibility and judgment are assigned lower numbers in these three lists, whereas functions that are less complicated have higher numbers. Thus, an occupation with a worker function rating of 084 would require a high level of interaction with data, a low level with people, and a medium level with things. Specifically, according to the *DOT*, this rating would require the worker to synthesize data, take instructions from or help people, and manipulate things. The last three digits of the occupational code number serve to differentiate a particular occupation from all others with the same characteristics; in essence, they are just a way to arrange occupations with the same six first numbers. With the development of O*NET, the Department of Labor will no longer be updating information in the *DOT*. It is expected, however, that the *DOT* will still remain in use as a resource for a number of years.

Another source of information is the *Occupational Outlook Handbook*. This document provides detailed information on the outlook for specific occupations as well as special feature sections on such topics as tomorrow's jobs, sources of career information, and related publications. The handbook is not designed to cover all occupations, but for the occupations it does feature, it provides information on the nature of the work, working conditions, the number of jobs in this area currently held, types of settings in which the workers are employed and trained, other qualifications, advancement, job outlook, earnings, related occupations, and sources of additional information. The handbook is available in hard copy and on the Internet.

The *North American Industry Classification System (NAICS)* provides common industry definitions that cover the economies of the three North American countries of Canada, Mexico, and the United States. The NAICS groups establishments with similar production processes and is organized in a hierachical structure with up to five digits of detail for classifying and grouping industries.

State Sources.   One of the major sources of occupational information at the state level is your State Occupational Information Coordinating Committee (SOICC). These groups are linked at the national level by the National Occupational Information Coordinating Committee (www.noicc.gov). This national website has information on each of the state-level committees, as well as information on other sources of occupational information. Each state also has one or more professionals designated as a labor market information specialist. This individual has a wealth of knowledge about employment trends in your state; these data are often also broken down by regions of the state.

State manufacturers' associations often have listings of companies, including products manufactured, services available, size of workforce, and names of key company managers. In addition, state industrial directories and other resources are available, such as *Moody's Industrial Manual, Thomas' Register of American Manufacturers, Encyclopedia of Business Information, Dun & Bradstreet's Middle Market Directory, The Wall Street Journal,* and *Business Week.*

Local Sources.   Some of the best local sources of information regarding occupational and labor market information are the adult providers with whom you work. These include workforce development centers, vocational rehabilitation, and other state and local agencies. These agencies are now attempting to work even more closely together to form a type of "one-stop-shop," or a *seamless* delivery system. These efforts may include locating their offices in the same building and sharing common databases, with the consumer's permission. This coordination of services and information will make them even more valuable as an information source.

Local advisory committees are an excellent source of information and connections for job placements, as well as a rich resource for input into your program. These committees are used much more frequently in career and technical education (CTE) than special education. An advisory committee is a group composed primarily of individuals outside the education profession who are selected because of their knowledge (and influence) in the community. Major types of people who should be represented on an advisory committee include (1) key employers in the community, (2) a representative from the Chamber of Commerce, (3) a representative from labor, (4) an individual with a disability, (5) a family member, (6) a school administrator, and (7) the vocational teacher or coordinator. Advisory committee members can provide a perspective for making placements that is difficult for school personnel to acquire. It is important to put time into recruiting the key representatives and organizing regular meetings of this group. Although this will require some effort on your part, the rewards will far outweigh the effort.

Other sources of information and connections for specific job placements include the Chamber of Commerce, service clubs such as Rotary and Kiwanis, and businesses with whom you interact on a daily basis. Because this interaction is so critical to your job placement efforts, we strongly recommend that you live in the community in which you work, or at least frequent the businesses in which you are placing your students. A trip to the dentist may result in a placement for one of your students in the office or lead to a placement elsewhere. A conversation with the person beside you at the ball game or civic club luncheon may lead to a whole new occupational area that you have never considered before. In addition, looking though the yellow pages of the telephone directory or city directory or the newspaper classified ads can inform you of specific sites or alternative groups of occupations that are just waiting to be explored.

Analysis of the Work Environment

A placement coordinator is going to have a great deal of difficulty making effective placements without some firsthand information on the work environments being considered. This stage of gathering information on the work environment focuses on the specific work environments you have identified using the sources of occupational and labor market information discussed in the previous section. Rogan, Grossi, and Gajewski (2002) identified four major focal points for a workplace analysis. Analysis of the specific job tasks will be covered under job analysis in the next section.

- Physical environment (accessibility, layout)
- Typical activities or work tasks (rate, sequence, quality, frequency, duration)

- People within the environment (age, gender, characteristics of supervisors and co-workers, nature of interactions)
- Climate and culture (customs, traditions, rituals, routines, rules, expectations)

Job Development and Selection

The task of *job development* is one of generating a pool of job placement alternatives so that there are real choices when looking for the best possible placement. This pool of job placement alternatives can be developed in several ways. One of the most commonly suggested activities for a placement coordinator who is new to a community or who is establishing a new work-training program is the community survey. A *community survey* identifies the local job areas that have vacancies, those that anticipate vacancies frequently because of high turnover rates, and those that hire entry-level employees. These three labor market variables reflect the starting point for placement personnel in knowing whether additional activities in job development are needed.

A community survey can involve both formal and informal information-gathering procedures. Mail or telephone surveys to employers or persons responsible for hiring, use of information from a Chamber of Commerce and workforce center, and regular and systematic analysis of newspaper classified ads will produce the bulk of the information needed. Some very helpful information on high-turnover occupations comes from workforce development center representatives and personal contacts with employers. It is helpful to organize this information in files or charts by occupational area (e.g., personal services, health occupations, construction/building trades, manufacturing, agriculture/agribusiness).

A community survey is only the first step in developing a pool of placement alternatives. For example, assume that a community survey reveals that a given community has no available jobs right now and that the high-turnover jobs are stabilizing because of the competition generated by high unemployment. Another procedure in job development in this situation is to identify areas for job *creation* within the community's labor market. This is a task requiring some skill in analyzing jobs and some creativity in using the analysis data for proposing new jobs. This can occur through the creation of a new job by combining elements of existing jobs or by creating entirely new jobs to fulfill unmet needs of the employer.

Building Relationships with Employers

Employers are generally willing to hire individuals with disabilities, but may continue to hold stereotypical beliefs about specific disability labels. Those who have previous experience with employees with disabilities express satisfaction with their performance and willingness to hire others with disabilities (Luecking, 2003). In reviewing the literature in this area, Leucking found that employer attitudes toward disabilities are less significant than the identification of workplace supports, accommodations, and training that can contribute to the companies' operation and organization.

As Luecking, Fabian, and Tilson (2004) mentioned, "There are almost no employers who are in the business of hiring people with disabilities" (p. 130). For-profit businesses are in the business of making money. Not-for-profit organizations are in business to address a specific societal or civic issue. Government agencies are in business to serve the public. In all of these cases, they employ individuals who will help them meet their goals (Luecking et al., 2004). Because of this, Luecking and associates proposed the following six strategies for getting to know the potential employers in your community:

1. Become knowledgeable about the business world and join business organizations.
2. Distinguish between the employer as an individual and the employer as an organization.
3. Learn how to translate your services into benefits for employers.
4. Learn the decision-making process for hiring.
5. Do your homework on particular companies.
6. Seek opportunities for information interviews. (pp. 131–137)

Luecking and associates (2004) also provided a number of strategies for marketing your services to businesses. We quote each specific strategy in italics directly from this source (pp. 149–157), and then summarize how you might implement this strategy in your program:

- *Conduct an image audit.* Review the language and materials that represent your program to the community, such as the program name and your informational materials.
- *Be on the lookout for "coffee stains."* Focus on things like dressing appropriately, being on time, and having a professional message on your answering machine.
- *Develop and use professional marketing materials.* Use language and images that appeal to the business audience.
- *Study and define the market.* Determine the types of businesses you want to target, and focus on them.
- *Consider your business card a marketing tool.* Exchange your card liberally with businesses, writing a brief note on the back reminding them of your initial interaction.
- *Develop an elevator speech.* Focus on explaining your services concisely and clearly enough to get your message across to a stranger in the time it takes to ride an elevator a few floors.

- *Use past placement partners as references.* Ask businesses who have worked with your students in the past if they would serve as a reference and/or contact their business colleagues.
- *Turn contacts into prospects, prospects into customers.*
- *Coordinate with your colleagues and keep track of your contacts.* Coordinate your job development activities with other placement specialists within your program and with those from other work-based learning programs in your school.
- *Use business letters as marketing tools.* Use letters on your school or program letterhead as cover letters for your marketing materials, to thank contacts for their time, and to restate in writing a verbal discussion you may have had. These letters need to be short, contain no grammatical or spelling errors, and end with clear next steps, such as "I will contact you next week."
- *Stay in touch with contacts.* Keep a file that reminds you to contact businesses at various intervals to find out whether their hiring needs have changed.
- *Build credit with your business partners.* Perform favors for employers, such as patronizing the business as often as possible or offering to provide training in areas such as interviewing or providing accommodations.
- *Conduct marketing presentations.* Make short presentations on your program at service club (Rotary, Kiwanis) and Chamber of Commerce meetings.
- *Ask for the sale.* Close the deal!!

Matching the Student with the Job

The task of matching job demands with individual interests, strengths, needs, and expectations brings together all the data available for a logical, intelligent placement. It is designed to take the guesswork and chance out of the process and replace them with reason. In the real world, however, it is never so simple. Decision making in any arena assumes that the decision maker can never know with certainty that he or she has made the right decision, but in following decision-making rules, the decisions can be judged as the best possible decisions, given the data available. This means that compromises may have to be made at times. The job match is rarely perfect, but more often the best possible job match. The assessment process discussed in Chapter 5 provides the foundation for making this match.

Identifying the Purpose of the Placement.   The type of job placement that school placement coordinators engage in most often is placement for exploration or training. Only those final-semester students who have been through a work-training program should be ready for long-term employment. Placement personnel and employers must not lose sight of the fact that the purpose of community on-the-job training placements is *exploration or training*. It is good to use the term *training stations* rather than *employees* for two reasons. First, if the job is not paid, the student is technically not an "employee" of the business. Second, it is important to convey to the business that it is an active part of the education process for the student.

Some placement personnel rely primarily on their experience in the work world, their ability to develop and use resources in the community, their instincts, their history of being at the right place at the right time, or all of these. Many of these persons are extremely effective and develop excellent reputations among their colleagues for their success in finding jobs. Persons in this league may find the challenge of the job hunt so satisfying that they vicariously experience the pleasure of finding someone else a job as if it were their own. In some cases, the jobs found are not necessarily an ideal job match, but a successful job finder is rarely criticized by administrators for that.

At the other extreme, there are placement personnel who rely primarily on their program visibility via high-probability employer contacts, community presentations to organizations to which employers belong, timely and effective media coverage, and sometimes the initiative of the students themselves in finding their own jobs. This type of placement person plants the seeds of labor supply and sits back and waits for people to contact the school. Some long-established programs move into this style because the program can begin to proceed on its own momentum in this way after a while. Again, in some cases, the desirability of job match may be sacrificed but is rationalized because of ease of placement or the need to please an employer who has taken the initiative to call.

Both of these placement styles appear to get the job done in terms of number of students placed while in the program. Whether these approaches are more effective in achieving transition outcome goals than a more systematic, technical approach is a researchable question. On the face of it, logic suggests that placement procedures designed to avoid mistakes in placements are more likely to be in the best interests of the individual student, the business, and the school. The systematic approach to job placement does not have to deny the effectiveness of personal charisma, persistent contacts and follow-through, "salesmanship," nor the obvious results of good public relations and advertising that attracts employers to the school program. A placement program should incorporate those important features into a systematic approach.

A systematic approach to job placement simply refers to the use of well-established procedures used successfully in employment training programs in the past—job analysis, work-site modification, and job carving and job sharing. Each of these will be introduced in the sections that follow.

Job Analysis. *Job analysis* has already been mentioned as a necessary element of the assessment process described in Chapter 5, in terms of "making the match" between the strengths, needs, preferences, and interests of the student and the demands of the job. The job analysis process, combined with the information that you have gathered on the student as part of the assessment process, will provide you with information that will help in determining the supports and accommodations the student will need on the job.

The job analysis process involves gathering information on what the worker does, how the work is done, and under what conditions the work is done. It also includes other areas, such as amount of supervision and production requirements. The job analysis process includes (1) directly observing the job during different times of the day; (2) talking with the worker (if possible) and the supervisor, to determine if there are job tasks that you did not observe; and (3) reviewing the company's written job description, if available.

We have included a sample job analysis form in Appendix 11A on the companion website. We have also included references on the job analysis procedure in the Resources section on this website. Whatever form you use, we suggest that you focus on the following specific areas of the job:

- The basic job tasks—those you observed as well as others who are involved.
- Specific reading, math, written and oral communication, and interpersonal skills, along with specific work habits and attitudes needed on the job. List *specific* skills, such as "reading labels on boxes" versus "5th-grade reading level" and "initiating conversation with customers" versus "good conversation skills."
- Other skills important to the job.

Work-Site Modification.   Work-site modifications, in one form or another, have been made by or for persons with disabilities for as long as people have worked. These accommodations were often made voluntarily by employers in the past when the person with disabilities was already an employee at the time of the modification or had high qualifications and potential for productivity. Since the passage of the Rehabilitation Act of 1973, the federal government has required reasonable accommodations in federal employment or any business or industry under contract with the federal government (Section 504). The Act also provided some financial incentives for work-site modification. Now, the Americans with Disabilities Act (ADA) requires any employer with 15 or more employees to make "reasonable accommodations" for a person with a disability if that accommodation will allow the person to perform the essential functions of the job. Appendix 11B provides a checklist of accessibility and usability of buildings and facilities that may assist you in identifying needed work-site modifications.

Work-site modifications range from the simplest and least costly ones (changing hours, changing work procedures, changing work locations, or changing task assignments) to the most complex and expensive ones using high technology or rehabilitation engineering for sophisticated equipment or building adaptations. Placement personnel should be alert to discrepancies in the job analysis and the analysis of an individual's strengths and needs that could be addressed through work-site modification. The Job Accommodation Network (JAN) is an excellent resource for making work-site modifications (janweb.icdi.wuu.edu). Your vocational rehabilitation counselor may also be able to link you with resources at the state level for work-site modification.

Job Carving and Job Sharing. Job carving and job sharing are two specific approaches to job placement that are particularly useful in working with students with significant disabilities. Both approaches require that you first conduct an analysis of the work environment and a specific analysis of the job within that environment. Both approaches require that you also have information on the strengths and needs of the student.

In *job carving*, you "carve" out specific tasks of existing jobs that could be completed by your student. These components are then combined into one total job for your student. For example, you might place a student with significant disabilities in a restaurant where his or her part-time job is to wrap the silverware and wipe down the menus to be used for lunch and dinner shifts. This frees the wait staff from this task and lets them focus on serving customers.

In *job sharing*, you combine the strengths of two or more students to address the demands of an existing job. An example of job sharing would be to combine the efforts of a student with significant physical disabilities with the strengths of a physically able student with very low reading ability. Together, their strengths would match the demands of the job.

Legal Aspects of Work-Based Learning

As you place your students in work-based learning sites either within the school system or the community, it is critical that you are aware of the legal issues that need to be considered. A number of excellent sources are available for in-depth information on these issues (Garfinkle, 1995; Love, 1995; National School-to-Work Office, n.d.; Pumpian, Fisher, Certo, Engel, & Mautz, 1998; Pumpian, Fisher, Certo, & Smalley, 1997; Simon & Halloran, 1994; Simon, Cobb, Halloran, Norman, & Bourexis, 1994). We will highlight the major issues you will need to consider; you are referred to these sources, however, for more in-depth information.

The key legislation in the area of work-based learning is the Fair Labor Standards Act of 1938 and its amendments, which established the guidelines for minimum wage regulations, child labor provisions, and distinguishing nonpaid instructional work experiences from paid employment. Appendix 11C on the companion website provides a summary of the child labor requirements in nonagricultural and agricultural occupations, respectively. You should pay particular attention to the issue of age requirements and hazardous occupations.

The other area with which you need to be concerned is the distinction between nonpaid instructional work experiences and paid employment. Pumpian and associates (1998) provided an excellent overview of this issue. As they stated, in the 1980s, large numbers of school programs were rapidly building and expanding job preparation, development, and support programs for individuals with disabilities. Many public school programs had established nonpaid exploration and training opportunities as part of their comprehensive service delivery models. At the same time, interpretation of the Fair Labor Standards Act varied considerably across Department of Labor wage and hour specialists. When the School-to-Work Opportunities Act of 1994 (PL 103-239) was passed, the issue of nonpaid experiences entered the arena of general education, as well. The use of nonpaid work experience seems to be an ongoing component of career development. It has been significant in disability-specific programs and its use will likely accelerate in school-to-work programs (Pumpian et al., 1998).

The Fair Labor Standards Act established the following six criteria that must be met if the trainees or students are not to be considered employees (who must then be paid):

1. The training, even though it includes actual operation of the facilities of the business or industry, is similar to that which would be given in a vocational education program.
2. The training is for the benefit of the students.
3. The students do not displace regular employees, but work under their close observation.
4. The business or industry person who provides training derives no immediate advantage from the activities of the students, and on occasion his or her operations may actually be impeded.
5. The students are not necessarily entitled to a job at the conclusion of the training period.
6. The students understand that they are not entitled to wages for the time spent in training.

In their article, Pumpian and colleagues (1998) interpreted various regulatory guidelines and court decisions related to the use of nonpaid work experience and provided additional information related to U.S. Departments of Labor and Education guidelines for work-training programs. They made three major points in their review: (1) all six criteria delineated in the Fair Labor Standards Act must be met in order to establish a training situation, (2) these criteria are interrelated, and (3) establishing an employee-employer relationship requires examination of the circumstances surrounding the whole activity rather than isolated factors. Pumpian and colleagues also proposed four questions central to every training situation. These questions are critical in determining if no immediate advantage accrues to the business or industry in which the student is placed:

1. Does the business or industry derive first and primary benefit? In other words, does the business or industry benefit more than the student?
2. Does the business or industry derive substantial benefit?
3. Does the trainee replace regular workers?
4. Is the experience educationally valid?

Inherent in all of these questions is the importance of planning work-based learning experiences that are designed specifically around the needs, preferences, and interests of the student and that are closely monitored to determine if the objectives of the experience are being met. The most essential aspect of the placement, training, and supervision process is that it be closely tied to the student's IEP. It is also critical for you to keep accurate records of all aspects of the placement, training, and ongoing supervision, if you are the person responsible for these activities. The next section presents the major steps in the placement and supervision process.

Steps in Placement and Supervision

Eleven basics steps are involved in placing and supervising students in the workplace. These steps are taken from the basic coordination techniques used by professionals in career and technical education and cooperative education programs. Modifications that are needed in working with students with disabilities are addressed under the specific steps.

The steps listed in the following sections are taken from the cooperative education approach initially developed in career and technical education. (See Chapter 6 for more information on this approach.) They are also related to the components of the school-to-work initiatives developed as part of the School-to-Work Opportunities Act and other federal- and state-level transition initiatives. In all of these approaches, there are three basic components: school-based learning, work-based learning, and connecting activities that tie the school and work site together. The work site and work-site personnel are seen as important partners in the training process, thus the terms *training station* and *training sponsor* are used throughout. The 11 steps are discussed in the following sections. They should be followed, regardless of the purpose of the work placement—exploration, work experience, or training.

- Assessment of the student
- Conference with the student
- Initial contact with the training sponsor

- Analysis of the work site
- Meeting to obtain the training station
- Student interview with the training sponsor
- Meeting to explain the role of the coordinator and training sponsor and the training agreement
- Meeting to develop and discuss the training plan
- Ongoing training of the student
- Continuing evaluation of the student
- Modification of the training program based on ongoing evaluation

Assessment of the Student

Assessment of the student was covered more fully in Chapter 5. The assessment of student needs, strengths, preferences, and interests is required by the Individuals with Disabilities Education Improvement Act of 2004 (IDEA, 2004). In working with students with disabilities, it is crucial to gather this information in cooperation with the student and family and use it to make the best possible match with potential work sites. This assessment is an ongoing process, however, and placement of students at work sites for exploration, for work experience, or for training can provide additional information on the students' needs, strengths, preferences, and interests and yield valuable information that can be used in transition planning and future placements for the students. It is important that the results of current assessment activities be included in the statement of the student's present levels of academic achievement and functional performance within the IEP.

A major part of the assessment may be conducted before the actual placement process is begun. It is still important, however, to review the assessment results carefully and to determine if further assessment needs to be carried out to fill in missing information or update the information previously gathered.

Conference with the Student

As mentioned in Chapter 5, involvement of the student in the assessment and overall placement process is critical. As the placement process begins, you must meet with the student to share the results of the assessments that were conducted and get input from the student regarding work sites that are of most interest to him or her. It is important at this point also to get the student's input on the type of work site at which he or she would like to be placed and the skills he or she would like to gain through this placement. This is an important time to discuss the goal of the placement with the student—whether it be exploration of possible jobs, gaining general work experience, or learning specific job skills through on-the-job training.

Initial Contact with the Training Sponsor

The formality of this step will depend on whether you have used the training station before and how much you know about the actual work site. Even if this training station does not work out for the specific student, you will have this information on file to use in future placements. Before conducting the work-site analysis, of course, you will need to meet with the training sponsor to inform him or her of what you are doing and why. If you have used this training station and this training sponsor before, then the initial contact will be mainly to set up a time to meet and discuss the student and the training process.

Analysis of the Work Site

If you have not used this training station before, or if you are using a different job within this site, it is important to conduct an analysis of the major components of the site. This process was covered in Chapter 5 and in earlier sections of this chapter.

Meeting to Obtain the Training Station

Again, how detailed this meeting is will depend on your previous experience with the training sponsor. In any meeting, however, you will need to cover or review three main types of information: (1) information on the student, (2) information on your program, and (3) overview of the role of the training sponsor.

Four types of information should be shared about the student: (1) his or her interests, (2) the student's strengths and challenges, (3) his or her previous experiences, and (4) the experiences and training you would like the student to gain at this training station. Much of this information can be obtained from the assessment activities you have conducted with the student. A good rule of thumb is to share with the potential training sponsor the information he or she will need in order to work with the student. Another rule of thumb is to share with the training sponsor what *you* would want to know about any new student. In small towns, the training sponsor may already know about the student; in larger settings, this will not be the case. We recommend not focusing on the disability label, but being honest about the challenges as well as the strengths the student will bring to the work site.

You will also want to share information on your program. In particular, you should outline the training the student has already received and will receive and the support that your program will provide while the student is at the work site. We have found that ongoing support provided by a program is often the factor most valued by training sponsors—over such factors as financial incentives and subminimum wage. You will, however, also want to cover any financial incentives that may be available for the training sponsor, such as tax credits and deductions.

Finally, you will need to cover the role of the training sponsor. You will go over this in more depth in a future step, but the businessperson needs to know that he or she will be an integral part of the exploration work experience, or specific skill or training program for the student.

Student Interview with the Training Sponsor

Once the businessperson has agreed to be a training sponsor, the next step is to arrange for an interview between the student and the relevant supervisor(s) at the business. Some programs prefer to have two or more students interview for the position. Others feel that the job match is so important that they would like to handpick the student to be placed on a specific job site. Whatever your approach, it is important to get students involved in this stage of the placement process. It allows them to practice the job interview skills they have been taught and also allows the potential training sponsor to see the student first-hand. Depending on the purpose of the job experience, the length, and whether it is paid or unpaid, the training sponsor may ask the student to complete a job application as part of the interview process.

Meeting to Explain the Role of the Coordinator and Training Sponsor and the Training Agreement

If the student interview goes well and the business agrees to serve as a training station, the next step is to meet with the training sponsor to explain his or her role and that of the other players in the training process. A key document to have as part of this process is a training agreement. Consult with your school district to determine if it has an existing format for this agreement that you can adopt or adapt. School-to-work and career and technical education programs are the programs most likely to have such agreements.

The training agreement, although not a legally binding document, does outline the roles of the key players in the exploration or training experience. Each training agreement should have the following sections:

- Introductory information, including the student's name, the business, training supervisor and title, job title, beginning and end of training period, and overall purpose of the experience
- Information applicable to all parties
- Responsibilities of the student
- Responsibilities of the parent or other family members

- Responsibilities of the training sponsor
- Responsibilities of the coordinator and school

In addition, every training agreement should have a nondiscrimination clause stating that the business and the school do not discriminate against individuals on the basis of race, color, national origin, gender, marital status, or disability. (You may want to consult with your administrator for examples of language used in other documents.) Finally, there should be designated lines for each party (student, parent, training sponsor, and coordinator) to sign and date the document.

It is important that the language of the training agreement be direct and to the point. It is also important that you, as the coordinator, sit down with each of the parties involved and explain his or her role in the exploration or training process. Your program should make needed modifications in training agreements based on whether the experience is paid or nonpaid and whether the goal is exploration, work experience, or specific skill training. Some programs use the term *exploration agreement* when the main goal of the placement is exploration. See Appendix 11D, on the companion website, for sample exploration and training agreements.

Meeting to Develop and Discuss the Training Plan

The next step in the placement process is to meet to develop and discuss the training plan. This plan lists the work habits, attitudes, and specific skills and knowledge that the student will develop on this particular training station. This is the document that is most closely tied to the IEP for students with disabilities. A number of individuals should have input into this plan. First, the student should help identify the general and specific skills he or she would like to develop at this site. Parents and other family members should also be consulted. The student's IEP or other planning documents should be reviewed, as well. As the coordinator, you will also have a set of work habits and attitudes that you want all students to develop. In addition, there may be specific areas on which you want the student to focus.

In terms of specific knowledge and skills related to the job, an array of sources may be of some help. First, career and technical education programs often have lists of competencies covered in each program. Second, the job may have a list of specific duties. Third, the work-site analysis you conducted while you were identifying this site will produce definite tasks. Finally, the training sponsor is an excellent source of skills and knowledge (as well as work habits and attitudes) that are expected on the job.

The training plan is one of the most important documents in determining the focus of the work-based learning experience and in monitoring the experiences and progress of the student. It is also the most effective tie to the IEP for students with disabilities. It forces you to identify why this training station was selected for the student. It is also excellent documentation (along with the training agreement) that the placement is, in fact, part of the student's curriculum and an educational experience. This documentation may be needed if there are questions regarding nonpaid placements or claims for unemployment insurance made by the student after the placement ends.

It is most effective for you to enter the meeting with the training sponsor with at least a draft of a proposed training plan. This will have been developed based on input from the student, the family, existing lists of competencies, and you. You can then seek the training sponsor's reaction to the identified skills and knowledge areas and add other competencies as needed. Again, the concept of the training plan can be modified to that of an exploration plan if the purpose of the placement is exploration. See Appendix 11E for a sample training plan.

Ongoing Training of the Student

Although the training sponsor will usually provide the actual training in the specific skills required by the job, it is important that you work closely with the training sponsor to ensure that the components of the training plan are carried out or revised as necessary. This revision may involve adding additional skills or knowledge to be learned, if the student progresses more quickly than planned. It may also involve deleting one or more skills or areas of knowledge from the training plan if the student requires additional time to learn a specific component of the job. It is important, however, that the training plan be referred to often so that the student does not just remain on certain job tasks he or she has already mastered.

You may also need to provide some instruction on the academic tasks related to the job, such as using metric measurements or mastering job-related vocabulary. In addition, you may be required to deal with job-related social skills or work habits and attitudes that you or the training sponsor identify as needing improvement. The areas of needed instruction should clearly emerge from the continuing evaluation of the student, which is described in the following section.

Continuing Evaluation of the Student

It is critical to monitor the student's performance on the work-based learning site. This monitoring should be done more frequently at the beginning of the placement and can be done less frequently as the placement progresses, if it is going well. You will need to make it clear to the training sponsor that he or she should contact you if any questions or concerns arise. Stress that it is important to catch problems as they are developing, rather than waiting until they become major concerns that may lead to the student being asked to leave the site. You should also contact the training sponsor fairly often, either by phone or stopping by the work site. In either case, these contacts should be made during the least busy time of the day for the training sponsor. You should also stop in to evaluate the student weekly if your schedule allows.

Each time you evaluate the student, there should be a written record of your comments and/or those of the training sponsor. This can be in terms of short notes made on a standard form or a formal rating scale. A formal rating scale should be used *at least* twice during the placement—midterm and at the end. If possible, it is good to use a formal rating scale even more often, particularly at the beginning of the placement.

It is important that the student, you, and the training sponsor each independently rate the student and then compare your ratings. One of the best methods of conducting this comparison is through a three-way meeting, once the ratings have been completed by each party. In addition to providing information to you and the student on how the placement is progressing, this is one of the best sources of ongoing assessment information on the student. These ratings will also be important to you if you need to assign a grade to the student for this placement.

The work habits, attitudes, and specific skills and knowledge identified on the training agreement make an excellent foundation for such a rating scale. You would need to add to this information the following: (1) name of the student, (2) training station, (3) training sponsor, (4) period over which the student is being evaluated, (5) overall job title, and (6) name and position of the person completing the evaluation. You would then need to develop the ratings to which you want the raters to respond, usually on a three- or five-point scale. It is also important to leave a space for comments underneath each item and at the end of the rating scale. (See Chapter 5 for more information on constructing rating scales.)

Modification of the Training
Program Based on Ongoing Evaluation

One of the main reasons for continuing evaluation of the student is to determine if the training program is working or if it needs to be modified. The training program in this instance is both the school-based component and the work-based component. If the student is having specific problems on the job, then possibly the problem areas could be addressed in the class session related to the work-based placement. In addition, additional support or instruction could be provided on the job either by the training sponsor, you as the coordinator, or by a co-worker. It is critical that the results of the ongoing evaluation be shared with family members and with the teachers who are working with the student in school.

Individualized Planning for Transition to Employment

The focus of any placement should be on the interests, preferences, and skills of the student, also taking into account his or her needs. Any placement you make should (1) capitalize on the specific talents of the student and (2) focus on the needs of the target business. For students with significant disabilities, the placement process may require even more effort, and you may need to utilize the concepts of job carving and/or job sharing, which were discussed in an earlier section. The term *customized employment* provides an excellent approach to placing all students, but particularly those with severe disabilities. This term is defined as follows:

> Individualizing the employment relationship between employees and employers in ways that meet the needs of both. It is based on an individualized determination of the strengths, needs, and interests of the person with a disability, designed to meet the specific needs of the employer. It may include employment developed through job carving, self-employment, or entrepreneurial initiatives, or restructuring strategies that results in job responsibilities being customized and individually negotiated to fit the needs of individuals with a disability. Customized employment assumes the provision of reasonable accommodations and support necessary for the individual to perform the function of a job that is individually negotiated and developed. (*Federal Register,* June 26, 2002, p. 43154)

One method of organizing any placement is the development of a business proposal. Luecking and colleagues (2004) presented the following steps in developing such a proposal:

- Visit company sites.
- Observe the environment and several jobs within the site.
- Identify all major tasks for each job.
- Order the tasks from most complex to least complex.
- Identify essential tasks from each job that could be reassigned to capitalize on the skill of the job seeker, while maximizing the company's resources.
- Combine tasks across different jobs.
- Determine reasonable time and wage to conduct these tasks.
- Prepare and submit a concise and professional proposal.
- Follow up.

The business proposal that you would prepare as a result of these steps should (1) request employment for a specific job candidate, (2) highlight the skills of the candidate, (3) explain your role as an employment specialist, (4) outline the benefits to the company, and (5) explain how you will follow up.

Use of Natural Supports

Another concept that you may find helpful in placing any students, but particularly students with significant disabilities, is the concept of natural supports (Butterworth, Hagner, Helm, & Whelley, 2000; Mank, Cioffi, & Yovanoff, 2000). Butterworth, Hagner, Kiernan, and Schalock (1996) defined *natural supports* as

> assistance provided by people, procedures, or equipment in a given workplace or group that: (a) leads to desired personal and work outcomes, (b) is typically available or culturally appropriate in the workplace, and (c) is supported by resources from within the workplace, facilitated to the degree necessary by human service consultation. (p. 106)

This definition places primary emphasis on the observed *outcome* of natural supports as experienced by the individual in the workplace. Butterworth and colleagues (1996) also proposed a multidimensional model of workplace support, which includes the dimensions of (1) support resources, (2) process, and (3) relationship to culture. *Support resources* are mechanisms though which support is provided; they include people, procedures and routines, and tools and equipment. The *process* dimension addresses how the support will occur. Supports may be spontaneous (developed by resources such as co-workers, supervisors, or family and friends with no input from a service provider), facilitated (provided through natural resources but as a result of intervention by a disability-related service provider), or substituted/imported (provided on site by a job coach, personal assistant, or other external resource). The third dimension, *relationship to culture*, characterizes supports as typical (commonly used within the workplace and considered part of the workplace culture), modified (individually developed or adapted in some way, but a logical extension of a typical practice), or anomalous (provided to only one employee with no roots or counterpart in typical practices of the workplace).

Butterworth and associates (1996) also stated that effective supported employment needs to balance the lessons learned over the past with an increased concern for the inclusion of the individual in the social culture of the workplace and the development of relationships for both workplace support and friendship. They listed three key points to consider relative to the use of natural supports: (1) the major purpose of engaging natural networks and resources is to enhance the community inclusion and quality of life of the individual, (2) the need for support may be of lifelong duration and may fluctuate during different stages of the individual's life, and (3) the goal is to maximize natural supports without any assumption or requirement that they will be fully adequate. External support resources remain an important service function; support is a *both/and* issue, not an *either/or* issue.

Butterworth, Whitney-Thomas, and Shaw (1997) suggested that the role of the job coach needs to shift from providing direct instruction to the employee with disabilities to facilitating problem solving and consultation with the employee, co-workers, and employers. Along this same line of thought, Ohtake and Chadsey (2001) described six types of strategies that co-workers and job coaches could implement when assisting supported employees, going from the lowest to the highest level of involvement of the job coach: (1) autonomous support by co-workers, (2) suggested support from job coaches to co-workers, (3) managed support of co-workers by job coaches, (4) instructional support by co-workers, (5) direct training by job coaches with consultation from co-workers, and (6) direct training by job coaches. Job coaches must decide which strategy is most appropriate for meeting the needs of a given supported employee, without being overly intrusive for the employment setting.

Work Incentives and Disincentives

The Social Security Administration (SSA) provides a number of programs that may benefit eligible individuals with disabilities throughout the transition process and in adulthood. These programs provide supplemental income and, more importantly, often medical benefits. The benefits commonly provided by the SSA, however, are often seen as disincentives to work because they are tied to the amount of income earned and because they are not clearly understood. We will summarize the basic programs offered by the SSA. These programs, however, are very complex, and the SSA considers many variables before determining if a person is eligible. Because of this, we would strongly encourage you to consult the SSA office in your area. Vocational rehabilitation and other adult providers who are involved in placing individuals with disabilities in community-based employment are very familiar with the programs administered by the SSA. They will also be a good resource for you, as you work with your students to take advantage of these programs as they transition to employment as young adults. The Social Security Administration and the Department of Labor are working together to establish a position, called the Disability Program Navigator or Navigator, within the one-stop career centers in selected states (Social Security Administration, 2003). Also, SSA maintains four websites that may also be helpful to you:

- www.socialsecurity.gov, which contains SSA publications and information
- www.socialsecurity.gov/locator, which will give you the address, telephone number, and directions to your local office, when you type in your zip code
- www.socialsecurity.gov/disability, which provides comprehensive information on SSA's disability benefits programs
- www.socialsecurity.gov/work, which provides information on SSA's programs to help individuals with disabilities enter the workforce

Supplemental Security Income (SSI). This program is the one most often accessed by students with disabilities exiting high school. The Supplemental Security Income program provides cash assistance to the elderly and individuals with disabilities (including children under age 18) who have limited income and resources. The program requires a financial needs test. Cash benefits are determined on a flexible scale based on "countable income." As wages increase, cash benefits decrease. Under Section 1619b, when the cash benefit reaches zero, recipients continue on the Social Security rolls, allowing them to continue working and still keep their Medicaid benefits. Medicaid benefits often continue as long as wages fall below the established threshold amount for earnings (Social Security Administration, 2003).

Social Security Disability Insurance (SSDI). This program is different from SSI because it considers the employment status of the student's parents. It provides benefits to persons (age 18 or over) who become disabled before the age of 22, if at least one of their parents had worked a certain amount of time under the Social Security system, but is now disabled, retired, and/or deceased. The SSDI program strictly limits the monthly income of participants with disabilities. Months in which wages are over the allowed amount are considered trial work months. After a set number of these trial months, if it is determined that the individual can work in spite of his or her disability, then SSDI benefits are terminated. As with SSI, eligibility for SSDI usually also makes an individual eligible for Medicaid benefits (Social Security Administration, 2003).

Impairment-Related Work Expenses (IRWE) and Plan for Achieving Self-Support (PASS). Impairment-Related Work Expenses (IRWE) and Plan for Achieving Self-Support (PASS) were created by the Social Security Administration to counter the "disincentives" to work associated with SSI and SSDI. Both programs allow the individual to set aside money that is not counted as part of the individual's income, when eligibility for continued funding is considered. Both programs can be a source of funds that can promote individual choice and control in the employment preparation process.

The IRWE program allows the individual to deduct the cost of certain disability-related items and services that he or she needs to be able to work. An example might be the cost of attendant care or a workplace accommodation. Impairment-Related Work Expenses is available to either SSI- or SSDI-eligible individuals. A Plan for Achieving Self-Support allows the individual to set aside income and/or resources for a specified time for a work goal. This might include setting aside money to pay expenses for education, vocational training, or starting a business, as long as the expenses are related to achieving the individual's work goal. Anyone may help the individual develop a PASS; the Social Security Administration then evaluates the plan to decide if it is acceptable. The PASS program is available only to SSI-eligible individuals (Social Security Administration, 2003).

Ticket to Work.   The Ticket to Work program is a voluntary program under which many SSI and SSDI recipients will receive a "ticket" that they can use to obtain services from an approved service provider of their choice. These approved providers are called *employment networks*. You can find current information about the Ticket to Work Program, including a list of approved employment networks, at www.yourtickettowork.com.

Conclusion

The responsibility for placing, training, and supervising students in community-based work-training programs cannot be taken lightly. The relative ease with which some individuals fulfill such responsibility is very deceiving. For most people, it is a major responsibility, especially when they realize all that it involves. It raises serious concerns that the vast majority of states across the nation do not value this professional role enough to recognize it as a legitimate, highly desirable public school position with appropriate certification requirements. It borders on malpractice that state and local education agencies permit individuals to function in such critical outcome areas with no more than some type of academic teaching endorsement, often with an elementary focus.

Until states and local communities take responsibility for ensuring appropriate training for work experience coordinators, the coordinators will have to be responsible for their own professional development. There is a rapidly growing body of literature that reflects an optimistic philosophy, a demonstrated technology, and a practical agenda for placing, training, and supervising youths with disabilities in community-based employment. Increasing numbers of colleges and universities are offering up-to-date training in vocational training and transition programming for students with disabilities. Individuals in public school roles requiring job placement, job training, and job supervision should seek out these sources of professional development for the sake of the youths they serve, for their own legal protection, and for their own professional pride.

CHAPTER

12

Issues in the Implementation of Transition Education and Services

It is difficult to say what is impossible, for the dream of yesterday is the hope of today and the reality of tomorrow.

—Robert H. Goddard

We will close this book by discussing some of the issues we feel need to be considered in providing transition education and services to youths with disabilities. These issues and our comments on them reflect the perspective we have gained while working as secondary special education teachers, vocational rehabilitation counselor, state department staff member, coordinator of follow-up studies, developer of assessment instruments, member of interagency councils, members of parent advisory groups, providers of in-service training, researchers in the area of transition, and university faculty members preparing future teachers, transition personnel, and other support personnel to provide effective transition education and services. Even more important is that these issues represent the outlook and opinions of the many families, professionals, and individuals with disabilities with whom we have worked. As you read through them, notice that many of these issues are interrelated.

Issues

Issue 1: The goal of improved adult outcomes often has to compete with the goal of improved academic outcomes.

At present, the relationship between a life-skills education curriculum approach and the traditional academic curriculum is a tenuous one. On the one hand, general education is moving toward a more rigorous academic model, and effective schools and outcomes-based education is focusing on fostering higher achievement scores in the traditional subject-matter areas, along with increased skills in higher-order thinking and problem solving. On the other hand, many educators are viewing outcomes-based education more broadly than simply increasing academic achievement scores. They are advocating functional, generalizable skills for responsible citizenship as the ends, and academic skills as the means to those ends. This broader view of outcomes for education provides educators and families who want a life-skills education approach a window of opportunity to choose to be a part of a single educational system that takes responsibility for *all* students.

Kochhar-Bryant and Bassett (2002b) advocated for a combined standards and opportunities-based education system that addresses (1) increased standards for all students included in the general education curriculum; (2) curriculum options that blend academic, career-technical, and community-based learning; (3) multiple outcome measures in multiple domains for all students; and (4) appropriate aids and supports that help students participate in general education.

To date, 17 states have developed specific workplace competency standards. Some have developed a separate set of competencies, whereas others have overlaid the workplace competencies on the state's academic learning standards (Williams, 2002). The competencies reviewed in Chapters 1 and 6 would be an ideal place to start in identifying such competencies. As Thurlow, Thompson, and Johnson (2002) stated, "Since state assessments primarily assess progress toward standards, and since progress toward standards is addressed in IEPs, and since IEPs for older students become transition plans, it all fits together" (pp. 96–97).

The flexibility of states to establish their own standards, however, may be in jeopardy. Although No Child Left Behind does not mandate graduation requirements or diploma, the Center on Education Policy (2003) found that it is influencing the performance goals, content, and timetables of state exit exam systems. Most states with current or planned exit exams intended to use these exams to comply with the NCLB's high school testing mandates. Most states, however, will need to modify their testing systems to do so. States with exit exams that cannot be easily adapted to NCLB requirements must decide whether to scrap their exams or forge ahead with two sets of high school tests.

Issue 2: Schools should be as accountable for the quality of delivery of transition services as they are for academic achievement.

There is considerable talk in education today about the expectation that instructional programs, strategies, and curricula be of the highest quality possible and represent evidenced-based efforts to demonstrate what works. We will find it difficult to survive as a field if we do not take our work seriously enough to demonstrate that what we do is effective. If we expect full support, our research must demonstrate the effectiveness of our transition interventions. This research must be designed under conditions that are replicated across programs. The results of this evidence-based research must be submitted to refereed journals within and outside the field of transition.

The field of transition service delivery has grown, but has had difficulty in advancing because of attention on program development, compliance, and litigation, and because of inadequate funding. Neither the U.S. Department of Education nor many state education agencies have put research on transition services effectiveness on its list of funding priorities. That is not surprising since general special education effectiveness has also not been a priority for funding (Gersten, Baker, & Lloyd, 2000).

We raise the issue here to acknowledge that this is a growing need area for our discipline and that professionals in the field are needed to initiate research efforts to demonstrate what works. We cannot continue to base our current practices on theory, logic, and inferences. We must establish a clear connection between transition education and services and adult outcomes. The National Longitudinal Study–2 (NLTS–2; Wagner, 2004) is certainly a good beginning to this research. However, states and districts need to document the outcomes of their students and the courses, programs, and activities that are effective not only in raising test scores but also in improving adult outcomes (Sitlington & Frank, 1998). The collection of outcome data should be fully integrated into the information management systems of states and districts. Researchers in the field need to supplement state and district efforts with quality research that meets the standards of "evidence-based" research.

Issue 3: The assessment of the transition education needs of individuals with disabilities is often left to chance. Transition assessment and involvement of students in state and districtwide assessments are often seen as separate processes.

We see two separate parts to the issue concerning the assessment of individuals with disabilities. The first issue relates to quality assessment of students' transition service needs to ensure good transition planning. In Chapter 5, we presented our approach to transition assessment. Models for assessing the present levels of academic achievement and functional performance of individuals with disabilities in the life-skills areas discussed in that chapter must be developed. Techniques should include not only formal and informal assessment instruments but also curriculum-based assessment measures. A number of valid instruments currently exist (Clark, 1998). In spite of this, IEP teams are using very few of these instruments for planning. Furthermore, there is still reluctance to use informal assessments and community-based assessments.

The second part of this issue relates to the relationship of transition assessment and the involvement of students with disabilities in state and districtwide assessments. The transition assessment process must be incorporated into the ongoing assessment efforts of the district and state, including those related to standards-based reform. If professionals in the field are successful in infusing content related to transition into state and district standards, then incorporating transition assessment into state and districtwide assessments will be much more straightforward. If transition-related content is not included in state and district standards, then the process becomes more complex. It is important to realize, however, that many of the academic competencies prevalent in existing standards are also critical in the transition process.

Issue 4: The effect of state and districtwide assessments and standards-based reform on school completion outcomes for students with disabilities is uncertain.

Graduation rates and dropout rates have been two major concerns for the field of special education over the past 15 years. Both school completion outcome data areas have not been considered satisfactory, although the trend has shown improvement. The 20th Annual Report to Congress on the Implementation of the IDEA provided a new benchmark on the progress the field is making in graduation rates. A highlight was the report information that the number of students with disabilities graduating with diplomas increased 31 percent from 1986–1987 to 1995–1996. The 23rd Annual Report to Congress for 1998–1999 data showed that increases, though much less dramatic, were up again with a record 57.4 percent of students with disabilities graduating from high school with a regular diploma. This is in contrast to 55.4 percent in 1997–1998 and 51.9 percent in 1993–1994 (U.S. Department of Education, 2002). The report indicated that dropout rates had fallen from 34.5 percent in 1993–1994 to 28.9 percent in 1998–1999.

The annual reports to Congress stay five years behind in currency of data, so there has been strong interest recently in knowing how the intensive reforms in school achievement accountability might have affected students with disabilities. The 2000 edition of this text reported only 17 states with high-stakes testing. In a survey of 46 states and the District of Columbia, 27 state education agencies were reported to have or expected to have exit exams that require students to take a high stakes assessment to receive a diploma (Johnson & Thurlow, 2003). Will these new conditions affect graduation and dropout rates?

The Center on Education Policy (2003) reported that evidence of both the positive and negative impacts of exit exams are accumulating. As discussed in Chapter 5, exit exams appear to encourage better coverage of the content in state standards, better alignment of curricula with state standards, and the provision of remedial and special courses for students at risk of failing. However, a moderate amount of data also suggests that these exams may be associated with higher dropout rates. We know that there are some stable, predictable factors associated with dropouts, including some relatively inalterable factors, such as socioeconomic and racial minority status (Kortering & Braziel, 1999). But other factors include absenteeism, course failure, and peer influence. Whether high-stakes testing can be added to this list is still a matter for research to determine. It seems logical to assume that failing courses, repeating grades, and insufficient evidence that school personnel care are considerations in whether graduation rates or dropout rates improve.

Large-scale assessment accountability standards are dissolving the general tolerance people have for differences in expectations and outcomes. The public's general concern for the low levels of expectations and outcomes is the force behind the new school reforms. Now, for the first time in many states, a high school diploma can be operationally defined by "performance level" in addition to an accumulation of credits or Carnegie units. This will undoubtedly benefit students with disabilities who are able to complete general education programs successfully. The issue under discussion here, however, is whether or not having arbitrary performance level standards devalues students with disabilities and at-risk students by denying them a regular diploma or forcing students to drop out of school.

To some degree, assessment and accountability standards for a specified core curriculum for *all* students are in conflict with the philosophy of the IDEA, which clearly mandates individualized determination of "appropriate education." Cut-off scores, based on a core curriculum that assumes everyone has the same needs, take the field of education back to elitism and education for a select population and raise the perennial issue of equity.

Freedman (1997) noted that a school district is not required to award a regular diploma to a student with disabilities who does not meet the academic requirements for a regular diploma, regardless of whether the student with disabilities has met the requirement of the IEP. The district must notify the parents in advance if successful completion of an IEP will not result in the awarding of a regular diploma. It seems reasonable to proceed on the basis that the awarding of a diploma to a special education student is at the discretion of state or local authority. If a decision is made by local school authorities not to award regular diplomas, but instead award "special" diplomas or certificates of completion to the special education students, the school must notify the student or parent well in advance of any expected graduation. As Johnson and Thurlow (2003) pointed out, however, little is known about the consequences of different diploma options in terms of access to employment and postsecondary opportunities.

Standards-based education with high-stakes assessments can be highly problematic for students with disabilities if the standards reflect primarily on a prescribed level of academic achievement, without regard to alternative performance outcomes or life skills. Alternative curricular requirements for students that could still lead to a regular diploma, appropriate modifications and accommodations in high school graduation exams, and a more comprehensive curriculum for all students must be adopted to ensure that reform efforts do not prove detrimental to students' successful graduations (Kochhar-Bryant & Bassett, 2002b).

Issue 5: Transition education and services compliance remains the most frequent local and state education agency area of noncompliance.

Although the Individuals with Disabilities Act and its Amendments mandated that a statement of transition service needs must be included in the IEP of all students with disabilities beginning at least at age 14, and a statement of needed transition services at least by age 16, the vast majority of schools have not complied. Noncompliance appears to be procedural violations and substantive omission violations. It also appears that negative consequences for noncompliance do not occur frequently enough or with enough effect to change the general response to transition planning.

Some parents have used their rights to challenge schools through the due process hearing approach and others have resorted to litigation. Only a small percentage of families do challenge the schools, but when they do so successfully, schools pay a high price for the noncompliance. Some parents are getting favorable rulings for their cases two and three years after their son or daughter graduated from high school because of school failure to inform parents of transition services (procedural omission) or provide any transition services (substantive omission).

The President's Commission on Excellence in Special Education report (Bellah, 2003) stated that schools under the IDEA are generally providing legal safeguards and access for children with disabilities, but that the current system often places process above results. It also found in its study that the culture of compliance has often developed from the pressures of litigation. Ultimately, compliance will save money and help make children and youths more successful. Providing individualized education programs, with appropriate related services and transition services is, in our view, a meaningful, systemic approach to doing the right thing. Complying with the law is not only the right thing to do but it is also the practical thing to do.

It appears that the IEP form or whatever is used to document transition service needs and needed transition services is the key to reasonable documentation for what was assessed, planned, and monitored during implementation. If states do not take the initiative to provide guidance to schools, the local school district must take responsibility for having a useful form. Iowa is one of the states that provide a model for schools to use. One of the six foundations on which the state model is based is that "the IEP reflects the student's and family's vision for the future" (Iowa Department of Education, 1998, p. 5). As part of the IEP meeting, the family, the student, and other members of the IEP team are given an opportunity to discuss their hopes, dreams, insights, and expectations for the student. This vision is written on the IEP document and is reviewed yearly. The vision statement focuses on the needs of the student and guides the student's IEP and the considerations for prioritizing needs. It is also used to design a program that meets the student's unique needs, taking into account the student's strengths, preferences, and interests. More states and local school districts need to follow this approach and ensure that transition considerations truly do drive the IEP process.

Issue 6: Formal training in self-determination is often not provided.

Ward and Halloran (1993) stated that "the ultimate goal of education must be to increase the responsibility of all students for managing their own affairs" (p. 4). As important and critical as self-determination is, training in self-determination must be infused into the IEP process for all students with disabilities and efforts must align with other reform efforts in general education to open this concept to *all* students.

Field, Martin, Miller, Ward, and Wehmeyer (1998a) summarized the major definitions of *self-determination* as follows:

> Self-determination is a combination of skills, knowledge, and beliefs that enable a person to engage in goal-directed, self-regulated, autonomous behavior. An understanding of one's strengths and limitations together with a belief in oneself as capable and effective are essential to self-determination. When acting on the basis of these skills and attitudes, individuals have greater ability to take control of their lives and assume the role of successful adults. (p. 2)

This view of self-determination emphasizes choice, control, and personally meaningful success.

As the DCDT Position Paper on Self-Determination for Persons with Disabilities (Field, Martin, Miller, Ward, & Wehmeyer, 1998b) stated, the focus on teaching self-determination skills has historical roots in the career-development and transition movement. We support DCDT's position that self-determination instruction during the elementary, middle, and secondary transition years prepares *all* students for a more satisfying and fulfilling adult life. Evidence increasingly shows that encouraging self-determination for *all* youths could help them be more successful in their educational programs as well as in their adult lives (Field, 1997). In addition, several curricula (e.g., Field & Hoffman, 1996; Halpern, Herr, Doren, & Wolf, 2000) have been implemented in inclusive environments and have resulted in positive outcomes for students with and without disabilities.

As Field and colleagues (1998b) stated, to teach self-determination skills and attitudes that generalize to real life, educators must realize that self-determination is a function of the interaction between an individual's skills and the opportunities provided by his or her environment. Specific assessments and lessons must be designed to focus on the acquisition of the knowledge, skills, and beliefs associated with self-determination. This includes activities such as student involvement in assessment and IEP transition planning and implementation. Grigal, Test, Beattie, and Wood (1997) found in their study of transition components of the IEP that not one IEP contained a self-determination or self-advocacy goal. Family members are also critical to self-determination. Turnbull and Turnbull (1996) listed a number of familial features: cultural values, beliefs and expectations, and coping styles; family interactions, such as role expectations and relationships; family functions, including economic and daily care needs; and family life-span issues, including developmental stages of family interactions and function over time. We agree with Field and colleagues that the important role that families play in the self-determination process needs to be supported and nurtured.

A closely related issue to self-determination is the transferring of parental rights at the age of majority, which was included in the IDEA Amendments of 1997 and IDEA 2004. When a student reaches the age of majority, schools are to provide a notice to the student and parents, and transfer rights of the parents to the student. If students are determined as not having the ability to provide informed consent with respect to their educational and transition programs, the state has to establish procedures to appoint the parent of the student or another appropriate individual as a legal guardian.

Issue 7: The availability of work-based learning programs in general education appears to be declining.

School-to-work and career and technical education initiatives offer a tremendous opportunity to include students with disabilities in general education, while providing them with the skills and experiences to transition successfully to adult life. In fact, at the time we were writing the 2000 edition of this textbook, we saw the passage of the School-to-Work Opportunities Act as an extremely encouraging influence on making transition education a priority for all students. Since that time, however, the school-to-work legislation sunset (in 2002). Programs, however, funded under this initiative are still in operation in many states.

In addition, the field of career and technical education is in a state of flux, as it attempts to determine its role within the standards-based reform movement. The recent *National Assessment of Vocational Education* (U.S. Department of Education, 2004) found that the average number of credits earned in career and technical education has declined, while the average number of academic credits earned by students has increased substantially. The absence of such programs would cause a serious dilemma for the field of special education as professionals attempt to provide students with disabilities the training and experiences they need to achieve their transition goals, while providing this training and experience in the least restrictive environment.

Issue 8: Postsecondary education programs are placing increasing emphasis on standard psychological tests to provide documentation of a disability, whereas programs at the secondary level are moving toward curriculum-based assessments and noncategorical labels.

As stated in Chapter 7, a number of current innovations in special education that are supported by IDEA 2004 offer both challenges and opportunities to the process of transition from secondary to postsecondary education. First, a district is required only to provide the exiting high school student with a summary of his or her academic achievement and functional performance, which shall include recommendations on how to assist the student in meeting his or her postsecondary goals. Second, special educators in many states are moving away from an emphasis on standardized assessments and toward use of curriculum-based assessment. Finally, many states are moving away from specific disability labels and toward the concept of *individuals with a disability* or a *noncategorical* label. We are certainly supportive of all of these innovations. Although they present challenges to the smooth transition of students with disabilities into postsecondary education, they also present opportunities to gather information that will be of assistance in documenting that the student's disability "substantially limits" a major life activity (e.g., learning) and that the student is "otherwise qualified." These innovations also provide an opportunity for determining the accommodations that are needed at the postsecondary level.

Those who stand to lose most in this emerging conflict of approaches are the student and the family. We strongly advocate that discussions intensify at the local, state, and national levels to narrow the ever-widening gap between secondary and postsecondary level education systems. In particular, we reiterate the three recommendations we made in Chapter 7, as the gathering of information is fully integrated into the ongoing transition assessment and planning process for the student. First, with the student, develop a process for determining what accommodations are most effective for him or her at the secondary level, and include only those accommodations in the student's IEP. Second, work with the postsecondary institutions in the surrounding area (those most often attended) to identify the format for providing the information they need. Third, if possible, involve a representative of the postsecondary institution in the IEP meetings in which transition to postsecondary education is being discussed.

Issue 9: In the area of transition to adult life, formalized preparation of special education personnel is inadequate.

Looking for a systemic factor that could be contributing to the issue of noncompliance in the area of transition services should start with the qualifications of the personnel expected to deliver transition services. Transition planning and life-skills content need to be infused into the college and university programs that prepare teachers to work with individuals with disabilities of all ages, as well as individuals without disabilities. When transition education and services issues are addressed in the majority of college and university programs preparing teachers of individuals with disabilities, they are usually addressed in an isolated course (usually only for those preparing to work with adolescents) or in isolated presentations, and account for little of the instructional time in methods or foundations courses. Seldom is the concept of transition education included at all in coursework for those being certified in general elementary or secondary education, even though general education teachers may be invited to be members of IEP teams considering transition needs and services.

The Council for Exceptional Children (1998) published a set of international standards for the preparation and certification of special education teachers. Infused in these standards are a number of knowledge and skill areas related to transition education. Examples of these include (1) life-skills instruction relevant to independent, community, and personal living and employment; (2) social skills needed for educational and functional living and working environments; and (3) creating an environment that encourages self-advocacy and increased independence. The standards also include knowledge and skills for beginning transition specialists.

We recommend that all trainees being prepared to work with individuals with disabilities (at both the elementary and secondary levels) be exposed to the concept of transition education and services through content infused in their curriculum and methodology coursework. Course requirements for special education teacher education programs spanning K–12 should include supervised practical experiences with adolescents with disabilities that include transition services activities. Course requirements for those preparing to be transition specialists should include supervised practical experiences involving actual transition assessment and planning, interagency collaboration, and community-based placements. In addition, we would recommend that those preparing to work with adolescents with disabilities as transition coordinators or specialists have at least three courses related to the provision of transition education and services. These courses should incorporate all components of the knowledge and skills standards proposed by the Council for Exceptional Children (1998) for transition specialists, including assessment of the student's strengths, needs, preferences, and interests.

The role of transition specialist or transition coordinator is still evolving, but many states have persons with this designation working in secondary schools. There are only a few states that have recognized certification plans in place for personnel whose primary responsibility is the provision of transition education and services (Anderson et al., 2004).

The Council for Exceptional Children (1998) standards for the preparation and certification of special education teachers include a listing of knowledge and skills for beginning transition specialists (see companion website Appendix 12A). This listing of knowledge and skills was developed by a group of individuals involved in providing transition education and services and in preparing transition personnel, with input from other practitioners in the field. We strongly support the knowledge and skills listed in this standards document. As we examined these knowledge and skills statements, however, we found ourselves thinking that all secondary special educators should have some of this knowledge and skills.

The role of transition specialist varies greatly across states, and even within states (Asselin, Todd-Allen, & deFur, 1998). In some cases, they basically establish policy and procedures, link with adult providers, and provide in-service training to staff, families, and individuals with disabilities. In other cases, they provide direct service to individuals with disabilities, in areas such as job placement and transition assessment. This variety in role and function makes it difficult to formulate a specific recommendation for certification and supports the suggestion that determining such a certification plan should be carried out independently by states.

We have two recommendations related to this area. First, we would encourage state departments of education to convene a working group composed of institutions of higher education and transition specialists in their state. The charge to this working group would be to examine the knowledge and skills identified by the Council for Exceptional Children (1998) for beginning transition specialists and to add other content areas typically required of transition specialists in their state. We would then recommend that each state identify an existing certification that would include these knowledge and skill areas or develop a new certification based on these areas. Second, we would recommend that the same or another working group identify the knowledge and skill areas from the beginning transition specialist area that should be incorporated into the certification requirements for all secondary special education teachers.

Conclusion

Many professionals in the field have been advocating for transition education and services for a number of years. Career education and other life-skills initiatives burst strongly onto the scene and then slowly died. The Individuals with Disabilities Education Act and its Amendments and other educational reform legislation, such as the School-to-Work Opportunities Act, provided a major impetus for transition education. Standards-based reform efforts and the academic emphasis of the No Child Left Behind legislation appear to have shifted the emphasis toward academic outcomes, rather than outcomes related to life as an adult. IDEA 2004 focuses transition services on improving the "academic and functional achievement" of the student to facilitate movement from school to postschool activities. Educators must work now with the federal government, state departments of education, universities, parent groups, individuals with disabilities, local school boards, administrators, and co-workers to ensure that the "spirit" of IDEA 2004 and its rules and regulations are implemented.

Transition planning must truly *drive* the individualized education program for all students with disabilities. As a student begins to receive special education services, the emphasis must always be on the skills and support needed for successful transition to the next environment and to the ultimate environment of life as an adult. As this planning occurs, the emphasis must remain not only on employment and postsecondary education but also on living independently and interdependently, becoming appropriately involved in the community, and experiencing satisfactory personal and social relationships.

It is easy to become pessimistic and lessen one's efforts. We feel, however, that we are at a crossroads for change in all education. If our efforts are lessened now, the battle could be lost. We need to become familiar with the reform agendas of the district, the state, and the nation, and integrate transition-related content into the standards being established. Often, the mandates for transition programs and better postsecondary outcomes have to compete with the mandates to raise academic standards. Efforts for transition education must be fully integrated into the ongoing standards-based reform efforts in the overall educational system. Transition education is critical for individuals with and without disabilities. It is imperative that this nation's educational system incorporate this concept into its standards and benchmarks to ensure that *all* students achieve the ultimate outcome of education—preparation for adult life.

GLOSSARY OF TERMS IN TRANSITION PROGRAMS AND SERVICES

adult services Adult services include support services and programs provided by both public and private agencies for persons with disabilities. Usually, these services are provided to individuals after they have exited the school system, but there are times when adult services and schools both provide needed services simultaneously. Most public adult service programs have eligibility requirements that vary across agencies.

advocacy/legal service needs Advocacy needs could be as simple as a student's need to learn how to advocate for self more effectively. Students may need specific planning for transition that relates to legal advocacy for themselves or specific legal services they will need. The individualized education program (IEP) team members and families may need to anticipate needs of current students as adults in the areas of guardianship and conservatorship, estate planning (wills and trusts), or parent surrogates. Planning decisions made for a student with disabilities in relation to certain legal issues may affect eligibility for programs and services.

alternate assessment An assessment designed for those students with disabilities who are unable to participate in general large-scale assessments used by a school district or state, even when accommodations are provided. The alternate assessment provides a mechanism for students with even the most significant disabilities to be included in the assessment system.

alternative curriculum This alternative curriculum varies from the general education curriculum. Such a curriculum may serve students with high cognitive abilities or lower functional levels. Alternative curricula may also address such areas as vocational and life skills.

assistive technology devices and services The Office of Special Education Programs (OSEP) has issued a policy ruling that "consideration of a child's need for assistive technology must occur on a case-by-case basis in connection with the development of a child's individualized education program (IEP)." An assistive technology device is any item, piece of equipment, or product system that is used to increase, maintain, or improve functional capabilities of individuals with disabilities. Assistive technology services include any service that directly assists an individual with a disability in the selection, acquisition, or use of an assistive technology device.

audiology Audiology services are generally provided by audiologists who screen, assess, and identify students with hearing loss. Audiological services also include referrals for medical or other professional attention for the habilitation of hearing, auditory training, speech reading, speech conservation, determining the need for group or individual amplification, and selecting and fitting a student for an appropriate hearing aid.

career education An educational emphasis stressing the teaching of life career roles (e.g., family member, citizen, community participant, worker, etc.) early in life, to be followed up throughout the student's education, in preparing him or her for those roles.

career planning options Students are provided with options for making tentative and, ultimately, realistic life-career decisions. Systematic provision of career information in coursework at school, occupational exploration opportunities through field experiences and job shadowing experiences, community experiences, and summer camps (art, music, computer, etc.) are examples of career planning options.

career and technical education Organized educational activities that (1) offer a sequence of courses that provides individuals with the academic and technical knowledge and skills he or she needs to prepare for further education and careers (other than careers requiring a baccalaureate, master's, or doctoral degree) in current or emerging employment sectors and (2) includes competency-based applied learning that contributes to the academic knowledge, higher order reasoning and problem-solving skills, work attitudes, general employability skills, technical skills, and occupation-specific skills of an individual (formerly referred to as *vocational and technical education* and *vocational education*).

collaborative consulting model Collaborative consultation is one of the administrative models used in inclusive education. It emphasizes consulting teachers working with general education teachers who have special education students in their classes. Both teachers collaborate in different ways to benefit all students.

community-based instruction Community-based instruction is a method of instruction in which a student is taught to perform skills in actual community environments, rather than teaching students skills in a classroom and expecting them to generalize to the community.

community participation options Students, are provided with opportunities to learn and develop age-appropriate life skills in real-life settings. Community-based experiences could include job training, job or work sample tryouts, living skills instruction, community survival skills, job search and application skills, leisure or recreational skills, and so forth. Instruction and experiences are acquired outside of the school environment (also referred to as *community-based instruction* and *community-based education*).

community-referenced instruction This method of instruction includes teaching a student to perform skills within the school setting in an environment as close as possible to the community. An example would include teaching the student to purchase lunch in the cafeteria rather than teaching the student to purchase lunch in a restaurant in the community.

continuing education This optional education service is offered to youths and adults who have completed or withdrawn from regular education programs. The programs offer training and knowledge in specific fields. Examples include adult education programs, institutes, colleges or other postsecondary education, community workshops, seminars, or correspondence courses.

counseling services Counseling services are typically provided by counselors who work with students to develop and improve students' understanding of themselves, their awareness of occupational alternatives, and their social and behavioral skills. Guidance and counseling techniques are used with students to assist them and their families in decision making about school and postschool options.

Dictionary of Occupational Titles Department of Labor publication providing extensive listing and classification of jobs in the United States.

Fair Labor Standards Act The Fair Labor Standards Act is commonly known as the Federal Wage and Hour Law. The act establishes minimum wage, child labor control, overtime, and equal pay standards for employment. The act applies to people with and without disabilities.

financial assistance/support Eligibility for certain programs is based on the individual characteristics and needs of each student. Some of the procedures for obtaining financial support are cumbersome and involve lengthy application periods. Planning may focus on need for Social Security Income, Social Security Disability benefits, Survivor's Benefits, home- and community-based waivers, food stamps, HUD Section 8 low-income housing eligibility, Medicaid, public health services, and so forth.

functional curriculum A functional curriculum is a purposefully designed program of instruction that focuses on teaching specific skills in daily living, personal and social interactions, and employability. Each individual student will have unique preferences and needs, which require individualization of functional curriculum and instruction. Functional curriculum instruction will occur both within and outside of the school setting.

functional evaluation A functional evaluation or assessment process is one that is an organized approach to determining the interests, needs, preferences, and abilities that an individual student has in the domains of daily living skills, personal-social skills, and occupational/employability skills. It is a continuous process, using both formal and informal assessment procedures, that provides a basis for planning and instruction.

independent living An expanded view of independent living is that it comprises all the demands of living on one's own. This includes residential choices and skills, economic decisions and money management, time management, maintenance of equipment or technological devices, community mobility, involvement in community activities and citizenship responsibilities, and so forth. Some agencies limit their meaning of this term to residential living, but that is not the case in IDEA.

independent living skills Independent living skills are those needed by persons so they can function in a home or community environment, with as few supports as necessary.

Individual Academic-Career Plan (IACP) A plan used in some comprehensive guidance programs with all students in Grades 6–12 to encourage students to commit each year to a tentative occupational choice and a course of study. Occupational choices are not binding, but students have the opportunity each year to look again at their options and make a choice while determining their courses of study. It is an attempt to help students see each year how they can and should be thinking of the relationships between their occupational choices and their educational experiences at school.

individualized education program (IEP) The IEP is a written document required of all individuals in school who have been classified as needing special education programs or related services because of some disabling condition. The document should include the student's present level of functioning in each identified needs area, a statement of annual goals for the student, a statement of appropriate short-term objectives (if receiving an alternate assessment), the evaluation approach and evaluation criteria for determining progress toward achievement of annual goals, a statement of any required related services and who will provide them, a statement of transition service needs (at least by age 16), and a statement that relates to the issue of least restrictive environment for the student relative to each program and service to be provided.

individualized education program planning meeting The IEP planning meeting is one that occurs at least once annually. The student's present level of functioning is discussed, progress made since the last meeting (for continuing students) is reviewed, and goals are established for the next year. Every

third year, the IEP planning group will conduct a review of the student's status based on appropriate reevaluation data.

individualized education program team The IEP team is a support and planning group made up of the student, his or her parents or guardians, the student's teacher(s), the person responsible for implementing or supervising the implementation of transition services, a school administrator, relevant school support services personnel, and other relevant agency representatives. The team is charged with the responsibility of developing and implementing an individualized education program for the student, based, on his or her needs, interests, and preferences.

informal assessment A procedure in which nonstandardized assessment tools are used to gather data on specific characteristics. Typical examples of informal assessments are teacher-made tests, rating scales, checklists, survey or interview forms, and observation forms.

insurance needs Insurance coverage should be active during school years while students are engaged in school programs. Community job training, transportation on field trips, and vocational education shops are examples of school-related insurance planning needs. Insurance needs for postschool life planning frequently include health and accident insurance and automobile liability insurance.

integrated employment Integrated employment is viewed in most cases as employment where a person with disabilities has real work opportunities in settings where the interactions are primarily with people who are nondisabled.

job coach A person designated as a supported employment work supervisor for a person in training or competitive employment. The job coach serves as an instructor and work model alongside the individual at work.

job sample A sample of a standard work activity that involves all or part of the total operations required of a particular job. Job samples are often used as an evaluation of a person's ability to perform certain tasks or to predict task performance in a real work environment.

job shadowing The process of following an employee performing his or her daily tasks. The goal is to gain an understanding of what the employee's job entails, and whether a person would be interested in or qualified to perform such duties.

leisure life skills Those life skills an individual uses in his/her time while not working or attending classes.

leisure/recreation needs Leisure and recreation are critical factors in the long-term success of persons with disabilities. Planning ahead for the skills needed to access and engage in leisure and recreation opportunities is a responsibility of the IEP team. There should be ongoing assessment of interests and encouragement of participation in a variety of activities. Accessing leisure and recreational activities through school clubs, parks and recreation programs, sport leagues, church groups, school and public libraries, and community facilities (movie theaters, bowling alleys, skating rinks, parks, etc.) should be planning and programming goals.

life skills Specific competencies that include knowledge, skills, and the application of life skills of local and cultural relevance needed to perform everyday activities across a variety of settings.

lifelong career development A lifelong approach for persons to acquire the skills and resources they need to acquire, maintain, or improve independent living and quality of life throughout their lives.

living arrangement options Planning for living options after leaving school depends on a variety of factors, beginning with the abilities and preferences of the student. In addition, the living alternatives vary from community to community. Planning should address the need to provide instruction in the basic skills necessary to take full advantage of the living options that are available, This might include the areas of consumer skills, home management skills (cleaning, cooking, laundry, use of appliances, etc.), safety, and dealing with emergencies. Planning for accessing living arrangement options would address the issues of living at home with parents, supervised apartment living, group home life, adult foster care, independent apartment with assistance services, and independent apartment options.

medical/mental health needs Planning for the current and future medical or mental health needs of an individual student must involve the student's family. In cases where parents are not well informed regarding the importance of continuing medical or mental health treatment or support, or of the resources in the community for their son or daughter, the IEP team should consider planning for accessing such resources as Arc-USA health insurance, Medicaid, sliding fee scale services (community mental health centers, public health centers, Easter Seal, March of Dimes, and some drug and alcohol centers), and state rehabilitation services.

medical services Medical services are considered a related service only under specific conditions. They are provided by a licensed physician, and at the present time, services are restricted to diagnostic and evaluation purposes. Services do not include direct, ongoing medical treatment. (See *school health services*.)

occupational therapy Occupational therapy services are provided by therapists who focus on assessing and training students whose disabilities impair their daily life functioning. Emphasis on motor functioning in everyday living demands helps individual students to be more prepared for functioning at home, school, and in the community.

outcome-based education Outcome-based education programs are based on predetermined outcome goals for students in a class. Instructional activities, materials, and assessments are designed with these outcomes in mind.

parent counseling and training Parent counseling and training is an increasingly important related service. Counseling and training may be provided when necessary to help the student with a disability benefit from the school's educational program. Specific areas of counseling and training include assisting parents in understanding the special needs of their child, providing parents with information about child/adolescent development, and providing parents with referrals to parent support groups, financial assistance and resources, and professionals outside the school system.

personal management needs Personal management needs overlap several other planning areas for IEP teams. Personal management of money, personal belongings, health care needs, personal hygiene needs, dental hygiene needs, and management and use of time are examples of needs in this area. Desirable personal habits—such as self-control of emotions and behaviors, responsibility, and honesty—are also examples of personal management needs to consider in planning for curriculum and instruction.

physical therapy Physical therapy services are provided by a therapist following a referral by a physician or other school or health-related professional. Emphasis is placed on increasing muscle strength, mobility, and endurance, and improving gross motor skills, posture, gait, and body awareness. Therapists may also monitor the function, fit, and proper use of mobility aids and devices.

postsecondary education or training Any education program beyond high school that has an academic, vocational, professional, or preprofessional focus is considered postsecondary education or training.

postsecondary education or training options Postsecondary education options include adult education, community college, or college or university programs. Any vocational or technical program beyond high school that does not lead to an associate of arts or baccalaureate degree is considered postsecondary training. Postsecondary training may be obtained in public vocational and technical schools, community college vocational or technical programs, private vocational or technical schools, labor union trades/skills training, military vocational or technical skills training, apprenticeship program, or state/federal employment training programs. Some of these programs require a license or certificate for an individual before being permitted to practice his or her occupational skills.

psychological services Psychological services are usually provided by a school psychologist. In addition to psychological testing and interpretation, school psychologists may obtain and interpret information about a student's behavior and conditions for learning or functioning in school environments. Psychologists consult with school staff, assist in planning individual educational programs, and provide counseling for students and parents or lawful custodians.

quality of life Quality of life is a subjective concept that should drive all outcome goals, programs, and services for adults and students with disabilities. It emphasizes personal choice and personal satisfaction with life experiences.

recreation therapy Recreation therapy is included as a related service because all children with disabilities need to learn how to use their leisure time and recreation time constructively and with enjoyment. For those students who need recreation therapy in order to benefit from their educational experience, the therapy usually focuses on improvement of socialization skills, as well as eye-hand coordination and physical, cognitive, or language skills. Recreation therapists assess students' leisure capacities and functions, give therapy to remediate functional difficulties, provide leisure education, and assist students in accessing leisure/recreation options.

rehabilitation counseling services Rehabilitation counseling services is a related service under IDEA. The services are defined in the regulations as "services provided by qualified personnel in individual or group sessions, that focus specifically on career development, employment preparation, achieving independence, and integration in the workplace and community of a student with a disability." The term also includes "vocational rehabilitation services provided to students with disabilities by vocational rehabilitation programs funded under the Rehabilitation Act of 1973, as amended" [IDEA, Sec. 602(A)(1)].

related services Those services, other than special education services, that are necessary for a student to benefit from special education. Examples of related services include speech therapy, physical therapy, and occupational therapy. Other related services include auxiliary services, computers, wheelchairs, summer schooling, and many others. Related services are those that are supportive of and may or may not be part of classroom instruction, including transportation, counseling, assistive technology, and so forth.

residential facility or institution A living arrangement in which individuals are housed most of the day in a protective environment. Examples include state schools/hospitals, intermediate care facilities for persons with mental disabilities/developmental disabilities, nursing homes, and so on.

school-based enterprise   A school-based enterprise is a school-sponsored, work-based learning opportunity in which a group of students (1) produce goods or services for sale or use by other people, (2) participate in multiple aspects of the enterprise, and (3) relate service and production activities to classroom learning. School-based enterprises must be student run. They give students real practice in entrepreneurship, accounting, budgeting, marketing, inventory control, and business-related skills. They also allow students to develop generic work skills in problem solving, communication, interpersonal relations, and learning how to learn in the context of work. A well-established example of a school-based enterprise program is the Junior Achievement model.

school health services   School health services are typically provided by a qualified school nurse or a specifically trained nonmedical person who is supervised by a qualified nurse. These services are available to those students who would be unable to attend school without such supportive health care and monitoring. Services may include clean intermittent catheterization, special feedings, suctioning, administering of medications, and planning for the safety and well-being of a student while at school.

self-advocacy needs   IEP planning for self-advocacy needs refers to instruction or related services that will help develop an individual student's skills in assuming responsibility for himself or herself at school and in the community. Skill training for self-advocacy in the IEP meeting is a starting goal that is recommended. Skill training should also include awareness of one's own needs and assertiveness training in other settings (also referred to as *self-determination*).

sheltered employment   A structured program of activities involving work evaluation, work adjustment, occupational skill training, and remunerative employment designed to prepare individuals either for competitive employment or for continued work in a protective environment (e.g., workshop).

Social Security Disability Insurance (SSDI)   This program is different from Supplemental Security Income (SSI), because it considers the employment status of the student's parents. It provides benefits to persons (age 18 or over) who become disabled before the age of 22, if at least one of their parents had worked a certain amount of time under the Social Security system, but is now disabled, retired, and/or deceased. The SSDI program strictly limits the monthly income of participants with disabilities. As with SSI, eligibility for SSDI usually also makes an individual eligible for Medicaid benefits.

social work services in schools   Social work services are provided when the whole welfare of the student with a disability must be addressed. Home, school, and community interactions result in complex problems, and educators may not be able to work effectively alone. Social work services in schools are performed by qualified personnel and are focused on mobilizing school and community resources to enable students to learn as effectively as possible in their school programs.

socialization opportunities   Successful transitions begin while students are still in school. IEP teams should look at each individual student's social skills with peers with disabilities, peers without disabilities, family members, adults at school and in the community, and children. Socialization opportunities can be made a part of the instructional program for a student at first as social skills training, but later as a maintenance activity through program and school activities.

speech-language pathology   Speech and language pathology services are provided by qualified professionals trained to deal with communication disorders in students. Speech-language pathologists screen, identify, assess, and diagnose communication problems, provide speech and language corrective services, consult on use of augmentative and alternative communication systems, and refer students for medical or other professional attention necessary for the habilitation of speech and language disorders. It is not necessary for students to be manifesting academic problems in addition to speech or language problems for them to be considered eligible for speech-language pathology services under the IDEA.

stakeholder   An individual or group that has a personal, professional, political, economic, or philosophical interest in an issue or event is a stakeholder in that issue or event. An individual or organization that is a stakeholder has the right and responsibility to participate in decisions or policies made regarding an issue or event.

Student Education and Occupation Plan (SEOP) See Individual Academic-Career Plan.

Supplemental Security Income (SSI) This program is the one most often accessed by students with disabilities exiting high school. The Supplemental Security Income program provides cash assistance to the elderly and individuals with disabilities (including children under age 18) who have limited income and resources. The program requires a financial needs test. SSI cash benefits are determined on a flexible scale based on "countable income." As wages increase, cash benefits decrease. Under Section 1619b, when the cash benefit reaches zero, recipients continue on the Social Security rolls, allowing them to continue working and still keep their Medicaid benefits. Medicaid benefits often continue as long as wages fall below the established threshold amount for earnings.

supported employment Supported employment is a work-based learning program typically used with individuals with more significant disabilities. The focus of supported employment is on placement in integrated jobs in the community, with wages and benefits commensurate with those of nondisabled coworkers. The consumer works with the service provider to identify and develop the supports needed to perform the duties of the job and participate in the other activities of the workplace.

task analysis The process of breaking down learning tasks into the smallest elements in the proper sequence. The resulting instruction involves systematically teaching specific elements in sequence.

transition councils Transition councils or teams are representative groups of persons at the local level who organize to promote, develop, maintain, and improve secondary special education, transition planning, transition services, and adult services for individuals with disabilities who move from school settings to adult living. The councils or teams are comprised of

persons with disabilities, their families, school personnel, adult service agency personnel, and members of the community who can contribute to the mission of the council.

transportation options Since transportation is key to mobility in a community, transportation options must be considered and planned for in the IEP. Instructional goals may be appropriate for skill training in accessing available transportation options. Related services goals and objectives may be needed to provide a transportation option that does not exist. Long-term planning should be initiated to try to ensure that appropriate transportation options will be available after the student leaves school. Transportation options include the following examples: driving one's own vehicle, taxi service, public transit service, and elderly/disabled transportation services.

transportation services Transportation services may be a related service provided to those students who need special assistance because of their disabilities or the location of the school relative to their homes. Not all identified special education students are eligible to receive special transportation services. For those who are, the school must provide travel to and from school and between schools, provide travel in and around school buildings, and provide specialized equipment, if required, to meet the special transportation needs of students.

vocational/applied technology training Training that may be offered at the secondary or postsecondary level to provide students with specific vocational or technical skills. These programs vary from semiskilled to skilled levels, and include such areas as building trades, industrial trades, printing and graphics production, commercial art, health occupations, cosmetology and barbering, food preparation, office machines, computer programming, marketing and distribution occupations, agriculture and agribusiness, mechanics, and automotive body repair.

work adjustment theory Work adjustment theory provides a conceptual framework that can be used in transition planning. It takes into account (1) work personality, (2) work samples, and (3) work goals.

work experience A program that helps a student acquire desirable job skills, attitudes, and habits and is provided through supervised part-time or full-time employment.

work-study program A method of teaching secondary-level students specific work skills by assigning them to employment in competitive jobs for partial days or sometimes full days. If they are assigned to partial days, the remainder of the day is spent in school (also referred to as *on-the-job training* and *community-based work experience*).

youth apprenticeship programs Youth apprenticeship is defined by the School-to-Work Glossary of Terms (National School-to-Work Office, 1996) as "typically a multi-year program that combines school- and work-based learning in a specific occupational area or occupational cluster and is designed to lead directly into either a related postsecondary program, entry-level job, or registered apprenticeship program. Youth apprenticeships may or may not include financial compensation" (p. 65). Registered apprenticeships are those programs that meet specific federally approved standards designed to safeguard the welfare of apprentices. These programs are registered with the Bureau of Apprenticeship and Training (BAT), U.S. Department of Labor, or one of 27 State Apprenticeship Agencies or Councils approved by BAT. Apprenticeships are relationships between an employer and employee during which the worker, or apprentice, learns an occupation in a structured program sponsored jointly by employers and labor unions or operated by employers and employee associations.

REFERENCES

Affleck, J. Q., Edgar, E., Levine, P., & Kortering, L. (1990). Postschool status of students classified as mildly mentally retarded, learning disabled, or nonhandicapped: Does it get better with time? *Education and Training in Mental Retardation, 25,* 315–324.

Agran, M., Snow, K., & Swaner, J. (1999). A survey of secondary level teachers' opinions on community-based instruction and inclusive education. *Journal of the Association for Persons with Severe Handicaps, 24*(1), 58–62.

Akan, G. E., & Grilo, C. M. (1995). Sociocultural influences on eating attitudes and behaviors, body image and psychological functioning: A comparison of African-American, Asian-American, and Caucasian college women. *International Journal of Eating Disorders, 18,* 181–187.

Albright, L., & Cobb, R. B. (1988a). *Assessment of students with handicaps in vocational education: A curriculum-based approach.* Alexandria, VA: American Vocational Association.

Albright, L., & Cobb, R. B. (1988b). Curriculum-based vocational assessment: A concept whose time has come. *The Journal of Vocational Special Needs Education, 10,* 13–16.

Allen, J. M. (2001). Counseling special needs students: In D. Sandhu (Ed.), *Elementary school counseling in the new millenium* (pp. 173–181). Alexandria, VA: American Counseling Association.

Allen, J. M. (2004). Career education for special education students. In S. M. Wakefield, H. Sage, D. R. Coy, & T. Palmer (Eds.), *Unfocused kids: Helping students focus on their education and career plans* (pp. 455–467). Greensboro, NC: CAPS Press.

Allen, J. M., & LaTorre, E. (1998). What a school administrator needs to know about the school counselor's role with special education. In C. Dykeman (Ed.), *Maximizing school guidance program effectiveness: A guide for school administrators and program directors* (pp. 117–122). Greensboro, NC: ERIC/CASS Publications.

Allen, S. K., Smith, A. C., Test, D. W., Flowers, C., & Wood, W. M. (2001). The effects of self-directed IEP on student participation in IEP meetings. *Career Development for Exceptional Individuals, 24*(2), 107–120.

Alliance for Technology Access. (1994). *Computer resources for people with disabilities.* Alameda, CA: Hunter House.

Alper, S. (2003). An ecological approach to identifying curriculum content for inclusive settings. In D. L. Ryndak & S. Alper (Eds.), *Curriculum and instruction for students with significant disabilities in inclusive settings* (2nd ed.) (pp. 73–85). Boston: Allyn and Bacon.

Alspaugh, J. W. (1998). Achievement loss associated with the transition to middle school and high school. *Journal of Educational Research, 92,* 20–26.

Alspaugh, J. W., & Harting, R. D. (1995). Transition effects of school grade-level organization on student achievement. *Journal of Research and Development in Education, 28,* 145–149.

American Educational Research Association. (2000). Position statement of the American Educational Research Association concerning high-stakes testing in preK–12 education. *Educational Researcher, 29*(8), 24–25.

American Occupational Therapy Association. (1994). Uniform terminology for occupational therapy. *American Journal of Occupational Therapy, 48,* 1047–1054.

American Physical Therapy Association. (1995). A guide to physical therapist practice. Volume I: A description of patient management. *Physical Therapy, 75,* 709–719.

American Psychiatric Association. (2000). *Diagnostic and statistical manual of mental disorders* (4th ed., text revision). Washington, DC: Author.

American School Counselor Association. (1997). *The national standards for school counseling programs.* Alexandria, VA: ASCA Press.

American School Counselor Association. (2001–2002). The professional school counselor and the special needs student (Position Statement adopted in 1999). In *ASCA membership directory and resource guide: 2001–2002* (pp. 59–60). Gainesville, FL: Naylor Publications.

American Vocational Association. (1998). *The official guide to the Perkins Act of 1998.* Alexandria, VA: Author.

Americans with Disabilities Act of 1990. 42 U.S.C., 12101. (PL101-336).

Anastasi, A. (1976). *Psychological testing* (4th ed.). New York: Macmillan.

Anderson, D., Kleinhammer-Tramill, P. J., Morningstar, M. E., Lehmann, J., Bassett, D. S., Kohler, P., & Wehmeyer, M. (2004). What's happening in personnel preparation in transition? A national survey. *Career Development for Exceptional Individuals, 26*(2), 145–160.

Aries, P. (1962). *Centuries of childhood: A social history of family life.* (R. Baltic, Trans.). New York: Vintage.

Arkansas Rehabilitation Research and Training Center. (1978). *The role of vocational rehabilitation in independent living.* Proceedings of the Fifth Institute on Rehabilitation Issues, Omaha, NE: May 23–25.

Ascher, C. (1994, January). Cooperative education as a strategy for school-to-work transition. *Centerfocus, 3,* 1–4. (ED 365 798).

Asselin, S., Todd-Allen, M., & deFur, S. (1998). Transition coordinators define yourselves. *Teaching Exceptional Children, 30*(3), 11–15.

Association of Higher Education and Disability (AHEAD). (1997, July). *Guidelines for documentation of a learning disability in adolescents and adults.* Columbus, OH: Author.

Austin Independent School District. (1996). *Curriculum design and management manual for guidance curriculum.* Austin, TX: Author.

Bailey, T. R., Hughes, K. L., & Karp, M. M. (2002). What roles can dual enrollment programs play in easing the transition between high school and postsecondary education? *Journal for Vocational Special Needs Education, 24*(2/3), 18–29.

Banks, R., & Renzaglia, A. (1993). Longitudinal vocational programs: A review of current recommended practices for individuals with moderate to severe disabilities. *Journal of Vocational Rehabilitation, 3*(3), 5–16.

Barrie, W., & McDonald, J. (2002). Administrative support for student-led individualized education programs. *Remedial and Special Education, 23,* 116–122.

Bassett, D. S., & Lehmann, J. (2002). *Student-focused conferencing and planning.* Austin, TX: Pro-Ed.

Beakley, B. A., Yoder, S. L., & West, L. L. (2003). *Community-based instruction: A guidebook for teachers.* Arlington, VA: Council for Exceptional Children.

Beisser, S. (1996). Service learning: Developing a curriculum for caring. *Delta Kappa Gamma Bulletin, 62*(2), 15–19.

Bellah, E. (2003). *A new era: Revitalizing special education for children and their families.* Report to the President by the President's Commission on Excellence in Special Education. Washington, DC: U.S. Government Printing Office.

Bellamy, G. T., Peterson, L., & Close, D. (1975). Habilation of the severely and profoundly retarded: Illustrations of competence. *Education and Training of the Mentally Retarded, 10,* 174–186.

Bender, W. N. (2001). *Learning disabilities: Characteristics, identification, and teaching strategies.* Boston: Allyn and Bacon.

Benz, M., Doren, B., & Yovanoff, P. (1998). Crossing the great divide: Predicting productive engagement for young women with disabilities. *Career Development for Exceptional Individuals, 21*(1), 3–16.

Benz, M., & Kochhar, C. A. (1996). School-to-work opportunities for all students: A position statement of the Division on Career Development and Transition. *Career Development for Exceptional Individuals, 19,* 31–48.

Benz, M., & Lindstrom, L. (1997). *Building school-to-work programs: Strategies for youth with special needs.* Austin, TX: Pro-Ed.

Benz, M., Lindstrom, L., Unruh, D., & Waintrup, M. (2004). Sustaining secondary transition programs in local schools. *Remedial and Special Education, 25*(1), 39–50.

Benz, M., Yovanoff, P., & Doren, B. (1997). School-to-work components that predict postschool success for students with and without disabilities. *Exceptional Children, 63,* 151–165.

Bergland, M. M. (1996). Transition from school to adult life: Key to the future. In A. L. Goldberg (Ed.), *Acquired brain injury in childhood and adolescence* (pp. 171–194). Springfield, IL: Charles C. Thomas.

Best, S. J., Heller, K. W., & Bigge, J. L. (2005). *Teaching individuals with physical or multiple disabilities.* Upper Saddle River, NJ: Prentice-Hall.

Black, R., Smith, G., Chang, C., Harding, T., & Stodden, R. A. (2002). Provision of educational supports to students with disabilities in two-year postsecondary programs. *Journal for Vocational Special Needs Education, 24*(2/3), 3–17.

Blackorby, J., & Wagner, M. (1996). Longitudinal postschool outcomes of youth with disabilities: Findings from the National Longitudinal Transition Study. *Exceptional Children, 62,* 399–413.

Blalock, G. (2005). Strategies for collaboration. In E. A. Polloway, J. R. Patton, & L. Serna (Eds.), *Strategies for teaching learners with special needs* (8th ed.). Upper Saddle River, NJ: Pearson Merrill Prentice-Hall.

Blalock, G., & Benz, M. R. (1999). *Using community transition teams to improve transition services.* Austin, TX: Pro-Ed.

Blum, R. W. (1995). Transition to adult health care: Setting the stage. *Journal of Adolescent Health, 17,* 3–5.

Bodner, J., Clark, G. M., & Mellard, D. F. (1987, November). *State graduation policies and program practices related to high school special education programs: A national study. A report from the National Study of High School Programs for Handicapped Youth in Transition.* Lawrence: University of Kansas, Department of Special Education.

Boesel, D., Hudson, L., Deich, S., & Masten, C. (1994). *National Assessment of Vocational Education final report to Congress. Volume II: Participation and quality of vocational education.* Washington, DC: U.S. Department of Education, Office of Educational Research and Improvement.

Boesel, D., & McFarland, L. (1994). *National Assessment of Vocational Education final report to Congress. Volume I: Summary and recommendations.* Washington, DC: U.S. Department of Education, Office of Educational Research and Improvement.

Bolt, S. E., & Thurlow, M. L. (2004). Five of the most frequently allowed testing accommodations in state policy: Synthesis of research. *Remedial and Special Education, 25*(3), 141–152.

Bos, C. S., & Vaughn, S. (2002). *Strategies for teaching students with learning and behavior problems* (5th ed.). Boston: Allyn and Bacon.

Bradley, D. F., King-Sears, M. E., & Tessier-Switlick, D. M. (1997). *Teaching students in inclusive settings: From theory to practice.* Boston: Allyn and Bacon.

Brannan, S. A. (1999). Leisure and recreation. In S. H. deFur & J. R. Patton (Eds.), *Transition and school-based services: Interdisciplinary perspectives for enhancing the transition process* (pp. 273–308). Austin, TX: Pro-Ed.

Braun, K. L. (2001). *Bullying in special education.* Master's thesis, University of Houston–Clear Lake, 1251.

Brendtro, L. K., Brokenleg, M., & Van Bockern, S. (1990). *Reclaiming youth at risk: Our hope for the future.* Bloomington, IN: National Educational Service.

Brinckerhoff, L. C. (1994). Developing effective self-advocacy skills in college-bound students with learning disabilities. *Intervention in School and Clinic, 29,* 229–237.

Brinckerhoff, L. C., McGuire, J., & Shaw, S. F. (2001). *Postsecondary education for students with learning disabilities: A handbook for practitioners* (2nd ed.). Austin, TX: Pro-Ed.

Brinckerhoff, L. C., McGuire, J. M., & Shaw, S. F. (2002). *Postsecondary education and transition for students with learning disabilities* (2nd ed.). Austin, Texas: Pro-Ed.

Brolin, D. E. (1978). *Life centered career education: A competency based approach.* Reston, VA: The Council for Exceptional Children.

Brolin, D. E. (1983). *Life centered career education: A competency based approach* (rev. ed.). Reston, VA: The Council for Exceptional Children.

Brolin, D. E. (1988, March). Personal communication.

Brolin, D. E. (1989). *Life-centered career education: A competency based approach* (3rd ed.). Reston, VA: Council for Exceptional Children.

Brolin, D. E. (1995). *Career education: A functional life skills approach* (3rd ed.). Englewood Cliffs, NJ: Prentice-Hall.

Brolin, D. E. (1997). *Life-centered career education: A competency-based approach* (5th ed.). Reston, VA: Council for Exceptional Children.

Brolin, D. E. (2003). *Life-centered career education* (revised). Arlington, VA: Council for Exceptional Children.

Brolin, D. E. (2004). *Life centered career education curriculum* (revised ed.). Arlington, VA: Council for Exceptional Children.

Brolin, D. E., & DAlonzo, B. J. (1979). Critical issues in career education for handicapped students. *Exceptional Children, 45,* 246–253.

Brolin, D. E., & Gysbers, N. C. (1989). Career education for students with disabilities. *Journal of Counseling and Development, 68,* 155–159.

Brolin, D. E., & Kokaska, C. J. (1979). *Career education for handicapped children and youth.* Columbus, OH: Charles E. Merrill.

Brolin, D. E., & Kolstoe, O. P. (1978). *The career and vocational development of handicapped learners.* The ERIC Clearinghouse on Adult, Career and Vocational Education, Ohio State University.

Brolin, D. E., & Loyd, R. J. (2004). *Career development and transition services: A functional life skill approach* (4th ed.). Upper Saddle River, NJ: Pearson Merrill Prentice-Hall.

Brolin, D. E., & Thomas, B. (Ed.). (1971). *Preparing teachers for secondary level educable mentally retarded: A new model.* Final report. University of Wisconsin-Stout, Menomonie.

Browder, D. M. (2001). *Curriculum and assessment for students with moderate and severe disabilities.* New York: Guilford Press.

Browder, D. M., Fallin, K., Davis, S., & Karvonen, M. (2003). Consideration of what may influence student outcomes on alternate assessment. *Education and Training in Developmental Disabilities, 38*(3), 255–270.

Brown, C. D., McDaniel, R., & Couch, R. (1994). *Vocational evaluation systems and software: A consumers guide.* Menomonie, WI: Rehabilitation Resource, Stout Vocational Rehabilitation Institute.

Brown, C. H. (2000). A comparison of selected outcomes of secondary Tech Prep participants and non-participants in Texas. *Journal of Vocational Education Research, 25*(3), 273–295.

Brown, L., Branston, M. B., Hamre–Nietupski, S., Pumpian, I., Certo, N., & Gruenewald, L. (1979). A strategy for developing chronological age-appropriate and functional curricular content for severely handicapped adolescents and young adults. *Journal of Special Education, 13,* 81–90.

Browning, P. (1997). *Transition in action for youth and young adults with disabilities.* Montgomery, AL: Wells Printing.

Bruder, M. B., & Walker, L. (1990). Discharge planning: Hospital to home transition for infants. *Topics in Early Childhood Special Education, 9,* 26–42.

Brunstein, M. (1998). *Analysis of 1998 Perkins Act.* October 20, 1998. www.vocserve.berkeley. edu/VOCNET.html.

Bryant, D. P., & Bryant, B. R. (2003). *Assistive technology for people with disabilities.* Boston: Allyn and Bacon.

Bryant, D. P., Patton, J. R., & Vaughn, S. (2000). *Step-by-step guide for including students with disabilities in state and districtwide assessments.* Austin, TX: Pro-Ed.

Bullis, M., & Fredericks, H. D. (2002). *Vocational and transition services for adolescents with emotional and behavioral disorders: Strategies and best practices.* Champaign, IL: Research Press.

Busch, T. W., & Espin, C. A. (2003). Using curriculum-based measurement to prevent failure and assess learning in the content areas. *Assessment for Effective Intervention, 28*(3&4), 49–58.

Butler, A. J., & Browning, P. L. (1974). Predictive studies on rehabilitation outcomes with the retarded. In P. L. Browning (Ed.), *Mental retardation: Rehabilitation and counseling* (pp. 198–227). Springfield, IL: Charles C. Thomas.

Butterworth, J., Hagner, D., Helm, D. T., & Whelley, T. A. (2000). Workplace culture, social interactions, and supports for transitioning-age young adults. *Mental Retardation, 38,* 342–353.

Butterworth, J., Hagner, D., Kiernan, W., & Schalock, R. (1996). Natural supports in the workplace: Defining an agenda for research and practice. *Journal of the Association for Persons with Severe Handicaps, 21*(3), 103–113.

Butterworth, J., Whitney–Thomas, J., & Shaw, D. (1997). The changing role of community based instruction: Strategies for facilitating workplace supports. *Journal of Vocational Rehabilitation, 8,* 9–20.

Carey, K. (1995). *A national study of the role and function of the school psychologist.* Paper presented at the annual meeting of the National Association of School Psychologists, Chicago.

Carl D. Perkins Vocational and Applied Technology Education Act of 1990, Public Law 101-392, 20 U.S.C., 2301.

Carl D. Perkins Vocational Education Act of 1984, Public Law 98-524, 98 STAT., 24345-2491.

Carnegie Foundation for the Advancement of Teaching. (1909, October). *Fourth annual report of the president and of the treasurer.* New York: Author.

Carnevale, A. P., & Desrochers, D. M. (2002). The missing middle economy: Aligning education and the knowledge economy. *Journal for Vocational Special Needs Education, 25*(1), 3–23.

Carter, S. L. (1998). *Civility: Manners, morals, and the etiquette of democracy.* New York: Basic Books.

Center on Education Policy. (2003). *State high school exit exams put to the test.* Washington, DC: Author. Retrieved May 1, 2004 from www.cep-dc.org.

Chaffin, J. D. (1968). *A community transition program for the mentally retarded.* Final Report RII NHO 1731, Parsons State Hospital and Training Center, Parsons, Kansas (supported in part by Social Rehabilitation Services, U.S. Department of Health, Education, and Welfare).

Chaffin, J. D., Spellman, C. R., Regan, C. E., & Davison, R. (1971). Two follow-up studies of former educable mentally retarded students from the Kansas work study project. *Exceptional Children, 37,* 733–738.

Chamberlain, M. A. (1988). Employers' rankings of factors judged critical to job success for individuals with severe disabilities. *Career Development for Exceptional Individuals, 11,* 141–147.

Chambers, A. C. (1997). *Has technology been considered? A guide for IEP teams.* Albuquerque, NM: Council of Administrators of Special Education and the Technology and Media Divisions of the Council for Exceptional Children, CASE/TAMS Assistive Technology and Practice Group.

Clark, G. M. (1996). *STUDY Project (Systematic Transition for Utah's Disabled Youth): Utah guidelines for appropriate practices in providing transition services and programs.* Salt Lake City: State Office of Education.

Clark, G. M. (1974). Career education for the mildly handicapped. *Focus on Exceptional Children, 5*(9), 1–10.

Clark, G. M. (1979). *Career education for the handicapped child in the elementary classroom.* Denver: Love Publishing.

Clark, G. M. (1980). Career preparation for handicapped adolescents: A matter of appropriate education. *Exceptional Education Quarterly, 1*(2), 11–17.

Clark, G. M. (1994). Is a functional curriculum approach compatible with an inclusive education model? *Teaching Exceptional Children, 26*, 36–39.

Clark, G. M. (1998). *Assessment for transitions planning.* Austin, TX: Pro-Ed.

Clark, G. M. (2005). Transition planning assessment for secondary-level students with learning disabilities. In G. Blalock, P. Kohler, & J. Patton (Eds.), *Transition and students with learning disabilities* (2nd ed.). Austin, TX: Pro-Ed.

Clark, G. M., Carlson, B. C., Fisher, S., Cook, I. D., & DAlonzo, B. J. (1991). Career development for students with disabilities in elementary schools: A position statement of the Division on Career Development. *Career Development for Exceptional Individuals, 14*, 109–120.

Clark, G. M., Field, S., Patton, J. R., Brolin, D. E., & Sitlington, P. L. (1994). Life skills instruction: A necessary component for all students with disabilities. A position statement of the Division on Career Development and Transition. *Career Development for Exceptional Individuals, 17*, 125–134.

Clark, G. M., & Knowlton, H. E. (1988). A closer look at transition for the 1990s: A response to Rusch and Menchetti. *Exceptional Children, 54*, 365–367.

Clark, G. M., Knowlton, H. E., & Dorsey, D. (1989). Special education for high school students with educational handicaps in a rural setting: A Vermont case study. In H. E. Knowlton & G. M. Clark (Eds.), *National study of high school special education programs for handicapped youth in transition: Volume 1, Qualitative component.* Lawrence: University of Kansas, Department of Special Education.

Clark, G. M., & Kolstoe, O. P. (1990). *Career development and transition education for adolescents with disabilities.* Boston: Allyn and Bacon.

Clark, G. M., & Kolstoe, O. P. (1995). *Career development and transition education for adolescents with disabilities* (2nd ed.). Boston: Allyn and Bacon.

Clark, G. M., & Oliverson, B. S. (1973). Education of secondary personnel: Assumptions and preliminary data. *Exceptional Children, 39*, 541–546.

Clark, G. M., & Patton, J. R. (1997). *Transition Planning Inventory.* Austin, TX: Pro-Ed.

Clark, G. M., Patton, J. R., & Moulton, L. R. (2000). *Informal assessments for transition planning.* Austin, TX: Pro-Ed.

Clark, S. G. (2000). The IEP process as a tool for collaboration. *Teaching Exceptional Children, 33*, 56–66.

Cobb, R. B., & Larkin, D. (1985, March). Assessment and placement of handicapped pupils into secondary vocational education programs. *Focus on Exceptional Children, 17*(7), 1–14.

Cobb, R. B., & Neubert, D. A. (1998). Vocational education: Emerging vocationalism. In F. Rusch & J. Chadsey (Eds.), *Beyond high school: Transition from school to work* (pp. 101–126). Boston: Wadsworth.

Combes, B., & Durodoye, B. (2002). Transitioning African American high school students with disabilities. In F. E. Obiakor & B. A. Ford (Eds.), *Creating successful learning environments for African American learners with exceptionalities.* Thousand Oaks, CA: Corwin Press.

Commission on Certification of Work Adjustment and Vocational Evaluation Specialists. (1996). *Standards and procedures manual for certification in vocational evaluation.* Washington, DC: Author.

Comprehensive Employment and Training Act of 1973, Public Law 93-203, U.S.C. 29 874, 918, 919 (1976).

Comprehensive Employment and Training Act Amendments of 1978, Public Law 95-524, U.S.C. 29 893, 899, 906, 942, 991: Supplement V (1981).

Constable, R. (1992). The new reform and the school social worker. *Social Work in Education, 14*(2), 106–113.

Conway, C. (1984). *Vocational education and handicapped students. Programs for the handicapped: Clearinghouse on the handicapped.* Washington, DC: Office of Special Education and Rehabilitation Services.

Council for Exceptional Children. (1998). *What every special educator must know: The international standards for the preparation and certifi-*

cation of special education teachers (3rd ed.). Reston, VA: Author.

Council for Exceptional Children. (2003). *Discover IDEA—Supporting achievement for children with disabilities: An IDEA practices resource guide.* Arlington, VA: Author.

Cox, A. W., & Sawin, K. J. (1999). School nursing. In S. H. deFur & J. R. Patton (Eds.), *Transition and school-based services: Interdisciplinary perspectives for enhancing the transition process* (pp. 167–205). Austin, TX: Pro-Ed.

Cozzens, G., Dowdy, C., & Smith, T. E. C. (1999). *Adult agencies: Linkages for adolescents in transition.* Austin, TX: Pro-Ed.

Cronin, M. E. (1996). Life skills curricula for students with learning disabilities: A review of the literature. *Journal of Learning Disabilities, 29,* 53–68.

Cronin, M. E., Lord, D. C., & Wendling, K. (1991). Learning for life: The life skills curriculum. *Intervention in School and Clinic, 26,* 306–311.

Cronin, M. E., & Patton, J. R. (1993). *Life skills instruction for all students with special needs: A practical guide for integrating real-life content into the curriculum.* Austin, TX: Pro-Ed.

Cronin, M. E., Patton, J. R., & Wood, S. J. (2005). *Life skills instruction: A practical guide for integrating real-life content into the curriculum* (2nd ed.). Austin, TX: Pro-Ed.

Cuningham, C. A., & Billingsley, M. (2003). *Curriculum webs: A practical guide to weaving the web into teaching and learning.* Boston: Allyn and Bacon.

Dahir, C. A. (2004). School counseling programs: Supporting a nation of learners. In S. M. Wakefield, H. Sage, D. R. Coy, & T. Palmer (Eds.), *Unfocused kids: Helping students focus on their education and career plans* (pp. 143–154). Greensboro, NC: CAPS Press.

Dahir, C. A., Sheldon, C. B., & Valiga, M. J. (1998). *Vision into action: Implementing the national standards for school counseling programs.* Alexandria, VA: American School Counselor Association.

Dake, J. A. (2003). Teacher perceptions and practice regarding school bullying prevention. *Journal of School Health, 73,* 347–355.

Dalaker, J. (1999). U.S. Bureau of the Census, Current population reports, Series P, 60–207, *Poverty in the United States: 1998.* Washington, DC: U.S. Government Printing Office.

D'Amico, R., & Maxwell, N. L. (1995). The continuing significance of race in minority male joblessness. *Social Forces, 73,* 969–991.

Darrow, M. A. (1990). *A Delphi approach to cross-validation of Halpern's general transition follow-along model for persons with disabilities.* Doctoral dissertation, University of Kansas, Lawrence.

Davis v. Southeastern Community College, 442 U.S. 397 (1979).

Day, S. L., & Edwards, B. J. (1996). Assistive technology for postsecondary students with learning disabilities. *Journal of Learning Disabilities, 29,* 486–492, 503.

deBettencourt, L.U. (2002). Understanding the differences between IDEA and Section 504. *Teaching Exceptional Children, 34*(3), 16–23.

deFur, S. H. (1997). Collaboration as a prevention tool for youth with disabilities. *Preventing School Failure, 41,* 173–184.

deFur, S. H. (2002). Education reform, high-stakes assessment, and students with disabilities. *Remedial and Special Education, 23,* 203–211.

deFur, S. H., & Patton, J. R. (1999). *Transition and school-based services: Interdisciplinary perspectives for enhancing the transition process.* Austin, TX: Pro-Ed.

deFur, S. H., Todd–Allen, M., & Getzel, E. E. (2001). Parent participation in the transition planning process. *Career Development for Exceptional Individuals, 24,* 19–36.

DeJong, G. (1980). The historical and current reality of independent living: Implications for administrative planning. In S. J. Sigman (Ed.), *Policy planning and development in independent living* (pp. 2–6). Proceedings of a Region V Workshop presented by the University Center for International Rehabilitation/USA, Michigan State University, East Lansing.

DeJong, G. (1983). Defining and implementing the independent living concept. In N. M. Crewe, I. K. Zola, & Associates (Eds.), *Independent living for physically disabled people* (pp. 4–27). San Francisco: Jossey-Bass.

Department of Education. (1992). *Federal Register 34 CFR Parts 300 & 301: Assistance to States for the Education of the Children with Disabilities Program and Preschool Grants for Children with Disabilities; Final Rule, 57*(189), 44804–44815.

Department of Education. (1997). *Federal Register 34 CFR Part 361 et al., The State Vocational Rehabilitation Services Program; Final Rule, 62*(28), 6308–6363.

Department of Education. (1999). *Federal Register 34 CFR Parts 300 and 303 et al.: Assistance to States for the Education of Children with Disabilities and the Early Intervention Program for Infants and*

Toddlers with Disabilities; Final Regulations, 64(48), 12420–12670.

Descoeudres, A. (1928). *The education of mentally defective children* (E. F. Row, Trans.). Boston: D. C. Heath.

Deshler, D. D., Ellis, E. S., & Lenz, B. K. (1996). *Teaching adolescents with learning disabilities: Strategies and methods.* Denver: Love Publishing.

Dever, R. B. (1988). *Community living skills: A taxonomy.* Washington, DC: American Association on Mental Retardation.

Dickinson, T. S. (Ed.). (2001). *Reinventing the middle school.* New York: Routledge Falmer.

Dinger, J. C. (1961). Post school adjustment of former educable retarded pupils. *Exceptional Children, 27,* 353–360.

Disability Statistics Abstract. (1991, December). Disability Statistics Program, School of Nursing, University of California, San Francisco.

Dole, R. L. (2004). Collaborating successfully with your school's physical therapist. *Teaching Exceptional Children, 36*(5), 28–35.

Dowd, L. R. (Ed.). (1993). *Glossary of terminology for vocational assessment, evaluation and work adjustment.* Menomonie, WI: Rehabilitation Resource, Stout Vocational Rehabilitation Institute.

Doyle, M. B. (2003). "We want to go to college too": Supporting students with significant disabilities in higher education. In D. L. Ryndak & S. Alper (Eds.), *Curriculum and instruction for students with significant disabilities in inclusive settings* (2nd ed). Boston: Allyn and Bacon.

DuChossois, G., & Michaels, C. (1994). Postsecondary education. In C. A. Michaels (Ed.), *Transition strategies for persons with learning disabilities* (pp. 79–117). San Diego: Singular.

Dugdale, R. L. (1910). *The Jukes: A study of crime, pauperism, disease, and heredity.* New York: Putnam.

Dukes, L. L. (2001). The process: Development of AHEAD program standards. *Journal of Postsecondary Education and Disability, 14*(2), 62–80.

Dukes, L. L., & Shaw, S. F. (1998). Not just children anymore: Personnel preparation regarding postsecondary education for adults with disabilities. *Teacher Education and Special Education, 21,* 205–213.

Dukes, L. L., & Shaw, S. F. (1999). Postsecondary disability personnel: Professional standards and staff development. *Journal of Developmental Education, 23,* 26–31.

Duncan, J. (1943). *The education of the ordinary child.* New York: Ronald Press.

Dunn, L. M. (1968). Special education for the mildly retarded: Is much of it justifiable? *Exceptional Children, 35,* 5–22.

Durlak, C. M., Rose, E., & Bursuck, W. D. (1994). Preparing high school students with learning disabilities for the transition to postsecondary education: Teaching the skills of self-determination. *Journal of Learning Disabilities, 27,* 51–59.

Dymond, S. K. (2004). Community participation. In P. Wehman & J. Kregel (Eds.), *Functional curriculum for elementary, middle, and secondary age students with special needs* (2nd ed.) (pp. 259–292). Austin, TX: Pro-Ed.

Eanes School District. (2004). "Eanespirational" Program of studies. Online resource: http://ee. eanes.k12.tx.us/eanespir.htm#Developing %20Self–Responsibility.

Eddy, J. M., Reid, J. B., & Curry, V. (2002). The etiology of youth antisocial behavior, delinquency, and violence and a public health approach to prevention. In M. R. Shinn, H. M. Walker, & G. Stoner (Eds.), *Interventions for academic and behavior problems II: Preventive and remedial approaches* (pp. 27–51). Bethesda, MD: National Association for School Psychologists.

Edgar, E. (1988, September). Employment as an outcome for mildly handicapped students: Current status and future directions. *Focus on Exceptional Children, 2*(1), 1–8.

Edgar, E. (1992). Secondary options for students with mild intellectual disabilities: Facing the issue of tracking. *Education and Training in Mental Retardation, 27,* 101–111.

Edgar, E., Parker., W., Siegel., S., & Johnson, E. (1993). *Developing curricula for alternative options: The belief academy.* Paper presented at the Blazing New Trails Specific Learning Disabilities State of Minnesota Conference, Brainerd, MN. Seattle: University of Washington.

Education Commission of the States. (2001). *Postsecondary options: Dual/concurrent enrollment.* Retrieved July 12, 2004, from www.ecs.org.

Education for All Handicapped Children Act of 1975, Public Law 94-142, 20 U.S.C. 1410(i), 1412(2),(A), 1414(a)(i)(C), (1982).

Education for the Handicapped Act Amendments of 1983, Public Law 98-199, 97 STAT., 1357– 1377.

Educational Testing Service. (1999). *Policy statement for documentation of a learning disability in adolescents and adults.* Retrieved June 1, 2003, from www.ets.org/disability/ldpolicy.html.

Elkind, D. (1981). *The hurried child: Growing up too fast too soon.* Reading, MA: Addison-Wesley.

Elksnin, N., & Elksnin, L. K. (1998). *Teaching occupational social skills.* Austin, TX: Pro-Ed.

Elliott, S. N., Braden, J. P., & White, J. L. (2001). *Assessing one and all: Educational accountability for students with disabilities.* Arlington, VA: Council for Exceptional Children.

Elliott, S. N., Kratochwill, T. R., & Schulte, A. G. (1998). The assessment accommodation checklist: Who, what, where, when, why, and how. *Teaching Exceptional Children, 31*(2), 10–14.

Elliott, S. N., & Marquart, A. M. (2004). Extended time as a testing accommodation: Its effects and perceived consequences. *Exceptional Children, 70*(3), 349–367.

Ellis, E., Deshler, D., Lenz, K., Schumaker, J., & Clark, F. (1991). An instructional model for teaching learning strategies. *Focus on Exceptional Children, 23,* 1–23.

Elswit, L. S., Geetter, E., & Goldberg, J. A. (1999). Between passion and policy: Litigating the Guckenberger Case. *Journal of Learning Disabilities, 32,* 292–303, 319.

Encyclopedia of Education. (1971). Public high school, United States. *Encyclopedia of Education* (Vol. 7). New York: Macmillan.

English, K. M. (1997). *Self advocacy for students who are deaf or hard of hearing.* Austin, TX: Pro-Ed.

Epstein, J. S. (2001). *School, family, and community partnerships: Preparing educators and improving schools.* Baltimore: Center on School, Family, and Community Partnerships, John Hopkins University, Westview Press (readings 2.1, 2.2).

Erikson, E. H. (1963). *Childhood and society* (2nd ed.). New York: Norton.

Erin, J. N., & Wolffe, K. E. (1999). *Transition issues related to students with visual disabilities.* Austin, TX: Pro-Ed.

Espelage, D. L., & Swearer, M. (2003). Research on school bullying and victimization: What have we learned and where do we go from here? *The School Psychology Review, 32*(3), 365–383.

Espin, C. A., Busch, T. W., Shin, J., & Kruschwitz, R. (2001). Curriculum-based measures in the content areas: Validity of vocabulary-matching as an indicator of performance in a social studies classroom. *Learning Disabilities Research and Practice, 16,* 142–151.

Espin, C. A., & Foegen, A. (1996). Validity of general outcome measures for predicting secondary students' performance on content-area tasks. *Exceptional Children, 62*(6), 497–514.

Espin, C. A., Skare, S., Shin, J., Deno, S. L., Robinson, S., & Brenner, B. (2000). Identifying indicators of growth in written expression for middle-school students. *Journal of Special Education, 34,* 140–153.

Espin, C. A., & Tindal, G. (1998). Curriculum-based measurement for secondary students. In M. R. Shinn (Ed.), *Advanced applications of curriculum-based measurement.* New York: Guilford Press.

Evers, R. B., & Elksnin, N. (1998). *Working with students with disabilities in vocational-technical settings.* Austin, TX: Pro-Ed.

Everson, J., & Reid, D. (1999). *Person-centered planning and outcome management: Maximizing organizational effectiveness in supporting quality lifestyle among people with disabilities.* Morganton, NC: Habilitative Management Consultants.

Fabish, D. (2004). Successful transitions for high school special education students from school to the workplace (emphasis on learning disabled, attention deficit, and behavior disordered youth). In S. M. Wakefield, H. Sage, D. R. Coy, & T. Palmer (Eds.), *Unfocused kids: Helping students focus on their education and career plans* (pp. 469–477). Greensboro, NC: CAPS Press.

Falvey, M. A. (1989). *Community-based curriculum: Instructional strategies for students with severe handicaps* (2nd ed.). Baltimore: Paul H. Brookes.

Family Educational Rights and Privacy Act (FERPA). PL 93-380.

Federal Register (August 19, 1991). p. 41272.

Federal Register (October 22, 1997). p. 55028.

Federal Register (June 26, 2002). pp. 43154–43190.

Fein, J. (1996). *Moving on: How to make the transition from college to the real world.* New York: Plume/Penguin Books.

Field, S., & Hoffman, A. (1994). Development of a model for self-determination. *Career Development for Exceptional Individuals, 17,* 159–169.

Field, S., & Hoffman, A. (1996). *Steps to self-determination: A curriculum to help adolescents learn to achieve their goals.* Austin, TX: Pro-Ed.

Field, S., Hoffman, A., & Spezia, S. (1998). *Self-determination strategies for adolescents in transition.* Austin, TX: Pro-Ed.

Field, S., Martin, J., Miller, R., Ward, M., & Wehmeyer, M. (1998a). *A practical guide for teaching self-determination.* Reston, VA: The Council for Exceptional Children.

Field, S., Martin, J., Miller, R., Ward, M., & Wehmeyer, M. (1998b). Self-determination for persons with disabilities: A position statement of the Division on Career Development and Transition. *Career Development for Exceptional Individuals, 21,* 113–128.

Findley, W. (1967). *A follow-up of the financial assets and liabilities of mentally retarded youth as related to the cost of vocational training in the public schools.* Unpublished doctoral dissertation, University of Northern Colorado.

Fisher, S. K. (1999). Assistive technology. In S. H. deFur & J. R. Patton (Eds.), *Transition and school-based services: Interdisciplinary perspectives for enhancing the transition process* (pp. 309–385). Austin, TX: Pro-Ed.

Fisher, S. K., Clark, G. M., & Patton, J. R. (2004). *Understanding occupational vocabulary.* Austin, TX: Pro-Ed.

Fisher, S. K., & Gardner, J. E. (1999). Introduction to technology in transition. *Career Development for Exceptional Individuals, 22,* 131–152.

Flannery, K. B., Newton, S., Horner, R. H., Slovic, R., Blumberg, R., & Ard, W. R. (2000). The impact of person centered planning on the content and organization of individual supports. *Career Development for Exceptional Individuals, 23*(2), 123–137.

Flexer, R. W., Simmons, T. J., Luft, P., & Baer, R. M. (2005). *Transition planning for secondary students with disabilities* (2nd ed.). Upper Saddle River, NJ: Pearson.

Frank, A. R., & Sitlington, P. L. (1993). Graduates with mental disabilities—The story three years later. *Education and Training in Mental Retardation, 27,* 75–80.

Frank, A. R., & Sitlington, P. L. (1997). Young adults with behavioral disorders—Before and after IDEA. *Behavioral Disorders, 23,* 40–56.

Frank, A. R., & Sitlington, P. L. (1998). *Young adults with mental disabilities—Does transition planning make a difference?* Manuscript submitted for publication.

Frank, A. R., Sitlington, P. L., & Carson, R. (1991). Transition of adolescents with behavioral disorders —Is it successful? *Behavioral Disorders, 16,* 180–191.

Frank, K., & Wade, P. (1993). Disabled student services in postsecondary education: Who's responsible for what? *Journal of College Student Development, 34,* 26–30.

Freedman, M. (1997). *Individuals with Disabilities Education Law Report: Special Report No. 18: Testing, grading and granting diplomas to special education students.* Horsham, PA: LRP Publications.

Friend, M., & Bursuck, W. D. (2002). *Including students with special needs: A practical guide for classroom teachers* (3rd ed.). Boston: Allyn and Bacon.

Friend, M., & Cook, L. (2003). *Interactions: Collaboration skills for school professionals* (4th ed.). Boston: Allyn and Bacon.

Fuchs, L. S., Fuchs, A., Eaton, S. B., Hamlett, C., & Karns, K. (2000). Supplementing teacher judgments about test accommodations with objective data sources. *School Psychology Review, 29*(1), 65–85.

Gajar, A. (1998). Postsecondary education. In F. Rusch & J. Chadsey (Eds.), *Beyond high school: Transition from school to work* (pp. 383–405). Belmont, CA: Wadsworth.

Gajar, A., Goodman, L., & McAfee, J. (1993). *Secondary schools and beyond: Transition of individuals with mild disabilities.* New York: Macmillan.

Garcia, L. A., & Menchetti, B. M. (2003). The adult lifestyles planning cycle: A continual process for planning personally satisfying adult lifestyles. In D. L. Ryndak & S. Alper (Eds.), *Curriculum and instruction for students with significant disabilities in inclusive settings* (2nd ed.) (pp. 277–306). Boston: Allyn and Bacon.

Garfinkle, L. (1995). *Legal issues in transitioning students.* Horsham, PA: LRP Publications.

Garnett, K. (1984). Some of the problems children encounter in learning a school's hidden curriculum. *Journal of Reading, Writing, and Learning Disabilities, 1,* 5–10.

Garriott, P. P., Wandry, D., & Snyder, L. (2000). Teachers as parents, parents as children: What's wrong with this picture? [Electronic version]. *Preventing School Failure, 45,* 37–50.

Gartin, B. C., Rumrill, P., & Serebreni, R. (1996). The higher education transition model: Guidelines for facilitating college transition among college-bound students with disabilities. *Teaching Exceptional Children, 29*(1), 30–33.

Gaumer, A. S., Morningstar, M. E., & Clark, G. M. (2004). Status of community-based transition programs: A national database. *Career Development for Exceptional Individuals, 27*(2), 131–149.

Geenen, S., Powers, L. E., & Lopez–Vasquez, A. (2001). Multicultural aspects of parent involvement in transition planning. *Exceptional Children, 67,* 265–281.

Gersten, R., Baker, S., & Lloyd, J. W. (2000). Designing high-quality research in special education: Group experimental design. *Journal of Special Education, 34*(1), 2–18.

Getzel, E. E., Stodden, R. A., & Briel, R. W. (2001). Pursuing postsecondary education opportunities for individuals with disabilities. In P. Wehman (Ed.), *Transition strategies for young people with disabilities* (3rd ed.) (pp. 247–259). Baltimore: Paul H. Brookes.

Gillet, P. (1981). Career education for exceptional children and youth. *Of work and worth: Career education for the handicapped.* Salt Lake City: Olympus Publishing.

Gilson, S. F. (1996). Students with disabilities: An increasing voice and presence on college campuses. *Journal of Vocational Rehabilitation, 6,* 263–272.

Ginzberg, E., Ginsburg, S. W., Axelrad, S., & Herma, J. L. (1951). *Occupational choice.* New York: Columbia University Press.

Goals 2000: Educate America Act, 20 U.S.C. § 5801 (1994).

Goddard, H. H. (1912). *The Kallikak family.* New York: Macmillan.

Gold, M. (1972). Stimulus factors in skill training of the retarded on a complex assembly task: Acquisition, transfer, and retention. *American Journal of Mental Deficiency, 76,* 517–526.

Gold, M. (1973). Research on the vocational habilitation of the retarded: The present, the future. In N. R. Ellis (Ed.), *International review of research in mental retardation* (Vol. 6, pp. 97–147). New York: Academic Press.

Gold, M. (1980). *Try another way: Training manual.* Champaign, IL: Research Press.

Goldhammer, K. A., & Taylor, R. E. (1972). Career education perspectives. In K. A. Goldhammer & R. E. Taylor (Eds.), *Career education: Perspective and promise* (pp. 1–12). Columbus, OH: Charles E. Merrill.

Gray, K. (2001). The role of career and technical education in the American high school: A student centered analysis. *Journal for Vocational Special Needs Education, 24*(1), 15–25.

Greenbaum, B., Graham, S., & Scales, W. (1995). Adults with learning disabilities: Educational and social experiences. *Exceptional Children, 61,* 460–471.

Greene, G., & Albright, L. (1995). "Best practices" in transition services: Do they exist? *Career Development for Exceptional Individuals, 16,* 1–18.

Greenspan, S., Switzky, H. N., & Granfield, J. M. (1996). Everyday intelligence and adaptive behavior: A theoretical framework. In J. W. Jacobson & J. A. Mulick (Eds.), *Manual of diagnostic and professional practice in mental retarda-* *tion* (pp. 127–135). Washington, DC: American Psychological Association.

Gregg, N., & Scott, S. S. (2000). Definition and documentation: Theory, measurement, and the courts. *Journal of Learning Disabilities, 22*(1), 5–13.

Gregory, G. H., & Chapman, C. (2002). *Differentiated instructional strategies: One size doesn't fit all.* Thousand Oaks, CA: Corwin Press.

Griffith, J. (2001). An approach to evaluating school-to-work initiatives: Post-secondary activities of high school graduates of work-based learning. *Journal of Vocational Education and Training, 53*(1), 37–60.

Grigal, M., & Neubert, D. A. (2004). Parents' in-school values and post-school expectations for transition-aged youth with disabilities. *Career Development for Exceptional Individuals, 27*(1), 65–85.

Grigal, M., Neubert, D. A., & Moon, M. S. (2001). Public school programs for students with significant disabilities in post-secondary settings. *Education and Training in Mental Retardation and Developmental Disabilities, 30*(3), 244–254.

Grigal, M., Neubert, D. A., & Moon, M. S. (in press). *Transition services for students with significant disabilities in community and college settings.* Austin, TX: Pro-Ed.

Grigal, M., Test, D., Beattie, J., & Wood, W. (1997). An evaluation of transition components of individualized education programs. *Exceptional Children, 63,* 357–372.

Guckenberger v. Boston University. 974 F. Supp. 106 (D. Mass. 1997).

Gysbers, N. C., & Henderson, P. (2001). Comprehensive guidance and counseling programs: A rich history and a bright future. *Professional School Counseling, 4,* 236–245.

Hagerty, G., Halloran, W., & Taymans, J. (1981). Federal perspectives on the preparation of vocational personnel to serve handicapped students. In C. A. MacArthur & C. Allen (Eds.), *Vocational education for the handicapped: Models for preparing personnel* (pp. 5–22). Urbana-Champaign, IL: Leadership Training.

Hagner, D., Helm, D. T., & Butterworth, J. (1996). "This is your meeting": A qualitative study of person-centered planning. *Mental Retardation, 34*(3), 159–171.

Hallahan, D. P., & Kauffman, J. (2004). *Exceptional children: Introduction to exceptional children* (9th ed.). Boston: Allyn and Bacon.

Hallahan, D. P., Lloyd, J. W., Kauffman, J. M., Weiss, M., & Martinez, E. A. (2005). *Learning disabili-*

ties: Foundations, characteristics, and effective teaching (3rd ed.). Boston: Allyn and Bacon.

Hallowell, E. M., & Ratey, J. J. (1996). *Answers to distraction.* New York: Bantam Books.

Halpern, A. S. (1985). Transition: A look at the foundations. *Exceptional Children, 51,* 479–486.

Halpern, A. S. (1988). Characteristics of a quality program. In C. Warger & B. Weiner (Eds.), *Secondary special education: A guide to promising public school programs.* Reston, VA: The Council on Exceptional Children.

Halpern, A. S. (1990). A methodological review of follow-up and follow-along studies tracking school leavers from special education. *Career Development for Exceptional Individuals, 13,* 13–28.

Halpern, A. S. (1994). The transition of youth with disabilities to adult life: A position statement of the Division on Career Development and Transition, the Council for Exceptional Children. *Career Development for Exceptional Individuals, 17,* 115–124.

Halpern, A. S., & Benz, M. (1987). A statewide examination of secondary special education students with mild disabilities: Implications for the high school curriculum. *Exceptional Children, 54,* 122–129.

Halpern, A. S., Herr, C. M., Doren, B., & Wolf, N. K. (2000). *Next S.T.E.P.: Student transition and educational planning.* Austin, TX: Pro-Ed.

Halpern, A. S., Yovanoff, P., Doren, B., & Benz, M. R. (1995). Predicting participation in postsecondary education for school leavers with disabilities. *Exceptional Children, 62,* 151–164.

Hamilton, M., & Hamilton, S. (1997). When is work a learning experience? *Phi Delta Kappan, 78*(9), 682–689.

Harris-Bowlsbey, J., Dikel, M. R., & Sampson, J. P. (1998). *The Internet: A tool for career planning.* Columbus, OH: National Career Development.

Hart, D., Pasternack, R. H., Mele–McCarthy, J., Zimbrich, K., & Parker, D. R. (2004). Community college: A pathway to success for youth with learning, cognitive, and intellectual disabilities in secondary settings. *Education and Training in Developmental Disabilities, 39*(1), 54–66.

Hasazi, S., Gordon, L., & Roe, C. (1985). Factors associated with the employment status of handicapped youth exiting high school from 1979 to 1983. *Exceptional Children, 51,* 455–469.

Haslam, H. A., & Valletutti, P. J. (2004). *Medical problems in the classroom: The teacher's role in diagnosis and management.* Austin, TX: Pro-Ed.

Hatzes, N. M., Reiff, H. B., & Bramel, M. H. (2002). The documentation dilemma: Access and accommodations for postsecondary students with learning disabilities. *Assessment for Effective Intervention, 27*(3), 37–52.

Havighurst, R. J. (1953). *Human development and education.* New York: Longmans, Green.

Heacox, D. (2002). *Differentiating instruction in the regular classroom: How to reach and teach all learners, grades 3–12.* Minneapolis, MN: Free Spirit Publishing.

Hegde, M. N. (2001). *Introduction to communicative disorders* (3rd ed.). Austin, TX: Pro-Ed.

Helmke, L. M., Havekost, D. M., Patton, J. R., & Polloway, E. A. (1994). Life skill programming: Development of a life skill science course. *Teaching Exceptional Children, 26*(2), 49–53.

Henderson, C. (Ed.). (1998). *Profile of 1996 college freshmen with disabilities.* Washington, DC: HEATH Resource Center, American Council on Education.

Henderson, C. (Ed.). (2001). *College freshmen with disabilities: A biennial statistical profile.* Washington, DC: American Council on Education.

Heron, T. E., & Harris, K. C. (2001). *The educational consultant: Helping professionals, parents, and students in inclusive classrooms* (4th ed.). Austin, TX: Pro-Ed.

Herr, E. L., Cramer, S. H., & Niles, S. G. (2004). *Career guidance and counseling through the lifespan: Systematic approaches* (6th ed.). Boston: Pearson/Allyn and Bacon.

Hershenson, D. B. (1981). Work adjustment, disability, and the three R's of vocational rehabilitation: A conceptual model. *Rehabilitation Counseling Bulletin, 25,* 91–97.

Hershenson, D. B. (1996). A systems reformulation of a developmental model of work adjustment. *Rehabilitation Counseling Bulletin, 40,* 2–10.

Hester, E. J., & Stone, E. (1984). *Utilization of worksite modification.* Topeka, KS: The Menninger Foundation.

Higgins, E. L., & Zvi, J. C. (1995). Assistive technology for postsecondary students with learning disabilities: From research to practice. *Tools for Remediation, 45,* 123–142.

Hodgkinson, H. L. (1985, June). *All one system: Demographics of education—Kindergarten through graduate school.* Washington, DC: Institute for Educational Leadership, Inc.

Hoover, J. (2004). Teaching study skills to students. In D. D. Hammill & N. Bartel (Eds.), *Teaching students with learning and behavior problems* (7th ed) (pp. 291–324). Austin, TX: Pro-Ed.

Hoover, J., & Patton, J. R. (2005). *Teaching students with learning problems to use study skills: A teacher's guide.* Austin, TX: Pro-Ed.

Hourcade, J. J., & Bauwens, J. (2002). *Cooperative teaching: Rebuilding and sharing the schoolhouse* (2nd ed.). Austin, TX: Pro-Ed.

Hoyt, K. B. (1975). *An introduction to career education.* Policy Paper of the United States Office of Education, DHEW Publications No. (OE) 75–00504. Washington, DC: U.S. Government Printing Office.

Hoyt, K. B. (1977). *A primer for career education.* Washington, DC: U.S. Government Printing Office.

Hughes, C., Kim, H., Hwang, B., Killian, D. J., Fischer, G. M., Brock, M. L., Godshall, J. C., & Houser, B. (1997). Practitioner-validated secondary transition support strategies. *Education and Training in Mental Retardation and Developmental Disabilities, 32,* 201–212.

Hughes, C., Pitkin, S. E., & Lorden, S. W. (1998). Assessing preferences and choices of persons with severe and profound mental retardation. *Education and Training in Mental Retardation and Developmental Disabilities, 33*(4), 299–316.

Hughes, K. L., Bailey, T. R., & Mechur, M. J. (2001). *School-to-work: Making a difference in education. A research report to America.* New York: Institute on Education and the Economy, Columbia University. www.tc.columbia.edu/~iee/PAPERS/Stw.pdf

Hungerford, R. H. (1941). The Detroit plan for the occupational education of the mentally retarded. *American Journal of Mental Deficiency, 46,* 102–108.

Hungerford, R. H. (1943). *Occupational education.* New York: Association for New York City Teachers of Special Education.

Idol, L. (2002). *Creating collaborative and inclusive schools.* Austin, TX: Pro-Ed.

Independent Living Research Utilization Project. (1978, May). *Final draft.* Houston: Texas Institute for Rehabilitation and Research.

Individuals with Disabilities Education Act Amendments of 1997, 20 U.S.C. § 1400 (1997).

Individuals with Disabilities Education Improvement Act of 2004, H.R. 1350, 108th Cong.

Individuals with Disabilities Education Act of 1990 (IDEA), P.L. 101-476 § 602(a) [U.S.C. 1401(a)].

Inge, K. J. (1995). *A national survey of occupational therapists in the public schools: An assessment of current practice, attitudes, and training needs regarding the transition process for students with disabilities.* Unpublished doctoral dissertation, Virginia Commonwealth University, Richmond.

Inge, K. J., Simon, M., Halloran, W., & Moon, M. S. (1993). Community-based vocational instruction and the labor laws: A 1993 update. In K. J. Inge & P. Wehman (Eds.), *Designing community-based vocational programs for students with severe disabilities.* Richmond, VA: Rehabilitation Research and Training Center on Supported Employment, Virginia Commonwealth University.

Ingram, C. P. (1960). *Education of the slow-learning child* (3rd ed.). New York: Ronald Press.

Iowa Department of Education. (1998). *Their future—Our guidance: Iowa IEP guidebook.* Des Moines, IA: Author.

Jackson, A. W., & Davis, G. A. (2000). *Turning points 2000: Educating adolescents in the 21st century.* New York: Teachers College Press.

Jageman, L. W., & Myers, J. E. (1986). *Counseling mentally retarded adults: A procedures and training manual.* Menomonie: University of Wisconsin—Stout Materials Development Center.

Jarrow, J. E. (2003, March/April). A word from the editor. *Disability Access Information and Support Newsletter, 7*(3/4). Retrieved from DAISlist@aol.com.

Job Training Partnership Act of 1982, Public Law 97-300, 29 U.S.C. 1512(a)(b), 1604, 1605, 1632 (1982).

Job Training Reform Amendments of 1992, 29 U.S.C. § 1501 (1992).

Johnson, D. R., & Sharpe, M. N. (2000). Results of a national survey on the implementation of transition service requirements of IDEA. *Journal of Special Education Leadership, 13,* 15–26.

Johnson, D. R., Stodden, R. A., Emanuel, E. J., Luecking, R., & Mack, M. (2002). Current challenges facing secondary education and transition: What research tells us. *Exceptional Children, 68,* 519–531.

Johnson, D. R., & Thurlow, M. L. (2003). *A national study on graduation requirements and diploma options for youth with disabilities* (Technical Report 36). Minneapolis, MN: University of Minnesota, National Center on Educational Outcomes. Retrieved January 10, 2004, from http://education.umn.edu/NCEO/OnlinePubs/Technical36.htm

Johnson, G. O. (1962). Special education for the mentally handicapped: A paradox. *Exceptional Children, 29,* 62–69.

Jordan, T. E. (1973). *America's children: An introduction to education.* Rand McNally.

Judith Fein National Institute on Disability and Rehabilitation Research. (1996). A history of legislative support for assistive technology. *Journal of Special Education Technology, 13,* 1–3.

Kagan, S. L. (1992). The strategic importance of linkages and the transition between early childhood programs and early elementary school. In *Sticking together: Strengthening linkages and the transition between early childhood education and early elementary school* (Summary of a National Policy Forum, pp. 7–9). Washington, DC: U.S. Department of Education.

Kagan, S. L., & Neuman, M. J. (1998). Lessons from three decades of transition research. *Elementary School Journal, 98,* 365–380.

Kampfer, S. H., Horvath, L. S., Kleinert, H. L., & Kearns, J. F. (2001). Teachers' perceptions of one state's alternate assessment: Implications for practice and preparation. *Exceptional Children, 67*(3), 361–374.

Kapes, J. T., & Whitfield, E. A. (2001). *A counselor's guide to career assessment instruments* (4th ed.). Columbus, OH: National Career Development Association.

Karan, O., & Knight, C. B. (1986). Developing support networks for individuals who fail to achieve competitive employment. In F. Rusch (Ed.), *Competitive employment: Issues and strategies* (pp. 241–255). Baltimore: Paul H. Brookes.

Kauffman, J. M. (1997). *Characteristics of emotional and behavior disorders of children and youth* (6th ed.). New York: Merrill.

Kaye, C. B. (2004). *The complete guide to service learning: Proven practical ways to engage students in civic responsibility, academic curriculum, and social action.* Alexandria, VA: Association for Supervision and Curriculum Development.

Kim, K. H., & Turnbull, A. (2004). Transition to adulthood for students with severe disabilities: Shifting toward person-family interdependent planning. *Research & Practice for Persons with Severe Disabilities, 29*(1), 53–57.

Kincaid, J. M. (1997). IDEA revisions may have "ripple effect" on college transition. *Disability Compliance for Higher Education, 3*(4), 1, 6–7.

Kinsley, C. W., & McPherson, K. (1995). *Enriching curriculum through service learning.* Alexandria, VA: Association for Supervision and Curriculum Development.

Kiser, K. (1999). Tapped out. *Training, 36*(7), 44–49.

Klein, H. B., & Moses, N. (1999). *Intervention planning for adults with communication problems: A guide for clinical practicum and professional practice.* Boston: Allyn and Bacon.

Kleinert, H. L., Green, P., Hurte, M., Clayton, J., & Oetinger, C. (2002). Creating and using meaningful alternate assessments. *Teaching Exceptional Children, 34*(4), 40–47.

Kleinert, H. L., Haig, J., Kearns, J. F., & Kennedy, S. (2000). Alternate assessments: Lessons learned and roads to be taken. *Exceptional Children, 67*(1), 51–66.

Kleinert, H. L., & Kearns, J. F. (1999). A validation study of the performance indicators and learner outcomes of Kentucky's alternate assessment for students with significant disabilities. *Journal of the Association for Persons with Severe Handicaps, 24*(2), 100–110.

Kleinert, H. L., Kearns, J. F., & Kennedy, S. (1997). Accountability for *all* students: Kentucky's alternate portfolio assessment for students with moderate and severe cognitive disabilities. *Journal of the Association for Persons with Severe Handicaps, 22*(2), 88–101.

Kleinert, H. L., Kennedy, S., & Kearns, J. F. (1999). The impact of alternate assessments: A statewide teacher survey. *Journal of Special Education, 33*(2), 93–102.

Kochhar–Bryant, C. A., & Bassett, D. S. (2002a). *Aligning transition and standards-based education: Issues and strategies.* Arlington, VA: Council for Exceptional Children.

Kochhar-Bryant, C., & Bassett, D. S. (2002b). Challenge and promise in aligning transition and standards-based education. In C. A. Kochhar-Bryant & D. S. Bassett (Eds.), *Aligning transition and standards-based education: Issues and strategies* (pp. 1–23). Arlington, VA: Council for Exceptional Children.

Kohler, P. D. (1993). Best practices in transition: Substantiated or implied? *Career Development for Exceptional Individuals, 17,* 187–202.

Kohler, P. D. (1998). Implementing a transition perspective of education. In F. R. Rusch & J. G. Chadsey (Eds.), *Beyond high school: Transition from school to work* (pp. 179–205). Belmont, CA: Wadsworth.

Kohler, P. D., & Chapman, S. (1999). Literature review on school-to-work transition. Retrieved

July 2, 2004 from www.ed.uiuc.edu/sped/tri/2stwresearch.htm.

Kohler, P. D., DeStefano, L., Wermuth, T., Grayson, T., & McGinty, S. (1994). An analysis of exemplary transition programs: How and why are they selected? *Career Development for Exceptional Individuals, 17,* 187–202.

Kohler, P. D., & Field, S. (2003). Transition-focused education: Foundation for the future. *Journal of Special Education, 37,* 174–184.

Kokaska, C. J., & Brolin, D. E. (1985). *Career education for handicapped individuals* (2nd ed.). Columbus, OH: Merrill.

Kolstoe, O. P. (1961). An examination of some characteristics which discriminate between employed and not-employed mentally retarded males. *American Journal of Mental Deficiency, 66,* 472–482.

Kolstoe, O. P. (1972). Special education for the mildly retarded: A response to critics. *Exceptional Children, 35,* 51–55

Kolstoe, O. P., & Frey, R. M. (1965). *A high school work study program for mentally subnormal students.* Carbondale, IL: Southern Illinois University Press.

Kortering, L. J., & Braziel, P. M. (1999). School dropout from the perspective of former students. *Remedial and Special Education, 20,* 78–83.

Kortering, L. J., Julnes, R., & Edgar, E. (1990). An instructive review of the law pertaining to the graduation of special education students. *Remedial and Special Education, 11*(4), 7–13.

Kovalik, S., & Olsen, K. (1994). *Integrated thematic instruction (ITI): The model* (3rd ed.). Kent, WA: Books for Educators.

Kranstover, L., Thurlow, M., & Bruininks, R. (1989). Special education graduates versus non-graduates: A longitudinal study of outcomes. *Career Development for Exceptional Individuals, 12,* 153–166.

Kroeger, S. D., Leibold, C. K., & Ryan, B. (1999). Creating a sense of ownership in the IEP process. *Teaching Exceptional Children, 32,* 4–9.

Lassiter, R. A. (1981, December). *Work evaluation and work adjustment for severely handicapped people: A counseling approach* (pp. 13–18). Paper presented at the International Roundtable for the Advancement of Counseling Consultation on Career Guidance and Higher Education, Cambridge, England.

Leconte, P. J. (1994a). *A perspective on vocational appraisal: Beliefs, practices, and paradigms.* Unpublished dissertation, George Washington University.

Leconte, P. J. (1994b). Vocational appraisal services: Evolution from multidisciplinary origins and applications to interdisciplinary practices. *Vocational Evaluation and Work Adjustment Bulletin, 27,* 119–127.

Lenz, B. K., & Deshler, D. D., with Kissam, B. (2004). *Teaching content to all: Evidenced-based inclusive practices in middle and secondary schools.* Boston: Allyn and Bacon.

Lever-Duffy, J., McDonald, J. B., & Mizell, A. B. (2003). *Teaching and learning with technology.* Boston: Allyn and Bacon.

Levine, P., & Nourse, S. W. (1998). What follow-up studies say about postschool life for young men and women with learning disabilities: A critical look at the literature. *Journal of Learning Disabilities, 31,* 212–233.

Levinson, E. M., & Murphy, J. P. (1999). School psychology. In S. deFur & J. R. Patton (Eds.), *Transition and school-based services: Interdisciplinary perspectives for enhancing the transition process* (pp. 53–76). Austin, TX: Pro-Ed.

Lewis, B. A. (1995). *The kid's guide to service learning.* Minneapolis: Free Spirit.

Lewis, L., & Farris, E. (1999). An institutional perspective on students with disabilities in postsecondary education. *Education Statistics Quarterly, 1*(3), 65–68.

Lewis, R. B. (1993). *Special education technology: Classroom applications.* Pacific Grove, CA: Brooks/Cole.

Lewis, R. B. (1995). *Special education technology: Classroom applications.* Pacific Grove, CA: Brooks/Cole.

Lindsey, J. D. (2002). *Technology and exceptional individuals.* Austin, TX: Pro-Ed.

Lindstrom, L. E., Benz, M. R., & Doren, B. (2004). Expanding career options for young women with learning disabilities. *Career Development for Exceptional Individuals, 27*(1), 43–63.

Linthicum, E., Cole, J. T., & DAlonzo, B. J. (1991). Employment and the Americans with Disabilities Act of 1990. *Career Development for Exceptional Individuals, 14*(1), 1–13.

Lohrmann-O'Rourke, S., & Gomez, O. (2001). Integrating preference assessment within the transition process to create meaningful school-to-life outcomes. *Exceptionality, 9*(3), 157–174.

Love, J. M., Logue, M. E., Trudeau, J. V., & Thayer, K. (1992). *Transitions to kindergarten in American schools.* (Final report of the National Transition Study). Washington, DC: U.S. Department of Education, Office of Policy and Planning.

(ERIC Document Reproduction Service No. ED 344 693).

Love, L. (1995). *Applying the Fair Labor Standards Act when placing students into community-based vocational education.* Stillwater, OK: National Clearinghouse of Rehabilitation Training Materials.

Loyd, R. J., & Brolin, D. E. (1997). *Life centered career education: Modified curriculum for individuals with moderate disabilities.* Reston, VA: The Council for Exceptional Children.

Luckkason, R., Coulter, D., Polloway, E. A., Reiss, S., Schalock, R., Snell, M., Spitalnik, K. K., & Stark, J. (1992). *Mental retardation: Definition, classification, and systems of support* (9th ed.). Washington, DC: American Association on Mental Retardation.

Luckner, J. L. (2002). *Facilitating the transition of students who are deaf or hard of hearing.* Austin, TX: Pro-Ed.

Luecking, R. G. (2003). Employer perspectives on hiring and accommodating youth in transition. *Journal of Special Education Technology, 18*(4), 65–72.

Luecking, R. G., Fabian, E. S., & Tilson, G. P. (2004). *Working relationships: Creating career opportunities for job seekers with disabilities through employer partnerships.* Baltimore: Paul H. Brookes.

Lytle, R. K., & Brodin, J. (2001). Enhancing the IEP team. *Teaching Exceptional Children, 33,* 40–44.

MacMillan, D. L. (1977). *Mental retardation in school and society.* Boston: Little, Brown.

Male, M. (1997). *Technology for inclusion: Meeting the special needs of all students.* Boston: Allyn and Bacon.

Male, M. (2003). *Technology for inclusion: Meeting the special needs of all students.* Boston: Allyn and Bacon.

Malian, I. D., & Love, L. (1998). Leaving high school: An ongoing transition study. *Teaching Exceptional Children, 30*(3), 11–15.

Mangione, P. L., & Speth, T. (1998). The transition to elementary school: A framework for creating early childhood continuity through home, school, and community partnerships. *The Elementary School Journal, 98,* 381–398.

Mank, D., Cioffi, A., & Yovanoff, P. (2000). Direct support in supported employment and in relation to job typicalness, co-worker involvement, and employment outcomes. *Mental Retardation, 38,* 506–516.

Marder, C., & D'Amico, R. (1992, March). *How well are youth with disabilities really doing? A comparison of youth with disabilities and youth in general.* A Report from the National Longitudinal Transition Study of Special Education Students. Menlo Park, CA: SRI International.

Markward, M., & Kurtz, D. (1999). School social work. In S. H. deFur & J. R. Patton (Eds.), *Transition and school-based services: Interdisciplinary perspectives for enhancing the transition process.* Austin, TX: Pro-Ed.

Marland, S. P., Jr. (1974). *Career education: A proposal for reform.* New York: McGraw-Hill.

Maslow, A. H. (1954). *Motivation and personality.* New York: Harper and Row.

Maynard, M., & Chadderdon, L. (n.d.). *Leisure and life-style: A cross national report on issues and models for people with disabilities.* East Lansing, MI: Michigan State University Center for International Rehabilitation.

McAfee, J. K., & Greenwalt, C. (2001). IDEA, the courts and the law of transition. *Preventing School Failure, 45,* 102–107.

McDonnell, J., Mathot-Buckner, C., & Ferguson, B. (1996). *Transition program for students with moderate and severe disabilities.* Pacific Grove, CA: Brooks/Cole.

McDonnell, J., Wilcox, B., & Hardman, M. (1991). *Secondary programs for students with developmental disabilities.* Boston: Allyn and Bacon.

McGuire, J. M., Madaus, J. W., Litt, A. V., & Ramirez, M. O. (1996). An investigation of documentation submitted by university students to verify their learning disabilities. *Journal of Learning Disabilities, 29,* 297–304.

McGuire, J. M., & Shaw, S. F. (Eds.). (1996). *Resource guide of support services for students with learning disabilities in Connecticut colleges and universities.* Storrs, CT: A. J. Pappanikou Center on Special Education and Rehabilitation.

McKenzie, R. G., & Houk, C. S. (1993). Across the great divide. *Teaching Exceptional Children, 25,* 16–20.

McKernan, J. R. (1994). *Making the grade: How a new youth apprenticeship system can change our schools and save American jobs.* Boston: Little, Brown.

McNair, J., & Rusch, F. R. (1991). Parent involvement in transition programs. *Mental Retardation, 29,* 93–101.

Mercer, C. D., & Mercer, A. R. (2001). Assessing students for instruction. In C. D. Mercer & A. R. Mercer (Eds.), *Teaching students with learning problems* (6th ed.) (pp. 97–144). Upper Saddle River, NJ: Prentice-Hall.

Michaels, C. A., Prezant, F. P., Morabito, S. M., & Jackson, K. (2002). Assistive and instructional technology for college students with disabilities: A national snapshot of postsecondary services providers. *Journal of Special Education Technology, 17*(1), 5–14.

Midgley, C., Anderman, E., & Hicks, L. (1995). Differences between elementary and middle school teachers and students: A goal theory approach. *Journal of Early Adolescence, 15,* 90–113.

Miller-Tiedeman, A., & Tiedeman, D. V. (1990). Career decision making: An individualistic perspective. In D. Brown, L. Brooks, & Associates (Eds.), *Career choice and development: Applying contemporary theories to practice* (2nd ed.) (pp. 308–337). San Francisco: Jossey–Bass.

Miner, C. A., & Bates, P. E. (1997). The effect of PCP activities on the IEP/transition planning process. *Education and Training in Mental Retardation and Developmental Disabilities, 6,* 105–112.

Mitchell, L .K., & Krumboltz, J. D. (1990). Social learning approach to career decision making: Krumboltz's theory. In D. Brown, L. Brooks, & Associates (Eds.), *Career choice and development: Applying contemporary theories to practice* (2nd ed.) (pp. 145–196). San Francisco: Jossey-Bass.

Mithaug, D. E., Horiuchi, C., & Fanning, P. (1985). A report on the Colorado statewide follow-up survey of special education students. *Exceptional Children, 51,* 397–404.

Mithaug, D. E., Martin, J., & Agran, M. (1987). A report on the Colorado statewide follow-up survey of special education students. *Exceptional Children, 51,* 397–404.

Moll, A. M. (2003). *Differentiated instruction guide for inclusive teaching.* Port Chester, NY: Dude Publishing.

Mooney, M., & Scholl, L. (2004). Students with disabilities in youth apprenticeship programs: Supports and accommodations. *Career Development for Exceptional Individuals, 27*(1), 7–25.

Morningstar, M. E. (1994). *Examining the transition process: What are the indicators of collaborative transition planning?* Unpublished manuscript. Lawrence: University of Kansas, Department of Special Education.

Morningstar, M. E., Turnbull, A. P., & Turnbull, H. R. (1995). What do students with disabilities tell us about the importance of family involvement in the transition from school to adult life? *Exceptional Children, 62,* 249–260.

Morris, M. (1992). Policy in the making: The right to take assistive technology home from school. *AT Quarterly: RESNA Technical Assistance Project, 3*(2), 5.

Mount, B. (1997). *Person-centered planning: Finding direction for change using personal futures planning* (2nd ed.). New York: Graphic Press.

Mountain Plains Regional Resource Center. (2003). The transition outcomes project. Retrieved August 26, 2004 from www.usu.edu/mprrc/curproj/sectrans/top/oleary.cfm.

Mull, C., & Sitlington, P. L. (2003). The role of technology in the transition to postsecondary education of students with learning disabilities. *The Journal of Special Education, 37*(1), 26–32.

Mull, C., Sitlington, P. L., & Alper, S. (2001). Postsecondary education for students with learning disabilities. *Exceptional Children, 68*(1), 97–118.

Murphy, S. T., Rogan, P. M., Handley, M., Kincaid, C., & Royce–Davis, J. (2002). People's situations and perspectives eight years after workshop conversion. *Mental Retardation, 40,* 30–40.

Murray, C., Goldstein, D. E., Nourse, S., & Edgar, E. (2000). The postsecondary school attendance and completion rates of high school graduates with learning disabilities. *Learning Disabilities Research, 15,* 119–127.

Muscott, H. S. (2002). Exceptional partnerships: Listening to the voices of families. *Preventing School Failure, 46,* 66–69.

Myles, B. S., & Simpson, R. L. (2003). *Asperger syndrome: A guide for educators and parents* (2nd ed.). Austin, TX: Pro-Ed.

National and Community Service Act of 1990 (PL 101–610), 42 U.S.C. 12572.

National and Community Service Trust Act of 1993 (PL 103–82), 107 Stat. 785.

National Association of School Nurses. (1996). *Issue brief: School nurses and the Individuals with Disabilities Education Act (IDEA).* Scarborough, ME: Author.

National Center for Education Statistics. (1994). *National Education Longitudinal Study of 1988, third follow-up survey (NELS: 88/94), data analysis system.* Washington, DC: U.S. Department of Education.

National Center for Education Statistics. (1996). *1995–96 National Postsecondary Student Aid Study (NPSAS:96), undergraduate data analysis system.* Washington, DC: U.S. Department of Education.

National Center for Research in Vocational Education. (1995). *Getting to work: A guide for better schools.* Berkeley: Author.

National Center for Youth with Disabilities. (1996). *Transitions from child to adult health care services: A national survey.* Minneapolis: Author.

National Center on Educational Outcomes. (2002). *Graduation requirements for students with disabilities*. Retrieved June 10, 2003, from www.education.umn.edu/NCEO/.

National Center on Educational Outcomes. (2003a). *Putting it all together: Including students with disabilities in assessments and accountability systems*. NCEO Policy Directions, 16, 1–6.

National Center on Educational Outcomes. (2003b). *Accountability for assessment results in the No Child Left Behind Act: What it means for children with disabilities*. Minneapolis, MN: University of Minnesota, National Center on Educational Outcomes. Retrieved January 6, 2004 from education.umn.edu/NCEO/OnlinePubs/NCLBaccountability.html.

National Center on Secondary Education and Transition (2002). *Youth with disabilities and the Workforce Investment Act of 1998*. www.ncset.org/publications/policy/2002_12.asp.

National Center on Secondary Education and Transition (2003). *Supplemental Security Income: A bridge to work*. Retrieved October 20, 2003, from http://ncset.org/publications/viewdesc.asp?id=937.

National Collaborative on Workforce and Disability (2003). *Serving youth with disabilities under the Workforce Investment Act of 1998: The basics*. Retrieved July 15, 2004, from www.ncwd-youth.info/enews2.html.

National Council on Disability. (2000a). *Back to school on civil rights*. Washington, DC: Author.

National Council on Disability. (2000b). *Transition and post-school outcomes for youth with disabilities: Closing the gaps to post-secondary education and employment*. Washington, DC: Author.

National Council on Disability. (2003). *People with disabilities and postsecondary education: A position paper*. Washington, DC: Author.

National Joint Committee on Learning Disabilities. (1994). Secondary to postsecondary education transition planning for students with learning disabilities. *Collective perspectives on issues affecting learning disabilities: Position papers and statements* (pp. 97–104). Austin, TX: Pro-Ed.

National Joint Committee on Learning Disabilities. (1999). Learning disabilities: Issues in higher education. *Learning Disability Quarterly, 22,* 263–266.

National Occupational Information Coordinating Committee. (1996). *The national career development guidelines K–adult handbook*. Washington, DC: Author.

National Organization on Disability. (2004). *2004 N.O.D./Harris survey of Americans with disabilities*. Washington, DC: Author. Retrieved August 15, 2004, from www.nod.org.

National School-to-Work Office. (n.d.). *School-to-work and employer liability: A resource guide*. Washington, DC: Author.

National School-to-Work Office. (July, 1996). *School-to-work glossary of terms*. Washington, DC: Author.

National Transition Network. (1993, Spring). Job Training Reform Amendments of 1992: Expanded opportunities for youth and adults with disabilities. *Policy Update,* 1–8.

National Youth Employment Coalition. (2004). *NYEC EDNet: NYEC Education Development Network* (2nd ed.). Washington, DC: Author. Retrieved July 9, 2004, from www.nyec.org.

Neubert, D. A. (1997). Time to grow: The history and future of preparing youth for adult roles in society. *Teaching Exceptional Children, 29*(5), 5–17.

Neubert, D. A. (2003). The role of assessment in the transition to adult life process for individuals with disabilities. *Exceptionality, 11,* 63–71.

Neubert, D. A., & Moon, M. S. (2000). How a transition profile helps students prepare for life in the community. *Teaching Exceptional Children, 32*(2), 20–25.

Neubert, D. A., Moon, M. S., & Grigal, M. (2002). Post-secondary education and transition services for students ages 18–21 with significant disabilities. *Focus on Exceptional Children, 34*(8), 1–12.

Neubert, D. A., Moon, M. S., & Grigal, M. (2004). Activities of students with significant disabilities receiving services in postsecondary settings. *Education and Training in Developmental Disabilities, 39*(1), 16–25.

Neubert, D. A., Moon, M. S., Grigal, M., & Redd, V. (2001). Post-secondary educational practices for individuals with mental retardation and other significant disabilities: A review of the literature. *Journal of Vocational Rehabilitation, 16,* 155–168.

Nippold, M. (1993). Developmental markers in adolescent language: Syntax, semantics, and pragmatics. *Language, Speech, and Hearing Services in Schools, 24,* 21–28.

NISH. (1996). Rehabilitation Act Amendments of 1992. *The Workplace, 22*(10), 4–8.

No Child Left Behind Act of 2001, 20 U.S.C. § 6301 (2002).

Noddings, N. (1992). *The challenge to care in schools: An alternative approach to education.* New York: Teachers College Press.

Nosek, M. A. (1992). Independent living. In R. M. Parker & E. M. Szymanski (Eds.), *Rehabilitation counseling* (2nd ed.) (pp. 103–133). Austin, TX: Pro-Ed.

Office of Educational Research and Improvements, U.S. Department of Education. (1994). *National Assessment of Vocational Education final report to Congress: Volume I: Summary and recommendations.* Washington, DC: U.S. Government Printing Office.

Ogbu, J. U. (1994). Understanding cultural diversity and learning. *Journal for the Education of the Gifted, 17,* 355–383.

Ohtake, Y., & Chadsey, J. G. (2001). Continuing to describe the natural support process. *The Journal of the Association for Persons with Severe Handicaps, 26*(2), 87–95.

Olson, J., & Platt, J. C. (2004). *Teaching children and adolescents with special needs.* Upper Saddle River, NJ: Pearson Merrill Prentice-Hall.

Osterman, P., & Iannozzi, M. (1993). *Youth apprenticeships and school-to-work transition: Current knowledge and legislative strategy.* Philadelphia: National Center on the Educational Quality of the Workforce.

Page, B., & Chadsey-Rusch, J. (1995). The community college experience for students with and with-out disabilities: A viable transition outcome? *Career Development for Exceptional Individuals, 18,* 85–96.

Paris, K., & Mason, S. (1995). *Planning and implementing youth apprenticeship & work-based learning.* Madison, WI: Center on Education and Work.

Park, J., Turnbull, A. P., & Turnbull, H. R. III. (2002). Impacts of poverty on quality of life in families of children with disabilities. *Exceptional Children, 68*(2), 151–170.

Patton, J. R., Cronin, M. E., Bassett, D. S., & Koppel, A. E. (1997). A life skills approach to mathematics instruction: Preparing students with learning disabilities for the real-life math demands of instruction. *Journal of Learning Disabilities, 30,* 178–187.

Patton, J. R., Cronin, M. E., & Wood, S. (1999). *Infusing real-life topics into existing curricula. Recommended procedures and instructional examples for the elementary, middle and high school levels.* Austin, TX: Pro-Ed.

Patton, J. R., & Dunn, C. (1998). *Transition from school to adulthood: Basic concepts and recommended practices.* Austin, TX: Pro-Ed.

Patton, J. R., & Trainor, A. (2002). Using applied academics to enhance curricular reform in secondary education. In C. A. Kochhar-Bryant & D. S. Bassett (Eds.), *Aligning transition and standards-based education: Issues and strategies* (pp. 55–76). Arlington, VA: Council for Exceptional Children.

Phelps, L. A., & Frasier, J. R. (1988). Legislative and policy aspects of vocational special education. In R. Gaylord-Ross (Ed.), *Vocational education for persons with special needs* (pp. 3–29). Palo Alto, CA: Mayfield.

Phelps, L. A., & Hanley–Maxwell, C. (1997). School-to-work transitions for youth with disabilities: A review of outcomes and practices. *Review of Education Research, 67,* 197–227.

Phillips, S. D., Blustein, D. L., Jobin–Davis, K., & White, S. F. (2002). Preparation for the school-to-work transition: The views of high school students. *Journal of Vocational Behavior, 61*(2), 202–216.

Pierangelo, R., & Giuliani, G. A. (2004). *Transition services in special education: A practical approach.* Boston: Allyn and Bacon.

Pisha, B., & Coyne, P. (2001). Smart from the start: The promise of universal design for learning. *Remedial and Special Education, 22*(4), 197–203.

Polloway, E. A., Patton, J. R., & Serna, L. (2005). *Strategies for teaching learners with special needs* (8th ed.). Upper Saddle River, NJ: Pearson Merrill Prentice-Hall.

President's Commission on Excellence in Education in Special Education. (2002). *A new era: Revitalizing special education for children and their families.* Washington, DC: U.S. Department of Education.

Price, L. A. (1997). The development and implementation of a code of ethical behavior for postsecondary personnel. *Journal of Postsecondary Education and Disabilities, 12*(3), 36–44.

Proctor, S. T., Lordi, S. L., & Zaiger, D. S. (1993). *School nursing practice: Roles and standards.* Scarborough, ME: National Association of School Nurses.

Pumpian, I., Fisher, D., Certo, N., Engel, T., & Mautz, D. (1998). To pay or not to pay: Differentiating employment and training relationships through regulation and litigation. *Career Development for Exceptional Individuals, 21,* 187–202.

Pumpian, I., Fisher, D., Certo, N., & Smalley, K. (1997). Changing jobs: An essential part of career development. *Mental Retardation, 35,* 39–48.

Raskind, M. H., & Higgins, E. L. (1998). Assistive technology for postsecondary students with learning disabilities: An overview. *Journal of Learning Disabilities, 31,* 27–40.

Raths, L., Merrill, H., & Sidney, S. (1966). *Values and teaching.* Columbus, OH: Charles E. Merrill.

Razeghi, J., Kokaska, C., Gruenhagen, K., & Fair, G. (1987). *The transition of youth with disabilities to adult life: A position statement of the Division on Career Development.* The Council for Exceptional Children. Reston, VA: The Council for Exceptional Children.

Redd, V. A. (2004). *A public school-sponsored program that serves students ages 18 to 21 with significant disabilities in a community college setting: A description of program characteristics and student experiences.* Unpublished dissertation, University of Maryland, College Park, MD.

Regents of the University of Minnesota. (1996). *School-to-work outreach project.* Minneapolis: College of Educational and Human Development.

Rehabilitation Act of 1973, PL 93-112, 29 U.S.C. 723(a), 721(a)(9), 793, 794, 795(a), 795(g) (1982).

Rehabilitation Act Amendments of 1984, PL 98-211.

Rehabilitation Act Amendments of 1986, 29 U.S.C. § 701, PL 99-506.

Rehabilitation Act Amendments of 1992, 29 U.S.C. § 701 (1992).

Reichard, C. L. (1979). *Project RETOOL Report.* Reston, VA: The Council for Exceptional Children, Teacher Education Division.

Reis, S., Neu, T., & McGuire, J. (1997). Case studies of high–ability students with learning disabilities who have achieved. *Exceptional Children, 63,* 463–479.

Reis, S. M., Kaplan, S. N., Tomlinson, C. A., Westberg, K. L., Callahan, C. M., & Cooper, C. R. (1998). Equal does not mean identical. *Educational Leadership, 56*(3), 74–77.

Reisner, E., McNeil, P., Adelman, N., Kulick, C., Hallock, R., & Leighton, M. (1993). *Using youth apprenticeship to improve the transition to work: An evaluation of system development in eight states.* Washington, DC: Council of Chief State School Officers.

Repetto, J. B., & Correa, V. I. (1996). Expanding views on transition. *Exceptional Children, 62,* 551–563.

Rich, J. (1997). *The everything college survival book.* Holbrook, MA: Adams Media Corp.

Richard, M. M. (1995). Pathways to success for the college student with ADD: Accommodations and preferred practices. *Journal of Postsecondary Education and Disability, 11,* 16–29.

Rief, S. (1998). *The ADD/ADHD Checklist: An easy reference for parents and teachers.* Paramus, NJ: Prentice-Hall.

Roessler, R. T., Schriner, K. F., & Price, P. (1992). Employment concerns of people with head injury. *Journal of Rehabilitation, 58*(1), 17–22.

Rogan, P., Grossi, T. A., & Gajewski, R. (2002). Vocational and career assessment. In C. L. Sax & C. A. Thoma (Eds.), *Transition assessment: Wise practices for quality lives* (pp. 103–117). Baltimore: Paul H. Brookes.

Rogers-Adkinson, D. L., & Griffith, P. (Eds.). (1999). *Communication disorders and children with psychiatric and behavioral disorders.* San Diego: Singular.

Roos, P. (1970). Normalization, de-humanization, and conditioning—Conflict or harmony? *Mental Retardation, 8*(4), 12–14.

Rose, D. H. (2001). Universal design for learning: Deriving guiding principles from networks that learn. *Journal of Special Education Technology, 16*(2), 66–67.

Rose, D. H., & Meyer, A. (2002). *Teaching every student in the digital age: Universal design for learning.* Alexandria, VA: Association for Supervision and Curriculum Development.

Rusch, F. R. (Ed.). (1986). *Competitive employment: Issues and strategies.* Baltimore: Paul H. Brookes.

Rusch, F. R., & Menchetti, B. M. (1988). Transition in the 1990s: A reply to Knowlton and Clark. *Exceptional Children, 54,* 363–365.

Rusch, F. R., & Millar, D. M. (1996). The transition to adulthood and the world of work by youth with mental retardation. *Current Opinion in Psychiatry, 9,* 328–331.

Rusch, F. R., & Phelps, L. A. (1987). Secondary special education and transition from school to work: A national priority. *Exceptional Children, 53,* 487–492.

Sabornie, E. J., & deBettencourt, L. U. (2004). *Teaching students with mild and high-incidence disabilities at the secondary level* (2nd ed). Upper Saddle River, NJ: Pearson Merrill Prentice-Hall.

Sale, P., Everson, J. M., & Moon, M. S. (1991). Quality indicators of successful vocational transition programs. *Journal of Vocational Rehabilitation, 1*(4), 47–63.

Salembier, G. B., & Furney, K. S. (1998). Speaking up for your child's future. *The Exceptional Parent, 28,* 62–64.

Salend, S. (2005). *Creating creative classrooms: Reflective and effective practices for all students* (5th ed.). Upper Saddle River, NJ: Pearson Merrill Prentice-Hall.

Salvia, J., & Ysseldyke, J. E. (2004). *Assessment in special education and inclusive education* (9th ed.). Boston: Houghton Mifflin.

Sampson, R. (2002). *Bullying in schools.* U.S. Department of Justice, Office of Community Oriented Policing Services. Online resource: http://purl.access.gpo.gov/GPO/LPS19843.

Sands, D. J., & Wehmeyer, M. L. (Eds.). (1996). *Self-determination across the life span: Independence and choice for people with disabilities* (pp. 8–9). Baltimore: Paul H. Brookes.

Sarkees-Wircenski, M., & Scott, J. L. (1995). *Vocational special needs.* Homewood, IL: American Technical Publishers.

Savage, H. J. (1953). *Fruit of an impulse: Forty-five years of the Carnegie Foundation, 1905–1950.* New York: Harcourt, Brace and Company.

Savage, R. C., & Wolcott, G. F. (1994). *Educational dimensions of acquired brain injury.* Austin, TX: Pro-Ed.

Sax, C. L. (2002). Person-centered planning: More than a strategy. In C. L. Sax & C. A. Thoma (Eds.), *Transition assessment: Wise practices for quality lives* (pp. 13–24). Baltimore: Paul H. Brookes.

Schirmer, B. R. (2001). *Psychological, social, and educational dimensions of deafness.* Boston: Allyn and Bacon.

School and Community Integration Project. (1992). *The School and Community Integration Project curriculum for students with severe disabilities.* Department of Special Education, University of Utah, Salt Lake City.

School to Work Opportunities Act, 20 U.S.C. § 6101 (1994).

Schuster, D. L., & Smith, F. G. (1994). The Interdisciplinary Council on Vocational Evaluation and Assessment: Building consensus through communication, advocacy and common goals. *Vocational Evaluation and Work Adjustment Bulletin, 27,* 111–114.

Schwartz, A. A., Holburn, S. C., & Jacobson, J. W. (2000). Defining person-centeredness: Results of two consensus methods. *Education and Training in Mental Retardation and Developmental Disabilities, 35*(3), 235–249.

Scott, S. S. (1991). A change in legal status: An overlooked dimension in the transition to higher education. *Journal of Learning Disabilities, 24,* 459–466.

Scott, S. S. (1994). Determining reasonable academic adjustments for college students with learning disabilities. *Journal of Learning Disabilities, 27,* 403–412.

Scott, S. S., Loewen, G., Funckes, C., & Kroeger, S. (2003). Implementing universal design in higher education: Moving beyond the built environment. *Journal on Postsecondary Education and Disability, 16*(2), 78–89.

Secretary's Commission on Achieving Necessary Skills. (1991). *What work requires of schools: A SCANS report for America 2000.* Springfield, VA: National Technical Information Service, Operations Division. (NTIS Number: PB92-146711).

Seidman, E., Allen, L., Aber, J., Mitchell, C., & Feinman, J. (1994). The impact of school transitions in early adolescence on the self-system and perceived social context of poor urban youth. *Child Development, 65,* 507–522.

Shafer, M. (1988). Supported employment in perspective: Traditions in the Federal-State Vocational Rehabilitation System. In P. Wehman & M. S. Moon (Eds.), *Vocational rehabilitation and supported employment* (pp. 55–66). Baltimore: Paul H. Brookes.

Shaw, S. F., & Dukes, L. L. (2001). Program standards for disability services in higher education. *Journal of Postsecondary Education and Disability, 14*(2), 81–90.

Shaw, S. F., McGuire, J. M., & Madaus, J. W. (1997). Standards of professional practice. *Journal of Postsecondary Education and Disability, 12*(3), 26–35.

Shepherd, J., & Inge, K. J. (1999). Occupational and physical therapy. In S. H. deFur & J. R. Patton (Eds.), *Transition and school-based services: Interdisciplinary perspectives for enhancing the transition process* (pp. 117–165). Austin, TX: Pro-Ed.

Shertzer, B., & Stone, S. C. (1981). *Fundamentals of guidance* (4th ed.). Boston: Houghton Mifflin.

Silverberg, M., Warner, E., Goodwin, D., & Fong, M. (2002). *National Assessment of Vocational Education Interim Report. Executive Summary.* Washington, DC: U.S. Department of Education.

Simon, M. (2001). Beyond broken promises: Reflections on eliminating barriers to the success of minority youth with disabilities. *Journal of the Association for Persons with Severe Handicaps, 26,* 200–203.

Simon, M., Cobb, B., Halloran, W., Norman, M., & Bourexis, P. (1994). *Meeting the needs of youth with disabilities: Handbook for implementing community-based vocational education programs according to the Fair Labor Standards Act.* Fort Collins: Colorado State University.

Simon, M., & Halloran, W. (1994). Community-based vocational education: Guidelines for complying with the Fair Labor Standards Act. *Journal of the Association for Severely Handicapped, 19,* 52–60.

Simpson, S. (1999). Early adolescent development. In C. W. Walley & W. G. Gerrick (Eds.), *Affirming middle grades education.* Boston: Allyn and Bacon.

Sitlington, P. L. (1996a). Transition assessment—Where have we been and where should we be going? *Career Development for Exceptional Individuals, 19,* 159–168.

Sitlington, P. L. (1996b). Transition to living: The neglected component of transition programming for individuals with learning disabilities. *Journal of Learning Disabilities, 29,* 31–39, 52.

Sitlington, P. L. (2003). Postsecondary education: The other transition. *Exceptionality, 11*(2), 103–113.

Sitlington, P. L., Brolin, D. E., Clark, G. M., & Vacanti, J. M. (1985). Career/vocational assessment in the public school setting: The position of the Division on Career Development. *Career Development for Exceptional Individuals, 8,* 3–6.

Sitlington, P. L., Clark, G. M., & Kolstoe, O. P. (2000). *Transition education and services for adolescents with disabilities* (3rd ed.). Boston: Allyn and Bacon.

Sitlington, P. L., & Frank, A. R. (1990). Are adolescents with learning disabilities successfully crossing the bridge into adult life? *Learning Disabilities Quarterly, 13,* 97–111.

Sitlington, P. L., & Frank, A. R. (1993). Success as an adult—Does gender make a difference for graduates with mental disabilities? *Career Development for Exceptional Individuals, 16,* 171–182.

Sitlington, P L., & Frank, A. R. (1994). Rural vs. urban: Does it affect the transition of individuals with disabilities? *Rural Special Education Quarterly, 13*(1), 9–15.

Sitlington, P. L., & Frank, A. R. (1998). *Follow-up studies: A practitioners handbook.* Austin, TX: Pro-Ed.

Sitlington, P. L., Frank, A. R., & Carson, R. (1992). Adult adjustment among high school graduates with mild disabilities. *Exceptional Children, 59,* 221–233.

Sitlington, P. L., Neubert, D. A., Begun, W., Lombard, R. C., & Leconte, P. J. (1996). *Assess for success: Handbook on transition assessment.* Reston, VA: The Council for Exceptional Children.

Sitlington, P. L., Neubert, D. A., & Leconte, P. J. (1997). Transition assessment: The position of the Division on Career Development and Transition. *Career Development for Exceptional Individuals, 20*(1), 69–79.

Sitlington, P. L., & Payne, E. M. (2004). Information needed by postsecondary education: Can we provide it as part of the transition assessment process? *Learning Disabilities: A Contemporary Journal, 2*(2), 1–14.

Skrtic, T. M. (1991). *Behind special education: A critical analysis of professional culture and school organization.* Denver: Love Publishing.

Smith, C. L., & Clark, P. J. (1999). Youth apprenticeship in Georgia: An assessment of students. *Journal of Cooperative Education, 34*(1), 7–16.

Smith, D. D. (2004). *Introduction to special education: Teaching in an age of opportunity* (5th ed.). Boston: Allyn and Bacon.

Smith, F., Lombard, R., Neubert, D., Leconte, P., Rothenbacher, C., & Sitlington, P. (1994). The position statement of the Interdisciplinary Council on Vocational Evaluation and Assessment. *The Journal for Vocational Special Needs Education, 17,* 41–42.

Smith, M. A., & Schloss, P. J. (1988). Teaching to transition. In P. J. Schloss, C. A. Hughes, & M. A. Smith (Eds.), *Community integration for persons with mental retardation* (pp. 1–16). Austin, TX: Pro-Ed.

Smith, P. K., Morita, Y., Junger–Tas, J., Olweus, D., Catalano, R., & Slee, P. (Eds.). (1999). *The nature of school bullying: A cross-national perspective.* London/New York: Routledge.

Smith, S. M., & Tyler, J. S. (1997). Successful transition planning and services for students with ABI. In A. Glang, G. H. S. Singer, & B. Todis (Eds.), *Students with acquired brain injury: The schools response* (pp. 185–200). Baltimore: Paul H. Brookes.

Smith, T. E. C., & Patton, J. R. (1999). *Section 504 and public schools: A practical guide.* Austin, TX: Pro-Ed.

Smith, T. E. C., Polloway, E. A., Patton, J. R., & Dowdy, C. A. (2001). *Teaching students with special needs in inclusive settings.* Boston: Allyn and Bacon.

Social Security Administration. (2003). *2003 red book: A summary guide to employment support for people with disabilities under the Social Security Disability Insurance and Supplemental Security Income programs* (SSA Pub. No. 64-030). Washington, DC: Author.

St. John, C., & Miller, S. M. B. (1995). The exposure of black and Hispanic children to urban ghettos: Evidence from Chicago and the southwest. *Social Science Quarterly, 76,* 562–576.

Staab, M. J. (1996). *The role of the school psychologist in transition planning.* Unpublished doctoral dissertation, University of Kansas, Lawrence.

State Vocational Rehabilitation Services Program, Final Rule, 66 Fed. Reg.7249-7258 (Jan. 22, 2001) (codified at 34 C.F.R. § 361).

Steere, D. E., & Cavaiuolo, D. (2002). Connecting outcomes, goals, and objectives in transition planning. *Teaching Exceptional Children, 34,* 54–59.

Steward, R. J., Gimenez, M. M., & Jackson, J. D. (1995). A study of personal preferences of successful university students as related to race/ethnicity and sex: Implications and recommendations for training, practice and future research. *Journal of College Student Development, 36*(2) 123–131.

Stodden, R., Ianacone, R. N., Boone, M. R., & Bisconer, W. S. (1987). *Curriculum-based vocational assessment: A guide for addressing youth with special needs.* Honolulu, HI: Centre Publications, International Education Corporation.

Stodden, R. A. (2001). Postsecondary education supports for students with disabilities: A review and response. *Journal for Vocational Special Needs Education, 23*(2), 4–11.

Stodden, R. A., Whelley, T., Harding, T., & Chang, C. (2001). Current status of educational support provision to students with disabilities in postsecondary education. *Journal of Vocational Rehabilitation, 16,* 1–10.

Super, D. E. (1953). A theory of vocational development. *American Psychologist, 8,* 185–190.

Super, D. E., Crites, J., Hummel, R., Moser, H., Overstreet, P., & Warnath, C. (1957). *Vocational development: A framework for research.* New York: Bureau of Publications, Teachers College, Columbia University.

Synatschk, K. O. (1999). Counseling. In S. H. deFur & J. R. Patton (Eds.), *Transition and school-based services: Interdisciplinary perspectives for enhancing the transition process* (pp. 231–271). Austin, TX: Pro-Ed.

Szymanski, E. M. (1994). Transitions: Life-span and life-space considerations for empowerment. *Exceptional Children, 60,* 402–410.

Szymanski, E. M., Hershenson, D. B., & Power, P. W. (1988). Enabling the family in supporting transition from school to work. In P. W. Power, A. E. Dell Orto, & M. B. Gibbons (Eds.), *Family interventions throughout chronic illness and disability* (pp. 216–233). New York: Springer.

Technology Related Assistance for Individuals with Disabilities Act of 1988. PL 100-497.

Thoma, C. A., Rogan, P., & Baker, S. R. (2001). Student involvement in transition planning: Unheard voices. *Education & Training in Mental Retardation and Developmental Disabilities, 36*(1), 16–29.

Thomas, A., & Grimes, J. (1995). *Best practices in school psychology III.* Washington, DC: National Association of School Psychologists.

Thomas, S. B. (2000). College students and disability law. *Journal of Special Education, 33,* 248–257.

Thompson, S. J., Quenemoen, R. F., Thurlow, M. L., & Ysseldyke, J. E. (2001). *Alternate assessments for students with disabilities.* Thousand Oaks, CA: Corwin Press.

Thompson, V. L. S. (1995). Sociocultural influences on African-American racial identification. *Journal of Applied Social Psychology, 25,* 1411–1429.

Throne, J. M. (1975). Normalization through the normalization principle. Right ends, wrong means. *Mental Retardation, 13*(5), 23–25.

Thurlow, M. L. (2000). Standards-based reform and students with disabilities: Reflection on a decade of change. *Focus on Exceptional Children, 33*(3), 1–16.

Thurlow, M. L. (2001). *Use of accommodations in state assessments: What databases tell us about differential levels of use and how to document the use of accommodations* (Technical Report 30). Minneapolis: University of Minnesota, National Center on Educational Outcomes. Retrieved May 20, 2004, from http://education.umn.edu/NCEO/OnlinePubs/Technical30.htm.

Thurlow, M. L., House, A., Boys, C., Scott, D., & Ysseldyke, J. (2000). *State participation and accommodation policies for students with disabilities: 1999 update* (Synthesis Report No. 33). Minneapolis: University of Minnesota, National Center on Educational Outcomes.

Thurlow, M. L., Lazarus, S., Thompson, S., & Robey, J. (2002). *2001 state policies on assessment participation and accommodations* (Synthesis Report 46). Minneapolis: University of Minnesota, National Center on Educational Outcomes. Retrieved November 15, 2003, from http://education.umn.edu/NCEO/OnlinePubs/Synthesis46.html.

Thurlow, M. L., Thompson, S. J., & Johnson, D. R. (2002). Traditional and alternative assessments within the transition process and standards-based education. In C. A. Kochhar-Bryant & D. S. Bassett (Eds.), *Aligning transition and standards-based education: Issues and strategies* (pp. 91–104). Arlington, VA: Council for Exceptional Children.

Thurlow, M. L., Ysseldyke, J. E., & Anderson, C. L. (1995). *High school graduation requirements: What's happening for students with disabilities?* Minneapolis, MN: National Center on Education Outcomes, University of Minnesota. (ERIC Document Reproduction Service No. ED 385 056).

Tindal, G., & Fuchs, L. (1999). *A summary of research on testing accommodations: What we know so far.* Lexington: University of Kentucky, Mid-South Regional Resource Center. Retrieved August 1, 2002, from www.ihdi.uky.edu/msrrc.

Tindal, G., & Fuchs, L. (2000). *A summary of research on test changes: An empirical basis for defining accommodations.* Lexington: Mid-South Regional Resource Center, University of Kentucky.

Tindal, G., & Nolet, V. (1995). Curriculum-based measurement in middle and high schools: Critical thinking skills in content areas. *Focus on Exceptional Children, 27*(7), 1–22.

Tomlinson, C. A. (1999). *The differentiated classroom: Responding to the needs of all learners. Strategies and tools for responsive teaching.* Alexandria, VA: Association for Supervision and Curriculum Development.

Tomlinson, C. A. (2001). *How to differentiate instruction in mixed ability classrooms* (2nd ed.). Alexandria, VA: Association for Supervision and Curriculum Development.

Tomlinson, C. A. (2003). *Fulfilling the promise of the differentiated classroom: Strategies and tools for responsive teaching.* Alexandria, VA: Association for Supervision and Curriculum Development.

Tomlinson, C. A., & Cunningham-Eidson, C. (2003). *Differentiation in practice: A resource guide for differentiating curriculum, grades 5–9.* Alexandria, VA: Association for Supervision and Curriculum Development.

Tomlinson, C. A., & Kalbfleisch, M. L. (1998). Teach me, teach my brain: A call for differentiated classrooms. *Educational Leadership, 56*(3), 52–55.

Turnbull, A. P., & Turnbull, H. R. (1996). Self-determination within a culturally responsive family systems perspective: Balancing the family mobile. In L. E. Powers, G. H. Singer, & J. Sowers (Eds.), *Promoting self-competence in children and youth with disabilities: On the road to autonomy* (pp. 195–220). Baltimore: Paul H. Brookes.

Turnbull, A. P., & Turnbull, H. R. (1997). *Families, professionals, and exceptionality: A special partnership* (3rd ed.) Upper Saddle River, NJ: Prentice-Hall.

Turnbull, A. P., & Turnbull, H. R. (2001). *Families, professionals, and exceptionality: Collaborating for empowerment* (4th ed.). Upper Saddle River, NJ: Prentice-Hall.

Turner, K. D., & Szymanski, E. M. (1990). Work adjustment of people with congenital disabilities: A longitudinal perspective from birth to adulthood. *Journal of Rehabilitation, 56,* 19–24.

U.S. Bureau of the Census. (2004). *Poverty thresholds for 2003 by size of family and number of related children under 18 years.* Retrieved July 24, 2004, from www.census.gov/hhes/poverty/threshld/thresh03.html.

U.S. Department of Education. (1983). *Report of services to adolescent handicapped, 1968–1982.* Washington, DC: U.S. Government Printing Office.

U.S. Department of Education. (1994). *School-to-Work Opportunities Act of 1994, PL No. 103-239.* (On-line). Available from: www.stw.ed.gov/factsht/act.htm.

U.S. Department of Education. (1995). *To assure the free appropriate public education of all children with disabilities: Seventeenth annual report to Congress on the implementation of the Individuals with Disabilities Education Act.* Washington, DC: Author.

U.S. Department of Education. (2002). *Twenty-fourth annual report to Congress on the implementation of the Individuals with Disabilities Education Act.* Washington, DC: Office of Special Education Programs.

U.S. Department of Education. (2003). *Federal Register,* December 9, 2003.

U.S. Department of Education. (2004a). *National Assessment of Vocational Education: Final report to Congress.* Washington, DC: Office of the Under Secretary, Policy and Program Studies Service.

U.S. Department of Education. (2004b). *A blueprint for preparing America's future: Summary of the Carl D. Perkins Secondary and Technical Education Act of 2004.* Washington, DC: Office of Vocational and Adult Education.

U.S. Office of Special Education Programs. (2004, April). *FACTS from OSEP's National Longitudinal Studies: Standardized testing among secondary school students with disabilities.* Washington, DC: Author.

Utah State Office of Education. (1991). *Utah State Office of Education mission statement.* Salt Lake City: Author.

Utah State Office of Education. (1998). *Utah model for counseling and comprehensive guidance.* Salt Lake City: Author.

Valdés, K. A., Williamson, C. L., & Wagner, M. (1990, July). *Statistical almanac, Vol. 2: Youth categorized as learning disabled. The National Longitudinal Transition Study of Special Education Students* (Contract 300-87-0054), SRI International, Menlo Park, CA.

Valdés, K. A., Williamson, C. L., & Wagner, M. M. (1990). *The national transition study of special education students.* Menlo Park, CA: SRI International.

Valletutti, P. J., Bender, M., & Sims-Tucker, B. (1996). *Functional curriculum for teaching students with disabilities: Functional academics* (Vol. 3, 2nd ed.). Austin, TX: Pro-Ed.

Van Reusen, A., Bos, C., Schumaker, J., & Deshler, D. (1994). *The self-advocacy strategy for education and transition planning.* Lawrence, KS: Edge Enterprises.

Vandercook, T., York, J., & Forest, M. (1989). The McGill Action Planning System (MAPS): A strategy for building the vision. *Journal of the Association for Persons with Severe Handicaps, 14*(3), 205–215.

Vocational Education Act of 1963, PL 88-210, 26 U.S.C. 5 (1964).

Vocational Education Act Amendments of 1968, PL 90-576, U.S.C. 1262(c), 1263(b), (F), (1970).

Vocational Education Act Amendments of 1976, PL 94-482, U.S.C. 2310(a), (b) (1982).

Vogel, S. A., & Adelman, P. B. (1992). The success of college students with learning disabilities: Factors related to educational attainment. *Journal of Learning Disabilities, 25,* 430–441.

Vogel, S. A., & Adelman, P. B. (Eds.). (1993). *Success for college students with learning disabilities.* New York: Springer-Verlag.

Wagner, M. (1991). *Dropouts with disabilities: What do we know? What can we do?* A report from the National Longitudinal Transition Study of Special Education Students. Menlo Park, CA: SRI International.

Wagner, M. (2004). National Longitudinal Transition Study–2. Retrieved February 2, 2004, from www.sri.com/nlts2/.

Wagner, M., & Blackorby, J. (1996). Transition from high school to work or college: How special education students fare. *The Future of Children, 6*(1), 103–120.

Wagner, M., Blackorby, J., Cameto, R., Hebbeler, K., & Newman, L. (1993). *The transition experiences of young people with disabilities: A summary of findings from the National Longitudinal Transition Study of Special Education Students.* Menlo Park, CA: SRI International.

Wagner, M., Cadwallader, T. W., Marder, C., Cameto, R., Cardoso, D., Garza, N., Levine, P., & Newman, L. (2003). *Life outside the classroom for youth with disabilities.* A Report of findings from the National Longitudinal Transition Study (NLTS) and National Longitudinal Transition Study–2 (NLTS2), Executive Summary. Menlo Park, CA: SRI International.

Wagner, M., Cameto, R., & Newman, L. (2003). *Youth with disabilities: A changing population.* A report of findings from the National Longitudinal Transition Study (NLTS) and National Longitudinal Transition Study–2 (NLTS2), Executive Summary. Menlo Park, CA: SRI International.

Wagner, M., D'Amico, R., Marder, C., Newman, L., & Blackorby, J. (1992). *What happens next? Trends in post-school outcomes of youth with disabilities: The second comprehensive report from the National Longitudinal Transition Study of Special Education Students.* Menlo Park, CA: SRI International. (ERIC Document Reproduction Service No. ED 356 603).

Wakefield, S. M., Sage, H., Coy, D. R., & Palmer, T. (2004). *Unfocused kids: Helping students to focus on their education and career plans.* Greensboro, NC: CAPS Press.

Walker, H. M., Ramsey, E., & Gresham, F. M. (2004). *Antisocial behavior in school: Evidence-based practices* (2nd ed.). Belmont, CA: Wadsworth/Thomson Learning.

Walker, M. L. (1991, Fall). Rehabilitation service delivery to individuals with disabilities: A question of culture competence. *OSERS News in Print, 4*(2), 7–11.

Wandry, D., & Pleet, A. (2004). *The role of families in secondary transition: A practitioner's facilitation guide.* Arlington, VA: Council for Exceptional Children.

Ward, M. J. (1992). OSERS initiative on self-determination. *Interchange, 12*(1), 1–7. Champaign, IL: Transition Research Institute, University of Illinois.

Ward, M. J., & Halloran, W. (1993, Fall). Transition issues for the 1990s. *OSERS News in Print, 6*(1), 4–5. (ERIC Document Reproduction Service No. ED 364 035).

Warren, F. G. (1976). *Report of the Kent County Educational Training Center.* Grand Rapids, MI.

Webb, K. W. (2000). *Transition to postsecondary education: Strategies for students with disabilities.* Austin, TX: Pro-Ed.

Wehman, P. (1981). *Competitive employment: New horizons for severely disabled individuals.* Baltimore: Paul H. Brookes.

Wehman, P. (1992). *Life beyond the classroom: Transition strategies for young people with disabilities.* Baltimore: Paul H. Brookes.

Wehman, P. (1996). *Life beyond the classroom: Transition strategies for young people with disabilities* (2nd ed.). Baltimore: Paul H. Brookes.

Wehman, P. (1997). *Exceptional individuals in school, community, and work.* Austin, TX: Pro-Ed.

Wehman, P. (Ed.). (1998). *Developing transition plans.* Austin, TX: Pro-Ed.

Wehman, P. (2001). *Life beyond the classroom: Transition strategies for young people with disabilities* (3rd ed). Baltimore: Paul H. Brookes.

Wehman, P. (2002). *Individual transition plans: The teacher's curriculum guide for helping youth with special needs* (2nd ed.). Austin, TX: Pro-Ed.

Wehman, P., Brooke, V., & Inge, K. J. (2001). Vocational placements and careers. In P. Wehman (Ed.), *Life beyond the classroom: Transition strategies for young people with disabilities* (3rd ed.) (pp. 211–246). Baltimore: Paul H. Brookes.

Wehman, P., Brooke, V., West, M., Targett, P., Green, H., Inge, K., & Kregel, J. (1998). Barriers to competitive employment for persons with disabilities. In P. Wehman (Ed.), *Developing transition plans.* Austin, TX: Pro-Ed.

Wehman, P., Everson, J., & Reid, D. H. (2001). Beyond programs and placements. In P. Wehman (Ed.), *Life beyond the classroom: Transition strategies for young people with disabilities* (3rd ed.) (pp. 91–124). Baltimore: Paul H. Brookes.

Wehman, P., & Kregel, J. (2004). *Functional curriculum for elementary, middle, and secondary age students with special needs* (2nd ed.). Austin, TX: Pro-Ed.

Wehman, P., Kregel, J., & Seyfarth, J. (1985). Transition from school to work for individuals with severe handicaps: A follow-up study. *Journal of the Association for the Severely Handicapped, 10,* 132–139.

Wehman, P., Revell, W. G., & Brooke, V. (2003). Competitive employment: Has it become the "first choice" yet? *Journal of Disability Policy Studies, 14*(3), 163–173.

Wehmeyer, M. L. (1997). Self-directed learning and self-determination. In M. Agran (Ed.), *Student-directed learning: A handbook of self-management.* Pacific Grove, CA: Brooks/Cole.

Wehmeyer, M. L., Agran, M., & Hughes, C. (1998). *Teaching self-determination to students with disabilities: Basic skills for successful transition.* Baltimore: Paul H. Brookes.

Wehmeyer, M. L., & Lawrence, M. (1995). Whose future is it anyway? Promoting student involvement in transition planning. *Career Development for Exceptional Individuals, 18*(2), 69–83.

Wehmeyer, M. L., Morningstar, M., & Husted, D. (1999). *Family involvement in transition planning and implementation.* Austin, TX: Pro-Ed.

Wehmeyer, M. L., & Ward, M. (1993). The spirit of the IDEA mandate: Student involvement in transition planning. *The Journal for Vocational Special Needs Education, 3,* 108–111.

Weir, C. (2001, May). *Individual supports for college success* (On-Campus Outreach, Fact Sheet #7). Retrieved June 28, 2004, from www.education.umd.edu/oco.

Weir, C. (2004). Person-centered and collaborative supports for college success. *Education and Training in Developmental Disabilities, 39*(1), 67–73.

Weiss, M., Hechtman,L., & Weiss, G. (2000). ADHD in parents. *Journal of the American Academy of Child and Adolescent Psychiatry, 39,* 1059–1061.

Will, M. (1984). *OSERS programming for the transition of youth with disabilities: Bridges from school to working life.* Washington, DC: Office of Special Education and Rehabilitative Services.

Williams, J. M. (2002). Using school-to-career strategies, workplace competencies, and industry skill standards to enhance the transition process in standards-based education. In C. A. Kochhar-Bryant & D. S. Bassett (Eds.), *Aligning transition and standards-based education: Issues and strategies* (pp. 77–90). Arlington, VA: Council for Exceptional Children.

Wolanin, T. R., & Steele, P. E. (2004). *Higher education opportunities for students with disabilities: A primer for policymakers.* Washington, DC: The Institute for Higher Education Policy.

Wolery, M., Strain, P. S., & Bailey, D. B. (1992). Reaching potentials of children with special needs. In S. Bredekamp & T. Rosengrant (Eds.), *Reaching potentials: Appropriate curriculum and assessment for young children* (pp. 92–113). Washington, DC: National Association for the Education of Young Children. (ERIC Document Reproduction Service No. ED 352 160).

Wolffe, K. E. (1999). *Skills for success: A career education handbook for children and adolescents with visual impairments.* New York: American Foundation for the Blind Press.

Wolinsky, S., & Whelan, A. (1999). Federal law and the accommodation of students with LD: The lawyers' look at the BU decision. *Journal of Learning Disabilities, 32,* 286–291.

World Health Organization. (1992). *International statistical classification of diseases and related health problems—Tenth revision.* Geneva, Switzerland: Author.

Younie, W. J. (1966). *Guidelines for establishing school work-study programs for educable mentally retarded youth.* Vol. 48 (10). Richmond, VA: Special Education Service, State Department of Education.

Zafft, C., Hart, D., & Zimbrich, K. (2004). College career connection: A study of youth with intellectual disabilities and the impact of postsecondary education. *Education and Training in Developmental Disabilities, 39*(1), 45–53.

Zhang, D., & Stecker, P. M. (2001). Student involvement in transition planning: Are we there yet? *Education and Training in Mental Retardation and Developmental Disabilities, 36,* 293–303.

Zigmond, N. (1997). Educating students with disabilities: The future of special education. In J. W. Lloyd, E. J. Kameenui, & D. Chard (Eds.), *Issues in educating students with disabilities* (pp. 377–390). Mahwah, NJ: Erlbaum.

AUTHOR INDEX

SUBJECT INDEX